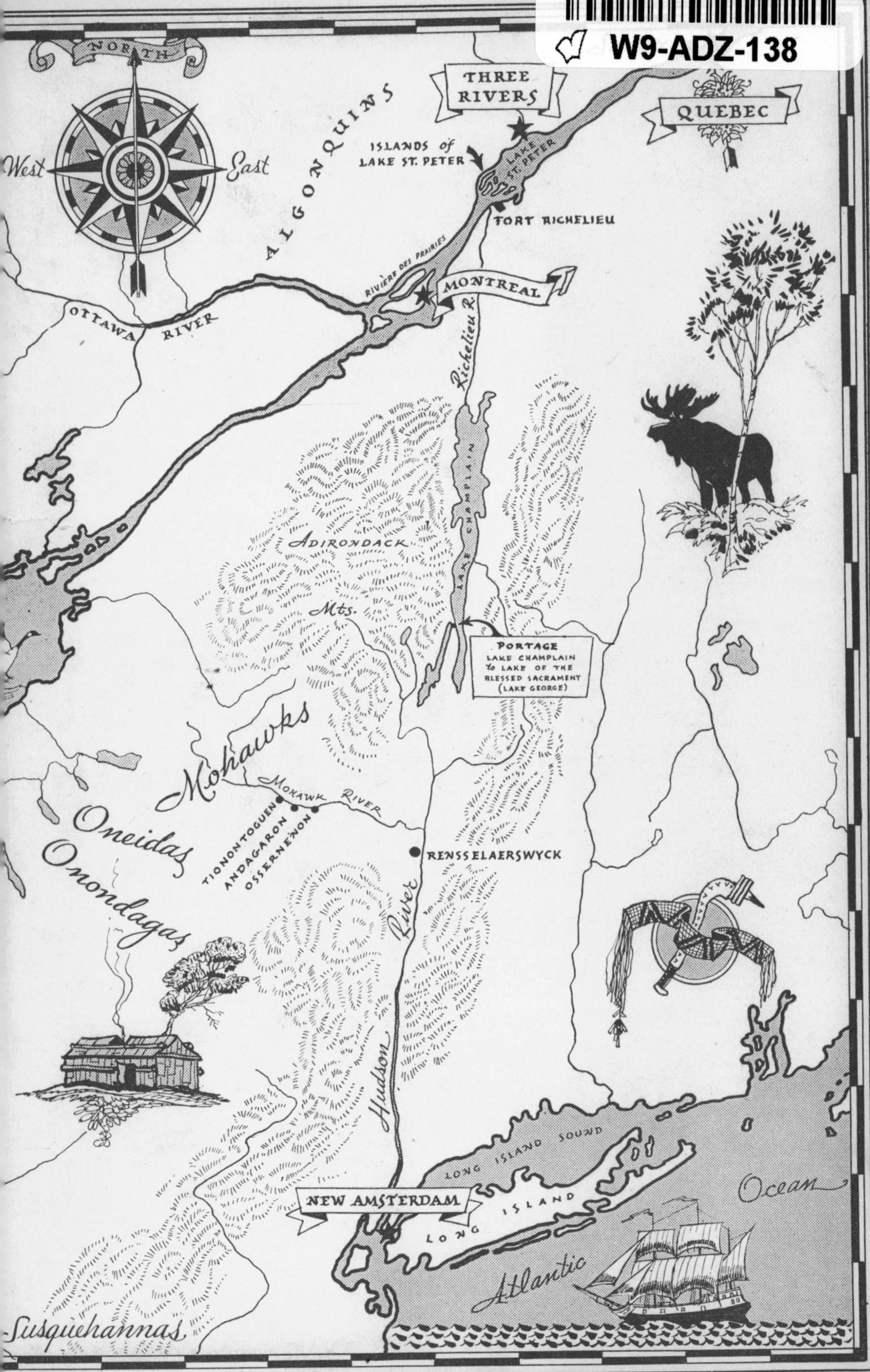
NORTH
West
East
ALGONQUINS
THREE RIVERS
QUEBEC
ISLANDS of LAKE ST. PETER
LAKE ST. PETER
FORT RICHELIEU
RIVIÈRE DES PRAIRIES
MONTREAL
OTTAWA RIVER
Richelieu R.
LAKE CHAMPLAIN
ADIRONDACK
Mts.
PORTAGE
LAKE CHAMPLAIN to LAKE OF THE BLESSED SACRAMENT (LAKE GEORGE)
Mohawks
MOHAWK RIVER
Oneidas
Onondagas
TIONONTOGUEN
ANDAGARON
OSSERNENON
RENSSELAERSWYCK
Hudson River
LONG ISLAND SOUND
LONG ISLAND
NEW AMSTERDAM
Ocean
Atlantic
Susquehannas

Saint Among Savages

ISAAC
1607 JOGUES 1646
S.J.

Saint Among Savages

THE LIFE OF ISAAC JOGUES

by

FRANCIS TALBOT, S.J

HARPER & BROTHERS PUBLISHERS

NEW YORK AND LONDON

1935

B
I

Saint Among Savages
Copyright, 1935, by Harper & Brothers
Printed in the United States of America
Third Edition
B-L

To

the Successors of Isaac Jogues

in Canada and the United States,

my Brothers

Acknowledgments

Facilities granted to me for the prosecution and completion of this biography require that I gratefully express my indebtedness to Edward C. Phillips, S.J., former Provincial of the Maryland-New York Province of the Society of Jesus, and to my immediate Superior, J. Wilfrid Parsons, S.J., Editor of *America*.

Most valuable assistance in the research work and in the earliest reading of the manuscript, and encouragement generously given, make me most thankful to John J. Wynne, S.J., Founder and Editor of the *Catholic Encyclopedia*, Vice-Postulator of the Cause of the American Martyrs and of Kateri Tekakwitha, and Honorary Chieftain of the Iroquois, called by them Ondesson, Ever-Bright-Light. Also, to Peter F. Cusick, S.J., Director of the Martyrs' Shrine, Auriesville, New York, I am indebted for help and continued coöperation. To Arthur Melançon, S.J., Archivist, Collège Sainte-Marie, Montréal, I am grateful for scholarly guidance, and to Alain de Becdelièvre, S.J., of Paris, who supplied me with information otherwise unavailable.

Among the many friends and associates who have contributed much and in diverse ways to the completion of this book, I am happy to mention: Thomas F. Meehan, K.S.G., Editor of *Historical Records and Studies*, and Trustee of the United States Catholic Historical Society; Sterns Cunningham, Treasurer and General Manager of the Catholic Book Club, Inc.; and Mrs. Florence Fitzmaurice Williams, who tirelessly typed, edited, and indexed the book.

Special acknowledgment is made to Burrows Brothers Company, of Cleveland, Ohio, for permission to make frequent and copious quotations from the translations in *The Jesuit Relations and Allied Documents*, edited by Reuben Gold Thwaites. This admirable work, consisting of seventy-three volumes, is of inestimable value not only because of the splendid English rendering, but also because of the comprehensiveness of the documents collected and of the scholarly editing of the French original texts. It is placed first in the Bibliography, and in the Notes and References at the end of this volume, where credit is given for the quotations. Additional references are listed so that the reader who is interested may be tempted to acquaint himself with the richness of the material that could not be quoted.

F. X. T.

Contents

~

Saint Among Savages

CHAPTER I

From Cradle to Cloister

I

ORLÉANS was at peace. In such a period as this, about the turn of the year 1600, it reposed serenely and prosperously as the queen city of the Loire. Encompassed within its tidy walls, it reigned over the countryside, content to let the rest of France fare for itself. It busied itself about its own gossips, made merry over its local festivals, drove its brisk provincial trades, married within its own families, and handed down from respected fathers to respectable sons its customs and fortunes and family heirlooms. It was mellow with memories of the glories of the past, for here had kings been consecrated, hither they had marched in triumphs, hither, too, in holiday mood they had often retired with their courts; and here they were borne to sleep within their tombs.

There were other marks that Orléans remembered. The most distant was in the time of Julius Cæsar when Orléans was Genebaum and the Romans were subjugating the savage Gauls. It was then little more than a trading-post, but it had the ill fortune to be a plotters' nest, and Cæsar leveled it to the sod. After the Romans had mingled with the natives and civilized them, Orléans was large enough to be an obstacle to Attila and his half-million Huns when they were cutting their devastating swath into the Roman Empire. It would have been left a mass of ruins had it not been rescued through the prayers and the courage of Bishop Aignan, who thereafter became its patron saint. Again miraculously, it was saved from ruin when Odoacer and his Saxons swooped down upon it. Later, the Norsemen sailed up the Loire in their sporadic incursions. Since there were no saints to oppose them, they brought terror to the people and carried off rich spoils.

Orléans was made forever famous on an April evening of 1429. The English and Burgundians sat about it, confident of its capture and, with it, of the control of France. God once more intervened through a saint. Jeanne d'Arc, gleaming in spotless armor, astride a snow-white horse, under the pale standard bearing the names of Jhesus and Maria, rode through the arched gateway and clattered up the cobbled streets to the Cathedral of the Holy Cross. "I bring you better ransom than ever came to knight or town, the succor of the King of Heaven," she announced. Within a week she had pried off the clamp of the enemies. Orléans, freed from the wars, rapturously thanked God and venerated Jeanne. On every May 8, during the century and more that followed, the town chanted its hymns of thanksgiving for the deliverance by the Maid.

The monument that had been reared to Jeanne d'Arc was tumbled down and insanely smashed into fragments, the old Cathedral of the Holy Cross where she had publicly worshiped was so completely wrecked that it was abandoned as a ruin, the walls that she had defended were battered apart in the latter half of the century which followed. For Orléans was gripped by civil war. Into the city had come disciples of Jean Calvin, the French savant who was living at Geneva and preaching the new religion. These propagandists militantly proclaimed a strange doctrine which denied the beliefs and the practices of the old Church, the while they bitterly denounced the corruption of the priests and the bishops and the Pope. Into Orléans, also, rode nobles and squires who were pledged in allegiance to the Prince of Condé and to Coligny, the High Admiral, against the royal authority.

Many of the people of Orléans avidly accepted the doctrines preached by Calvin's disciples; the majority violently condemned them as innovations of the devil. Some of the important personages of the district of the Loire allied themselves to Condé, while the rest maintained fidelity to the Dukes of Guise, the champions of the Catholic cause. The religious differences soured into political feuds. Disputes multiplied, rioting and street fighting flared up vindictively, and Orléans fell apart into chaos. By 1562 the storm that had been gathering throughout the whole of France was detonating along the Loire. The followers of Condé and the House of Bourbon established themselves in Orléans. Duke Francis of Guise laid siege to the walls. Though he himself was assassinated on the banks of the river, his Catholic forces captured the city.

Orléans, however, by no means simmered down into peace, for

the Huguenots were a strong and militant people. Within five years they gained the ascendancy, wreaking their vengeance on all that was Catholic. They built Orléans into a fortification against the King. It was then that Charles IX ordered that the city be recaptured, that the walls and towers be razed to the ground. In 1569, the Catholic party once more held firm control over the government.

The Huguenots were resurgent. They made themselves so feared and hated that resentment against them easily exploded into an hysterical madness. Orléans had word of the massacre of the Huguenots in Paris and its environs on August 24, 1572. The bloodlust raged uncontrollably. Remembering the insult to Jeanne d'Arc, looking upon the ruins of the Cathedral of the Holy Cross, wishing to avenge the sacrileges committed against its sacred shrines, mindful of the arrogance and cruelty of their Huguenot townsmen and of Calvin's disciples when they held power, in a furious burst of barbarism, Orléans hunted down and slew the promoters and the supporters of the Calvinistic Huguenots all through a bloody week. Before order was restored, the toll of murders had mounted up to several hundred.

This bleeding did not cure the ills of France. Political and religious wars broke out anew. The weak kings, swayed by malicious favorites, were overawed by plotting nobles. The people were restless and lawless in the anarchy caused by the conflict of allegiances. Charles IX died in impotence. Henry III left no legitimate offspring when he was stabbed to death by Jacques Clement in 1589. No heir, in the direct line, remained to mount the throne of France.

The Catholic nobles, under the leadership of the Guises, proclaimed the aged Cardinal Bourbon as Charles X. The Huguenots raised their leader, Henry of Navarre, as the legitimate king. Though Henry could prove the best claim, he held the support of only a few of the first houses, the fidelity of only a small number of the petty nobility, and the following of less than one-tenth of the populace. He could force his rule solely on one-sixth of the kingdom. Against him, the Catholics forged themselves into the Holy League and swore that Henry the Calvinist would never be accepted by them as the King of France. Henry marched his army through northern France and threatened Paris; whatever victories he won were desultory and unimportant. He issued manifestoes declaring that he would not molest his Catholic subjects in the practice of their religion, that he would not favor Calvinism against Catholicism; but the Holy League refused to listen to his pledges.

Henry of Navarre was the greatest general of France. He was also the greatest diplomat. Thrice in his young life, as he found change expedient, he had swerved in his religious affiliations. Clearly, he recognized the fact that his Calvinism barred him from the throne. Therefore, he would profess Catholicism. If he had to go to Mass publicly to be king, he would go to Mass. In 1593, he asked to be instructed in Catholic doctrine. He abjured his Calvinistic heresy in the year following. This strategy split the Holy League. Henry was crowned King of France in the Cathedral of Chartres, and then triumphantly rode through the open gates of Paris.

It was the peace established by Henry IV that Orléans enjoyed at the turn of the year 1600. During the forty years before his accession, eight civil and religious wars had ruined France, about 800,000 people had perished, 100,000 homes had been ruined, some 250 villages were wrecked, and Orléans and the larger towns were partially destroyed. Though he loved the game of war, Henry devoted himself to peace, within and without the realm. At his crowning he had expressed the wish that "soon there might be a fowl in the pot of every peasant on a Sunday." He made his wish turn true. He quelled the battling noblemen, pacified the hostile religious factions, put down banditry, guaranteed justice in the courts, reconstructed roads and built up towns, and so regulated finances that he spared his people from exorbitant taxes.

Orléans was prosperous and happy. Peasants tilled the soil with a certainty they would reap a harvest. Graziers bred their cattle with an assurance that soldiers or brigands would not slaughter them. Craftsmen and laborers had steady work and fair wages. The numerous officers of the King and the Commune were well paid. Money being plentiful, the tradesmen flourished, as always in the periods of peace.

Prominent among the merchants, because of his character, his family connections, and his reputed wealth, was the young man named Laurent Jogues. He traced his ancestors back to about 1489. There lived then a Georges Jogues, who worked as a laborer in the employ of a tradesman of Tremblevif, a market town near Orléans. He thought to better his fortunes by removing himself to Orléans, where he opened a little shop. So well did he prosper that he could educate his son Pierre, who filled the office of notary from 1525 till his death in 1544. Pierre fathered a family of six children, among them Philippe and Pierre junior. These rose to the estate of the better bourgeois society. In 1568, Pierre was named with Jacques des Comtes as a deputy from Orléans to the States General in Tours. Philippe flourished in business and was heard in the civic affairs of the town. Upon his marriage with Claudine Javary in 1566, he founded a new branch of the family, and was blessed with four sons, Laurent, Philippe, François, Claude, and a daughter, Marie.

All the numerous cousins of the Jogues name were well respected and comfortably established, some of them as notaries or councilors of law, some as apothecaries or drapers or silk merchants or general dealers. Not one, however, bore a better reputation for honesty and ability than Laurent. He had succeeded to the lucrative business of his father, Philippe, in general merchandise; he had already been chosen by his fellow burghers to fill some of the lesser municipal offices; it was taken for granted that, when he would be a little older, he would be elected Mayor of Orléans.

Coming to his maturity in the years when Henry IV had instituted the reign of peace, Laurent had prospect of a life of security. He took as wife Marthe, the daughter of Aignan Seurat, in the closing years of the century. She bore him two daughters, Marthe and Marie. But she did not long survive. Laurent, at the age of thirty, was left a widower with two little babes to provide for. It was needful, thought everyone, that Laurent Jogues should seek another marriage.

In the same quartier of Orléans dwelt a merchant with whom Laurent had some dealings and whom he respected highly. François de Saint-Mesmin, though a tradesman, was derived from an ancient and honorable family of aristocrats. A century before Jeanne d'Arc rescued Orléans, Estienne de Saint-Mesmin was inscribed on the annals of the city, for 1312, as Provost Guard. The family de Saint-Mesmin, during the next two hundred years, continued to be prominent in the affairs of the Loire district. François de Saint-Mesmin, in 1523, was recorded as holding the traditional office of Provost Guard, and in addition was Seigneur de la Cloye, licentiate at law, and Councilor of the King in the Grand Council. Nicholas, his son, in 1563, ranked likewise as knight, and among other functions exercised that of Grand Steward of Woods and Forests. But the religious and civil wars that raged about Orléans in his time wasted his substance, as it did that of all the landed squires.

François, the son of Nicholas, was heir to little except the title of Sieur de la Bressière. Men of his standing were forced to devote themselves to some gainful occupation, or to a more assiduous farming of their estates. Thus it happened that François sought a livelihood as a merchant in Orléans. His wife, Michelle de Comte, also belonged to the rather impoverished aristocracy of the Loire, but she loyally shared the fortunes of her husband. He located his place of business in the parish of St. Paul, close to the remains of the old walls along the bank of the Loire, near to one of the far gates of the southwest district of the city, the quartier du Châtelet.

While the de Saint-Mesmins had let down some of the barriers of caste, the Jogues had risen socially. It was not to be wondered at, then, that the young widower, Laurent Jogues, should aspire to a union between himself and the daughter of François de Saint-Mesmin, the Mademoiselle Françoise, who was then in her sixteenth year, and thus of marriageable age. Laurent sought some indications as to the possibilities for such an arrangement from François. These showed favorably. Laurent paid a formal call upon François and respectfully declared his desire to wed Mademoiselle in honorable fashion. Monsieur, her father, revealed that he deeply appreciated the honor. The proposal was discussed in the family councils. Laurent was able to prove that he was of irreproachable character, that he could support Mademoiselle in comfort, even in luxury. François agreed to grant an adequate dowry and stated that he would express his paternal will to Françoise. With the consent of Mademoiselle given, with the contractual obligations arranged, the betrothal was duly announced and ratified.

On September 30, 1602, Laurent and Françoise were solemnly married in the parish church of St. Paul, before the altar at the foot of which Jeanne d'Arc had prayed privately so often during her week in Orléans. The priest who performed the ceremony duly recorded it in the parish register:

Laurent Jogues, son of the honorable Philippe Jogues, merchant citizen of this city of Orléans, and of Claudine Javary, of the parish of St. Hilaire.

And, Françoise de Saint-Mesmin, daughter of the honorable François de Saint-Mesmin, merchant citizen of Orléans, and of the defunct Michelle de Comte, her father and mother, of this parish.

For both families it was a happy and memorable occasion. Festively, they escorted the young bride across the flagged streets which stretched along the embankment of the Loire to the home of Laurent, a half-mile distant. It was an overhanging gabled house with the lower front opening into the dark store. Most advantageously was it situated, in the same southwest quartier du Châtelet. Around the corner toward the city was the Grand Marché, where noble and burgher and peasant and laborer haggled over prices. The house faced the rather wide cobbled street which sloped down toward the river. A hundred paces away were the remnants of the old city wall which had been dismantled during the Huguenot wars. To the rear of these was le Châtelet, a grim, gray little castle that had been spared ruin. Abutting one side of the castle was the archway of the gate called La Rose. This opened out on the stone bridge which humped over the Loire to the south bank.

The duties of Françoise were not trivial. Though she was a competent young person and experienced, for she had the cares of her father's establishment after the death of her mother, she was well tested by the management of Laurent's large household, of his infant daughters, his ageing mother and younger brothers and sisters, of the maidservants and apprentices who lodged with their master.

In due time, there came the increase to the family. Madame Françoise, to the great joy and pride of Laurent, bore a son on March 11, 1604. He was baptized the same day in the parish church of St. Hilaire and given the name of his maternal grandfather, François. A year and one-half later, she presented a second son to Laurent, and had him christened Jacques. As December, 1606, drew to a close, Madame Françoise was in expectation of her third child.

II

Madame Françoise Jogues was a robust young matron of twenty-one years. She was safely delivered of her third son in the dark hours of Wednesday morning, January 10, 1607. During the preceding weeks she had settled that her child, if another boy, would be named after her brother Isaac. So he was christened when, later in the same day, Grandmother Jogues held him in her arms for the baptism. A Canon of St. Euverte, who ministered at the parish church of St. Hilaire, crossed the new Jogues baby with the holy oils, put a pinch of salt between his lips, and poured the cold water on his head, baptizing him in the name of the Father and of the Son and of the Holy Ghost. He entered the event in the baptismal register of St. Hilaire:

> The 10th of January, was baptized Isaac, the son of the honorable Laurent Jogues, merchant citizen of this city, and of Françoise de Saint-Mesmin, born on this same day, Wednesday, at the second hour of the morning. His godfathers were his two uncles, brothers of the aforesaid Françoise, known to be honorable men, François de Saint-Mesmin and Isaac de Saint-Mesmin, and his godmother, his grandmother, mother of the said Laurent, an honorable woman, Claudine Javary, wife of Philippe Jogues.

Laurent was festive over the advent of this third son to carry on his name and family. Well might he be congratulated by the many brothers and sisters of Françoise and himself, by the numerous aunts and uncles and cousins, by the friends and neighbors gathered in the large living-room where they made merry that January evening before the roaring fire. He was a man blessed by God, with a well-born, healthy, and devoted wife, with the three sons born of her, with the two beautiful daughters by his first wife, with a large, solid house, with a lucrative business, with the respect of his townsfolk, with the honors of the public offices that he held. They raised their pewter cups then, and drank a hearty health to Monsieur and to Madame, and to the new baby.

From his birth, Madame Jogues felt a most particular love for her little Isaac, *mon cher Isaac,* as she began to call him. He was so good and so quiet, so little trouble, so very adorable. It seemed to her that, in some strange way, she were more a part of him and he was more hers than were her older sons, François and Jacques. He reigned the idol of the household for eighteen months.

Isaac ceased to be of much interest and was moved from his cradle to give place to a baby sister, Françoise, who was born on July 10, 1608. She, in turn, retired as the center of attraction before Philippe, the fourth son, who was ushered into the family on August 13, 1609. The fifth boy came on November 25, 1612, and was called after his father, Laurent. Still another boy, Samuel, was born two years later. Thus, with her stepdaughters, Marthe and Marie, growing up to marriageable age, with her six sons and her daughter, ranging down from ten years, with the houseful of servants and shop assistants, with some concern about Laurent, who was engaged in many matters and not so strong as he had been, Madame Françoise had few moments of idleness.

Her household and the children she ruled rigidly, albeit affectionately. As Madame la Mère, she was totally responsible for the order and the management of the home, for the proper upbringing of the children in obedience, in politeness, in gentility, as well as for their bodily care. These things were not to be a trouble on Monsieur le Père, nor was the deportment of the children to be an annoyance to him. He was the master, and was to be treated with the greatest deference and was to be obeyed instantly when he spoke. Seldom did he unbend, even in the privacy of the home; always was he waited upon with the most active solicitude when he retired after the labors of the day; never was he to be disturbed through the evening when he sat in his great chair before the fireplace and conversed with his relatives and friends.

Under the careful tutelage of Madame la Mère, Isaac emerged as a well-behaved and attractive lad. As the middle child in the family of nine, he had the disability of older brothers and sisters overawing him, and the drag of younger ones distracting him. Until he reached the age of six or thereabouts, he was bundled in a heavy smock. Then he was initiated into the more manly costume of bloomer and coat, most often those which François and Jacques had outgrown. Shortly after, he was inducted into the mysteries of reading and writing, at first under the instruction of his older brothers, or even of Monsieur le Père; and then under the care of a tutor who visited the house.

In Orléans, as in the larger centers of the realm, the function of education was under the control of the university schools. These had degenerated from the monastery schools of the Middle Ages, and were but loose assemblages of instructors and pupils, with no well-defined curriculum, with teachers too often brutal and ignorant, with discipline so lax that morals were destroyed rather than safeguarded. The Society of Jesus, through the establishment of colleges in Paris and the large provincial cities, revolutionized education. The Jesuit teachers vitalized whatever was good in the old system and introduced a balanced and progressive course of studies. They emphasized high moral and spiritual ideals, and maintained a strict though paternal form of discipline. So vastly superior were their colleges that the sons of the greatest houses, from the best of the nobles to the best of the bourgeoisie, were put under their tutelage.

For Isaac Jogues, when he had come to the school age, about his tenth year, there occurred a most fortuitous event. The Fathers of the Society of Jesus were opening a college in the city. Negotiations for this had been begun as far back as 1608. But the General Assembly of Orléans, which was strongly tinctured by Calvinism and included many Huguenot members, refused to guarantee the funds required for financing the college. In 1617 the leading Catholic citizens prevailed upon the Assembly of Orléans to support a college of the Society of Jesus. The Queen Regent, Marie de Médicis, in the name of Louis XIII, confirmed the permission granted by Henry IV in 1609, and assigned that the sum of 2,345 livres be taken from the city receipts as an annual revenue for the college. In April, three members of the Society, Fathers Lalemant, Dinet, and Demassau, arrived in Orléans. On May 12 they formally installed themselves in a residence on rue Sainte Anne. All the chief personages of Orléans, except the Huguenots, attended the solemn dedication.

Early that summer, Lalemant secured a more spacious, better adapted site for the college in a house on rue de la Veille-Monnaie, near les Quatre Coins. Over the doorway was placed the inscription: *Collegium Societatis Jesu Virgini Deiparae Sacrum*. The Calvinists broiled with indignation at this Jesuit invasion and began a persistent sabotage. Father Lalemant endured it until one morning he found they had defaced the inscription by smearing out the word *Jesu* and printing in *du diable*. He appealed to the Lieutenant Criminel and thereafter had some protection against the fanatical petty persecution.

Isaac Jogues was one of the first students listed on the registers of the new college. He was a lad approaching his eleventh year. He felt somewhat lordly as he walked up to the college on rue de la Veille-Monnaie on the morning of October 18, 1617. But he and the other boys of Orléans were expeditiously and efficiently garnered into their classes by the strange, positive priests. Succinctly, the Father Rector informed them of the ideals they must strive to attain and of the faults that would in no wise be tolerated. Isaac and the other students learned that they were being admitted into the college not only to be educated as learned gentlemen, but primarily to be trained in piety and all the virtues. He was given to understand that he must be docile, obedient, silent when silence was imposed, orderly in his deportment, diligent in his studies. He would attend Mass at the times appointed, and would go to Confession and Holy Communion at stated intervals.

With some misgivings, Isaac listened to the catalogue of things forbidden him: he must not swear or curse; he must not tell lies or be deceitful; he must not attend evil performances, must not frequent shady places; he must not act the braggart, must not carry a sword, dagger, or like weapon within the school premises; he must not deface the tables, walls, by writing, whittling or in any other way. These and others were the rules and regulations. Any violations, he was warned, would merit a specific number of strokes with a whip, administered by a school officer appointed for that purpose.

With these points firmly settled in the minds of pupils and teachers, the classes began. Isaac spent the first two years of 1617 and 1618 in the elementary grades and was prepared for entering the lowest class prescribed in the Ratio Studiorum of the Society of Jesus. He proved to be a diligent student, acquisitive and plodding. He was of a gentle, affable, rather retiring disposition, but with a quiet assertiveness and a determination and a perseverance that was called stubborn. He was good without being priggish, studious but not an anemic bookworm.

Ever since he had been a tiny lad, he and the boys of the neighborhood had played along the sandbanks of the swift-flowing Loire, just a few hundred yards from his home, and he had developed into an expert, vigorous swimmer. He was ingenious, so that he excelled in the games of the children about his house and in the college playground, where the masters superintended the physical exercise. He was remarkably fleet of foot, so that he could outrun the boys of his own age. Though robust, he was a wiry and agile rather than a large-limbed, rugged type of boy. His skin was fair, his features fine and delicate, and his manners, due to the sharp eyes of Madame la Mère and the Jesuit teachers, were courteous and even elaborately punctilious.

Two months after the college began to function, on December 23, 1617, Canon Raoul de Gazil, Councilor and Almoner of the King, signed the document by which he donated to the Society of Jesus the Priory of Saint Samson of Orléans, of which he was Prior Commendatory, and the Priory of Saint Sulpice de l'Aigle, to which he held title. Saint Samson was admirably located in the northwest quartier, not far from l'Hôtel de Ville. It was a spacious, firmly constructed building, but had been so long neglected that it was falling into ruin. The Canon added a gift of 2,000 livres for the needed repairs, and Father Martellange, a noted architect, was brought up from Paris to rehabilitate the ancient monastery. He designed fitting classrooms, built a theater, and reconstructed the chapel which had been destroyed during the religious wars by the Huguenots. The new college was formally opened on March 14, 1619.

Isaac continued with his classes in the new premises. In the grade of Infima Grammatica he was thoroughly grounded in the rudiments of Latin, the basic study; he was introduced to the elements of Greek and was given practice in the use of the vernacular. Other subjects, such as history and geography, were incidental to the teaching of the classical languages. Religion was never forgotten, for the teachers were enjoined to deduce salutary moral and doctrinal reflections in all the secular studies. He progressed through Media and Suprema Grammatica, at the end of which he had a finished command of Latin, a sufficient familiarity with Greek to read the simpler texts, and an extensive general knowledge.

In the uppermost two grades of humanities and rhetoric, he absorbed the beauty and the culture inherent in the orations, the tragedies, the histories, the philosophies, the poetry of the ancient civilizations, the great thoughts, the noble ideals of the pagan world, translated into the Christian concept and supernaturalized. He had formed in him an esthetic appreciation, and had rounded out his French style, both in prose and poetry, so that he wrote and orated fluently and with a flourish. His years at the Jesuit college had developed him into a brilliant young scholar and a courtly gentleman of the Renaissance.

During these years subtle changes had been working in him. In his exterior he was one of the young bloods of Orléans. His family was one of the most respected among the commoners and was linked with the local nobility. He had the distinction of having been educated at the Jesuit college, to which all the best people sent their sons, not only in Orléans, but in Paris, Rheims, and Rouen. Dressed elegantly in his brocaded coat with the flaring skirts, in his tight breeches and silken stockings and high-lipped boots, in his ruffled collar and lace front, with a smart cap resting upon his flowing curls, with a sword at his side, he swaggered somewhat with an air of distinction as he strolled about the streets.

His inclinations, however, were to serious pursuits. He enjoyed most the conversations he had with his Jesuit masters. He read as much as he could from the books in the library which Canon de Gazil had donated to the college, and frequently haunted the bookstalls located in the cloister of the Cathedral of the Holy Cross. His choice friends were similarly minded, so that when they could secure a prized volume they would gather with him in his home to read it aloud to one another. Definitely religious in his aspirations, he was attracted to the exercise of virtue, to a practical charity, to a militant hostility toward the Calvinism which was prevalent in Orléans, to the frequentation of the Sacraments of Penance and the Eucharist, to attendance at Mass, and he was more than ordinarily devoted to the Blessed Virgin, Mother of God.

At seventeen he decided about his future. There was place and opportunity for him in Orléans. His father, Laurent, had died a few years back, but left the family well provided for. Isaac might continue the tradition of being a merchant; or turn, as his uncles, to that of the law; or seek a government post. These ambitions did not attract him strongly. As far back as he could remember, he felt instinctively drawn to the Church. By the time he had completed college his desires for a priestly life had crystallized. By then, too, he was quite well determined to be a priest of the Society of Jesus.

To Madame la Mère, when he revealed it to her, his ambition caused no surprise. It was what she had prayed for secretly. Gently she questioned him, however. Would it not be better to be a priest of Orléans, a canon, perhaps a bishop? Were there not monasteries near by which he might enter? Did he realize he must leave her and his family forever, if he became a Jesuit, for they traveled everywhere and were sent to the far ends of the earth as missioners? Did he not think their rule of life too strict? They had so many enemies, they were accused of so many crimes, they had been expelled from France by Henry IV, they were always putting themselves in some kind of danger. Isaac settled her doubts; he had thought of everything; he wanted nothing except to become a Jesuit.

On the side of the Society of Jesus there was no obstruction. Isaac's masters knew his ultimate decision even before he had made it. He was a boy in every way fitted to join their company. He was intelligent and studious above the average, his morals and character were spotless, he was tractable though of strong will, was balanced in his judgments, and had no mental or emotional instabilities. His piety had been evidenced through the seven years he had attended the college. That he was called to be a Jesuit the Jesuits at Orléans had no doubts. Accordingly, they recommended to the Father Provincial that he be received into the Novitiate.

A sense of finality came with the instructions Isaac received early that summer of 1624 that he was to report at the Novitiate of Rouen in October. He was almost the first young man from Orléans to go off with the Jesuits, and that seemed adventurous. He must leave the cozy familiarity of home, must bid farewell to Madame la Mère, to Françoise, who was celebrating her sixteenth birthday that July, to the younger boys. There were things to prepare, and things to complete, and calls to make on the host of relatives, so that it was a short summer, and October came with its autumn tang as if unexpectedly.

Madame Jogues, proud though she was of her dear Isaac, and happy in the thought that he was preparing to be a priest, had watery eyes. She did not feel so well when the morning came for his departure. Many guests filled the Jogues house to say the last adieus. Marthe and Marie, now young matrons, and Françoise, bustled about to welcome the uncles and aunts and cousins; François and the older boys busied themselves with the baggage and the weather and numerous details. Isaac was tremulously excited, but strove to cover his shyness and nervousness with an air of manly decisiveness.

When the stage-coach drew up before the door he was folded in the last embrace of Madame la Mère and released with her kisses upon his cheeks and her blessings on his head. He shivered a little when he stepped out from the dark living-room into the street. François and the boys fastened his trunk under the benches, all the relatives shouted their Godspeeds, and he mounted to the straw-strewn coach. He waved back his farewells as the stage lumbered up the street.

Isaac looked his last on the narrow, winding thoroughfares of

Orléans. The coach progressed up past l'Hôtel de Ville and the Jesuit college near by, out through the arched gateway to the north, on the road to Paris. They rocked along past the farms and vineyards. Isaac looked back sadly through the lengthening vistas at the peaked roofs of the houses, at the slender steeples of the churches, at the bulk of the cathedral walls, which seemed to settle lower in the countryside. He felt a heaviness within him, for all that he was nearing his eighteenth birthday.

About the second evening, they drove into Paris, where Isaac visited some relatives and was welcomed by his Jesuit friends at the College of Clermont. Thence, in a few days, he trundled out through the long streets to the yellow road which unrolled between the high-walled fences and turreted castles to the open country of the fields and through the narrow defiles of the hamlets and villages. After leagues of riding, he sighted the cluster of steeples and the towers of Rouen. Huge and dominating over all was the lofty bulk of the famous cathedral. The city came nearer as he gazed upon it from the bowling stage-coach. They were before the gray, mossy walls, entering the battered gates, picking a way between the fronts of the grim houses.

Isaac stood before the entrance to the Jesuit College of Rouen, securely guarded by a tall encircling wall. He was ushered into a dark and stately parlor. He was acutely ill at ease; this was so different from the easy comfort of home. A priest, youthful-looking, thin, ascetic, came quietly into the room and greeted Isaac affectionately. He introduced himself as Father Louis Lalemant, the Master of Novices. Isaac, studying him with the sharp eyes of youth, instinctively trusted him. After the short exchange of greetings he was guided out of the parlor into the corridor and escorted to the section of the building reserved for the Novices.

III

At the time Isaac Jogues entered the Novitiate at Rouen on October 24, 1624, the Society of Jesus was firmly implanted in France. Some seventy-five years earlier, the disciples of St. Ignatius of Loyola fought for an entry into the realm. They were distinguished as the arch-enemies of all the current heresies of Luther and Calvin. They were the champions of the inner reformation of the Church. From the beginning, in France, they were violently assailed by the Calvinist theologians and the Huguenot nobility; they were opposed by the compromising corporations of Catholics who controlled the parliaments and universities; they were condemned by the unsteadier and laxer bishops.

They came to France, however, with special delegations from the Holy See. They won the patronage of the loyal members of the French hierarchy, were befriended by the more zealous higher ecclesiastics, and were received as allies by the Catholic majority of the nobility. Royal favor was showered upon them, both through appointments as Court preachers and confessors, and through generous permissions to establish their colleges in Paris and the metropolitan cities.

During the latter half of the sixteenth century they were the sustaining force of the Catholic ascendancy in the religious wars. They were responsible for forging the Holy League against the Huguenot threat of seizing, or at least controlling, the throne. They roused the nobility and the populace against Henry of Navarre, and raised the cry that no Protestant would sit upon the throne of Catholic France. Henry circumvented them by renouncing his Calvinism and professing himself a Catholic. It followed inevitably that Henry must crush them. Shortly after his coronation he suppressed the Society of Jesus in France. He confiscated their colleges and residences, which were quickly ransacked by the rabble, and expelled all the members from the kingdom.

Though destroyed materially, and though banished, the Jesuits had achieved their higher purpose. Henry IV was a professing Catholic, pledged to hold France loyal to the Papacy. The Jesuits came to believe in the sincerity of Henry's abjuration, and Henry recognized in the Society of Jesus a powerful army for the spiritual good of his people. The Superiors of the Society petitioned His Holiness, Clement VIII, and negotiated directly and indirectly to bring about the solemn absolution of the King. Henry, on his side, determined that as soon as he was strong enough to withstand his Huguenot supporters and the hostile Catholics of the parliaments and universities, he would revoke the decrees of banishment against the Jesuits.

In 1601 he drew up proposals to this effect, but such were the restrictions he imposed that they were rejected by the Society of Jesus and the Pope. In September, 1603, Henry brushed aside the objections, and issued the Edict of Rouen whereby the Society of Jesus was permitted by law once more to exist in France. He was following a devious policy, one calculated to quiet the fears of the enemies of the Jesuits and one designed to win the confidence of the Jesuits. Within two years he had leagued them so closely to him that Father Coton could write: "His Majesty takes glory in the title of Jesuit which the heretics confer on him."

Before his assassination in 1610 he had so encouraged and personally subsidized the educational institutions of the Society in France that the Order was greater and more flourishing than it had been when he suppressed it. By 1624 its membership had increased to 1,400, distributed in forty-five colleges and residences, divided under five administrative provinces. Ardent young men of the best blood, of the finest talents and promise, sought for admission and were apportioned between the two Novitiates, at Rouen and Paris. So many were the applicants that the Superiors were forced to exercise the most rigid tests in their selections. And then, after admission, they sedulously weeded out those who did not most fully attain the ideals of the Society.

As to the fitness of Isaac Jogues, there was never any question. From the morning in October, 1624, when he first garbed himself in the soutane, he proved to be an intense, earnest Novice, striving after sanctity and strictly following the rules. Easily and happily he submitted to the rigid, undeviating routine which clicked all day long in a minutely ordered schedule of time. He was wholly controlled by an exacting discipline, by a system that never let him escape but kept molding him every instant, kept correcting his faults in character, kept impressing him with the necessity and practice of obedience, of self-control, of all the virtues, kept always in his soul noble aspirations and spiritual ideals.

Brother Isaac found happiness and a profound peace in the two years at the Novitiate. Not only had he no inclination to violate the code of action and the prescriptions, but he inclined to be exaggerated in his meticulous observance of the smallest rules. He had to be restrained, rather than urged, in his observances and his pieties. It was his good fortune to be under the direction of Father Lalemant, a priest totally immersed in God. Sanctity was in his soul, and communicated itself to the Novices under his charge. He knew instinctively, as it were, the deepest recesses of their characters, their weaknesses, their strengths; as one inspired, he accorded to each the treatment needed.

As with most Novices, the thoughts of Isaac visioned a future in which he might spend himself utterly in the service of God. He conceived the ambition of faring out into the far lands of the pagans and infidels as a missioner. His imagination carried him off to the apostolate of India, where St. Francis Xavier had converted thousands; to China and Japan, where the Jesuits were combating the bonzes; to the Americas, where were whole continents yet unknown and millions of souls to save. He began to concentrate his ambitions on the conversion to Catholicism of the infidels in Constantinople, and through the Levant, where the French Jesuits were already laboring.

Isaac revealed his secret longings to Father Lalemant, and begged that he would be accepted as a volunteer to these foreign missionary fields. It was no new story to Father Louis Lalemant. Twenty years before, he too had pleaded with his Superiors to send him out to the East where he could devote all of himself to the spread of the Faith. His request was never granted, but he could sympathize with Isaac and could encourage him the while he taught him to accept whatever obedience imposed on him. He told Brother Isaac to live so that he might be prepared for such arduous enterprises for God.

The Novices were thrilled in 1625, and their thoughts turned to missionary exploits in the New World, when Fathers Charles Lalemant, Massé, and de Brébeuf passed through Rouen on their way to Dieppe, where they were to embark for New France. Brother Isaac hoped one day to be a missioner like them, but he felt called toward Constantinople. He renewed his supplications to the Master of Novices. Father Lalemant looked into his eager eyes and was silent for a moment. "Brother Isaac," he said, "you will not die anywhere but in Canada."

On October 24, 1626, Isaac pronounced his first vows. Kneeling upon the altar step, in the presence of the Blessed Sacrament, he bound himself to the perpetual service of God, in poverty, chastity, and obedience in the Society of Jesus. It was not for him an act of sacrifice, but one of joy and exaltation of soul. As God had given him all, so would he give all of himself to God. A few days later he was sent from Rouen to Anjou, to the College of La Flèche, there to pursue a three-year course in philosophy.

This college was the supreme gift of love which Henry IV made to the Society of Jesus. As far back as 1601, while the Jesuits were banished from France by the order of Henry, he declared that "he considered them better qualified and more capable than any others to instruct youth." He nursed an ambition to rear up a university that would be the greatest in Europe, and to put it completely under the charge of the Society of Jesus. Since La Flèche had been the happiest of the many homes he had had as a child, he wished to perpetuate his memories. He planned schools of arts and sciences, medicine and law, philosophy, theology, and Sacred Scripture. He erected magnificent buildings, among them a masterpiece of a church and a hospital most modernly equipped. *Tous les jours,* attested Father Coton, Henry discussed how *mon collège de la Flèche* could be made into *le plus beau qui fût au monde*. His last letter before his assassination had to do with the college. His will directed that his heart be preserved forever at La Flèche.

The Jesuits did not fail Henry. They assigned their greatest scholars as professors and applied their system of education in all its details at La Flèche. Within three years the college had attracted more than a thousand students drawn from the first nobility of the kingdom. Twenty years later, when Isaac Jogues began there his study of philosophy, the College of La Flèche was of established reputation. He was one of some two hundred young Jesuits who comprised a little world in the larger, secular college life. While they mingled in the classes with the concourse of other students, they were otherwise segregated in their own religious community.

Isaac passed through a well-graded philosophical course. After being grounded in the fundamentals of logic and correct reasoning, he had opened before him the questionings of the more metaphysical ontology, the theories of cosmology, the speculations of psychology, the principles of general ethics, and the practical applications of special ethics, the rationalizations of natural theology. He was introduced to the sciences, especially of physics and astronomy and mathematics, and was encouraged to continue the reading and study of the Greek and Latin classics, and of the purer examples of contemporary French.

During these three years at La Flèche Isaac also advanced spiritually. He still cherished the hope of a missionary career in Ethiopia or Constantinople. As his special patron he venerated Father Charles

Spinola, who was put to death in Japan in 1622, as a martyr, everyone believed. He carried about with him a little picture showing Father Spinola tied upright to a pole, with the red flames leaping up about his legs. Below the picture was printed the verse from the psalm, *Laudate pueri Dominum*. Isaac prayed to Father Spinola and visioned a similarly glorious ending for his own life.

He did not merely dream, but endeavored to persuade his Superiors to assign him definitely as a candidate for missionary work among the infidels. Frequently he talked of his ambition to his spiritual advisers, and stubbornly he refused to be put off with evasive answers. Father Dattichs, a famed Ethiopian missioner who resided for the time being at La Flèche, was rather amused by Isaac's zeal and insistence, and laughingly used to say: "I shall certainly take him along with me when I return to Ethiopia."

At La Flèche the great missionary enthusiasm was for New France. This had been cultivated by Father Ennemond Massé, who had first gone out to the New World in 1611, to Acadia, and was shipped back by the English in 1613. For twelve years he held the office of Assistant Rector at La Flèche and talked everlastingly of his experiences and his hopes once more to return to the copper-colored savages. In 1625 the opportunity came, and Father Massé, though fifty-two years of age, sailed for Canada and his pagans. His influence was perpetuated at La Flèche by the young Jesuits, scores of them, who were bent on following Father Massé to New France. Isaac, though he did not relinquish his desire for Constantinople, began to think more of the possibilities of a future life in Canada.

Having successfully completed his course of philosophy, Isaac was advanced to the next stage of his life as a Jesuit. For the scholastic year beginning in the autumn of 1629 he was assigned as Master of the Class of Fifth Grammar in the College of Rouen. He was approaching his twenty-third year, but seemed younger, for his skin and features were youthfully fresh, he was slimly built and not tall. It was with trepidation that he ascended the rostrum as a master and faced the young Normans in his class, shiny-faced youngsters of ten or eleven years. He had an air of assurance, an abundance of confidence, however, and magisterially surveyed his charges. Their young eyes estimated him. Master Isaac and his pupils soon came to mutual understandings and affectionate regards.

During four years he continued as Master of the same class of boys. He drilled them in the beginnings of Latin and Greek, and led them up through the fifth, fourth, third and second classes, through all the complexities and intricacies of the grammar and the writings of classical authors. With his quick mind and his nervous vitality, with his earnestness and sincerity, he was an inspiring teacher. Though a conscientious disciplinarian, he was invariably kindly and patient, that is, beyond the times when his naturally quick, violent temper flared out. He had a sense of justice, a self-sacrificing generosity, an amiability, a modesty tempering his official assertiveness that won the confidence and the love of his pupils. While he made them learned, he shed on them his own piety and religious spirit.

For his own spiritual direction at Rouen he had the advantage of consultation with his former Master of Novices, Father Louis Lalemant, who now filled the office of Instructor of the young priests in their third year of probation. He had also the wise counsel of Father Julien Haineuve, then the Master of Novices, who was generally regarded as a saint and an inspired guide of the interior life. Master Isaac, with his tender conscience and his exalted idealism and his passion for spiritual perfection, would easily have developed an over-scrupulosity were he not kept in balance by the sane advice of these two directors. His ardent nature drove him to excesses. Their counsels kept him vividly aware of realities, preserved him in his fervor, but restrained him from delusions.

Late in the autumn of 1629 the Canadian missioners, crestfallen, passed through Rouen. Charles Lalemant, Massé, de Brébeuf, and Vimont, who had voyaged with such high hopes to Canada, were forcibly returned to France when the English captured Quebec the preceding July. Their work among the red savages was totally ruined. France was driven out of the New World. But they were not disheartened. Cardinal Richelieu would force England to return Quebec; then they would sail back to their beloved missions. Master Isaac listened to them with a glowing heart. By the time he would be ordained the Jesuits would be back in Canada. Perhaps he might join himself with Father Massé along the St. Lawrence; he might be the companion of Father de Brébeuf among the Huron nations, deep in the center of the continent.

For the present, however, he contented himself with his duties as Master. He had to concern himself with controlling his mischievous boys and forcing them to study. Occasionally he was perplexed with other duties, such as those of appearing publicly before the joint assembly of teachers and scholars. On the opening of schools one year, he recited with great acclaim a long Latin poem which he had composed about the child martyr of Constantinople, Nicephorus. This lad, Master Isaac narrated in sonorous Latin verses, the son of a Jewish glass-blower and a Christian mother, had received in the company of Christian children a fragment of the Sacred Host. His Jewish father was so infuriated that he cast his son into a burning furnace. Nicephorus remained untouched by the flames. While imprisoned thus, he was visited by a beautiful lady clothed in purple, who gave him food and drink for three days and preserved him until he was miraculously rescued. Master Isaac thrilled all by his skill in Latin versification. In his subdued way he was so proud of his achievement that he sent the poem to his mother at Orléans, and she was so proud of her gifted son that she cherished it as a valued family possession.

Upon the completion of his four-year period of teaching at the College of Rouen, Isaac was called to Paris, to the College of Clermont, there to enter the classes of theology in preparation for his ordination to the priesthood. In a letter to his mother, dated October 10, 1633, he reflected:

After having been a master, here I am become a student again. This employment is all the more agreeable to me because it applies me to the study of the holy and sacred theology, a science which ought to make me more than ever fitted to work for the glory of God, since it will enable me to be advanced to Holy Orders within a few years. That is the grace to which I have aspired. May it be granted to me, and then, may it give more efficacy than ever to the prayers which I offer to the Lord for you and all your household. The only thing I need is the help of your prayers. I beg you to continue them in behalf of your very humble son and servant in Our Saviour,

Isaac Jogues, of the Company of Jesus.

Clermont College lay in the heart of Paris. From its earliest organization, seventy-five years before, it had rivaled and been attacked by the University of Paris and the Parliament. Under Henry IV it had been reduced to debris by the rioting mobs at the time of the suppression of the Jesuits. In the later years of Henry, through his help, it had been resurrected and now held rank as the first Jesuit college of France, surpassing even La Flèche. Its most renowned courses were those of theology. With Isaac Jogues were associated the most brilliant students of the younger generation.

Theology, he learned, was as exact a science as philosophy. The teachings of Christ, the Scriptures, and tradition, were analyzed into strictly defined terms, into stern propositions, each one of which could be clearly proved in perfect syllogism and defended against the objections of heretics. Morality as well as dogma was treated with precision and made practical in its human applications. Sacred Scripture was searched for its moral and dogmatic content. The lecturers sought not so much to inflame the heart as to inform the intellect.

Isaac followed the processes of the reasoning of his professors, but he drew from their lectures a deeper love of religion. He incorporated his theology and scriptural and moral learning into his prayers and meditations. He had no ambition to be a great scholar. He recognized his limitations as compared with his fellow students. He sought to be a priest who was learned enough to instruct simple-minded lay folk, and holy enough to lead souls to God.

Relentlessly he cherished his ideals as a religious. Jacques Buteux, who was then living at Clermont, awaiting his appointment to go as a missioner to Canada, recalled: "He was sent to Paris to undertake the study of theology. It was at that time that I first met him, and from that time, also, I sought to know him. It was his prudence, most of all, that attracted me. His remarkably exact and continued observance of the rules was particularly noteworthy because, in the surroundings of the college in which he lived, the observance of the rules is wont to suffer, if I may use the phrase, some eclipse or other. I also admired as well as venerated the humility which characterized him. Oftentimes he begged that he should be withdrawn from the study of theology because he lacked the ability to master it, and that he should be sent off to the barbarians in New France."

As at La Flèche, the young Jesuits led a circumscribed life at Clermont. They went out into the streets of Paris, but only with downcast eyes and religious demeanor, for exercise and mild relaxation. Neither mentally nor emotionally were they part of the throbbing city which enclosed them about. Isaac was forced to mingle with the young Parisians, however, for he was appointed to act as a prefect of discipline over the lay students at Clermont. His presence was required about the halls and on the recreation grounds as a check upon these spirited students who belonged to that ebullient young generation born into the prosperous era that followed Henry IV and made grandiosely ambitious and proud by Cardinal Richelieu. They had need of control. Master Isaac found them far more difficult to manage than the provincial lads of Rouen.

It was in his second year at Clermont that he received the announcement of the marriage of his younger brother, Philippe, to Elizabeth, the daughter of Claude and Marie Jousse Caillard. It was a notable marriage in Orléans society, and Madame la Mère urged Isaac to attend the ceremony on February 18, 1635. He paid little attention to her suggestion. Madame Jogues was hurt, and reproached him for his neglect. On April 25, 1635, he returned an answer:

> It never entered my mind to speak of the matter to my Superiors. The urgent duties of my work do not permit me to leave the house even for a single day. Moreover, my presence at this ceremony was not at all necessary. The prayers that I am able to offer for the happy result of this marriage are as helpful from afar as they would be near, and they are all the most affectionate indications that I can give you, to show the interest that I have in you. I beg my brothers and sisters to receive kindly the assurance which I give them, that my prayers are often offered up for the intention of their welfare. I shall be able to help in this way with still greater efficacy in this coming year when, I believe, I shall receive the blessing of being promoted to the priesthood, unworthy though I am of such a grace.

That grace was granted sooner than he anticipated. Normally, he would have been ordained priest later in 1636. But in the beginning of January he was informed that he would be priested within a few weeks. Not only that, but his repeated requests to be sent out of France as a missioner to the pagans in far countries were also answered. Because of the needs of the Fathers in New France and in view of their demands that helpers be sent them, Isaac was informed by the Father Provincial, Estienne Binet, that he must make himself ready to sail in the early spring to Canada.

CHAPTER II

The Portals of New France

I

FROM time beyond remembrance, Breton and Norman fishermen had been sailing their tubby boats far out into the ocean. They would leave early in the spring and return in the autumn, loaded down with a cargo of the finest fish. The location of their fishing-grounds they kept a secret among themselves. Jacques Cartier, as a young sailor, had adventured out in these expeditions. He had never gone beyond the gray fogs where the haul was so plentiful, but he was convinced that land lay not far beyond. He was resolved to explore the northern waters, with the hope of discovering gold and precious stones, and eventually of penetrating through these countries to India and Cathay. King Francis I listened to Cartier's vision, and empowered him to claim for France all the New World that he found on the western rim of the Atlantic Ocean.

In 1534 Cartier piloted out of the estuary of St. Malo two ships which measured not more than fifty feet in length and twenty-five in beam. By July he came up out of the sea before a headland. This he named Gaspé. It marked the entrance to a gulf which he called after St. Lawrence. He planted a cross and a banner upon the hill, and proclaimed Francis King over all the territories of this further world. In the following year, equipped by the King with three larger vessels, he nosed a way up the Gulf of St. Lawrence till it narrowed into a river. By September, he approached a towering promontory. "Que bec!" shouted the pilot in his Norman dialect. Cartier mounted the summit of the wall of rock and once more subjected all the known and unknown lands and peoples to France and the King.

Autumnal storms would be raging over the ocean, so Cartier decided to risk spending the winter in the wilderness. He followed the river up 150 miles till he reached an island dominated by a cone-shaped mountain, to which he gave the name of Mont-Réal. Returning to Quebec, he built a camp near the great rock. The rigors of the months that followed nearly destroyed him and his men. When he arrived in France the following summer he failed to interest the King in his story. He brought no cargo of precious metals and jewels, he had not opened the short route to Cathay.

In France there were foreign wars to wage. Then there were civil and religious conflicts to split the kingdom. The new world of Cartier was abandoned. Not until seventy years had passed, until Henry IV brought peace and stability, were any sustained efforts made to confirm the claims of Cartier. About 1603, a Company of Merchants interested in furs planted a habitation at Port Royal, in Acadia. The enterprise was preëminently commercial and Calvinistic. It created strife in France, especially when two Jesuits, Pierre Biard and Ennemond Massé, were forced on the directors by Henry IV. They were reluctantly transported to Port Royal in 1611, and barely tolerated by the colonists.

The Marquise de Guercherville obtained from Louis XIII superior rights over all the lands of Acadia, from the St. Lawrence to Florida. Her ambition was not mercenary, but religious. In 1613 she sent thirty pioneers under La Saussaye to establish a center for the conversion of the natives. Three Jesuits were of the party, in addition to the two missioners who were salvaged from Port Royal. They located at Saint Sauveur, on Mount Desert Island, near the mainland. The savages welcomed them, but the English of Virginia, regarding them as squatters, burned their habitations, and returned them through devious routes to France.

Samuel Champlain had been Chief Geographer of Port Royal. He had fought as a Catholic with the Holy League, had battled for France along the Spanish main, and proved himself an adventurer with a clear brain, an imperial vision, and a will of iron. He believed that the destiny of France should be plotted along the St. Lawrence. In 1608 he commanded a party which wintered at Cartier's old camp beneath the rock of Quebec. In 1609 he piloted a shallop up the St. Lawrence, turned down the river of the Iroquois, and discovered the lake thereafter called Champlain. On its shores he fought the first battle with the Iroquois. In the following years he struck out to the west and familiarized himself with the lands a thousand miles to the interior. He was hindered in his tremendous projects by the changes of governors in France, as well as by the greedy and mercenary policy of the Company of Merchants which held the fur monopoly.

At the invitation of Champlain, four Récollets sailed for Quebec in 1615. They had unbounded hopes of converting the natives. Father Joseph Le Caron traveled up the rivers to the Hurons; Father Jean d'Olbeau followed the Montagnais into the forests; Father Denis Jamay and Brother Pacifique du Plessis shepherded the French and savages at Quebec. They spared no labor, they feared no danger in their supernatural ambition. For ten years, these apostolic Récollets struggled heroically, with Champlain, to evangelize New France. But the continued obstruction of the Calvinist majority of the Company of Merchants reduced them to despair and practically nullified all their efforts.

By themselves, they realized they could not master the situation. Their rule forbade them to have a permanent endowment for support; hence, financially they must depend on the Merchants. They had no influence at Court; hence, they could obtain no redress against the Calvinists from the King. They were not a numerous religious body; hence they could not guarantee a steady increase in the number of missioners. They resolved to seek the Jesuits as allies. Ever since the collapse of the colonies in Acadia, the Society had been longing to return to Canada. They accepted the invitation of the Récollets enthusiastically, and in 1625 sent out Fathers Charles Lalemant, Ennemond Massé, Jean de Brébeuf, and Brothers Gilbert Burel and Nicholas Charon, under the sponsorship of the Récollet Father Joseph de la Roche. The Calvinist directors in France tried to prevent the departure of the Jesuits; those in Quebec strove to prevent their landing and remaining.

The Jesuits arrived early in the summer. In the autumn Lalemant took ship back to France. He demanded that the Huguenots be ousted from the control of the Company of Merchants; Cardinal Richelieu suppressed the Company of Merchants and organized his Company of One Hundred Associates, entirely Catholic, to hold full authority over all of New France. Lalemant sought support for the Récollets and Jesuit missioners; he was guaranteed generous amounts by the Hundred Associates and other benefactors. He aimed to educate France to the plan of building a great empire in the New World; Richelieu and Louis XIII caught his vision. The Hundred

Associates engaged to ship two hundred colonists to Quebec in 1628, and to transport five thousand settlers before 1633. The dreams of Samuel Champlain through twenty-five years, the hopes of the Récollets during thirteen years, were being fulfilled through their Jesuit allies.

About the time the first transports in the new régime were sailing from France, David Kirk, a French Calvinist from Dieppe, with his brothers, Louis and Thomas, was leaving London with authorization to destroy all the French occupations in America. The Kirk brothers demolished the abandoned settlements in Acadia, captured the French transports at the mouth of the St. Lawrence, and threatened Quebec. Champlain was helpless and desperate. He was forced to surrender on July 19, 1629, and the colonists, Jesuits and Récollets, with a few exceptions, were shipped back to France. Cardinal Richelieu raged at this violation of peace by England. He demanded the immediate return of New France and an indemnity. England engaged in diplomatic conversations. Three years passed, then Richelieu let it be known he was arming ten battleships to recapture Quebec. England promptly signed an agreement, on March 29, 1632, whereby Canada was returned to France.

In his reorganization of the Company of the One Hundred Associates, Cardinal Richelieu decided there must be unity of control in every department. The missionary activities, as the commercial and governmental, must be under single heads. He offered the apostolate of New France, as a religious monopoly, to his favorite Capuchins. When they begged to be excused, his choice lay between the Récollets and the Jesuits. Since the Jesuits were not a mendicant order, and thus could support themselves and be no burden to the colony, and since they were stronger numerically, Cardinal Richelieu, despite the pleas of the intrepid and apostolic Récollets who so eagerly desired a share in the evangelization of New France, ruled that the Society of Jesus must be the sole Missionary Order to labor under the French government.

The first ships leaving France in 1632 to take over Quebec from the English carried Fathers Paul Le Jeune, Anne de Nouë, Antoine Daniel, Ambroise Davost, and Brother Gilbert Burel. In 1633 Massé returned for his third attempt, and de Brébeuf for his second. Six more missioners went in 1634. Seven more sailed in 1635. They sent back across the ocean their cry for even more missioners. So insistent was their demand for helpers, so vitally important seemed their work, that eight more priests and Brothers were appointed to the Mission of New France in 1636.

Isaac Jogues was of this number. When his Provincial, Father Binet, consulted him about his willingness to go to Canada as a missioner, he answered with a burst of enthusiasm and gratitude. He had wished it, begged for it, prayed for it through long years. He was twenty-nine years old, in the best of health. Certainly he would be glad to sail in the spring. The invitation, also offered to three of his classmates, was accepted as eagerly. Charles Garnier, a pink-checked, delicately formed man, two years the senior of Isaac, belonged to a distinguished family of Parisian lawyers. Pierre Chastellain, a year older than Jogues, was born at Senlis, and was derived from a hardy stock that begot strong bodies and undaunted wills. Paul Ragueneau was twenty-eight; he was of Paris, sturdy, broad-shouldered, keen of mind and sure in his judgments.

Clermont College was hugely excited when it learned that four of its theological students were being sent as missioners to Canada. The young men were excused from the lectures in early January. Toward the end of the month, after they had passed the examinations of various sorts, the days were set for their ordinations. Isaac Jogues knelt and prostrated himself before the altar of the College Chapel, and was raised up successively as sub-deacon, deacon, and priest. He became the anointed of God, bearing the indelible mark of the priesthood upon his soul, having the Divine power to change bread and wine into the Body and Blood of Christ, deputed to absolve from sin, commissioned to go forth and teach all nations, baptizing them in the name of the Father and of the Son and of the Holy Spirit.

When Isaac apprised his mother of his ordination, and of the reason for it so early, her joy of the one was mingled with her sorrow because of the other. She wanted him a priest, but not a missioner among savages. She craved, then, all the more to see him as soon as could be. After his answer to her at the time of Philippe's marriage, she did not trust him to secure the required permissions. And so she directed her requests to the Jesuit Superiors.

Isaac was ordered home to Orléans for the celebration of his first Mass. On February 1, 1636, he wrote to his mother saying that, "since his Superiors had judged reasonable the petition which she had made to them, he was held bound to give this comfort to her." He informed her that he expected to be ready to journey to Orléans within a few days. Meanwhile, he begged her to seek prayers for him from every source, "so that God might bestow on him the graces necessary for a ministry so sublime and so exalted."

Carnival time held sway in Orléans when the lumbering coach rattled through the north gate and halted before the grilled doors of the Jesuit College. Fresh from the quiet of the cloisters of Clermont, under the spell of his first priestly ecstasy, Orléans seemed to Isaac to have gone wildly mad. Yet, he remembered, it was as if long ago, he had taken part as a boy and a young man in the fun and merry-making before Ash Wednesday. His delight now was singly in his priesthood. He retired to the seclusion of his room at the College. Madame la Mère had little more than a glimpse of him during his first few days in Orléans. From Wednesday until Sunday, February 10, he spent in a spiritual retreat in order the better to prepare himself for the first Solemn Mass.

On the first Sunday of Lent he vested himself in purple. His features were tense, his virginal eyes bright, his stride was firm as he followed the acolytes and ministers of the Mass across the sanctuary of the College Church and ascended the altar. He was enwrapt in this tremendous experience of pronouncing the awesome words of consecration. His mother watched him through tear-dimmed eyes. *"Mon cher Isaac,"* she mumbled with her lips, as so often she had repeated over him as a child. At Communion time, she walked, faintly, to the sanctuary step and there received the Sacred Host from his fingers. That hour compensated for her years of loneliness. It strengthened her for those years to follow.

Later, there were festivities in the Jogues household down near the Grand Marché. All the dozens of families closely related to the Jogues and the de Saint-Mesmins, all the old friends and neighbors, offered their felicitations to Isaac and Madame Jogues, and expressed their grief that Père Isaac must so soon depart, and for the far-away New World. During the days that followed, Madame la Mère was truly broken-hearted. She pleaded with Isaac that he remain in France, at least for a few years. She was growing old, she loved him best of all her children, she could not part with him.

Patiently, Isaac tried to reconcile her with all the spiritual motives which seemed to him so convincing. He told her, calmly, of the abandoned souls he must go out to save; he tried to arouse her to a realization of the exceptional grace God had tendered him; he pointed out the marvelous opportunities for renunciation and sacrifice, and how God must bless her and him in this world and the next. He was tender, and grief-stricken at her sorrow. But he could not sincerely dampen the ardor of his own spiritual jubilation.

Madame Jogues accepted the inevitable. There was no moving Isaac, once he had made up his mind. She knew him as having always been that way. After listening to his talk, in the quiet hours they had together, after watching him in his eagerness for this future he prized, she consoled herself and resolved that she must not be an obstacle to him. She distracted her mind by busying herself with getting clothes and other things ready to make his journey a little more comfortable.

One gift only did he desire. He had been told that it would be possible for him to say Mass on board the ship. He had to supply himself, however, with the chalice, vestments, and other necessaries. Marthe, his stepsister, the wife of Arnout Houdebine, the treasurer of Orléans, insisted on bearing the expense, and she, with Madame Jogues, set to work to prepare all that was needed for the chapel set.

A short week only was allowed Father Isaac in Orléans. He then had to hurry back to Paris, to gather baggage, to pay official calls on his Superiors, to bid farewell to his friends. He was dispatched up to Rouen, with orders to await there the word to go on to Dieppe, from which port the fleet of that year was to sail. To Isaac, Rouen was a second city of home, for here he had been born to his religious life in 1624, and here he had passed his four years as a Master. It was all so familiar to him when he rode into the Norman streets on this chilly day in late February. Though brief, his stay would be a period of peace and quiet after the past six weeks of feverish excitement. He must immerse himself in a Spiritual Retreat; must spend all his remaining days in France in prayer and meditation, in silence, self-mortification, and retirement from everything mundane; must build up virtues against the dangers of a life among the savages.

Ordinarily, after the completion of his studies, Isaac would have been held to a full year of further ascetical training, commonly referred to as the Tertianship—a year that would have been wholly and exclusively concerned with completing the spiritual life which he began in the Noviceship. Since he was being rushed prematurely to Canada, the normal routine of the year of Tertianship was commuted. But he was not excused from the chief essential of this year, that of the Thirty-day Retreat. Under the direction, then, of Father Louis Lalemant, the Instructor in the Tertian House of Rouen, his former Novice Master, Isaac applied himself to a deeper understanding of the principles and ideals in the Jesuit handbook of spirituality as outlined by Saint Ignatius, the "Spiritual Exercises to Conquer Oneself and Regulate One's Life, and to Avoid Coming to a Determination through Any Inordinate Affections."

Isaac was thoroughly familiar with the method of prayer and the exercises programmed by St. Ignatius. He had learned them when he first entered the Society twelve years before, and each year he had spent at least eight days in their practice in his annual Retreat. They formed the basis of his daily meditations. But now, in view of his future, he must find new and pertinent applications. For the first few days, he pondered the question of his destiny, so simply stated in the "First Principle and Foundation."

In the words of St. Ignatius, he found the simplest possible answer to the problem of existence: "Man was created to praise, reverence, and serve God our Lord, and by this means to save his soul; and the other things on the face of the earth were created for man's sake, and in order to aid him in the prosecution of the end for which he was created." There followed a conclusion of inescapable logic: "Whence it follows, that man must make use of creatures in so far as they help him to attain his end, and in the same way he ought to withdraw himself from them, in so far as they hinder him from it." This was reduced to a practical procedure: "It is therefore necessary that we should make ourselves indifferent to all created things, in so far as it is left to the liberty of our free will to do so, and is not forbidden; in such sort that we do not for our part wish for health rather than sickness, for wealth rather than poverty, for honor rather than dishonor, for a long life rather than a short one; and so in all other things, desiring and choosing only those which most lead us to the end for which we were created."

Vividly could Isaac exemplify these considerations in his own case. From them, he entered into the series of meditations upon sin and the eternal punishment of hell, upon death and the Divine judgment. Never, he resolved, would he offend God through sin; bitterly did he repent of his transgressions in the past. Chastened in soul, with such thoughts absorbing him for the greater part of a week, he progressed to the second period of the Spiritual Exercises, the contemplation of Christ, his Master.

In the primary meditation on "The Kingdom of Christ," he protested that he desired "to signalize himself in every kind of service to his Eternal King and Universal Lord"; he offered himself wholly to imitate his King, "in bearing all insults and reproaches, and all poverty as well actual poverty as poverty of spirit, if only Thy Divine Majesty be pleased to choose and receive me to this life and state."

Through a few days, he dwelt in quiet contemplation on the applicable events in the early life of Christ. He then vowed anew his unreserved and unflinching loyalty to Christ in the meditation: "On Two Standards, the one of Christ, our sovereign Leader and Lord; the other of Lucifer, the mortal enemy of our human nature." Through several more days, prayerfully he studied his King in the three years of His public life. Then, calmly, with balanced mind, cold-bloodedly, he made his own the highest aspiration contained in the meditation on "The Three Degrees of Humility." He affirmed: "the better to imitate Christ our Lord, and to become actually more like to Him, I desire and choose rather poverty with Christ poor, than riches; contempt with Christ contemned, than honors; and I desire to be esteemed as useless and foolish, for Christ's sake, Who was first held to be such, than to be accounted wise and prudent in this world."

Such determinations as these were leading Isaac to New France, and such as these were now hardening his soul against all worldly allurements. He made his list of practical resolutions, convinced of St. Ignatius' proposition that "he will make progress in all spiritual matters in proportion as he shall have divested himself of his own self-love, his own will, and self-interest." Then he entered into the third period of the Spiritual Exercises, the contemplation of the physical tortures endured by Christ, of His mental anguish, in His Passion and death. Isaac held colloquy with Jesus his Master, asking the fullness of grace whereby he would desire "sorrow with Christ Who is full of sorrow, anguish with Christ in anguish, tears and interior pain that Christ has suffered for me."

From the glowing depths of these days of sorrow, Isaac rose to the fourth period of his Retreat, the vision of the glorious life of Christ in His Resurrection. Finally, he approached the concluding ecstasy, the "Contemplation for Obtaining Love." He loved God beyond himself and all things created. He sought only God's love for him. He read from St. Ignatius that "love ought to be found in deeds rather than words"; and again, "that love consists in mutual interchange on either side." He thought of all God had done for him. What could he offer in return to God? Only himself. Solemnly he repeated the supreme oblation: "Take, O Lord, and receive all my liberty, my memory, my understanding, and all my will, whatsoever I have and possess. Thou hast given all these things to me; to Thee, O Lord, I restore them; all are Thine, dispose of them all according to Thy will. Give me Thy love and Thy grace, for this is enough for me."

Three weeks had passed while Isaac prayed thus, alone with God, in silence and seclusion even from his fellow Jesuits at Rouen. The summons came for him to proceed to Dieppe, where the fleet was making ready to sail. One more bond with the Society of Jesus was necessary for him. At the end of his Novitiate, in 1626, he had pronounced his simple, though perpetual, vows of poverty, chastity, and obedience. Now that he had finished with all his studies and his years of training, he was ready to utter his final vows. He was acceptable for the Solemn Profession in all requisites save one: he had not finished his full course of theology nor had he passed the comprehensive examination of all philosophy and theology. He had the privilege, in some future day, since his life was to be spent in the foreign missions, of substituting proficiency in the native languages for excellence in the higher studies. Instead of taking advantage of the extraordinary circumstances, he simply offered himself to God as a Formed Spiritual Coadjutor with vows that linked him closer than ever to his God.

II

Into Dieppe trundled the coaches bearing the adventurers who were sailing out to New France. Young men they were, mostly, and men of middle age. They were masons, carpenters, farmers, workers who could turn a hand to anything. Of good character they were, too, and of steady habits, for the Hundred Associates would ship no riffraff to Quebec. Their ambition was to better their fortunes in the New World, to settle a home and later bring out their womenfolk. A goodly number were young aristocrats, hardy and reckless spirits inspired with grand visions. Such were the brothers-in-law, Pierre le Gardeur, Sieur de Repentigny, a gentleman of twenty-six, and Jacques le Neuf de la Poterie. They were tearing up their family roots in the old country and were claiming the seigniories granted them in the environs of Quebec. With their six baby children, their wives, mothers, and sisters, their servants and dependents, their party included forty-five people.

A new Governor-General, Charles Hualt de Montmagny, Chevalier of the Military Order of St. John of Jerusalem, was sailing for Canada. Samuel Champlain was dead. After laboring more than thirty years to build an empire for his King, after seeing his efforts first nullified and then smashed, after witnessing the restoration of 1632 and visioning a glorious future, he was stricken with paralysis in October, 1635, and on Christmas day passed quietly to the God whom he had so zealously served through all his seventy years. Cardinal Richelieu sought a man of the same heroic mold as Champlain. He fixed his choice upon de Montmagny, and on March 10, 1636, formally commissioned him as Governor of New France under the authority of the King and the Company of the One Hundred Associates.

About the time Chevalier de Montmagny was arriving in regal state in Dieppe, Isaac Jogues and his classmates, Garnier, Chastellain, and Ragueneau, were assembling in the little Jesuit residence in the old seaport town. There they found their fellow voyagers. Father Nicholas Adam was a stout, ruddy man of forty-eight; he had become a Jesuit the year Isaac Jogues was born. Father Georges Alexander d'Eudemare had passed twenty-four of his forty-six years in the Society in various avocations. Brother Ambroise Cauvet was a vigorous thirty, and Brother Louis Gaubert was just past twenty-eight. Only three months previously he had entered the Novitiate with the intention of being assigned to the Mission of New France. They were, all of them, jubilant over their good fortune of voyaging out into the wilderness to convert the nations of those far-off countries to the true God.

Admiral Guillaume Guillemot, Sieur Duplessis-Bochart, had assembled the eight vessels of his fleet in the harbor. He had superintended the overhauling of the ships from the keel to the topmost spars; he had the cargoes packed and fastened; he had the crews at their posts. He had set the date of departure for the week following Palm Sunday, March 16. But the weather was adverse. March winds blew in a gale from the sea, dark clouds lowered over the waters, rain beat down incessantly, through Holy Week, all of Easter day, and through the next week.

With the beginning of April came a break in the stormy weather. A favorable land breeze sprang up, the sun reappeared, the seas subsided. Duplessis-Bochart sent criers through the town calling on the passengers and crews to hold themselves in readiness for the signal to board the ships. Isaac had been waiting for this last moment to write his final letter of farewell to his mother. He addressed her:

Madame and most honored Mother:

It would be to fail in the first essential duty of a good son toward a good mother if, being ready to set sail, I should not bid you the last adieu. I wrote to you last month from Rouen, through the kindness of Mons. Taureau, who offered to take charge of my letters, and told you that I was leaving for Dieppe, from which port we hoped to embark about Holy Week. But the winds were contrary and the weather was not right for us, so that we were detained up to the present time and could not leave. I trust that God is going to give us a prosperous and happy voyage, for one reason because we sail in a number of vessels assembled together, but principally because many persons who are pleasing to God, are praying for us. Try, also, if you please, to contribute something by your prayers for the good success of our voyage, and more than that, by the generous submission of your will to the Divine Will, accommodating our desires to the desires of the Divine Goodness, which cannot but be very sacred and very respected by us, since these come from a Heart most desirous for our good. I trust, as I have already told you many times, that if you accept this little sorrow as you should, it will be an act extremely pleasing to God; since, for the love of God, not only would it be right for you to give one son, but all the other sons, and even life itself, if that were necessary. For a little gain, some men traverse the seas and endure as much as we, at least; and we, for the love of God, we do not do as much as these men do for the affairs of this world. Adieu, Madame ma mère, I thank you for all the great love that you have always given me, and mostly for the love shown at our last meeting. May God reunite us in His holy Paradise if we do not ever see each other here on earth. Please offer my most humble remembrances

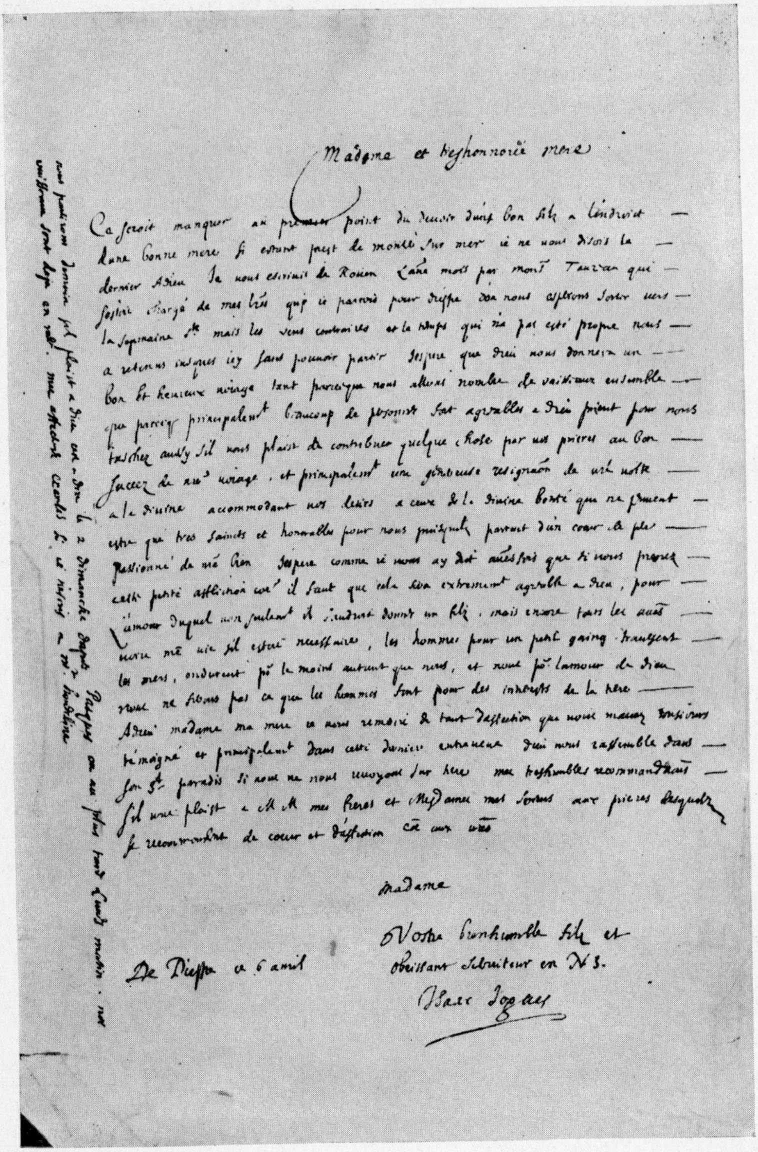

Madame et treshonnorée mere

Ce seroit manquer au premier point du devoir d'un bon filz a l'endroit d'une bonne mere si estant prest de monter sur mer je ne vous disois le dernier Adieu. Je vous escrivis de Rouen l'autre mois par monst Tauvan qui s'estoit chargé de mes lres quand je partois pour dieppe ou nous esperions sortir vers la Septmaine Ste mais les vents contraires et le temps qui n'a pas esté propre nous a retenus jusques icy sans pouvoir partir. J'espere que Dieu nous donnera un bon et heureux voiage tant parceque nous allons nombre de vaisseaux ensemble que parceque principalement beaucoup de personnes fort agreables a Dieu prient pour nous. Taschez aussy s'il vous plaist de contribuer quelque chose par vos prieres au bon succez de nre voiage, et principalement une genereuse resignation de vre volonté a la divine accommodant vos desirs a ceux de la divine bonté qui ne peuvent estre que tres saincts et honnorables pour nous, puisqu'ils partent d'un coeur le plus passionné de nre bien. J'espere comme je vous ay dit aultrefois que si vous prenez cette petite affliction come il faut que cela sera extremement agreable a Dieu, pour l'amour duquel non seulement il s'est donné un filz, mais encore tous les autres voire mesme sa vie s'il estoit necessaire. Les hommes pour un petit gaing traversent les mers, endurent pour le moins autant que nous, et nous pour l'amour de Dieu ne ferons pas ce que les hommes font pour des interests de la terre. Adieu madame ma mere je vous remercie de toute l'affection que vous m'avez tousiours tesmoigné et principalement dans cette derniere entreveue. Dieu nous rassemble dans son St paradis si nous ne nous voyons sur terre. Mes treshumbles recommandations s'il vous plaist a MM mes freres et Mesdames mes soeurs aux prieres desquelz je recommande de coeur et d'affection ceux de vous.

Madame

Vostre treshumble filz et obeissant serviteur en N. S.

Isaac Jogues

De Dieppe ce 6 avril

[illegible] nous partirons demain s'il plaist a Dieu. C'est aujourd'huy le 2 Dimanche d'apres Pasques [illegible] plus tard demain matin. nos vaisseaux sont deja en rade. mes affectionées [illegible]

Letter of Isaac Jogues to His Mother

Courtesy of Collège Sainte-Marie, Montréal

to MM. mes frères and Mesdames mes sœurs, to whose prayers I recommend myself from the heart and with affection as to your prayers,

Madame,

Your very humble son and
obedient servant in Our Lord,
Isaac Jogues.

From Dieppe, April 6.

Later in the day, Admiral Duplessis-Bochart sent out the criers to announce that embarkation would follow Mass on the morrow. Isaac added a postscript, hurriedly, in the margin of his letter:

We depart tomorrow, if it please God; that is to say, the 2nd Sunday after Easter, or at the latest, Monday morning. Our vessels are already in the roadstead. My affectionate excuses that I do not write M. Houdebine.

Folding the sheet in the form of an envelope, he sealed it and inscribed the address:

A Madame
Madame Jogues
demeurant près le grand marché devant
La Rose
à Orléans.

Isaac Jogues, with his last letter written, felt that he was finished with France, with his mother and his family, forever. He and his Jesuit companions assembled down by the quay, and were rowed out to the ships which lay anchored a little way off in the harbor enclosure. Isaac was detailed to the vessel that would visit the sea coast settlement at Miscou. Eighty people, among them the distinguished Sieur François de Champflour, formed the ship's company. Father d'Eudemare was on the boat that was to call at Cape Breton Island, the first of the French outposts in the New World. Father Adam and Brother Cauvet were assigned to the vessel of the Vice-Admiral, M. de Courpon; Father Ragueneau and Brother Gaubert were to board the flagship of the Admiral; and Fathers Garnier and Chastellain were appointed to the ship carrying Governor de Montmagny.

They did not sail on Sunday, nor yet on Monday. But on Tuesday, April 8, Admiral Duplessis-Bochart ran the signal up the mast of his flagship. His cannon thundered their farewell. The other ships crashed out their salute. The guns of the castle and the fort responded and rocked the air. The white sails of the flagship lifted and bellied, the keel cut a straight path toward the narrow passageway between the protruding seawalls. One by one the other vessels showed their sails and pointed their prows along the bubbling waters toward the open sea. With the white pennants of France fluttering in the breeze, the fleet for New France proudly and confidently rode out from the port of Dieppe.

Isaac stood upon the deck, and looked down upon the square roadstead, back at the waves playing about the jetties and sprawling over the shore, up at the gables and slanting roofs, and at the frowning turrets of the castle and the fort. He was free as the white gulls which circled above the masts. He had one bond, his vows to God; one ambition, to lead souls to God. Dieppe, Rouen, Paris, Orléans, his home, mother, all were slipping on the other side of the horizon, all were fading into memories. He said his adieu to France happily.

They were out in the ever-changing circle of the green ocean. Some days, when the breeze was favorable, they advanced upward of a hundred miles; but on other days they labored to progress fifty miles. The little flock of eight ships clustered together in the vastness of the waters, rising with the heaving of the waves and hiding in the hollows, kicking a way forward against the billows. The ships rolled and floundered, and the passengers as well as the crews were wracked with sickness. Not Isaac, however, for he boasted: "I astonished everybody, since it is no ordinary thing to make such a long voyage without experiencing the least feeling in the stomach or the least nausea."

On mornings when the sea was calm, Father Jogues set up an altar in the dark cabin and celebrated Mass. This was the first year that the Fathers enjoyed this privilege of offering the Holy Sacrifice on board the ships. He often thanked in his heart his mother and Marthe, his stepsister, who had provided him with the altar-stone, the chalice and vestments. On May 1, the Feast of the Ascension, and then on Pentecost and Trinity Sunday, all the eighty persons of his ship confessed and received Holy Communion. It was a new, a profound, an ecstatic experience for Isaac, ordained priest but these three or four months, to murmur the words of absolution over sinners, to pronounce the words of Consecration in the Mass; and that, when the little boat was surrounded by such an infinity of the ocean.

The days slipped by into weeks. April turned into May. Seven weeks out of Dieppe, they ran into the fog that hung low over the Newfoundland banks. Now they were out of the void of the sea; now they were at last in the waters of the New World. They plotted their course parallel to the dim shadow of the Newfoundland shoreline and pointed toward the entrance of the Gulf of St. Lawrence. Then, one of the vessels veered off to the left and sailed its own route to the settlement of Ste. Anne, at the tip of Cape Breton Island, the most seaward of the outposts of New France. A day or two later, Jogues' ship signaled its farewells and cut across the horizon away from the rest of the fleet, bound for the second of the settlements, that of St. Charles, on the island of St. Louis de Miscou, near the southern promontory of the Baye des Chaleurs.

Father Jogues saw the low, gray strip rise indistinctly out of the misty horizon. He and the others crowded the deck, deliriously shouting "Land!" It was their eighth week of voyaging. They drew up in the quiet waters of the circular harbor on June 2. French shallops darted out from the strand to greet them. Little barks—they were canoes—paddled by dark-skinned men, fluttered about nearer the shore. Jogues climbed down the ladder and into the shallop, and leaped out to the sand of the shore. Two black-robed priests were waiting for him, were throwing their arms vigorously about his shoulders, were implanting resounding kisses on both his cheeks. Fathers Charles Du Marché and Charles Turgis, they had been studying theology with him at Clermont just a year ago; they had spent a winter among the savages here at Miscou; they were welcoming him as a fellow missioner. His head was whirling with the joy and triumph.

Their first greetings over, the three young priests climbed the hill to the cluster of log cabins. In the rude hut where they lived they all three knelt humbly before the Blessed Sacrament and recited a fervent *Te Deum* of thanksgiving. Then Du Marché and Turgis plied him with questions innumerable. They had had no communications from the rest of the world for a full year, for only once a year did a ship come from France, and rarely did one arrive from Quebec. They told him of Miscou. Twenty-three Frenchmen lived there, carrying on a fair trade in furs, and shipping these, together with fish and lumber, to France. It was not healthy. There had been much scurvy and other sicknesses during the two years that the post had been settled. They had some success with the Algonquin natives who came to trade their furs and peltries for French goods, in making friends with them, in learning their language, in teaching them some knowledge of God.

Flocks of these natives emerged out of the forests and loitered in Miscou after the arrival of the French ship. Jogues was curiously observant of them. Their naked bodies were a reddish, dull copper color. Their faces were heavy, barbaric-looking, with large, hooked noses, spreading nostrils, and bulbous lips, with high cheekbones, with narrow slits for eyes. Their hair was straight, wiry as the mane of a horse. Scarcely a one of them but had streaked his face and body with greasy paints of white, black, red, blue, in most grotesque, most comical, most ferocious designs. He listened to the grunting sounds of their speech. They seemed to talk from their bellies, or from the gorges of their throats, without moving their lips. Happy beyond telling was he to mingle with these nations he had come to save.

When he was leaving Paris, Isaac understood that he was to be assigned to the mission among the Hurons. Shipping at Dieppe, he was put on the ship stopping at Miscou. His unexpected arrival, at first, seemed to solve a difficulty. Du Marché was obliged to go to Quebec, to consult with Father Le Jeune on matters connected with the St. Charles Mission at Miscou. His absence would leave Turgis alone, certainly for the summer, probably for the winter, since it might not be possible to find passage back. It was proposed, then, that Jogues remain at Miscou with Turgis. He was willing, but he preferred to go on to Quebec, as ordered, and thence to the Hurons. After some consultation, the three young priests decided that Jogues should follow the instructions he had received.

Two weeks after his arrival, then, on June 13, Du Marché and Jogues sailed from Miscou. They crossed the gaping mouth of the Baye des Chaleurs, rounded the Cape of Gaspé, and sailed into the lower widths of the St. Lawrence. After a few days they saw the far bank of the river appear like a black line above the level waters. Toward the end of June they came up to the trading village of Tadoussac, on the north bank, where the Saguenay debouches into the St. Lawrence. Throngs upon throngs of natives crowded the shores of the two rivers with their canoes and pointed tents. From time immemorial, Tadoussac had been the rendezvous for summer trading among the nations of this region, and the French found it convenient as a market. There, also, the larger vessels of the French fleet anchored for the summer.

Father Isaac remained at Tadoussac but a day or two, then sailed up the one hundred and twenty miles to Quebec. The St. Lawrence, called Sacqué by the natives because of its powerful current, seemed to stretch inland interminably. Never could he have imagined a river so magnificent, so enormous. On Wednesday morning, July 2, through the pearly mist half shrouding the shores, he saw outlined in the grayness the famed rock of Quebec, upright, like the walls of a giant castle. His ship drove across the basin formed by the juncture of the St. Lawrence and the St. Charles Rivers toward the rim of land at the foot of the beetling rock, and there tied up at the wharf.

Jogues and Du Marché tramped up the dirt road along the bank of the St. Charles to the residence of the Fathers, Notre Dame des Anges, a mile or two away, near the little river Lairet. Arrived, and greeted affectionately, Father Jogues said Mass. "I do not know what it is to enter Paradise," he wrote to his mother, "but this I know, that it would be difficult to experience in this world a joy more excessive and more overflowing than that I felt when I set my foot in New France and celebrated my first Mass here at Quebec on the feast of the Visitation. I assure you it was, indeed, a day of the visitation of the goodness of God and Our Lady. I felt as if it were a Christmas day for me, and that I was to be born again to a new life, and a life in God."

After his Thanksgiving, Jogues was overwhelmed with the fervor of the welcome accorded him by Father Charles Lalemant, by Massé, lively as a boy, by Anne de Nouë, the one-time gentleman at the Court of Henry IV, by Paul Ragueneau and Brother Gaubert, who had arrived just four days earlier. Father Le Jeune, the Superior of the Mission of New France, and Father de Quen, added their embraces later in the morning when they came down from their residence of Notre Dame de Recouvrance. "These meetings in a country so far from our native land," Le Jeune once remarked, "after having crossed so many seas, affect sometimes the eyes as well as the heart." Of Isaac's coming, he wrote: "On the second of the same month (July), Father Jogues and Father Du Marché came to add to our great joy, which we felt all the more deeply, since Our Lord brought them both to us in good health."

Notre Dame des Anges was the residence first built by the Jesuits on their arrival in 1625. Since they were not wanted then, they were assigned this plot of land, the site of Cartier's old fort, about half a league away from the cluster of houses beneath the Quebec rock. Their home was wrecked by the English in the occupation of 1629, but was restored in 1632 by Le Jeune. The building was ten to twelve feet high, constructed of logs and mortar, and covered with a slanting thatched roof. It contained four rooms. The largest was the chapel. Adjoining this was the refectory and community room, along the sides of which were partitioned off by rough boards four cubicles; two of these were about six feet square, and the other two, a few feet longer, were large enough for two occupants. The third room was the kitchen, and the fourth was given over to the servants and laborers. There was a garret, reached by a ladder, but it was so low that a cot could scarcely be stretched in it. Normally, there were accommodations for six Jesuits in the community. Jogues' arrival brought the number to be housed up to ten.

Across from this building was another, originally of the same size, but not yet reconstructed since the English burned it. A barn and workshop were thrown up crudely on the foundations. Round about the two structures was a fence, about fourteen feet high and one hundred feet square, composed of twelve hundred fir poles. The entrance to this stockade was through a gate, hung and bound with iron. Beyond the fenced plot were the vegetable gardens, the orchard, the grazing-lands for the cows and pigs along the banks of the St. Charles River and the Lairet stream.

To Isaac, it was a garden of Paradise. He exulted in it, and regarded Quebec as the gate to the promised land. He strode down the road toward the log cabins of the settlement, past the sprawling warehouses and trading-place, along the sagging wharves. He swung up the road from the lower town to the heights where the new town contemplated by Champlain was being built. On the summit Champlain had placed his fort and so perched his guns that he could drop cannon balls far out into the river. Near to the fort was his residence, and a few steps away was the Jesuit residence of Notre Dame de Recouvrance, built by Champlain in fulfillment of a vow that he would raise a chapel to Our Lady if ever France should recover

Quebec from the English. As yet, it was a tiny chapel, and the house of the priests was but a cabin large enough for two. But, thanks to the Company of One Hundred Associates and generous benefactors, it had promise of being the principal religious structure in all of New France.

Le Jeune, when Isaac visited him in his hut atop the rock, extolled with enthusiasm the achievements of Champlain, and prophesied a glorious future of expansion under Governor de Montmagny, whom he regarded as a man of God, an inspiring and trustworthy leader. He rejoiced over the virtues of those who had settled in Quebec during the past four years, and was elated by the arrivals of this summer, by their numbers, their quality, their evident goodness. "The inhabitants of New France have multiplied far beyond our hopes," he declared. "A great number of very honorable persons are landing here every year. They come to cast themselves into the bosom of our great forests as if into the bosom of peace, to live here with more piety, more immunity, more liberty. The din of palaces, the great uproar of lawyers, litigants, and solicitors, is heard here only at a thousand leagues' distance. Exactions, deceits, thefts, rapes, assassinations, treachery, enmity, black malice, are seen here only once a year—in the letters and Gazettes which people bring from Old France."

All this piety, all this security, all this progress and culture in Quebec, was apparent to Jogues. He could honestly join his voice to the voices of the Fathers in thanksgiving to God. But he was not content with Quebec. His ambition lay beyond. He wanted to minister to the natives, not to the French; wanted to journey up into the interior, into the dark density of the forests, up the rivers and lakes, to live in a Huron village, to teach all the barbaric nations of the West the knowledge of the true God. To him Quebec was but a stage in his journey, like Paris, like Rouen, like Dieppe.

In answer to his urgent petitions to be assigned to the Mission of the Hurons, that very summer, Father Le Jeune could give him no definite assurances. Garnier and Chastellain were already on their way to the Hurons; they had left Quebec just the day before Jogues had arrived. It was hardly possible to spare a third missioner, since the needs of Quebec and Three Rivers were most important. However, Le Jeune promised him kindly that if an opportunity presented itself, if it were at all possible to arrange for him to go to the Hurons before the summer closed, he would certainly be the first choice. Meanwhile, advised the Superior, it would be well for Isaac to quiet his mind and to be patient, and await orders down at Notre Dame des Anges.

III

Father Jogues clung to the gunwale of the shallop as it bowled and splashed against the rippling current of the St. Lawrence. His soul was calm and steady as the deep waters of the river, but, like the surface, glinting in the morning sun and wrinkling with the breeze, his face and gestures glowed with excitement. He had received his orders from Father Le Jeune, who had gone to meet the Huron traders at Three Rivers. The advance party of the Hurons, wrote Le Jeune, were conveying Garnier and Chastellain back with them to their villages. The main flotilla of the Hurons was expected, and there were hopeful prospects that they would be willing to accept another missioner. Therefore, Father Jogues was directed to present himself at Three Rivers. Immediately, on Monday, July 21, then, Jogues made haste to leave Quebec.

Three Rivers had been turned into a permanent settlement two years before. It lay at the juncture of the St. Maurice River emptying into the St. Lawrence, some eighty miles inland from Quebec, and was a prehistoric trading and assembly-place of the natives, who called it Metaberoutin, the "Spot Exposed to All the Winds." The French named it Three Rivers because the St. Maurice, divided by projecting islands, had the appearance of three distinct rivers at its mouth. Jacques Cartier had planted a cross on the more forward island in 1535, and Samuel Champlain, when he explored the area in 1603, planned to build a fort and habitation on the hill which sloped up from the bank. The Récollets evangelized the Algonquins there in 1615, and in the following year built themselves a trapper's lodge. But it was not till 1634 that Champlain sent the first colonists, among them Fathers Le Jeune and Buteux.

Thither the shallop bearing Jogues was cutting its way. On Tuesday evening, they bore across the wide St. Lawrence to where the shores closed in, and rounded the curve of the north bank. There beyond the three mouths of the St. Maurice tumbling between the low-lying, wooded islands, was the crest of the hill on which, amid the dark trees, fluttered the white flag of France. Along the water's edge were strewn the pointed tents of the savages. The shallop floated slowly to the wickerwork wharf and Jogues climbed over the rim to the pebbly beach. Le Jeune was there to welcome him, and there, too, was the dearest friend of all, Jacques Buteux, whom he had known so intimately at Clermont College.

They led their fresh missionary recruit up the slanting path to the hilltop. Arrived on the level plateau, Jogues could see all of Three Rivers in one glance of the eye. To the left of the road was the squatty block of the fort, with the black cannon raised on a platform above the low walls. A dozen or more small cabins, built of shaggy logs plastered between with clay, and thatched with straw, lined the pathway. To the right was a larger frame building, the new chapel and residence of Notre Dame de l'Immaculate Conception, Buteux proudly announced, completed last autumn. Beside it was the log cabin, twelve feet square, which had been the first residence of the priests and their workmen. Beyond the chapel, a half-hundred paces along the road, was the other recent improvement, the warehouse and trading-post. Isaac felt strange and happy; Three Rivers was the last stopping-place; from here, if he were to go, he would leave for the Huron country.

The talk at Three Rivers was mostly about the arrival of the Hurons. Le Jeune and Duplessis-Bochart were much worried. The first detachment, Le Jeune told Jogues, was detained by the Island Algonquins, who controlled the passage down the Ottawa River. This nation was envious of the Huron trade with the French, and exacted high tribute from the Huron canoes that passed through their waterways. This year their demands were exorbitant. It was doubtful, even, if the Algonquins would let the main Huron body through. But in these troubled times, Le Jeune explained, and with these fickle savages, nothing was ever certain except that which was most unexpected.

It happened that way in regard to Garnier and Chastellain, who had left on July 21. Le Jeune had anticipated the greatest difficulty in persuading the Hurons to carry the two priests back with them to their village. And yet, he told Jogues: "It seemed so easy of accomplishment that we almost suspected something was wrong. The affairs of God are generally crossed in the beginning, but they do not fail in the results. See how times are changed! In the past few years we had to go here and there, to interpose the authority of everyone, to secure the affection of many more, in order to find a place for one of our Fathers among these barbarians. And this year, the first seven Huron canoes which have come down to Three Rivers have asked for the Fathers, on their own initiative." It might be the same with the main flotilla, Le Jeune assured Jogues. They, too, might be begging for a Blackrobe instead of refusing to take one.

A lone Huron canoe paddled down to the strand of Three Rivers on August 13. It brought promise that the Huron fleet would soon be following. The chief gave Le Jeune a note, scribbled on a piece of cardboard, from Chastellain and Garnier. The Hurons said they met these two Blackrobes far up the Ottawa, in the land of the Island Algonquins. "The bearers of this will tell you, better than we can, the name of the place where they met us," the message read. "We are in good health, thank God. We are gliding along swiftly in our gondolas of bark. We are flying to this paradise so long desired with an increase of courage that God has given us. Kionché shows at least as good treatment to Father Garnier, as Aënons does to Father Chastellain. They have managed our provisions well, we still have a little bread. . . ." The rest was blotted out and indecipherable.

On the next day, Three Rivers became a bedlam. A flotilla of Algonquin canoes came floating proudly down the St. Lawrence. The warriors chanted vociferously and pounded their paddles in unison against the birch-bark boats. Twenty-eight scalplocks fluttered from as many poles, upraised in the canoes. As the boats neared the land, the native women on the shore threw off their clothes and swam out to snatch and fight for these scalps which they prized as trophies for their cabins. An Iroquois man and a squaw were standing up in the canoe, singing as lustily as their Algonquin captors. As soon as the boats touched the strand and the Iroquois brave stepped out, the Algonquin squaws and children leaped on him.

They beat him with clubs and lashed him with heavy ropes and iron chains as he walked forward singing a chant of defiance. They thrust firebrands against his naked flesh and put fire in his mouth and crushed his fingers between their teeth. One squaw cut off his thumb and stuffed it into his mouth, commanding him to swallow it. He tried, but could not; she then roasted it and gave it to the children to suck upon. Some of the braves bit greedily the arms and legs of the captive, and shook him like rabid wolves.

The three priests rushed to the scene. Father Le Jeune hurled himself among the Algonquins and commanded them to stop their cruelties. He threatened that if they continued such practices, the French would no longer love them and be allied to them. Reluctantly they ceased the torture then, but carried their Iroquois off to their own camp. Jogues marveled as much at the courage of Le Jeune as he was nauseated by the savagery. He spoke of it that evening, and Le Jeune explained the manner of dealing with the natives: "We have gained the courage and the authority to reprimand them when they commit these great wrongs. The first year we came among them, even if I knew the language perfectly, I would never have dared to assume the ascendancy I can now take with my stammerings, for they would have soon shut me up. But we have fed them when they were hungry, and clothed them, so that we can demand some courtesy in return. Of course, when we reprimand them, we must never threaten them with any violence, for that would finish our influence. And so, I generally tell them that if they are going to be stubborn about their customs, we will hold fast to ours; that if they do not love us enough to stop their acts of cruelty, we will not harm them, but we will not love them enough to take the food from our own mouths and feed them; that we are going to find out who it is among them who perpetrates the public indecencies or who acts outrageously and insanely, and then we will close our doors against them, but will keep the doors open to those who are good."

Sickened though he was by the barbarous cruelties he had that day witnessed, Father Jogues did not despair of civilizing these savages. As the good Le Jeune admitted to him, and warned him, these natives were vicious and utterly without a moral sense; they were proud, arrogant, intractable, and wild as beasts; they were liars and thieves and murderers; they were superstitious to an amazing degree, and ruthless and cruel; they had every vice that the teaching of Christ condemned. Yet they were not to be condemned, nor were they to be despised. Among themselves they were gentle, and they could be made docile as children, and they did have keen minds. Father Jogues pitied them in their ignorance, and longed to soften their hearts and tame their wild savagery.

While he waited at Three Rivers, he wrote the first letter since his arrival, to Madame his mother. It would be carried back to her by the fleet returning in October. He thought to console her in the sorrow that he brought her by his departure. And so, seated at the rough-hewn table in the dark room of the residence, he related to her:

Madame and most honored Mother:

At last it has pleased Our Lord to allow me to stand on the soil of New France, a blessing for which I have been hoping for many years. We left Dieppe on April 8, eight vessels in the fleet. We arrived eight weeks after our departure. I debarked on an island named Miscou, where there are two of our Fathers engaged in rendering service to the French who have a settlement there, and in attempting the conversion of the savages. After spending fifteen days with them, I embarked in another vessel, which brought me to Tadoussac. This is the place where the larger vessels lay to while the barques and smaller vessels ascend the St. Lawrence up to Quebec—a French settlement that is growing every day. I arrived there on the second of July, the day of the Visitation of Our Lady. I have been in such good health continually on sea and on land, thank God, that I astonished everybody, since it is no ordinary thing to make such a long voyage without experiencing the least sick feeling in the stomach or the least nausea. The vestments and utensils for Mass have been most useful, for I said Mass every day that the weather was favorable, a happiness of which I should have been necessarily deprived if our family had not provided me with the Mass things. This was a great consolation for me; it was a favor that our Fathers did not enjoy in former years. The officers and crew profited by it; otherwise, the eighty persons who were on our vessel would have passed more than eight weeks without assisting at the Holy Sacrifice; instead of that, owing to the faculties I had of celebrating, they all confessed and received Holy Communion on Pentecost, Ascension and the Feast of God. God will reward you and Mde. Houdebine for having contributed to this great good. For the rest, Madame, every year, with the grace of God, you will receive a letter from me and I shall await letters from you, also, once a year. Please forward these to Paris in the beginning of March, in order that they may reach Dieppe before the departure of the vessels. It will always be a consolation to receive news of you and of our family, for I have no hope ever to see you again in this life. May God in His Goodness unite us all in His holy abode, where we may praise Him through all eternity. This it is for which we must earnestly strive as long as we are alive. So well must we use the time that is accorded us that we must do that in our life which we would have wished that we did at the moment of our death. What comfort there is for a person who is dying, what satisfaction of conscience he has, in the knowledge that he has served God with the smallest imperfection possible for him, and that he has tried in everything and everywhere to do that which is most agreeable to His Divine Majesty? I believe that such were the thoughts and the reasons which forced us to demand so insistently that we be sent to these lands where, as there is much for us to suffer, so we may testify more sincerely to God the love which we have for Him. If I were capable of giving you good advice, or if you were in need of it, I would counsel you to put yourself under some holy director to whom you would entrust the guidance of your soul, and to whom you would promise to frequent the Sacraments more. This piety of life, in which you yourself have always been most faithful, should be your endeavor more than ever. Your advanced age and the leisure which you now enjoy make it all the more easy for you. I write this to you separated from you by more than a thousand leagues. It may happen, this year, that I shall be sent to a nation which is called the Huron. It is distant from here by more than 300 leagues. They show good disposition to embrace the Faith. It matters not where we may be, provided we may always be in the hands of Providence and in God's holy grace. That is the intention which I make for you every day at the altar, and for all of our family.

Your humble and affectionate servant and
son according to God,
Isaac Jogues, of the Society of Jesus.

He did not seal the letter then, for he thought he might have more news to add later. Besides, Monsieur Duplessis-Bochart, who would command the fleet for France, still lingered at Three Rivers awaiting the arrival of the Hurons with their cargo of peltries and furs. All the French, through those August days, scanned the St. Lawrence continuously. At last they spotted a canoe rounding the belly of the north shore and driving resolutely nearer, as if in flight. It was recognized as Huron. It landed, and the paddlers told that they alone had been allowed by the Island Algonquins to pass through the Ottawa, but that their companions were forbidden to advance.

They carried letters from Father Daniel to Father Le Jeune and to Monsieur Duplessis-Bochart. These, dated August 7, were written from a place 450 miles up the rivers. Daniel informed his Superior of the troubles which the Island Algonquins were causing. These savages had absolutely forbidden the Hurons to pass through their land, and had forced some of the canoes to turn back. Daniel said that he himself was granted leave to continue on his way by the chief of the Island nation; but he refused to take advantage of this permission unless all the Hurons were allowed to go with him. He had persuaded the chief to permit this one canoe to carry his message to the French; he was hoping that he might succeed in regard to the rest of the Huron canoes. To Duplessis-Bochart, Daniel wrote that there were not many Hurons traveling down to Three Rivers, but that they were, nevertheless, carrying a great amount of merchandise.

There was some hope at Three Rivers upon the receipt of these letters; but the Island Algonquins were known to be a haughty, deceitful race and, though presumably friendly to the Hurons, were always obstructing their relations with the French. Three days passed. On August 19, the St. Lawrence was dotted with the advancing flotilla of the Hurons. They swept down proudly, chanting, raising echoes along the shores. In the foremost canoe stood upright a bearded man. He was waving his paddle with a happy, vigorous flourish. Father Antoine Daniel it was. The French and the natives danced along the shore with joy and shouted out their welcome vociferously.

Daniel was smiling and gay, as he had ever been. But he was a specter, a skeleton with scarcely enough flesh on him to cover his bones. His skin was the color of leather, rough and wrinkled. His eyes were deep sunk in their sockets, his cheeks hollowed, his beard and hair unkept and matted. His bare arms and legs showed through his cassock, which was torn almost to shreds, and his only other garment, a shirt, was literally rotting. About his neck, tied with a thong, was his breviary. In his hand was the paddle he had been wielding.

He stepped out of the canoe, and with the grace and courtliness of old France he made his salute. They crowded about him and hugged him to their breasts. During four years he had lived in the wilderness among the Hurons. He was reduced to a wreck of a man in God's service. Father Jogues shivered; this was not the man he had seen departing for New France back in 1632. He was aghast, and approached Father Daniel as timidly as one would address a saintly hero. Daniel was returning from the Hurons. Jogues hoped with all the fervor of his soul that he would be sent back with these very Hurons to take the place of Antoine Daniel.

CHAPTER III

In the Huron Cabins

I

THE Hurons swarmed about the chapel and fort and warehouse of Three Rivers. They were naked except for a breech-clout, though some of them, in vanity, wore a robe or a blanket slung loosely about their shoulders. Sturdy, loose-limbed men they were, with bulging muscles, somewhat taller than the majority of stocky Frenchmen. Their faces, heavy and impassive, were made grotesque by daubs of many-colored paint. One had a blue nose and a jet-black chin, with white circles about the eyes and mouth. Another was livid white on one side of his face, and coal black on the other. Here went one with stripes of red, blue, white, gray, black across his features, and here was another with the bands criss-crossing, and here a third with variegated dots and circles weirdly mingled. Their arms, their legs, their torsos were garishly smeared with greasy colors, and were tattooed in flaming splotches of many designs. Pendants dangled from their ears, necklaces of bright porcelain beads hung down over their chests, bracelets and gaudy bands clasped their arms.

They were easily distinguished from the Algonquins by their fashion of wearing their hair. Some were completely shaved on one side of the head, while on the other the straight, black locks flowed to the shoulder. The majority wore ridges of hair, an inch or two wide, from the forehead to the nape of the neck, with furrows of the same width cut to the scalp. It was these ridges that suggested the name of Huron to the French, for one of Champlain's men noted the resemblance to the tufts of *la hure*, and so nicknamed them. Feathers of various hues were rakishly stuck in the ridges of their hair, and those of importance wore a head-dress of shiny quills.

Upon their arrival, with the usual courtesy between friendly nations, they held council with the French. Solemnly, the Hurons and French sat before the council fire in the courtyard of the fort.

The Huron orator held before him a wampum belt. With that present, he declared, he dried the tears of the French and helped them swallow the bitterness caused by the death of Champlain. With other gifts of porcelain beads he pledged the love of his peoples to the French and bound them and the French into one nation. On the following evening, under the presidency of Admiral Duplessis-Bochart, the French returned their answers in the second council. Through an interpreter, he assured the Hurons that the French loved them equally. "Here is a present," he told them, "to grease your arms and limber them, and to relax them from the labor they have had on the journey. Here is another present to fasten a rope to your canoes to pull them down here next year."

One chief proposition of the French was that the Hurons send some of their boys to Quebec, where they might be educated in the school for the native children which the Blackrobes had built. Father Daniel had had hopes of bringing down this year twelve lads, but he had gathered only three, nor was he certain that these would remain with him. Duplessis-Bochart exhorted them: "If you really love the French, why do you not show your friendship? You give beaver robes to the French, and they give you hatchets and other goods; all this is by way of traffic and trade. These are not the evidence of real love that I seek; the real love is to visit and to help one another, to go into each other's country, to ally ourselves together like the fingers of the hand; these are acts of friendship. That is what we are doing; we are going into your country; we are sending the Blackrobes there, our fathers, our teachers, those whom we hold most dear, those who show us the way to heaven. And not one of you will live with our French. Why do you not trust as much in us as we do in you? Why is there only one village, Ihonatiria, among the Hurons that loves us? We show in this respect our friendship toward you; why do you not act likewise?"

With great reluctance, the Hurons agreed to allow the three boys to live with the French at Quebec for that winter. The councils concluded on August 19. Nothing was said about Father Jogues. The Hurons extended no invitation to him, nor to any other Frenchmen, to reside in their villages. Duplessis-Bochart, having secured his cargo of furs and peltries, prepared to sail next morning for Quebec. Fathers Le Jeune and Daniel, who were leaving with him, invited the Hurons to a farewell feast in their cabin.

When the Hurons had eaten their fill, one of the chiefs spoke privately to Father Daniel. He was irked by the reference which Duplessis-Bochart had made to the village of Ihonatiria, as being more friendly than the village of Ossossané, to which he and his comrades belonged. He presented himself as the spokesman of the people of Ossossané. He demanded to know, on the word of his brother Antwen, why the French loved Ossossané less than Ihonatiria. Daniel assured him that the French had the greatest affection for the people of Ossossané. Why, then, asked the chief, did the French not give some of their brothers to reside in Ossossané?

This was the invitation which the Blackrobes sought. Daniel informed Le Jeune of the chief's request. Le Jeune answered that he would prove he and all the French loved Ossossané dearly. He would give one of his sons, the Blackrobe Isaac Jogues, to the chief, to travel back with him and to live among the nation of the Bear at Ossossané. Overjoyed at this testimony of friendship, the chief announced it grandiosely to the other Hurons. "Behold them the happiest people in all the world," Le Jeune related with a smile. Daniel confirmed the agreement by offering valuable presents to them so that they would treat his brother, Isaac Jogues, as their own kinsman. The Hurons accepted his presents, and thus pledged their word.

This was an ecstatic moment for Father Jogues. What he had prayed for had come. He was appointed, at last, to accompany the Huron flotilla to the Huron country. As soon as he could absent himself from the feast, he rushed to the chapel and offered there his most fervent thanksgiving. Then he drew out the letter which he had written some days previously to his mother, and scribbled hurriedly a postscript at the bottom of the page:

P.S. I have just received, within this very hour, the order to prepare myself to depart in 3 or 4 days for to go among the Hurons.

From Three Rivers, 20 August, 1636. Isaac Jogues.

It had been agreed, also, that the French would further show their affection for the Hurons by entrusting to them the French boy, Jean Amyot, a lad of ten or eleven years. This act, the French assured the Hurons, was in appreciation of their generosity in allowing their children to live at Quebec and thus more closely joining together the two nations. The intention of the French in sending Jean and other boys among the savages was that they might learn the language perfectly and habituate themselves to the customs and mental attitudes of the savages, so that later they might be interpreters and intermediaries in the dealings of the colonists with the Hurons.

Left to himself, Isaac found little to prepare in a material way. All he needed was the little bag in which were packed his winter clothes, few enough they were, and a parcel of beads and trinkets for use as presents to the savages. His chief preparation was spiritual. He needed strength of soul. He remembered Le Jeune's words: "The altogether angelic chastity demanded by our Constitutions is necessary here; one needs only to extend the hand to gather the apple of sin." Four virtues, he had been told, were especially required: affability, humility, patience, and charity. Long and arduously he prayed in the presence of the Blessed Sacrament, for it would be weeks before he could say Mass again or seek the help of confession and Communion.

Second to the spiritual preparation was the study of how to act toward the Hurons. He learned much from the conversations he held with Le Jeune, Buteux, and Daniel. He must not try to dominate the natives, but he must not be servile; he must be gentle, but determined; he must adapt himself to their ways in order to lead them to his thoughts. Most helpful, because most definite, were a set of instructions drawn up by Father de Brébeuf. These were written that spring and were brought down by Daniel. They were to be sent over to France, but Le Jeune allowed Isaac to make a copy. "Instructions for the Fathers of Our Society who shall be sent to the Hurons," de Brébeuf headed them. "You must have sincere affection for the savages," the veteran counseled. To conciliate them, never make them wait in embarking; have a tinder box to light their pipes and fires for them; eat their sagamité "although it may be dirty, half-cooked, and very tasteless"; eat all they offer, and when they offer it; do not carry water or sand into the canoe; do not be troublesome, do not ask too many questions, do not criticize; be and appear to be always cheerful; make presents to them of pocket knives, fish-hooks, colored glass beads; do not stand on ceremony; wear a nightcap in the canoe rather than a broad-rimmed hat; help carry the baggage at the portages, "if it be only a kettle."

"Finally, understand that the savages will retain the same opinion of you in their own country that they will have formed on the way," de Brébeuf wrote. "And one who has passed for an irritable and troublesome person will have considerable difficulty afterwards in removing this opinion. You have to deal not only with those of your canoe, but also, if I may say it, with all the inhabitants of the country; you meet some today and others tomorrow, and they do not fail to inquire from those who brought you what sort of man you are. It is almost incredible how they observe and remember, even to the slightest fault. When you meet savages on the way, as you cannot yet greet them with kind words, at least show them a cheerful face, and thus prove that you endure gayly the fatigues of the voyage. You will thus have put to good use the hardships of the way, and have already advanced considerably in gaining the affection of the savages.

"This is a lesson which is easy enough to learn, but very difficult to put into practice. For, leaving a highly civilized community, you fall into the hands of barbarous people who care nothing at all about your philosophy and your theology. All the fine qualities which might make you loved and respected in France are like pearls trampled under the feet of swine, or rather of mules; they utterly despise you when they see that you are not as good pack animals as they are. If you could go naked and carry the load of a horse upon your back, as they do, then you would be wise according to their doctrine, and would be recognized as a great man; otherwise, not. Jesus Christ is our true greatness; it is He alone and His Cross that should be sought in running after these people; for if you strive for anything else, you will gain naught but bodily and spiritual affliction. But having found Jesus Christ in His Cross, you have found the roses in the thorns, sweetness in bitterness, everything in nothing."

Jogues, the Blackrobe, was formally accepted by the Hurons at a feast which they held for him. Later on, in their village they would adopt him into their nation and give him a name. Temporarily, however, they had to have some way of addressing him. They told him to repeat his name: Isaac Jogues. They could not say that; but it reminded them of a word in their language; and this word fitted him, with his keen eye and his nervous gestures. They then solemnly pronounced his new name: Ondessonk, Bird of Prey.

Ondessonk strove to make himself agreeable to his Hurons. He mingled with them in the settlement and visited them in their summer tents down along the river shores. Of special interest to him were their canoes, so fragile and yet capable of bearing up under the weight of many men and heavy baggage. He marveled at the ingenuity with which the pieces of birch bark, as thin as cardboard, were fitted about the framework of slender poles, and made watertight. Most of them were eight to ten feet long and could carry six men. Some were large enough to hold twenty men and their bundles. He was eager to be in one of them, speeding up the river.

Sunday, August 24, the Huron flotilla got under way. Father Jogues said his last Mass, that of the Apostle Saint Bartholomew, ate heartily of his last French breakfast, and with singing heart walked down the hillside to where the canoes were already bobbing in the shallow inlet. Jean Amyot, frisky as a kitten, ran before him and stared wide-eyed at the doings of the Hurons. On the damp grass near the canoes, the Hurons held their parting council. This finished, in silence they climbed into the barks. Father Jogues, wearing a night cap, with his breviary tied with a thong about his neck, tucked his soutane about his waist, cleansed the sand from his feet, and climbed into the canoe. At the signal of the chief, the little boat shivered under the first impulse of the paddles and slid into the river.

Jogues looked back. He bowed his head as Father Buteux raised his hand in blessing. He heard the farewell shouts of the French and Algonquins, the salute of muskets, and looked back upon the hill and fort of Three Rivers, and the flag, white against the green trees. Peace flowed through him as he sat huddled in the pointed stern. After all the uncertainties, after all the preparations since January, here he was at last on his way to the Huron country. The canoe lapped against the ripples and passed by the trees that lined the shore. In rhythm, the naked, reddish backs of the paddlers swung back and forth as they dug and pulled their blades. They sat on their heels, he observed, their knees and shins resting on the ribs of the frame. He was uncomfortable, with his knees drawn up to his chin, but he feared to move a muscle lest he disturb the balance of the nervous bark.

The cool of the early morning melted before the summer sun. The heat grew intense, with the sun beating down on his head and back, and the reflection from the waters blinding his eyes. The Hurons were silent, save for an occasional grunting word. Their eyes roamed continually over the river and along the shore. A speck on the water, a twirl of smoke in the sky, a footprint on the shore, a broken twig, a suspicious sound, that might betray the presence of the Iroquois, their bloody enemies who were known to be lurking about.

In the middle of the morning, they emerged from the narrows of the St. Lawrence into the open expanse of the river known as Lake Saint Peter. They circled along the north shore and could scarcely see the dim outline of the other shore, ten or twelve miles over. All the day they advanced, past bays and inlets, projecting points, rocks and yellow sand and black swamps, until in the late afternoon they approached the barrier of marshy islands at the head of the lake and nosed the canoes among the sedge grass at the mouth of a little river. They had covered some thirty miles in this first day of the journey.

Their supper was a mush of powdered corn, and Ondessonk as well as the Hurons ate ravenously after the day's fast. Father Jogues ached through all his body after the rigor of sitting cramped in the canoe. Before the night blackened, the savages were breathing heavily in sleep. Jogues stretched himself on the hard earth under the trees. The woods vibrated with the shrill hum of the insects; the darkness was punctuated with the scream of a night bird or the wail of a wolf. Mosquitoes and flies and bugs swarmed about him and stung viciously. He thought that he was not afraid being alone with the savages, except for little Jean. The Hurons had been kindly thus far. But they were like sullen mastiffs, quick to anger, irresponsible, easily irritated. Praying softly to the God above him, he dozed into sleep.

The earliest lifting of the night was the signal for the camp to wake. Expeditiously the Hurons prepared the morning meal of crushed corn soaked in water, and gulped it down voraciously. It would be the last food until evening. Shortly, they were again in the canoes and were stealthily paddling through the waving water grass to the channel between the mainland and the marshy islands that closed in about the lake. The passage between the islands was hazardous. A hundred battles had been fought on these banks, for the channels and promontories and bays offered fine play for ambushes. They passed through the dangerously narrow channel, and by noon were once more on the wide bosom of the St. Lawrence.

At eventide the Hurons relaxed from the grind of paddling and turned in toward a rim of yellow sand for the second night's camp.

In the days that followed, Jogues hardened himself against the long hours of crouching in the canoe, to the gnawings of hunger, to the monotonous sway of the boat, to the scorching heat of the sun, to the desolate loneliness, the profound silences, his own speechlessness; and in the nights he learned not to be disturbed by the fearsomeness of the terrible blackness, of the breathing forests, by the wail of the beast, the screech of the bird, by the shrill treble of the insects, and by the sting and burn of their bite. Before the end of the first week the flotilla had turned from the St. Lawrence up the Rivière des Prairies which cut off the island of Montreal. Here the current lashed down in swirling furrows and tormented itself against the boulders. Dexterously the Hurons pushed the prows of their canoes against the foaming water and sped them along the quiet stretches. At times they pulled up into a pool and taciturnly unloaded the canoes. Shouldering their baggage and tossing the boats over their heads, they picked their way along the slimy banks or climbed the rocks to the level above the cascades and waterfalls. From here on, the monotony of the journey was broken by spells of paddling and portages.

From the Rivière des Prairies they advanced into a wide lake of waters streaked yellow and green, formed by the downflow of the River of the Algonquins, the Ottawa. The currents were treacherous, but the Hurons battled their way around the points and bays till they were within the river confines. They were pointing to the north and west. The air grew chilly and damp in the forests that shrouded them. Rapids and falls confronted them day by day, and portages through tangled underbrush and intertwined trees and vines were three or five or six miles.

In the lower regions of the Ottawa they encountered a large Huron flotilla on its way to Three Rivers. Jogues thrilled with excitement. Accompanying the party was Father Ambroise Davost, who was returning to the St. Lawrence after three years of labor among the Hurons. He had followed shortly after Father Daniel, but his band had been delayed interminably by the troublesome Algonquins of the Islands. They had been finally allowed to pass through after paying an exorbitant tribute. Davost related that he had met Garnier and Chastellain in the country of the Nipissings. They were well, he said, and by this time were nearing the Huron villages. Jogues listened and talked like a man starved of human contact. As he had venerated Father Daniel and been shocked by his appearance, so was he affected by Father Davost, who was gaunt and hollow-cheeked, and sick in addition to being exhausted by the fatigues of the journey. Their meeting was not for long. Davost floated down with his Hurons to the St. Lawrence. Jogues adventured upward, bursting with eagerness to carry on what Ambroise Davost had been forced, against his will, to relinquish.

A day or two after this happy meeting, little Jean Amyot was fairly worn out. The lad was getting no nourishment from the mashed corn, their only food; he suffered from the exposure to the heat of the day and the cold of the night. The arduous tramps of the portages were too much for his eleven years. He became so weak he could scarcely lift himself from the canoe or drag himself along the banks. In the first few portages, one of the Hurons had carried Jean on his back. But the Huron soon tired of this for the law of the forest was not merciful to the sick and the burdensome. Such a one, as he grew helpless, might just as well as not be left along the route.

The burden of carrying Jean fell on Father Jogues. He had the strength and the will to transport the boy, even though he was, by this time, also weakened by the ceaseless hardships. But he feared for the safety of the youngster, since he was not used to the slippery rocks and the boulders and the narrow ledges they must clamber over in their detours and portages. A stumble or a misstep, and both he and Jean would be injured or killed. The Hurons would not be bothered with the boy, and Jogues was terribly concerned about him. Happily, he effected a trade with one of them: the Huron agreed to carry Jean, if Ondessonk would carry the Huron's bundles of hatchets, a load far heavier than the boy.

They climbed up to the barrier of the Algonquins of the Islands, but were not delayed beyond the ordinary limits of courtesy. From here they picked their way against the current, defiled through more gorges, portaged over the rapids and waterfalls until they turned left into a series of black little lakes and finally into the stream that meandered down into the Ottawa from the toplands about Lake Nipissing. The taxing fatigues of the ascent were lessened, the air was bracing, the tenseness relaxed. They were now in the territory of the friendly Algonquin nation of the Nipissings. They dawdled a space in the early mornings and at nightfall to fish. Under the influence of the purer air and the fresh food, little Jean regained his strength and Jogues himself partook of new vigor.

Coming out of the hemmed in waters of the French River, they burst into the spreading horizon of the famous *mer douce*, the Lake of the Hurons. Hugging the shore to their left, they needled between the ten thousand islands that spotted the lake. Autumn had touched the foliage and turned it into brilliant crimsons and russets, which contrasted with the somberness of the firs and pines. The lake gleamed and sparkled far, far out.

Then the Hurons shouted with joy and chanted a merry rhythm. They had sighted La Pointe, the tip of their peninsula. Vigorously they dug their paddles into the choppy waves. Now they were cutting across from the mainland, across the bay that washed against their peninsula. The rough currents bounced their canoes crazily. They saw the smoke curling up over the low headlands, up from the tree tops. With sweeping strokes they fared into the quieter waters and through the passage by Ondiatana, the Island Beyond Our Point. A twist of the prow headed the canoes behind a hook of land, and they drifted into the sand cove beneath the hill of Ihonatiria.

II

This day of his arrival, September 11, was the opening of a new paradise for Father Jogues. He felt dazed under the tremendous fulfillment of his years of hope. His hero, the giant Father de Brébeuf, bundled him into his arms. Fathers Le Mercier, Garnier, and Chastellain embraced him in a heartfelt welcome. Earlier that summer de Brébeuf had written:

"When you reach the Hurons you will indeed find hearts full of charity. We will receive you with open arms as an angel from Paradise." And Le Mercier, in his Relation of that year, confessed: "The joy which is experienced in these reunions seems to be some image of the happiness of the Blessed upon their arrival in Heaven, so full is it of sweetness." He records that when Father Jogues arrived, "it was a tremendous consolation on his side; and on our side was so much the more deeply felt because—two days before we had received any news that he was coming—we had quite given up hope for any new helpers; we were expecting none till next year. God be infinitely blessed."

Their first act, when they reached their bark cabin, dedicated to St. Joseph, was to crowd into the partitioned room of the chapel, and there thank God for the safe arrival of Father Isaac and Jean. Then they scurried about to prepare a feast, the best luxuries they could provide, smoked fish cooked with flour, fresh corn roasted in the embers, a head of squash, and a dessert of their precious store of prunes and raisins. Their faces beamed with the supreme joy of it as they sat about the cabin fire; their talk rambled on vivaciously, their laughs rang merrily.

Jogues surveyed the cabin with puckered eyes. It was a tunnel-like structure some fifty feet in length and about eighteen in width and in height. At each end of it there was a door, but there were no windows, only openings at the top to let the smoke of the fires escape. The interior was a rough framework, with sturdy, slim tree trunks and saplings as uprights, supporting a network of poles and beams and crossbars. This skeleton was sheeted over with strips of bark, sewn neatly together with roots and tendrils, and seamed with gum and resin. "It was no Louvre, and no palace," de Brébeuf could remark; "it would be hard to find a hut in France wretched enough with which to compare it." It was, however, immeasurably superior to the old cabin, only thirty-two feet long, in which the Fathers had lived for four years. It was fairly weather-proof, at least. It had been built the preceding autumn by the Hurons, in the space of three days, but only after interminable argument with them.

The interior design, the Fathers told Isaac, was the marvel of the savages. Each door opened into a vestibule, in which were stored wood and bark barrels of corn. The vestibule of the main entrance led into the living-room, which extended more than half the length of the cabin. Open fires gleamed along a center aisle, on both sides of which were wooden benches a few feet high. On these were stored the boxes and trunks containing clothes and other needed articles. Under the benches, de Brébeuf indicated, "in the place where the Hurons keep their wood, we have contrived some little bunks to sleep in, and to store away some of our clothing from the thievish hands of the Hurons. They sleep beside the fire, but still they and we have only the earth for bedstead, some bark or bough covered with a rush mat for mattress and pillow, and our clothes and some skins for sheets and blankets."

Beyond the living-room was the partition which formed the chapel, a room some fifteen feet long and about twelve wide. A bit of carpentry, de Brébeuf noted, gave it a fairly good appearance and made it the wonder of the savages. For floor it had the packed earth, and for walls the birch bark. The altar was solid but crude, and about it were a few holy pictures of Our Lady and St. Joseph, the patron of the cabin, and some smaller prints. Adjoining the chapel was a large closet, quite securely barricaded against the Hurons, in which were hidden the axes, hatchets, and other precious utensils.

Isaac had written to his mother from Three Rivers, telling in a postscript the good news of his appointment to the Hurons. He could forward no further word of himself till the following spring, but in the few days after his arrival at the residence at Ihonatiria, he jotted down an account of his journey:

I departed, then, from Three Rivers, a settlement of the French on the Great river St. Lawrence, on the 24th of August, the day of St. Bartholomew. I got into a canoe of the savages, a kind of boat made out of bark, very light, which is able to hold five or six persons. It would not be easy to give you in detail all the discomforts of such a voyage, but the love of God which has called us to these missions, and the desire which one has to contribute some little thing to the conversion of these poor barbarians, render all these discomforts so sweet that we would not wish to change the sufferings for all the pleasures of the earth. The food of the travelers is a little Indian corn, crushed between two stones and boiled in plain water without any other seasoning. We sleep either on the earth or on the rough rocks which are on the shore of the great river, in the sight of the moon. The posture that you take in the canoe is the most uncomfortable; you are not able to stretch your legs, so small and crowded is it. You dare not move, even a little, for fear of causing the canoe to turn over in the water. I was forced to keep a profound silence, being able neither to understand our savages nor to make them understand me. Another source of suffering and fatigue is met in the journey. Sixty or eighty rapids, or waterfalls, drop from such a height and rush with such great force that, if one were to go too close, the canoes would be carried over and sunk beneath the falls. It is true that, going against the current of the river, we were not exposed to this danger, but we were, nevertheless, obliged quite frequently to land on the earth and to climb over the rocks and to walk through the woods, in detours of a league or more, burdened down with all the baggage, and with the canoe itself. As for me, I not only carried my own little packages, but I also helped our savages, and relieved them as much as I could. A boy of ten or eleven years, who belonged to our company, fell sick. I was obliged to carry him on my shoulders during the marches occasioned by the rapids of which I have spoken. We made finally such great effort that, instead of the twenty-five or thirty days that this journey ordinarily requires, it did not take more than nineteen days to bring us to the place where five of our Fathers resided, some of whom have already counted five or six years' residence in this land. The two last had arrived only about a month before me.

Eleven Frenchmen were to be living during that winter at St. Joseph's cabin in Ihonatiria. The Superior was Father Jean de Brébeuf, whom the Hurons addressed as Echon. Next in authority was Father François Le Mercier, known to the savages as Chaüose. Father Pierre Pijart was the third of the veterans; he was then absent, for it was his duty to journey down along the St. Lawrence, gathering and seeing to the transportation of the supplies. Assisting these veterans in their ministries were the three newcomers—Father Charles Garnier, who had received the name of Ouracha from the Hurons; Father Pierre Chastellain, called Airoo by them; and Father Jogues, who bore the title of Ondessonk.

In addition to the six priests, there were four *engagés*, and little Jean Amyot. The workmen, François Petit-Pré, Simon Baron, Dominique and Mathurin, were employed by the Huron Mission to do the manual work about the cabin and to serve as companions for the Fathers in their travels through the country, as well as to assist them as catechists. Mathurin, that September, was at Three Rivers with Father Pijart, but he would return to the community before the cold set in. Eleven white men they would be, hidden in the forests a thousand miles away from the nearest French settlements, alone and at the mercy of the savages.

Appraisal of Ondessonk had been made by the Hurons with whom he had journeyed up to Ihonatiria. They spoke of him favorably. But the villagers were eager to make their own estimates. Strong-limbed braves and tottering old men, squaws, children of all sizes, swarmed through the cabin and stood stolidly about Ondessonk and the boy Jean, staring at them. Ondessonk, like all the white men, was not too attractive. He had pale skin and blue, open eyes; he had hair on his lips and chin; he did not have much hair on his head. They preferred their own men with their heavy heads of hair ridged and shaved, with their faces not disfigured by beards, with small, sharp eyes, with good, dark skin. He did not impress them by his size; but he was strong, they were told, and had carried the baggage well over the portages. He had not been troublesome in the canoe. He had shown himself pleasant and agreeable.

Father Jogues, with equal curiosity, observed the Hurons as they milled about and discussed him. The braves he knew, for he had seen them both in their holiday attire at Three Rivers and stripped during the stress of the journey. The women were clothed in loose-fitting skins which reached from the shoulders to the knees. They were large-featured like the men, with high cheek bones and beady, black eyes, with sprawling noses and bulbous lips. Their hair, jet black and coarse as thread, they wore drawn back tightly from the forehead and braided in the back. Some of them had thongs about the forehead which held suspended down along their backs their baskets and cradle board. Tucked into these bags were the babies, chubby-faced, black-eyed little things, with olive skin. The larger children, free of all clothing, poked unabashed among the elders. They were barbaric, no doubt, but they had souls to save, Jogues concluded.

Freeing himself from the rout in the cabin, Jogues walked out from the gloom and the damp darkness into a morning that sparkled with brilliance. He looked about at the maze of huts strewn about in haphazard positions. They were all of bark, streaked and shaggy, and most of them were ragged and dilapidated. Some were oblongs twenty or thirty feet in length, while others spread out more than a hundred feet and were quite twenty feet in height. Some forty large and small cabins were clustered thus in Ihonatiria. A palisades enclosed them, but this, too, was in a wretched condition, with large gaps in it, with poles askew and the crossbars loosed from their supporting thongs. All of Ihonatiria was disintegrating, Jogues learned. It had been occupied now for about ten years, and after that span of years a village was abandoned. For the cabins would then be falling into ruin, the filth and refuse would have accumulated everywhere, the firewood would grow scarce, and the soil become exhausted. Plans were being discussed even then in councils to merge Ihonatiria with some neighboring hamlets and to build a new village.

Jogues walked into the cabins of the savages, for the Blackrobes adopted the Huron custom of wandering in and out at will. If he thought the cabin of the Fathers was smoky and grimy, he was nauseated by the stench and the grease and dust and disorder he saw in the huts of the natives. They looked like long tunnels, free from door to door of all obstructions save the upright logs that served as columns and the interlaced rafters and ridge poles. Down the center, every five or six feet, a fire glowed and lit up the heavy air about it. One family lived on each side of the fireplace and slept crowded in the space between the fire and the wall. There was no pretense of privacy anywhere in the cabin and no attempt to preserve order, for meat and fish and furs and garments and bags of corn and implements and trinkets and scalps and innumerable other things were strewn about or suspended from the poles of the skeleton framework. Father Jogues had experience, almost as soon as he stepped within the door, of the horde of insects that infested the cabin. He was glad to emerge once more into the sun-bathed morning.

In company with some of the Fathers, he strayed beyond the palisades across the trodden earth to the edge of the promontory on which Ihonatiria was built. On three sides there spread out before him the vast expanse of this huge bay of the Lake of the Hurons. The sides of the hillock on which he stood had been hollowed out by the storms, and the beach below was leveled by the waves. Ihonatiria lay at the northernmost point of the Huron peninsula. It was the last stopping-point of the canoes loaded down with furs and skins on their way to the trading; and it was the first place of welcome to the parties returning from a journey. With appropriateness, it bore the name of Ihonatiria, The-little-hamlet-above-the-loaded-canoes.

Due to its location as well as to the fact that the first Hurons they met chanced to be from this village, the French had located themselves in Ihonatiria. It was not a populous village, for the inhabitants numbered less than five hundred, nor was it an important center, for it boasted of no influential warriors and chiefs. It was, however, a major hamlet of the Nation of the Bear, the Attignawantans, who, with the southernmost Nation of the Cord, the Attigneenongnahacs, formed the original stock of the Wendat peoples whom the French referred to as Hurons. From Ihonatiria, the missioners planned to penetrate down through the peninsula to the twenty or more villages of the four nations of the Hurons. The distance was not great, for all the Huron land was not more than seventy-five by twenty-five miles in extent, and could be traversed, as de Brébeuf stated, in three or four days.

In his calculations, the people of these villages and nations speaking the Huron tongue approximated some thirty thousand. Beyond them to the west were other allied nations who were descended from the same stock and spoke dialects of the same language, such as the Petuns, the Neutrals, and the Eries. The missioners hoped that they might advance through the evangelization of the Hurons to that of these other peoples. Then to the south were the five nations of the Iroquois, also of the same blood as the Hurons and using a variation of the same root language. These, at present, were hostile to the Hurons, but preliminary negotiations for peace were being undertaken. So that, if peace came, the Hurons would be the door through which the Gospel could be preached to these more distant natives.

Such were the prospects that fired the soul of Jean de Brébeuf, the bulwark of the Huron mission. He had come up to the Huron country ten years before with that intrepid Récollet, Father Joseph de la Roche d'Aillon. Three winters he had spent living in the cabins with the savages, and the last of these he was the only white man in this far wilderness. He returned to the St. Lawrence only at the insistent order of his Superiors, in 1629, and arrived in Quebec just two days before it was captured by the English. Transported back to France, he was there forced to wait until the French again occupied Canada. He was appointed as Superior of the Huron Mission in 1634, and here he had remained. He spoke the native language better than any alien who ever came into the country. He was taller than any of the savages, broader in shoulder, and more tremendous in his strength. Though he was kindly and patient with them, he was their master. Echon, as they called him in their corruption of his name of Jean, was beloved and feared by all the Hurons.

By the missioners, also, he was revered as a father and a teacher. Of an evening after Jogues' arrival, he sat before the fire of the cabin and initiated the three young priests into the apostolate of the Hurons. "Instead of being a great master and a great theologian as in France," began de Brébeuf, "you must reckon on being here a humble scholar; and then, good God, with what masters!—women, little children, and all the savages—exposed to their laughter. The Huron language will be your Saint Thomas and your Aristotle. Clever men as you are, and speaking glibly among learned and capable persons, you must make up your minds to be mute for a long time among the barbarians. You will have accomplished much if you begin to stammer a little, at the end of a considerable time."

He prepared them for some of the experiences they could expect: "I tell you without exaggeration that the five or six months of winter are spent in almost continual discomforts, excessive cold, smoke, and the annoyance of the savages. We have this cabin built of simple bark; you will notice it is so well joined that we have to send some one outside to learn what kind of weather it is. The smoke is very often so thick, so annoying, and so obstinate that, for five or six days at a time, if you are not entirely proof against it, you are so blinded that you can scarce read a few lines of your breviary. Besides, from morning until evening our fireplace is almost always surrounded by savages; above all, they seldom fail to be here at mealtimes. If we happen to have something more than usual, be it ever so little, we must count most of these gentlemen as guests. If we do not share with them, we are considered stingy. As regards the food, it is not so bad, although we usually content ourselves with a little corn, or a morsel of dried, smoked fish, or some vegetables.

"You must realize," he leaned over to say to Isaac and the others, "that our lives depend upon a single thread. We are told to expect death every hour and to be prepared for it, no matter where we are in the world; that applies particularly here. I do not need to mention that our cabin is only chaff, and that it might be burned down at any moment, despite all our care to prevent accidents. The malice of the savages gives us special cause for almost perpetual fear; a malcontent may burn you down or may cleave your head open in some lonely spot. Then, too, we are responsible for the sterility or the fecundity of the earth, under the penalty of our lives. We are the cause of droughts; if we cannot make rain, they speak of nothing less than murdering us."

He laid before them the spiritual safeguards they had in France, and contrasted those with their present state. In France, he said, "you were almost beyond the danger of sinning; at least, the falls are insignificant and you have help immediately at hand. Here, we have nothing which incites toward good. We are among a people who are astonished when you speak to them of God and who often have only horrible blasphemies in their mouths. Often you are compelled to deprive yourself of the Holy Sacrifice of the Mass. I pass over the small chance of seclusion there is among the barbarians who scarcely leave us. Especially, I hardly dare to speak of the danger there is of ruining oneself among the impurities of these savages, in the case of one whose heart is not sufficiently full of God to resist firmly this poison."

Thus he recounted all the frightfulness of life among the Hurons, all the sufferings and the dangers to body and soul. Jogues and Garnier and Chastellain assured him they were not fearful. They protested that they sought even greater labors, more harrowing sufferings for the love of that God which brought them to these savages. "It is workmen such as you that we seek here," de Brébeuf exclaimed. "It is to souls like yours that God has appointed the conquest of so many other souls whom the devil holds yet in his power. Fear no difficulties, there will be none for you since it is your whole consolation to see yourself crucified with the Son of God.

"The Divine Goodness makes everything easy here," de Brébeuf continued. "The sleep we get lying on our mats seems to us as sweet as if we were in a good bed. The food of the natives does not nauseate us, although there is scarcely any other seasoning than that which God has put into it. Notwithstanding the cold of a winter six months long, passed in the shelter only of this bark cabin, we have still to experience its evil effects. No one complains of his head or his stomach; we do not know what diarrhea, colds, and catarrh are. I am tempted to say that delicate persons in France do not know how to protect themselves from the cold. Those rooms are so well carpeted, those doors so well fitted, those windows closed with so much care, that they serve only to make the effects of the cold more keenly felt. Cold is an enemy from whom one wins almost more by holding out one's hand to him than by waging a war on him."

Father de Brébeuf stirred the embers of the fire meditatively for a moment, then opened his hands in a gesture and smiled: "As for the dangers of the soul, to speak frankly, there are none—for him who brings to the country of the Hurons the fear and love of God. On the contrary, I find unparalleled advantages for acquiring perfection. Is it not a great deal to have in one's food, clothing, sleep, no other attraction than bare necessity? Is it not a glorious opportunity to unite oneself with God when there is no other creature whatsoever that gives you reason to spend your affections upon it?"

Isaac felt himself uplifted under the inspiration of this steady, vibrant voice of de Brébeuf. He listened with rapt attention, forgetful of all else: "If the question is of the fundamental virtues, I will glory not in myself, but in the portion which has fallen to me. Or, if I must, acknowledge it humbly beside the Cross which Our Lord in His blessing gives us to carry after Him. Certain it is that this country and our work here are much more fitted to feed the soul with the fruits of heaven than with the fruits of earth. I may be deceiving myself, but I imagine that here is a grand means of increasing the soul in faith, in hope, and in charity. Should we scatter the seeds of faith without ourselves profiting by them? Could we put our confidence anywhere but in God in this region where everything is lacking to us, as far as man is concerned? Could we wish a nobler opportunity to exercise charity than amid the roughness and discomfort of a New World, where no human art or industry has yet provided any conveniences? and to live here that we may bring back to God men who are so unlike men that we must live in daily expectation of dying by their hand if the fancy of murder should seize them?"

Silence brooded without over Ihonatiria, as Father de Brébeuf spoke on, rather hesitatingly: "There seems to be one thing which might give apprehension to a Son of the Society, to see himself in the midst of a brutal and sensual people whose example might tarnish the luster of the virtue that is the most delicate and the least delicate of all the virtues, unless special care is taken. I mean chastity. I would make bold to say, in regard to this danger, that if there is any place in the world where this most precious virtue is safe—for any man among us who wishes to be on his guard—it is right here."

His voice sank low and tense as he fondly recounted the strength to practice purity which comes from God. Then, more lightly, he exclaimed: "I imagine that all the Guardian Angels of these neglected and abandoned nations are perpetually endeavoring and laboring to save us from these dangers. They know very well that if there were anything in the world that ought to give us wings to fly back whence we came both by obedience and our own inclination—it would be this evil; that is, if we were not shielded from it by the protection of Heaven. It is this which arouses these Angels to procure means for us to guard against this evil, so that they may not lose the brightest hope they ever had, by the grace of God, for the conversion of these people."

Father de Brébeuf rose from his mat before the fire. His eyes were like burning coals as he concluded: "Now, at the vision of these difficulties and crosses that are prepared and waiting for us, if some one feels himself so strengthened from above that he can exclaim: 'It is too little'; or like St. Francis Xavier can call out: 'More, more'; I hope that Our Lord will also draw from his lips, as a result of the consolations which He will give to him, this other confession, that the consolation is too much for him, that he cannot endure more joy, that he can cry: 'It is enough, Lord, it is enough.' "

Under the spell of this spiritual exaltation Father Jogues lifted his cramped body upright and stood erect. He was upraised in soul and spirit, ready to dare and to suffer and to die for the Christ. The soft bronze hue cast by the fire dimly illumined the posts and rafters and walls of the cabin. In the duskiness the Fathers moved down the cabin toward the cool chapel and disappeared in its solemn darkness. One by one they emerged after a time, and still in the freighted silence of the night they lay down to rest on their mats beneath the benches.

III

When Father Jogues stepped out of the canoe on the sandy beach below Ihonatiria, on Thursday, September 11, he was utterly fatigued. Nineteen days of continuous struggle up the waterways had sapped his strength. Though worn in body and famished, the joy of his arrival lifted him up with a specious vitality. Sleep and food knit up his nerves during the few days that followed, and the inner happiness glowed through him like a bracing tonic. He was exalted in spirit. Out of the thousands of Jesuits who aspired to make an oblation of themselves, he was chosen. He was one of the six elected to the apostolic work of bringing the knowledge of the true God to the Huron nations, of converting not only the Hurons, but the tribes of barbarous peoples living to the west and the south and the north in this vast, unknown continent.

For a few days he was bursting with vigor, exhilarated by the mellow sunshine and the fresh breezes bearing the scent of the woods and the autumn. From Thursday to Sunday, these were but days of grace. On Monday and Tuesday there began a reaction. A deadening lassitude gripped him. He fought against it, and tried to throw off the sick feeling that was in every part of his body. By Wednesday de Brébeuf was somewhat concerned about his illness and discovered that he was in the throes of a burning fever. He was ordered to repose himself on his mat that very day. Father Le Mercier assumed the duties of infirmarian with much merriment; during the past year he held the office, but complained that everyone had been in such perfect health that he had had no practice. Now he had a minor patient in little Jean, who was still convalescing, and a major patient in Isaac Jogues.

Le Mercier, however, became much worried within a day or two. Being historian, as well as infirmarian of the community, he wrote:

As for Father Jogues, God brought him to us in very good health, but it was only for a few days. This would make me readily believe that, if he did not feel any ill effects of the fatigues of his journey at the time of his arrival, it was because he was so overjoyed and so elated at finding himself in possession of the blessing and grace that he had so long ambitioned, a blessing that had nearly slipped out of his hands. Miscou had almost detained him while he was on his way over here. And then, Fathers Pierre Chastellain and Charles Garnier, who had arrived first, had already directed so many entreaties to Heaven for the Huron Mission that, when he arrived after them, the conclusion had almost been reached that he was to remain at Quebec. But your Reverence took into consideration his holy desires, and above all, the request we had made to you to send us, if it were at all possible, three or four of our Fathers. At all events, his coming here was a very great consolation on his side—and on our side was felt all the more deeply because, two days before we had received any news of his coming, we had almost given up all hope, and we were only waiting for next year. God be infinitely blessed. On the 17th, he fell sick, and although at first it was apparently only a slight indisposition, yet at the end of some days, the fever appeared daily and quite violently. Of all the countries of the world, it is true that here it is most desirable, perhaps, that a sick person should be able to say, and to mean to say, "Thank God, in the place and in the condition in which I am, I have no other physician than His Paternal Providence; and of all the comforts which a sick person may desire, to speak rightly, I have none except those which come to me directly from heaven."

On the same day on which Father Jogues collapsed, the workman Mathurin was deposited on the shore of Ihonatiria by his Huron fellow travelers. He had accompanied the native traders down to Three Rivers. On his return along the River of the Algonquins he was seized with a debilitating fever. His Hurons treated him well enough, but they would not be burdened with a sick man during a journey. Accordingly, they abandoned him and his four large bundles of mission supplies at Lake Nipissing. Here he found some care in the cabin of some Nipissings. His fever abated, so that he could attach himself to another band of Hurons on their route home. But he was still shaken and weak when he arrived at St. Joseph's. Mathurin became the third patient of Father Le Mercier.

That September there was much sickness among the people of Ihonatiria. It had begun late in the summer and was affecting more and more at the change of the season. Reports came in that the large village of Ossossané, twelve miles down along the shore of Nottawasaga Bay, was afflicted. Visitors from villages near and far were telling of relatives stricken by the influenza. Braves who had travelled among the Nipissings and the Island Algonquins related that multitudes of these natives were dying. The Hurons grew apprehensive. They had had experience of these contagions and pestilences in years gone by. A great fear hovered in their hearts.

Isaac grew steadily worse during the latter part of the week. He was wracked by a burning fever. Neither Le Mercier nor any of the others had any knowledge or experience in ministering to sickness. Besides, they had no remedies or medicines that would avail anything. By Monday, Father Jogues appeared to be in a critical condition. The lad, Jean, had a relapse, and suffered miserably in his corner of the cabin. Mathurin's fever returned with a terrible violence. During that night, the *engagé*, Dominique, who had been helping Father Le Mercier tend the sick, showed signs of the disease. On Tuesday morning he was so ill that he could not rise from his mat.

On that Tuesday morning, Jogues' temperature was frightening. He was soaking with sweat, and so continually coughing that he almost strangled. For three or four days he had been bleeding from his nose so copiously and steadily that he could scarcely take any food. De Brébeuf and Le Mercier, looking at him in the dim light cast by the fire, saw that he was ghastly, dangerously sick. It was the influenza prevalent among the natives. What could they do for him, how treat him? They had no medicines except purges. There was only one remedy for a fever that they knew, and that was to bleed the patient. But how did one safely bleed a sick person?

Not one of the community had ever attempted to do it, and they hesitated about experimenting on Father Isaac. They decided, nevertheless, that if there were not soon a change for the better, they must make this last desperate attempt to save him. That evening they waited anxiously. One of them was always by his mat, watching over him and easing him in his coughing. Shortly after midnight, Father de Brébeuf, clothed in surplice and stole, brought Holy Communion to Father Jogues. The other priests knelt about his mat and prayed; they feared that this would be his Viaticum. Isaac received his Lord with a smile of peace. He lapsed into quiet, then, and the other priests retired for a few hours' rest before the hour of Mass at daybreak.

He was breathing heavily, and was restless and still hot with the fever when morning came. He was nearing the end. It was absolutely necessary to bleed him. But who would be the surgeon? If the cut were bungled, he would die. Each of the priests shrank from the duty; nevertheless, each was ready to take up the lancet and save the others from the responsibility. They waited for Father de Brébeuf to make a choice from among them. He knelt down on the mat near Isaac and roused him from the torpor into which he was fallen. He asked him if there might be anyone in whom he had confidence for the operation. Father Jogues understood the love and the fear that made them hesitate to pierce the vein.

He told Father de Brébeuf that he would make the cut himself; he had bled one of the savages on the journey; it had been successful; he believed he could do it on himself. De Brébeuf with some reluctance agreed. They raised Isaac up to a sitting posture then, and spread the cloths and the receptacles on his knees. His hand was shaking with the illness when he took the lancet. They held the candles near so that he might see more clearly. He poised the blade above his arm, and made the stroke. The blood poured out copiously. When it was drained off, they bound the wound and settled him on his mat. He relapsed into a coma. For the rest of the day he lingered on in a crisis. By the next day the fever was much abated.

On that day, Thursday, September 25, Father Chastellain contracted the influenza. He had been tireless in helping Le Mercier, in tending to the sick, cooking, gathering wood for the fire. All that day he felt the disease creeping through him and the fever consuming him. At nightfall he had to stretch himself out on the skin against the wall, and submit. Garnier, meanwhile, was engaged in the spiritual exercises of his annual retreat. When Chastellain was stricken, he begged to be allowed to interrupt his days of prayer and help in the nursing. Even then, he also was gripped by the influenza, but he persuaded himself that it was nothing but a passing weakness and concealed his condition from the others. As Le Mercier remarked, he judged there was a greater demand for nurses than for patients. He could not continue his deception. On Saturday, after he had almost fainted while saying Mass, he groped his way to his bed.

There were now six sick people. De Brébeuf, Le Mercier and Petit-Pré, the *engagé*, were alone on their feet. Father Pijart and Simon Baron were away. When Jogues first was stricken, Petit-Pré was sent out to scour the woods for game. "It was from this that we expected all our succour, after God," said Le Mercier. But Petit-Pré, through several days, could sight neither bird nor animal at which to take a shot. It was imperative that the growing number of patients should have nourishing food. "We had nothing to give our invalids only some broth of pursley weed stewed in water, with the dash of the juice of unripe native grapes," the infirmarian related. "We had one hen, but she did not give us an egg every day; and, well, what is one egg for so many sick people? It was most amusing to see those of us who were well, waiting for that egg. And when it was laid, we had to consider to whom we should give it and to decide who needed it most. As for our patients, the question among them was who should not eat it."

De Brébeuf heard of a man who was raising a bustard in his cabin, and went to buy it. At first the Huron refused to sell it under any condition. Echon argued with him. Finally the savage agreed to give it up in exchange for a deer skin. The man got his price, Le Mercier comments: "a deer skin is precious in this country; but what would we not have given in these circumstances? Had it not been for that, we were just about to kill one of our dogs. They do not have the same aversion to them here as in France. We would not have hesitated to cook a broth of it for our invalids."

Meanwhile, Pijart returned from Three Rivers. He and Petit-Pré scouted the woods from morning till night, walking miles through brambles and swamps, in search of game. After the first week or two, the ducks and geese were passing the Huron land in their migrations south. They bagged many, says Le Mercier: "We saw plainly the paternal providence of God over this little house, for the game kept on increasing in proportion to the increase of our patients."

But the sick lingered on. The single room of the cabin was dark and heavy with the smoke of the fires. As de Brébeuf and Le Mercier knew, the patients needed perfect quiet and should not be disturbed. But that was made impossible by the savages. These crowded the cabin from sunrise till they thought it time to go to bed. They had never seen the French demons sick on their mats and dying. Strangely, these white foreigners lay stretched out on their backs when sick; the proper Huron way was to sit with the knees drawn up to the chin. These Blackrobes kept the cabin silent; but the Hurons thought it better to chant and dance and feast about the sick, in order to drive away the evil demons. The French were peculiar. It was a sight well worth remembering to watch them when they were ill. Men, women, children, and dogs packed into the cabin and raised continual uproar and turmoil about the beds and the fires.

De Brébeuf and Le Mercier reasoned with the savages and did their best to prevent them from swarming through the doors. Since they could not prevent their entry, they tried to persuade them to leave quickly, or at least to talk quietly and not to kick up the dust. The savages were offended; when anyone was sick, everybody visited him; the Blackrobes were queer and impolite and inhospitable. Le Mercier was in desperation; de Brébeuf was angry. They could avail nothing; the savages poured into the cabin day after day, even while the sick hovered between life and death. One of the Hurons was one day shouting at the top of his lungs, and Le Mercier restrained himself enough to remonstrate: "My friend, I pray of you to speak in a little lower voice." The man looked aggrieved and, pointing to the rooster perched on the crossbeams, replied: "Chaüose, you have no sense. There is a bird that talks louder than I do, and you do not reprehend him."

Father Chastellain was sinking fast. He became delirious and tortured himself tossing restlessly on his deerskin. They thought, at times, that he could not live. De Brébeuf bled him; that quieted him for a day or two. Again, the fever flared up, and they bled him a second time. Father Garnier lay in a deathly coma, unable to lift an arm. His temperature was not high, but he was utterly weak, exhausted, and his pallor was ghastly. De Brébeuf cut a vein in his arm, but the blood was sluggish. Again, a second time, later, he opened the skin; but the blood would not flow. Dominique, the workman, was in a still more serious condition. His was a purple fever that discolored all his face and body. Alternately, his temperature rose to the limit and beyond; then the fever would leave him, paralyzed and scarcely breathing. They bled him once, then again, and again, but with no good results. It seemed a matter of hours; he could not be saved. Father de Brébeuf administered Extreme Unction and gave him Viaticum. Dominique sank into his last agony, and those who could joined in the prayers for the dying.

Thus two weeks passed since Jogues fell sick. Through those terrible days Le Mercier had nursed his six patients indefatigably day and night. On October 1 his head was throbbing and he was streaming with perspiration. He kept to his duties, however, and tried to work off the influenza. By evening he felt himself beaten, and crept into his bunk. His developed into a violent fever, but he retained consciousness throughout. He begged them to lance his vein; the blood refused to flow. The temperature lowered, then rose rapidly; again the fever disappeared, and again spread through him for a third assault. His symptoms were so puzzling that they perturbed de Brébeuf terribly. But a crisis came on the third day, and suddenly, for no apparent reason, he was freed of the alarming signs and became normal, though quite weak.

The two priests left, Fathers de Brébeuf and Pijart, kept up the nursing and the care of the cabin. Petit-Pré, out with his arquebus all the days, brought home big bags of game in the evening. During the first week of October not one of the seven invalids was out of danger; and yet, not one but gave signs of recovery. In the second week they were all definitely recuperating. "We are under great obligations to the Divine Goodness," recounts Le Mercier, "which overwhelmed us with consolation during this little domestic affliction. We were never more cheerful, one and all. The sick were as content to die as to live, and by their patience, piety, and devotion greatly lightened the little trouble we took for them day and night. As for our Fathers, they enjoyed a blessing which is not a common one in France, that of daily receiving the Holy Sacrament of the altar, Father Superior or some one else carrying It to them during the night. It was from this treasure-house that they drew so many resolutions and so many pious sentiments, which made them delight in, and tenderly cherish, their condition, and which made them prefer their poverty to all the comforts of France."

All the sick survived, and the three well ones were not attacked. In the aftermath, the scourge of the epidemic was regarded as a blessing of God and a lesson of the Divine Providence. The Great Physician, they believed, "was not content with restoring us to complete health, but has so disposed this slight affliction that, in whatever manner we look at it, we must regard it as a very notable favor." No human remedies were available, they noted, yet they all recovered. The time in which they were stricken was the most favorable of all the year, since game is most plentiful in the autumn. François Petit-Pré, the hunter, was preserved in the best of health. Father de Brébeuf, the Superior, the one who was needed most while the others were ill, who was most valuable because of his skill in speaking Huron and of his power over the savages, was never sick a day. Then, they told each other, it was amazing that God should have been so good as to send them the influenza in the first appearance of the epidemic, which thereafter swept the entire country; through their own experience, they learned how best to treat the sickness. Finally, they were convinced that their affliction was a most loving dispensation of Divine Providence. If they had not been sick unto death, they would certainly have been massacred.

CHAPTER IV

Under the Shadow of Death

I

FEAR, then hysteria, followed by madness and despair, paced in equal step with the influenza through the Huron lands. The first victims fell in early September, after the return of the traders who had passed through the infected territory of the Island Algonquins. During the latter weeks of September the disease slowly became more prevalent. In Ihonatiria, the numbers of the sick increased and not a few died. So it was, also, in the hamlet of Wenrio, three miles inland to the southeast, and in that of Anonatea, the same distance due south, in the village of Onnentisati, seven miles off near the head of Penetanguishene Bay, and in Angwiens, a few miles beyond. From Ossossané, twelve miles to the southwest, along the lake shore, the most populous and important of all the towns in the district, came most alarming reports. The whole northern section of the Huron peninsula was stricken.

The savages turned with hope to the sorcerers. They begged the medicine-men to drive away the plague. In Ihonatiria, in Ossossané, in all the country, sorcerers rose up and boasted unlimitable powers. Tonnerauanont, an odiously misshapen hunchback, was a leader among the oracles. He had had the audacity to offer to cure the Blackrobes, in payment of ten glass beads, through his incantations, a dance about the invalid, and a special sweat which he himself would perform. De Brébeuf drove him off as a charlatan, but did learn from him of some natural remedies, of juices from the small branches of the fir and cedar, from wild sorrel and other plants and roots. But these were only incidental remedies to Tonnerauanont, who solemnly declared: "I am not like other men. I am a demon," and wove a fantastic story of his preternatural origin.

He was the devil's mouthpiece, alleged the Fathers; but he was a good demon and a deity to the Hurons. He announced that the cure for the plague was the game of la crosse which all the men of the villages must play. They played till their arms ached; the disease increased, but Tonnerauanont castigated them for failing him. He boasted that he would forbid the disease to enter the palisades of his village of Onnentisati. It was a challenge; the Fathers vowed thirty Masses in honor of St. Joseph that the devil and his agent be confounded. Though Onnentisati was stricken as the other villages, the sorcerer still enthralled the savages.

Other sorcerers, likewise, plied their grotesque superstitions and were accorded implicit faith by the people. Sometimes they demanded gifts of beads and furs; or prescribed the playing of the game of dish or of straw; or exerted themselves by blowing violently about the sick one, thus driving off the disease, which they believed was a true devil; or staged ritual dances about the patient, in which friends and relatives joined. Sometimes, the sorcerers claimed to cure through the interpretation of the dreams and the deliriums of the sick; whatever the sick person dreamt, that had to be done, no matter how impossible, how ridiculous, how tragic. Then again, they commanded feasts, and especially eat-all feasts, in which, according to Le Mercier, the diners "had to disgorge at intervals, but not ceasing to empty plate after plate. Meanwhile, the sick man thanked them, assuring them that they were doing well and that he was indebted to them."

The more the epidemic raged, the more the sorcerers reigned supreme. They disguised themselves and the villagers in masks, and distorted their bodies; then, with rods in their hands they beat about the cabin of the sick and howled and danced till they fell exhausted. They had driven away the evil spirit, they announced, and to keep him away they hung the masks on the doorposts. They instituted ritual sweats; into little tents in which were piled roasting stones, the sorcerer led a dozen men clothed in the heaviest robes. They danced, they shrieked, they sweated until the vital moment; then the sorcerer threw tobacco on the stones and addressed the devil: *"Io sechongnac."* In the smoke he claimed that he learned the remedy for the plague.

They held the sabat, the orgy of the Aoutaerohi. Le Mercier tells of one such witch's vigil in the cabin of a dying girl: "The women sang and danced while the men struck violently against drums of bark. Never have I heard such a din, nor shouts so raucous. As if keeping time, they took burning embers and red-hot cinders in their

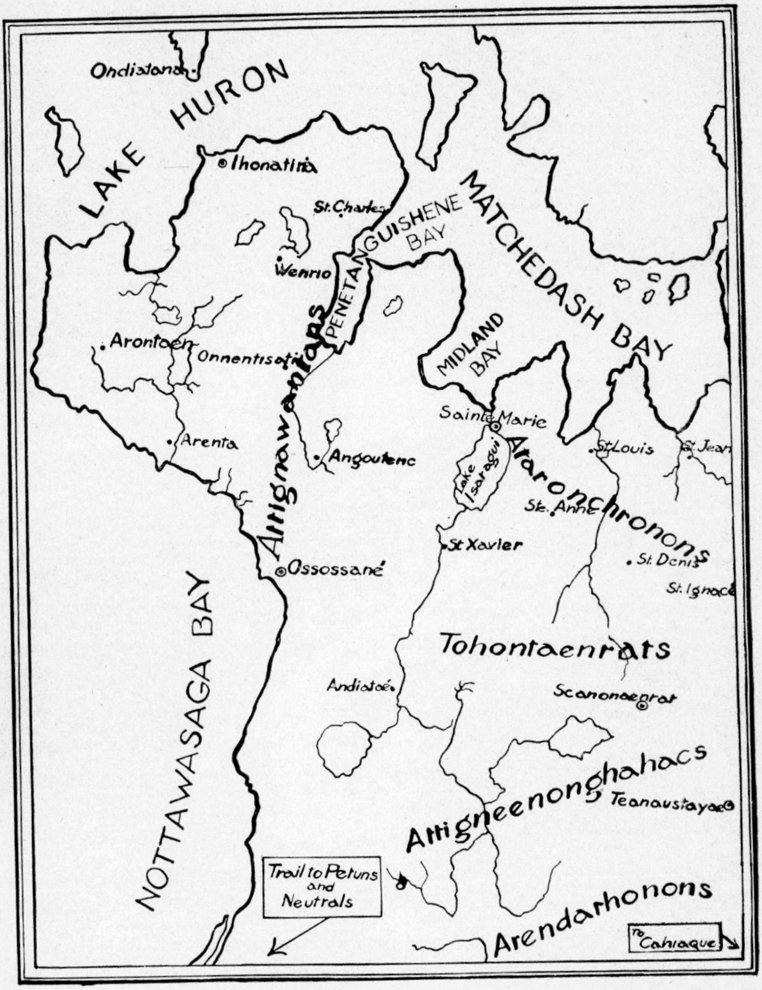

The Huron Country
Adapted from map by Arthur E. Jones, S.J.
Drawn by Marie Marique

bare hands, and then passed their hands over the stomach of the patient, who, as part of the ceremony, tossed like a maniac and kept shaking her head incessantly." They made hideous the days and the nights with their mad shrieks, their plaintive, their despairing, their wild chants, with the beating of the drums and the rattles, with the pounding dances and the furious rampages, with feasts and rituals and incantations. The sick died, the well became insane.

The Blackrobes, meanwhile, argued and pleaded with the savages. They pointed out how useless, how nonsensical were the remedies of the sorcerers, how all their efforts failed to stop the course of the influenza. Their words had no hearers. They endeavored to teach the Hurons their own natural remedies. They cooked broths and carried them to the sick; the savages swallowed the essences greedily, but complained that the Blackrobes were mean and stingy, since they kept the best part of the soup, the heavy grease, for themselves, and would not share the fat and the meat with the poor sick people.

Another of their medicines was eaten greedily, the prunes and raisins. Since the Blackrobes had but a small store of these, says Le Mercier, "everything was given by count, two or three prunes, or five or six raisins, to one patient. This was restoring life to him. Our medicines produced effects which dazzled the country, and yet I leave you to imagine what sort of medicines they were! A little bag of senna served over fifty persons; they asked for it on every side." Their most efficient treatment was that of bleeding the savages; blood-letting was a thing the Hurons could understand, and it produced such immediate effects that it was much sought after.

Jogues was the first of the French to recover. His progress was so rapid that he was able to minister to the sick of Ihonatiria early in October. He with de Brébeuf and Pijart made rounds of the cabins in the morning and the evening. While they tended to the physical needs of the natives, they were concerned mostly about their spiritual condition. They exhorted and instructed the sick who would listen to them; they sought the consent of the dying adults to baptism and, over the infants and children, when in extreme danger, they poured the saving waters. As for the adults, there was little success in persuading them to be baptized, or in making them understand the delights of heaven or the pains of hell. "I have no desire to go to heaven," one of the sick replied, "for I have no acquaintances there and the French would not give me anything to eat." Another would not go to heaven because his relatives would not be there, and another refused because he understood there were no fields, no corn, no trading or fishing or hunting, and that there was no marriage. While some were simple and ignorant, others refused with a rage and a malice that was truly diabolic.

The missioners hoped that the influenza epidemic would pass away with the change of the season, as in France. The first frosts were on the earth about November 10, and winter was being heralded by winds and storms. But as the weather became colder the terrible plague increased in violence. The Fathers resolved, now that all were fully recovered, to extend their aid to the other villages. On Monday, November 17, Father de Brébeuf, Father Jogues, and Petit-Pré made the first excursion to Ossossané. They followed the narrow path through the bare woods in the teeth of an icy wind that bit their faces and ears. The trail, not more than two feet wide, was littered with leaves and difficult to trace, as it undulated over the hills and through the ditches of the streams. Jogues, strong again, was nevertheless tried in legs and muscles by this twelve-mile walk and the rapid pace, but he was borne along by an exultant soul on this his first adventure into the wilds of the country.

The trail ascended through thick woods to a broad plateau, along the upward swell of a lofty hill. The village spread out along the level fields. It was one of the largest in the Huron Confederation, with a population of two or three thousand housed in a hundred and more cabins. A stout palisade, twice the height of a man, built of logs closely woven together, with a moat running along the base, enclosed it. On the other side of the plateau was a precipitous descent to the shores of Nottawasaga Bay. Jogues could well understand why the French named the place La Rochelle, for the headland was bold and sweeping like that of the famed port of France.

De Brébeuf and Jogues were welcomed by the people. They admired Echon and they were curious to see Ondessonk who had traveled with their warriors. The two Blackrobes visited the cabins and distributed their stores of raisins and prunes to the sick. Echon talked to them of how they must nurse the afflicted, of how they must distrust the sorcerers, of how wise it was to be baptized. He was heard kindly, and succeeded in baptizing six adults and three children who were dying. But they were treated badly by some who were under the domination of the wizards, and were told disquieting rumors. When they returned to Ihonatiria on Thursday, they learned that the same reports were being widely circulated. The Hurons were divided in opinion: some claimed the Blackrobes were responsible for the plague, and therefore were to be killed; others contended they were powerful magicians who could drive the disease away, and therefore to be cultivated.

The Huron sorcerers fanned the hostile mood against the Blackrobes. One claimed he saw the disease sweeping down the lake from the direction whence the Blackrobes arrived. The sickness was a huge, poisoned cloak, he said. Another asserted Champlain died with a determination to return and kill all the native peoples. They warned the people that the broth of the Blackrobes was poisoned. They recalled that Echon made them a present as a token that he would "open the way to heaven"; smartly they concluded that he meant the way to heaven was through death. Then, most of all, the Blackrobes caused people to die by pouring water on their heads; practically every one they baptized died soon after.

These and like accusations, flung about secretly and openly, roused hatred against the Blackrobes. The Fathers countered them by a feast of deer meat which they prepared on November 27. De Brébeuf, after the savages had gorged themselves, assured them of the sympathy and goodwill of the Blackrobes, and in testimony offered them four hundred wampum beads, many hatchets, and a moose skin. He exhorted them, in this crisis, to believe in the true God and make a vow to serve him. After holding a council among themselves, they promised to believe in the God of the Blackrobes and, if the influenza disappeared, to build a chapel in His honor the following spring. They proclaimed their vow, despite Echon's warning "that they were dealing with a God who could look down into the depths of their hearts, and that this God would punish them severely if they did not respect Him." But on the next day they donned their masks and chanted their ritual dance to drive the disease away. The Fathers, on their side, took a vow to offer masses and prayers in honor of Our Lady and St. Joseph.

When the village of Wenrio heard of the vow made by Ihonatiria, the people there also wanted to take the vow which would dissipate the sickness. On December 5, de Brébeuf visited them. They wished to pledge themselves to build a chapel for the God of the Blackrobes in order to be rid of the plague. But Echon surprised them by demanding that they must believe in this God and keep His commandments. He proposed "that they give up their beliefs in dreams, that their marriages should be binding and for life, that they observe conjugal chastity; he told them that God forbade vomiting feasts and those shameless assemblies of men and women, and the eating of human flesh, and the feasts they call Aoutaerohi."

The Hurons, troubled, debated these propositions in a council among themselves. Aënons, the chief, answered Echon: "I consider that what you propose will prove to be only a stumbling-block. We have our ways of doing things, and you have your ways, as all nations have. When you speak to us about obeying and acknowledging as our Master Him Who you say has made heaven and earth, I imagine you are talking of overturning our country. Your ancestors assembled in earlier times and held council, where they resolved to take as their God Him Whom you honor, and arranged all the ceremonies that you observe. As concerns us, we, too, have learned our ceremonies from our ancestors." But a friendly old chief persuaded the council to accept Echon's proposals, for, he said, all things considered, it was better to endure a little trouble and live, rather than to die miserably.

Father de Brébeuf also secured the acceptance of his proposals by Ossossané. On December 12, the chiefs deputed a medicine-man, Okhiarenta, to go through the streets and paths, "crying in a loud voice that the people of Ossossané took God as their Lord and Master, that they renounced all their errors, that from now on they would not believe in dreams, that they would not make any more feasts to the demon Aoutaerohi, that their marriages would be binding, that they would not eat human flesh, and that they bound themselves to build a cabin in God's honor next spring, on condition that God be pleased to stop the progress of the disease."

For the next few weeks the Blackrobes were regarded affably. They were welcomed in the cabins and allowed to minister to and instruct the sick. But baptism they did not administer, except under certainty of death. On one occasion, Father Jogues found a savage named Sononresk favorably disposed and sufficiently instructed, who was gasping his last breath. All through the night the man kept repeating *"Rihouiosta"* (I believe). Ondessonk baptized him, and the man suddenly recovered. He announced that baptism cured him; the water that had been poured on his head by Ondessonk had flowed down through his throat, so that he felt no more pains. His rejoicing in this life was not for long, however, for he died the next day.

Two days after Christmas, Jogues again went to Ossossané with Father de Brébeuf and Simon Baron. Snow blanketed the forests and the cold bit bitterly. They detoured to Anonatea, and found sick in every cabin. They turned off to a winter encampment of Algonquin Nipissings, where thirty or forty had recently died. They failed to persuade the Algonquins to listen to their words or to accept their gifts. They passed on to Onnentisati. The influenza ravaged whole families. Here they learned that the sorcerer Tonnerauanont, over in Ossossané, was accusing them of being poisoners. They hurried off to confront the charlatan. Under the menacing height of Echon, the little hunchback denied he had spoken the calumny.

Ossossané, for the most part remained friendly. De Brébeuf and Jogues doled out their bits of senna, dried fruits, and French snow, or sugar, which the savages loved, while Simon Baron bled as many as fifty people a day. "They emulated each other in holding out their arms to him," the Fathers reported, "those who were well wishing to be bled as a precaution, and those who were sick considered themselves half cured when they saw their blood flowing. Among others was an old man who was half blind; as soon as he was bled, he exclaimed, 'My nephew, ah, you have restored my sight. Now I see.' " The priests labored over the spiritual welfare of the victims. Some seemed predestined for salvation, so perfect were their dispositions. Others were willing to enjoy the happiness promised by baptism, but they flatly refused to admit that they had ever committed a sin or done any wrong. Some would have none of baptism, since they believed it would cause their death.

When they returned to Ihonatiria, on January 4, 1637, they found the village rabidly aroused. The chiefs had held a public feast and publicly denounced the Blackrobes as the authors of the plague. One of them, Achioantaeté, declared that if he were the Aondechio, the Great Chief, he would be finished with the Blackrobes and would fix them so they could do no more harm. The leader, Taretandé, hurled burning fagots at the Blackrobes and threatened that if one of his family died, he would split the head of the first Frenchman he met. He later burst into the Fathers' cabin and shouted at them that they must either cease their witchcraft or they would be killed. It was resolved to be rid of them, either to murder them outright or to drive them down to Three Rivers as soon as the spring came.

Taretandé, meanwhile, was concocting a plot with the chiefs of the neighboring villages to massacre all the French. The Fathers knew of it, and all the people discussed it placidly. "Even the children spoke of us only as persons who were soon to have our heads split," reports Le Mercier. "One Sunday, toward evening, when they heard us chanting the Litanies of Our Lady, they believed that we were weeping in expectation of the hour when the chiefs were to come and cut all our throats or burn us in our cabin."

The crisis passed, through the affliction of Taretandé. Rapidly, one by one, his family became sick and he himself died within a few days. The other chiefs feared and repented. Aënons, who professed no great love for the French but yet claimed he had no part in the plot, made the Blackrobes a long speech, entreating them, "in the name of every one of the people to think no more of what had passed, and not to reveal the evil designs upon their lives" to the French at Three Rivers. Echon accepted the apology, but took the occasion to berate them for practicing the grotesque superstitions ordered by the sorcerers, for calling on the devil for aid by their dances and feasts and incantations. Aënons' only answer was "*Onanonharaton*—what can you expect? Our brains are muddled." And an old chief made the excuse: "My nephew, we do not know what we are doing. There is nothing we would not do to preserve our lives. If it be necessary to dance night and day to drive away the disease, I will begin first, all decrepit as I am, in order to save the lives of my children."

As soon as Ihonatiria quieted, de Brébeuf and Jogues, with Maturin, on January 17, fared on another apostolic journey. The snows were waist deep. The trees of the forest were coated with ice crystals. They visited Wenrio, the first village that had accepted Echon's proposals a little more than a month before. Not one of the savages would tolerate any words from the Blackrobes. They went on to Angwiens, where they remained the night. The natives were hostile, but the missioners managed to baptize two dying children. They crunched through the banks and drifts of snow to Ossossané where, as they said, "they found the devil let loose."

A new sorcerer was in the ascendancy, Tehorenhaegnon, who had fasted ten days in a divining cabin and had learned the cure of the disease from the demons who visited him. Though Ossossané had publicly proclaimed its belief in God and its rejection of superstitions and devil-worship only a month before, it now just as publicly worshiped at the shrine of Tehorenhaegnon, the oracle of the demon. He himself would not deign to enter Ossossané as its savior, but he would depute his disciple, Saossarinon, as his ambassador and would communicate to him his powers.

Fathers de Brébeuf and Jogues reached the village at the time the town-crier was proclaiming that Saossarinon was come to vanquish the plague. They were informed that the great feast ordered by the sorcerer would be held that night in the large cabin where they usually lodged. They elected to stay there. At nightfall the men of the village assembled for their feast; and later in the night the women were to gather for theirs. When all were crowded in, a chief climbed on a beam above their heads, and cried the invocation: "Come now, demons, see us here assembled. Listen, you demons whom Tehorenhaegnon invokes, behold we are about to make a feast and have a dance in your honor. Come, let the contagion cease and leave this town. If you still have a hunger to eat human flesh, carry yourselves off to the country of our enemies. We now join ourselves with you, to bring the sickness to them and to destroy them."

They chanted in slow rhythmic beats, groaning from their bellies and beating time on their drums of bark and skin. They swayed in unison, and raised their knees, and pounded their heels in the earth. The mass of almost naked men moved along the aisle and about the fireplaces, raising, lowering their voices in the barbaric chorus, pounding on the tomtoms, bending and writhing, slowly pushing this way, milling that way, singing the monotonous hymn. Saossarinon left the cabin to visit the sick of the village. A chief commanded silence and offered an incantation to the demon. The dance and chant were resumed. The night wore on, the chanters waited for the sorcerer's return. The gray of the morning leaked through the doors and apertures: "Come, great Arendiowane, come, behold the day begins to dawn." They were now exhausted, but they urged one another on in the orgy.

At last, Saossarinon stood at the door of the cabin. Silence reigned. With one hand he waved the bow of Tehorenhaegnon, as a symbol of power, and in the other carried a turkey wing and a kettle of mystic water. He passed gravely down the lines of savages, giving each a few drops of the water to drink. They were enraptured. The demon had heard them, the demon would fly away, carrying the disease with him. Saossarinon gravely withdrew from the assembly, and the men fell on the kettles of food ravenously. After they had finished, the women made like invocation to the demon. But they had no feast that morning, since the men had left no food.

On two successive nights the same ritual was transacted. Saossarinon departed, leaving two disciples to continue the dissipation of the sickness. As many remained sick as professed themselves cured. He returned within a few days, and, instead of visiting the sick, ordered that they be carried to his presence. In the process, a few died; not one was bettered. Opinion veered, and Saossarinon left the village hurriedly while his two delegates threw away their turkey wings and renounced their distinction of being sorcerers, since the penalty of failure was a split skull.

De Brébeuf and Jogues waited for the hysteria to pass. They had the consolation of baptizing a few souls and sending them to God. One was a squaw who had resisted all their attempts to talk to her until just before her end, when she begged to be baptized. Another was a young brave who eagerly wished for baptism, but whose relatives guarded him against the approach of Echon and Ondessonk. De Brébeuf waited until the relatives were absent from the cabin, and then poured the saving waters on his head a moment before his mother-in-law returned to prevent him. As he related: "The Divine Goodness had prepared this moment for an act of mercy to this poor young man, doubtless through the merits of St. Joseph, who was invoked very especially on this occasion, as well as on the preceding one."

II

When February came in 1637, the influenza epidemic had almost spent itself. The fear that had alternately driven the Hurons to despair and to fury, now gave place to a lethargic calm. They no longer threatened to massacre the Blackrobes, and they paid little attention to the weird superstitions ordered by the sorcerers. They mourned over the hundreds who had died, and were depressed. But the winter was near gone. Soon it would be the spring, soon the trails would be cleared of the snow and the waterways of the ice. When the sun shone warmly, they would leave their cabins and take to their canoes and travel off to the fishing-haunts.

Relief came also to the missioners. The threat of being murdered was not so often hurled at them. The duty of visiting the cabins and seeking out the sick in Ihonatiria and the other villages was not so insistent. Despite the obstacles and the conflict, they had been successful enough in their ministrations to be satisfied. From October to the end of January they counted more than two hundred and fifty baptisms which they had administered to those about to die. That was a harvest of souls for heaven. Le Mercier remarked about the sick: "It is well for us that they are not all in heaven." But those who recovered, after having been baptized in their last agonies, became an acute problem.

Now that the stress of the active apostolate had ceased, the Fathers turned to a more intensive study of the Huron tongue. This was their single occupation from about February 20, just before Lent, till Easter. Father de Brébeuf was the teacher. Both he and Daniel had acquired considerable fluency, and together they had labored to compile a dictionary and to discover the rules of grammar and syntax that governed the language. In conjunction with a Huron boy, Louys de Sainte Foy, who had been taken over to France some years before, they had reduced to script the questions and answers essential for baptism, as well as some few necessary prayers. They had also put into Huron a short narrative of the life of Our Lord.

A curious and an amazing language it was to the French. As for the alphabet, there were only eight consonants: D, G, H, Khi, N, R, S, T. There were no labials, since the savages did not use their lips in speaking. Their words seemed to be composed almost entirely of vowels, and were spoken from the gorge of the neck. Compound words, made up of substantives joined with adjectives and pronouns, abounded. The mastery of these, according to de Brébeuf, was the secret of the language. There were genders, as in French, and numbers and cases as in Greek. What astonished the French was that all the words were inflected. The verbs were conjugated in tenses and numbers in as many ways as in Greek; more than that, there was a double conjugation, one direct and the other reciprocal; and then, in addition, a feminine conjugation, at least in some persons. The more they learned of the native tongue, the more the Fathers realized that this was no barbarous language but one of regular construction, richer than the French in its complex shades of meaning.

Years before, Father Biard observed that the Algonquins had no abstract words and de Brébeuf discovered the same lack in the Huron tongue, though they sprang from diverse roots. Biard had written: "Their conceptions are limited to sensible and material things. There is nothing abstract, internal, or spiritual. Good, strong, red, they will repeat to you in their language; goodness, strength, redness, they do not know what they are. As to all the virtues you may enumerate to them—wisdom, fidelity, justice, mercy, etc.—these are not to be found among them at all except as expressed in the words, happy, tender, love, good heart, etc. Likewise, they will name to you a wolf, a fox, a squirrel, a moose; but as to words expressing universal and generic ideas, such as beast, animal, body, substance, and the like, these are altogether too learned for them."

De Brébeuf and the other Huron missioners struggled to discover the Huron equivalents which would express the doctrines of religion and the precepts of virtue. Because of the fact that such universal terms as father or son could not be comprehended or expressed by them, and that a noun always had a pronoun attached, it was impossible to translate the words of the sign of the cross. The nearest approach, and de Brébeuf inquired of the theologians of France as to its propriety, was: "In the name of our Father, and of His Son, and of Their Holy Spirit."

By Easter Sunday, April 12, Le Mercier, the diarist of the Community, could report: "We have not failed, through God's holy grace, to make great progress in the language. So that now, if there is a question of making little trips to visit and instruct some savage, the Father Superior finds all of us ready to go. And there is not one of us who does not consider himself happy to go and coöperate in the salvation of some soul. We have good reason to thank this Infinite Goodness which gives us so great a liking for this language of the barbarians. After our devotional exercises, we have no greater consolation than to devote ourselves to this study. It is our most common subject of conversation, and we gather up all the words from the mouths of the savages as so many precious stones, that we may use them afterwards to display before their eyes the beauties of our holy mysteries."

His tongue itching to use the knowledge he was acquiring in the language for the service of God, Jogues made a round of the nearby villages on April 23, under the tutelage of Le Mercier. The results were the persuasion of the parents to allow the baptism of four babies in danger of death. One continued to live, but as for the other three, Le Mercier writes: "What a favor from Heaven for these little angels, and what a consolation for us!" On May 12 Jogues and Garnier were deputed to go to Anonatea without any of the veterans. They poured the water on three persons desperately sick. The same two were companions, on May 28th, on a visit to an old man who lived in Arontaen, one of the hostile villages. The man, however, was not averse to listen to his nephews, Ondessonk and Ouracha. He found them interesting, and professed his willingness to go to heaven. After they had baptized him, he thanked his nephews, the Blackrobes, most cordially and affectionately.

For the most part, however, the Blackrobes were persons to be suspected. To have the name of being a sorcerer, among the savages, and to be suspected of using witchcraft against the people rather than in their aid, was equivalent to a death sentence. As stated by Le Mercier, "the prominent and chief men of the country show us quite plainly that they do not share the belief that we are devils and evil sorcerers, but nevertheless intimate that they fear some heedless fellow will commit some foul deed that will cause them to blush. We are in God's hands and all these dangers do not make us forfeit a moment of our joy. It would be too great an honor for us to lose our lives while employed in saving some poor soul."

Since Ihonatiria had turned bitterly hostile to the Blackrobes, and since, also, the villagers were negotiating plans to abandon their identity and merge with some neighboring hamlets in a new village, the Fathers looked about for a cabin elsewhere. Invitations had been extended them to establish themselves among the Arendarhonons, the Rock Nation, who occupied the eastern region below the peninsula. The Attigneenongnahacs, the Cord Nation, which inhabited the far south also besought them. But the most generous offers came from the Bear Nation, the Attignawantans of Ossossané. "For this we have to praise God," exclaimed de Brébeuf, "that He gives us the favor to be loved and sought after throughout the country; there is strife as to who will have us in his village." He realized, nevertheless, that the chiefs wanted them mostly because of the preferences they could thus secure in trade with the French along the St. Lawrence.

The missioners selected Ossossané. It was large, it was important, it offered easy access to the villages and nations of the east and south, and its people were hospitable. During April and May de Brébeuf held council with its chiefs, and on May 17 reached an agreement by which the chiefs bound themselves to erect, immediately, a cabin seventy feet long for the Blackrobes. They apologized for not building a larger residence, begging the Blackrobes to consider that the plague had killed off many of their men, and that a great number, just then, were away fishing and hunting. Next year, they promised, they would make the cabin as long and as wide as the Blackrobes desired.

As soon as the final resolution was passed, the chiefs and braves seized their hatchets and flowed out to the site which de Brébeuf had chosen, a grove about a musket-shot from the palisades. They felled trees, stripped sheets of bark, gathered the poles and thin branches and saplings, wove the roots and vines into thongs, and began to fashion the house. Father Pierre Pijart and two *engagés* supervised the construction. He found that the first enthusiasm did not persist, for two weeks later, on June 4, he sent a note to the brethren at Ihonatiria: "I am here in the midst of extraordinary confusion. On the one hand, I have to keep them at work upon our cabin, and on the other I have the sick to visit. The former do only a part of what they attempt; and I encounter near the latter more sorcerers and Arendiowane than occasions to speak to them of God and of the matter of their salvation."

At Ihonatiria, on Trinity Sunday, June 7, a most imposing and most significant ceremony was enacted. "It was perhaps one of the most beautiful days we have ever had in this country," exclaims Le Mercier. Tsiouendaentaha, a man about fifty years of age, highly intelligent, very prudent and discreet, exercising great influence in the councils of the nation, was baptized publicly and with all the ceremonies of the Church. For three years he had sought knowledge of the doctrines of the Blackrobes, and, after mature consideration, had asked to be baptized. He was the first adult Huron, in good health, to seek to become a Christian. The Fathers, aware of the fickleness and inconstancy of the savages, of their habitual deceit and cupidity, which would lead them to seek baptism for the material advantages that would accrue, knowing well the temptations of sin in the loose environment and in the atavistic pull of superstitions and devil-worship, had hesitated to baptize the man, and had refused to do so until they had instructed him completely and tested his fidelity. So eager, so sincere, so intelligent and firm proved the man that they could not in conscience reject him. And so important a conquest was he, that they used the occasion for a public demonstration.

On Trinity Sunday, the Fathers decorated their cabin in gala fashion. Over the chapel door they wove a bower of green leaves and flowers entwined with tinsel. They decked the little chapel with all their sacred pictures and statues, and massed the altar with flowers and candles. Father de Brébeuf baptized Tsiouendaentaha and gave him the name of Peter, the first Christian. Simon Baron was his godfather. At the Mass which followed, Peter received his first Holy Communion. The chapel and cabin shook with the mobs that came to witness the solemn services. They were reasonably quiet, so impressed that they did not create the usual turmoil. One old man, Tendoutsahoroné, however, insisted on breaking into exhortations. He kept telling the people that it was much better to be baptized this way than in sickness, for sickness takes away one's brains; and everybody should follow the lead of Tsiouendaentaha and be baptized immediately.

Following the Mass was a great feast at which Peter and Echon delivered speeches and were roundly applauded. For the remainder of the day the cabin and chapel were left open to the admiring gaze of the visitors. The pictures and images in the chapel were the focal points of attention, for the natives had heard of these from the sorcerers. Some feared their baneful influences, remembering that the sorcerers declared the disease emanated from them. One squaw, in particular, was terrified. She wanted to satisfy her curiosity by a nearer view, yet she feared to contract the sickness. For a long time she stood at the threshold of the chapel, but finally, in despair, she cried out: "There is no help for me; I must take a chance; I have to get a good look, even if it costs me my life."

One picture, however, did create an unfortunate opinion. Le Mercier tells: "We had exhibited an excellent representation of the Judgment, where the damned are depicted; some had serpents and dragons tearing out their entrails, and the greater part had some kind of instrument of their punishment. Many savages obtained some benefit from this spectacle; but others persuaded themselves that this multitude of men, desperate and heaped one upon the other, were all those whom we had caused to die during the winter. They conceived the idea that these flames represented the fires of this pestilential fever, and that these dragons and serpents were the venomous beasts that we made use of in order to poison them." The result was a new crop of rumors and suspicions.

Two days later, about fifty villagers of Ossossané, braves and squaws, invaded Ihonatiria. They loaded on their shoulders the baggage and food and furniture and chapel goods, practically all the contents of the Blackrobes' cabin, and carried them off along the twelve-mile trail to their own village. They deposited them that night at the new residence in the grove near Ossossané. When the Fathers had arranged all their belongings in place and had set up their altar and pictures and decorations in the chapel, which was partitioned off and took up half the cabin, the people of Ossossané were in amazement before the magnificence of it all. Before long, the cabin became the mecca for sightseers from all the country of the Hurons. The visitors gave the Fathers much occupation, for their hands and feet had to be watched constantly, lest they steal all the furnishings.

During early June, the Fathers were busy with the annual reports and letters which would be carried by the canoes to Quebec, and thence to France, in the autumn. Le Mercier, the historian of the house, labored over two or three hundred pages of the Huron Relation of the year. De Brébeuf was composing in elegant Latin his official letter to the Father General of the Society, in Rome, Mutius Vitelleschi. Of the five priests associated with him he wrote: "These are in every way extraordinary laborers, who in the highest degree combine prayer and union with God with a burning zeal for souls. In the one or two years that they have been here they have made such great progress in the language, still rudely known and not reduced to rules, that it is truly marvelous; the persistence of all of them in this study is remarkable."

Father Jogues was writing to his loved ones in France. His longest letter was to his mother. He began it in a most filial and respectful tone:

Madame and most honored Mother in Our Lord:

As there does not present but one occasion each year to write to you, it is not proper that I let it pass without acquitting myself of the duty that I owe to one who is so good a mother. I am sure that you will be happy to recognize the Special Providence with which the Divine Goodness has guided me, for God has given me the grace of a safe arrival in the land of the Hurons. I wrote to you last year, in the month of August, just at the moment when I was about to prepare to take the road here. . . .

He continued by recounting some of the experiences of the trail up from Three Rivers. But he omitted the narrative of what he had since suffered, of the sickness that laid him low upon his arrival, of the influenza epidemic that had carried off hundreds of the savages, of the threats on his life made by the enraged savages, of the filth and squalor of the cabins he visited and in which he lodged, of the cold and wretched food and the journeys and the hardships. It was sufficient for her, and better for her, perhaps, not to know too much of life among the Hurons. From the recital of his upward journey he abruptly turned to something joyous:

It is thus that Providence has preserved me up to the present, full of strength and health. It has granted me the grace of the greatest happiness and peace, a thousand times over, amid the inconveniences inseparable in our situation—a greater happiness than if I had in my possession all the riches of the world. Here, God makes himself felt with an abundance of consolation. He protects us among the barbarians with so much love, He consoles us with such great tenderness in the little afflictions that we have to endure, that there is not the slightest regret over that which we have given up for him. Nothing can equal, or even approach, the satisfaction that our hearts feel in revealing the knowledge of the true God to these infidels. We have baptized about two hundred and forty of them this year. Among these are some whom I have washed in the waters of baptism, and who are assuredly in Paradise, since some of them were small babies of one or two years of age. The life of a man, could it be better employed than in this noble work? What am I saying? All the labors of a million persons, would they not be well compensated for by the conversion of one single soul gained for Jesus Christ? I have always had a great love for this kind of life and for this vocation, so grand and so much like that of the Apostles. So that, if I had only to seek for happiness here below, I would make every effort possible before God and man to obtain the favor that I now possess, and I would buy it at the price of a thousand lives. I beg of you, Madame, if these lines fall into your hands, by the bowels of the charity of Jesus Christ, to give thanks to the Saviour for this extraordinary favor that He has conferred on me, a favor that so many of the great servants of God, endowed with qualities more noble than mine, desire and crave so ardently.

Your humble and affectionate servant and son according to God,

Isaac Jogues.

Residence of St. Joseph in the
village of Ihonatiria, 5 June, 1637.

For the present, Jogues and Chastellain were left with Le Mercier in the ruined cabin of St. Joseph's in Ihonatiria. De Brébeuf took Pijart and Garnier with him to the grand new residence of the Immaculate Conception at Ossossané. After the dread, dreary winter there bloomed for them a lovely spring. Peace was in the Huron land, persecution had passed. The Blackrobes of Ossossané and Ihonatiria looked forward to a still greater harvest of souls.

III

Most of the men departed the villages about the beginning of June. They were journeying the waterways, fishing, scaring up guerrilla warfare with the Iroquois, trading with the Algonquins, visiting the French down along the St. Lawrence. Only the old men and the squaws and the children lingered about the cabins and in the adjacent fields. A torrid, blistering summer was setting in, and already was baking the land and hovering over the rippling, green lake.

In the new life that came with the spring the epidemic seemed to have been checked. But, when summer began, a few of the women and children fell sick, then a few more. Within a week or two it became evident that a new wave of the contagion was breaking over the country. Ihonatiria and Ossossané were relatively immune. But the villages within the radius of a few miles from Ihonatiria, those especially of Anonatea and Andiatae and Onnentisati and Angwiens, reported an ever-increasing number of deaths. So, too, were the villages near Ossossané stricken. Reports were current that the

Huron nations to the south and the east were being destroyed by the plague. By the beginning of July the sickness was as prevalent as it had been in the winter.

With its increase started new fears and hysteria. The sorcerers were invoked. They sought again to discover the cause of the disease. They learned from friendly demons that the Blackrobes were the cause. The pictures in the Blackrobes' cabins blew out the pestilence. The kettles which the French sold them exuded virulent poison. The piece of black cloth hung on a fir tree near the cabin at Ossossané, which the Blackrobes declared was to show the way the wind blew, was a sign to the bad spirits as to whither they should send the disease. The box in the cabin, which mysteriously beat tick, tick, all day and all night, was a demon striking out death. The Blackrobes forbade the people to enter their cabin early in the morning, before daybreak; it was then they wove their evil spells for the day. The Blackrobes chanted together in the evening; these were incantations calling up the devils. The Blackrobes walked about in silence and moved their lips as they held a little book before them; they were talking to the spirits. The Blackrobes brought a corpse from France and were hiding it in a little closet in their chapel. The Blackrobes took a child into the woods and stabbed it to death with a sharp bodkin; this was to bring about the death of innumerable children.

To little avail did the Fathers remonstrate against these hideous accusations. The only answer they received, when they sought for proof, was, "These things are being said by everyone." They ceased to be welcome in their visits. Doors were slammed to, and held, when they approached a cabin. They were driven away from others, with shouts and gestures. One warrior stood at his door, flourishing his hatchet, and threatened to split the head of any Blackrobe that came near. If they did manage to enter a cabin, the sick drew the blanket over their heads and refused to speak or listen. Their few friends assured them that all the people were firmly convinced that they were the authors of the disease, and therefore must be killed as sorcerers or else driven out of the land. In view of the public sentiment, Le Mercier states: "We judged that our visits might be prejudicial to the progress of the Holy Gospel." Hence, he continues, "we judged it wise to desist entirely from our visits. We remained for some time at anchor during the tempest."

Jogues, who remained at Ihonatiria with Le Mercier, was in the first storm center of this wild tempest, for it was in the near-by villages that the slanders originated. He was assured by his friends that the people of Ihonatiria did not believe what was said. Nevertheless, he found even his friends growing colder and colder, and many of the cabins closed to him. Father de Brébeuf ranged the country, now at Ossossané, now at Ihonatiria, now in the hamlets. He explained everywhere why the Blackrobes were living among the Hurons, why they visited the sick and tried to talk to them and baptize them, what it meant to save the soul, and who was the God he believed in. The chiefs who listened were impressed, but their attitude, as expressed by one of them, was: "The young men should be very careful not to strike a blow for which the whole country might groan."

On Tuesday night, August 4, there convened at Ossossané a general council of all the Huron nations. Two questions were to be debated: that of war or peace with the Iroquois; that of the guilt of the plague. Thither came, as guests of the Attignawantans, the civil chiefs and the ancients of the Arendarhonons of the east; of their neighbors, the Ataronchronons; of the southern Attigneenongnahacs. Their minds were settled on the question of the guilt. They had no doubt but that the Blackrobes were white devils. De Brébeuf mingled with the visiting chiefs, and as Le Mercier states, "endeavored to clear us in private talks with various persons from the slanders that had been loaded on us. But they were already so bitter that the chiefs most favorable to us told him plainly that the greatest favor we could hope to gain was to be driven out of the country and sent back to Quebec."

The council debated through the night. It was agreed that no final condemnation should be made of the Blackrobes until the war chiefs and the important leaders who were absent, trading at Three Rivers, should return. There was general disappointment at this resolution. The chief who had brought Father Jogues up to Ihonatiria the year before, was especially chagrined that the Blackrobes were not murdered. He was sorry that he had not put Ondessonk to the torture, he confessed, "to draw from him the whole truth which his brothers conceal from us. I would certainly have ruined him, and caught him up in some of his words." To which Le Mercier responds: "What knowledge could he have gained from a man who could not yet know nor understand what was asked of him?"

On September 1, the first canoes back from the trading at Three Rivers landed at Ihonatiria. With this contingent came Father Paul Ragueneau, who had left France the preceding summer with Isaac Jogues. A week or two later, Father Pierre Pijart returned, bringing the winter supplies and the letters from home. He had gone down in June with the chief, Aënons, who had succumbed to the influenza at Three Rivers. He himself was stricken with the disease, but had recovered. Ragueneau and Chastellain went on to Ossossané to reside, while Jogues and Pijart remained at Ihonatiria. More Huron canoes kept arriving during September and October, until, about the middle of the month, the main body of about one hundred and fifty braves landed their canoes below the various villages.

With the return of the men, the wave of hate and hostility against the Blackrobes ebbed away. "They were the most contented men in the world," the missioners remarked. "They no longer believe, they say, that we caused their death, since they neither saw nor heard anything at Three Rivers and Quebec which did not greatly drive out of their minds their sinister suspicions." They were impressed by the fact that the Blackrobes on the St. Lawrence spoke of the disease precisely as the Blackrobes in their own country. Since they had held friendly council with the French and were well feasted, they were all in favor of tolerating the Blackrobes.

While this lull was on, Jogues and Pijart were exploded out of their sense of security. All of a sudden their cabin at Ihonatiria was crowded by a furious mob of young warriors. One of the savages held his bow stretched, ready to discharge an arrow. He looked from Jogues to Pijart, as if deciding which one to shoot first. He pointed an arrow at Pijart. "That is the man," he announced. "Yes, that is the man," his companion assured him. The two priests stared back at the savage, mystified yet unafraid. He drew back the string and aimed the arrow. Just then a commotion arose in the far end of the cabin. The braves had entered the chapel and spied the sacred pictures on the wall. The mob rushed down to the new excitement. They talked together in low tones, as if plotting some mischief.

The man with the bow and arrow was left facing the two Blackrobes alone. When the others finally sauntered out of the cabin, he followed them. "I do not know what deterred the man from discharging that fortunate arrow at me," Pijart remarked later. They learned afterwards that the braves were from Wenrio, and that the would-be murderer was a relative of Aënons, the chief who had died at Three Rivers. The brave, holding Pijart responsible for Aënons' death, was demanding a life for a life.

Endlessly the influenza lingered in the veins of the people. Death was always in their cabins. The warriors had come back from their summer trade in good health and feeling friendly to the French. But on their return they learned of the deaths of their squaws and their children, their parents and their relatives. They were mystified and saddened. Before long they were as crazed as those who had remained at home in the midst of the plague all the summer. Their sureness that the Blackrobes were not at the bottom of the pestilence dwindled away.

Toward the end of October Father de Brébeuf was visiting Jogues and Pijart at Ihonatiria. In the evening, as the sun was setting among the trees beyond the lake and all was peace, Le Mercier burst into the cabin. Father de Brébeuf had to rush back to Ossossané immediately; that day a friendly old chief had excitedly given them warning: "My nephews, you are dead men," he cried out to them. "The Attigneenongnahacs are coming to split your heads while the people of this village are away fishing. I have just learned this from the chief of that nation." Le Mercier believed the old man spoke the truth, for this nation of the south had been the most threatening at the August council. He had assembled the Fathers and workmen within the cabin, he related, and told them to be prepared for the attack; then, he had run all the way to Ihonatiria to bring back the Superior.

This was the greatest crisis yet, the four priests agreed. The Attigneenongnahacs were thirsting for their blood. They were restrained with difficulty during the summer. They could march into Ossossané without let or hindrance, and could massacre the French and burn their cabin. Not a person in Ossossané would withstand them, for that would be an unfriendly act to a brother people. All four priests realized the danger. De Brébeuf decided that he and Le Mercier would hurry back to Ossossané and face the savages. Jogues and Pijart were to remain at Ihonatiria. It was likely that the savages, after murdering all at Ossossané, would press on to Ihonatiria and kill the two survivors. Jogues and Pijart assured de Brébeuf they were ready to die. De Brébeuf gave them final instructions, in the event of their being spared, and took the trail that night to Ossossané.

Meanwhile, the Attigneenongnahacs had arrived and held council. They demanded the immediate execution of all the Blackrobes. A friendly native summoned the young Blackrobes, Garnier, Chastellain, and Ragueneau. "Come quickly and answer the council," he told them. "You are dead men!" They went boldly and faced their enemies. If they had wavered, if they had cringed, they would have been tomahawked on the spot. They were as stoical as any Huron. They demanded that the Blackrobes be heard before a general council of the Huron nations. This was agreed, and the chiefs were being summoned when de Brébeuf and Le Mercier arrived.

De Brébeuf strode in among the chiefs and ancients. To his greetings they merely bowed their heads, their sign that all was over with Echon and his Blackrobes. The only friendly chief in Ossossané was absent. Everybody had turned hostile. The council was scheduled for the night of October 28. The death sentence was prearranged. "We prepared our domestics," said Le Mercier, "to be ready to conform to the Holy Will of God no matter what happened. In truth, they prepared themselves reverently, but they determined, nevertheless, they said, not to die with their arms folded. They were not willing to let themselves be murdered without making some defense. As for ourselves, we were resolved to await death calmly before the Holy Altar."

All day Wednesday the priests made their final preparations. De Brébeuf composed a letter, addressed to the Superior at Quebec, Father Le Jeune, informing him: "We are, perhaps, at the moment of shedding our blood and sacrificing our lives to the service of our good Master, Jesus Christ." Speaking in the name of all the Fathers, he declared: "If He wills that at this hour we should die, oh, fortunate hour for us! If He wills to reserve us for other labors, may He be blessed! If you hear that God has crowned our insignificant labors, or rather our desires, bless Him; for it is for Him that we desire to live and to die, and it is He Who gives us Grace therefor. For the rest, if any survive, I have given orders as to all they are to do." This last testament before death, dated "In this Residence of la Conception at Ossossané, this 28th of October," was signed by de Brébeuf, Le Mercier, Chastellain, Garnier, and Ragueneau. A postscript was added: "I have left Fathers Pierre Pijart and Isaac Jogues in the residence of St. Joseph, with the same sentiments."

Fearing that an assault would be made on the residence, even before the council convened, de Brébeuf advised the priests and workmen to disperse themselves in the cabins of their friends among the Hurons. He entrusted his letter to Peter, the Christian of Ihonatiria, who promised to carry it down to Three Rivers. He also persuaded some of the Ossossané Christians to carry the chapel goods over to Peter's lodge, and asked them "to be especially careful to put our dictionary and all that we have of the language in a place of safety." De Brébeuf hoped and prayed that, though he and his four companions at Ossossané be killed, Jogues and Pijart would be spared. He turned, in his extremity, to their great heavenly patron, Saint Joseph. That day, the feast of Saints Simon and Jude, they vowed to begin a novena of Masses in his honor.

After dark had set in, the Hurons assembled in the long cabin of the chief of Ossossané. On one side of the council fire sat the people of the Attignawantan, and with them Echon and the Blackrobes. Opposite, their faces stolid and grim in the flickering of the flames, haunched the Attigneenongnahacs. They sat a while in silence, smoking their calumets. Then orators on both sides spoke and, fixing the guilt of the pestilence on the Blackrobes, demanded that they be put to death. No one defended them; no one spoke against the sentence. The night wore on. The chiefs and ancients hesitated to pronounce the final sentence of death, though all were convinced that death was the just penalty and would alone save the nation from further ruin. They were stayed by the larger issue of thus nationally fracturing their alliance and forfeiting their privileges with the French. They broke up the assembly, irresolutely, and postponed the decision till the next night.

It was but a question of time, both the Hurons and the Blackrobes believed. That day, October 29, the Fathers adopted the Huron custom of holding their Atsataion, or Farewell Feast. They invited friend and enemy alike to their cabin, as was the propriety for people about to die, and offered bounteous supplies of fish, corn, and other vegetables. The cabin overflowed with guests. They ate in silence and mourning. Echon and the other Blackrobes made their final addresses and exhorted the people to believe in the one true God in Whose name they were about to die. The Hurons looked sullen and troubled.

In that same mood, they gathered again that night for the second council. Early into the morning they harangued. They convinced themselves more than ever that the Blackrobes should be struck down. But again they could not, strangely, nerve themselves, as a nation, to pass the decree. If an individual committed the murder, they would not object, for that would not carry with it the responsibility of the chiefs and ancients. They adjourned without commanding the death of the Blackrobes.

The Fathers said the second of their votive Masses to St. Joseph. They walked about the village, where they were met with scowls and silence, but were not otherwise molested except for occasional threats and warnings. That day, the Attigneenongnahacs padded out of Ossossané. The villagers looked on their departure with surprise. They were amazed that the Blackrobes were allowed to live. Everybody understood that permission to kill them had been granted, though the order was not officially given. "One, two, then three days slipped away," wrote Le Mercier, "to the astonishment of our entire village, without these gentlemen menacing us with threats of death in their council. I do not know whether the devil had aroused these barbarians against us, but I can say that we had not completed our novena before all these tempests were quieted, so that the savages even wondered at it among themselves, and with reason."

During these days of excitement at Ossossané, Jogues and Pijart waited at Ihonatiria in a grueling uncertainty. Many of the people had gone to attend the council and to witness the murders. Reports came back, all dire, all certain. Echon and the Blackrobes would surely be tomahawked today. The morrow came. They would have their heads split without doubt today. Jogues and Pijart prayed to St. Joseph, and waited along the Ossossané trail. Peter the Christian came to them with a sad face. Not yet were the Blackrobes killed, but who could tell how soon? Then, the villagers returned. They were mostly silent and perplexed. The Blackrobes lived.

CHAPTER V

Powers of the Other World

I

A PERIOD of quietude hovered over the Huron land while autumn turned to winter and the new year of 1638 came in. Father Jogues lived at Ihonatiria with Pijart and Chastellain. They had for their care their own village and the hamlets in the neighborhood. Daily they made their rounds of the cabins. They entered the huts without remonstrance, but were received stolidly and without enthusiasm. The men might grunt a formal greeting, the women would stare coldly through the slits of their eyes, the children scampered away, except those of the malicious age, who mimicked them and played little tricks.

They learned, however, much of the strategy to be followed. Their first point of attack was against the men. These dominated opinion entirely, and in all except the domestic affairs of the cabin ruled the lives of their families. The good-will of the squaws was essential, and the friendliness of the children was an asset for the future, but the braves and chiefs were the ones who must first be convinced and converted. Hence, the Blackrobes sedulously sat about the cabin fires and talked to the men during their winter inactivity.

The Hurons loved arguments and the telling of wondrous tales. They came to enjoy the talk of Ondessonk and the Blackrobes who now could express themselves with some ease. As a result, the Fathers and the savages grew in mutual esteem. One missioner could write: "They nearly all show more intelligence in their business, speeches, courtesies, intercourse, tricks, and subtleties than do the shrewdest citizens and merchants of France." And another averred: "I can say in truth that, as regards intelligence, these savages are in no wise inferior to Europeans and to Frenchmen. I would never have believed that, without instruction, nature could have supplied a most ready and vigorous eloquence, which I have admired in many Hurons, or more clear-sightedness in affairs, or a more discreet management in things to which they are accustomed."

On occasions, the Fathers prepared feasts in their cabins. Always they were assured of a plentiful company, for never would a Huron refuse food. They used the opportunity to explain their beliefs and doctrines and to contradict the notions of the savages. The guests were most content to smoke the calumets which the Blackrobes filled with tobacco for them, and to listen and question for further knowledge. They began to be impressed.

From the interest evoked in private discourses and at feasts, the Blackrobes gradually, as the winter months wore on, attracted a goodly number of the men into their cabin for more formal exercises. The assembly would begin with a prayer in the Huron language, spoken in the tone used in the council. Then would be chanted in the native rhythm the Apostles Creed. There followed the catechism lesson, carried on by a staged dialogue or one that arose naturally. The Hurons enjoyed these displays of intelligence immensely. Thereafter, the Fathers would sing a hymn in the French style and chant a closing prayer in the native cadence. The old men more than others, even though they would not accept baptism, proved great aids in pointing out the wisdom and the reasonableness of the Blackrobes' words, and often urged the young men to pay heed to them.

All this, however, was by way of sowing the seed. The Fathers proceeded very slowly and most cautiously in receiving the natives into the Church. For the danger of perversion, through the nature as through the environment of the Hurons, was always imminent. "The nature of the savage," one missioner summarized, "is patient, liberal, hospitable; but it is importunate, visionary, childish, thievish, lying, deceitful, licentious, proud, lazy." And another sharply remarked: "All these barbarians have the law of wild asses: they are born, live, and die in a liberty without restraint. They do not know what is meant by a bridle or a bit. With them, to conquer one's passions is considered a great joke, while to give free rein to the senses is a lofty philosophy."

They lied brazenly, and, the missioners conjectured, for the pleasure of deceiving. They not only stole, but practiced thievery and boasted of their skill. "They used to steal with both their hands and their feet, in the presence and in the absence of the owner, not from actual utility but from pure vice," one of the Fathers stated with acerbity. A prospective chief was asked if, when he had power, he would punish thievery by death, as in France. He answered with a smile: "In that case, the country would very soon be depopulated, for it would be necessary to kill everyone. A Huron and a thief are almost the same."

In the matter of sexual relations, the Hurons were notorious among all the native nations for their immoralities. Outside of marriage there was neither curb nor disapproval of any licentiousness on the part of either sex, so that never did the child reach the age of puberty in a virginal state. Marriage was seldom contracted because of romance or love, but was entered into for utility. Polygamy was not usual, but divorce occurred for the most trivial of reasons. The utter lewdness, the free mingling of the sexes, the instability of the marriage tie made the missioners most wary about administering baptism.

That the Hurons were men of violence and cruelty, the Blackrobes had had tragic experience. The spilling of blood, the smashing of skulls, the shooting with arrows, the stab of the knife or the spear, the giving of poison—they were accustomed to these things from childhood. Still, the murder of their own people was not over-prevalent. It was not punished by death through a community decree. It was a private affair, and the relatives of the slain person were free to kill the murderer or to condone the act by accepting presents. For the killing of a sorcerer, or of one suspected of weaving evil designs through witchery, there was universal approbation. Toward enemies of other nations, the traditional rule was that of diabolical cruelty.

The deadliest obstacles, the missioners found, to their efforts to civilize and Christianize the Hurons were the multitudinous forms of superstition, sorcery, and devil-worship. Faith in dreams was the least harmful, but it led to dreadful crimes. For a dream to the Huron was a revelation from a god that must be obeyed no matter how fantastic or how impossible or how woeful in its results. They placed implicit faith also in the unseen demons who were everywhere. The oki "that which is above" was to be feared and flattered, for it perpetrated evil and was propitious if treated well. The oki were of a universal nature, such as the sun; or local, such as the demon of a lake or tree; or personal, attached to a family or an individual. These deities were believed to exercise perpetual influence and domination. The savages were craven under them or arrogant because of them.

Controlling, and an essential part of, this system of preternatural influences were the sorcerers. They were usually men, and usually the more esteemed the more hideous their bodily deformity. They interpreted dreams, foretold the future, revealed the past, rendered favorable the deities of war and the chase and fishing, controlled the weather, cured the sick, and in general dispersed good luck. For these blessings, they were courted and revered. They were always feared for their malice and the evil they might concoct.

Almost all of them claimed a preternatural origin and boasted of being in communication with the spirits. The missioners discovered that many of their practices were trickery and charlatanism, but attributed others to the direct intervention of the devil. The cabins and huts where they held their seances were oftentimes violently shaken; they themselves would stuff live coals into their mouths without being burned, or would thrust their arms into boiling water without being scalded. The rites and ceremonies they conducted were so indecent and revolting that they surpassed unaided human invention.

Quietly, for the most part, the battle of forces waged that winter in the cabins of the Hurons. Not many of the savages were willing to submit to the religious demands of the Blackrobes, and they, on their part, were unwilling to accept those who sought baptism until they had absolute proofs of the understanding and the moral strength of the catechumens. In Ihonatiria, Jogues was highly edified by the piety and steadfastness of the first Christian, Peter. In Ossossané, there occurred a more notable conversion.

Chihwatenhwa was a man of about thirty-five, the nephew of the great chief of the Bear Nation, "of superior mind, not only as compared with his countrymen, but even, in our judgment, he would pass as such in France," attests Le Mercier. During the preceding August, when he was thought to be dying from the influenza, he had been baptized and given the name of Joseph. He recovered, and continued faithful to his baptismal promises. During October, when the death decree was being passed on the Blackrobes, he was unfortunately absent. His voice, the only one, would have been raised in their defense. That winter he championed their cause. In the services and disputations, the chronicler records, "our Joseph does wonders; for sometimes acting as objector, sometimes as ignoramus, and anon as doctor, he gives opportunity to our catechist to explain by dialogue and with more clearness what otherwise would be only half understood." In March, 1638, his wife, Aonetta was baptized, together with Theresa, his daughter, and his little sons. Then, he and Maria Aonetta were solemnly married at the first such ceremony in the Huron land.

Thus, through the icy months of winter, Jogues and his companions were seekers of souls in all the cabins and villages. The mildness of spring then clothed the earth with green and decked the bleak limbs of the trees with baby leaves. A warm sun and cooling breezes evoked the heavy fragrance of the forests and lulled nature into mellowness. It was then that there occurred to Father Jogues an experience which he himself put into writing:

On the eleventh of May, which fell on Tuesday, the day before the vigil of the Ascension of Our Lord Jesus Christ, on an afternoon when I was studying the Huron language with Father Chastellain, I was overcome with drowsiness. I asked him whether he would mind if I took a little rest. He advised me that I should go into the chapel, and there I could satisfy the demand of nature for a little while before the Most Blessed Sacrament. He said that he was accustomed to rest before the Blessed Sacrament when he was sleepy, not without a great feeling of piety, and even, in such naps, he had sometimes enjoyed celestial happiness. I rose up; but, since I judged that I could not sleep in the presence of the most awe-inspiring and adorable Majesty of my God without irreverence, I went out to a neighboring woods. I was wholly stricken with great confusion, since others, even in their sleep, were more united to God than I was in my prayers. I lay down, accordingly, about the hour of vesper time. While drowsing, I seemed to myself to be singing the psalms of vespers, in my accustomed way, with the other Fathers and domestics. On one side was Father Pijart. He was close to the door, and I was farther in the chapel; who the others were on the other side and in what order they were, I do not know. Father Pijart began the first verse of the psalm *Verba mea auribus percipe, Domine*. Since he could not continue it alone, we two finished it. When that verse was ended, now, no longer, did I seem to myself to be in our cabin, but to be dwelling in some other place unknown to me.

Then, suddenly, they were chanting the remaining verses. I do not recall which ones, but they referred to the happiness of the saints and to the joys which they experience in the kingdom of God. The chanting had such beauty and the harmony of the voices and the instruments were so sweet that never before could I remember ever having heard anything like it. Indeed, all human melody, however enthrallingly beautiful, seemed to be discordant in comparison with this; I would do it a grave injustice if I even compared it to human melody. However, through that most exquisite, angelic harmony, I was lifted up to God in such a great, vehement, burning love, that, since I was not able to bear such great sweetness of the overflowing Divine Love, all my little heart dilated and melted away under the immensity of this inexplicable Divine Love. Most particularly, I experienced this when they chanted this verse, which I remembered well: *Introibimus in tabernaculum ejus: adorabimus in loco, ubi steterunt pedes ejus*. When I heard this, while yet half-asleep, I kept thinking to myself that I could trace that which I had received to the words of Father Chastellain. Then, when I awoke, all of that passed away. But such sweetness remained that even now the memory of so much consolation fills my soul with some strangely incredible sweetness. The result is that I seem to myself to be more drawn by love of Our Lord to the heavenly fatherland and the celestial joys. Happy the hour, brief the space, for I do not think it endured longer than the Hail Mary, Holy Mary. "If thou dealest with us thus in our exile, how much greater in the palace of the Most High."

May was the time to think about the annual letters for France. On the seventh, Father Jogues wrote to his mother, in respect to the epidemic:

Although we were every day and all day close to the dying, in order to try to gain these for Jesus Christ, and in spite of the infected air which we were breathing at their sides and in the midst of them, not a single one of us was stricken with the contagion. After that, we would be most ungrateful if we did not thank God for protection so visible on His part, and if we did not, for the future, place all our confidence in His Fatherly Goodness.

As regards the danger of death from the savages, he states in the same exalted strain:

The evil designs of our enemies have vanished, their plots against us have all gone up in smoke. God has been more powerful in protecting those who, for His Glory, have thrown themselves in the arms of His Divine Providence than men have been wicked in injuring them.

In the following week, on Ascension Thursday, May 13, he addressed a letter to his younger brother, Samuel, who had become a Capuchin:

In spite of the fire of persecution, the zeal of the missioners did not relax. They baptized more than 1,200 persons during the epidemic. And in that very village where they were most exposed, at the very height of the hate and ill-will of the inhabitants, there were always some who were desirous of following our instructions. I have regenerated about one hundred of these in the waters of baptism, among whom were twenty-two little children who are raised up in the Blood of the Lamb. But, as the entrance of the other villages has been closed to us, it was impossible for us to go and take care of them, so that we had the sorrow of seeing die, so to speak, under our very eyes, more than a hundred of the unhappy ones who called out in vain for our assistance.

For more than two years, now, the missioners had been planning to remove their cabin from Ihonatiria. The village had disintegrated. The palisades were fallen apart, the cabins were beyond repair, the filth was piled high, the stench was unendurable, the fields and woods were exhausted. More than half the inhabitants had died during the epidemics, and the remaining people were demoralized. The residence of St. Joseph was tumbling apart. It was necessary either to build a new lodge or to seek a cabin in another village. Even from their first arrival, the missioners regarded Ihonatiria only as a temporary location, as a gateway where they might pause and plan their further penetration into the Huron land. In 1638 they found a further reason to depart, namely because of "the lack of inhabitants there, and of people capable of profiting by our labors, nearly all being scattered or dead from the plague. This would seem to be, not without reason, a punishment from heaven for the contempt that they showed for the favor of the visit that the Divine Goodness had procured for them."

"When we resolved to abandon the dwelling at Ihonatiria, on account of its lack of inhabitants, the majority of them having been carried off or scattered by the disease," says the chronicler, "we were not long in deciding to what place it would be wise to go. We believed that the village of Teanaustayaé was the most important in the whole country, and one which, consequently, being once won to God, would give a strong impulse to the conversion of all the rest." There was a grave difficulty. Teanaustayaé was the capital town of the Attigneenongnahacs, the most hostile of the four Huron nations, the people who had gone to Ossossané in October resolved to massacre the French. "What a poor prospect in undertaking this project, and still less of succeeding in it!" the Fathers remarked. "For this village, a little while before, had been one of the principal shops in which the blackest calumnies and the most pernicious plots were forged against us. Nevertheless, He to Whom nothing is impossible, made this enterprise easy both in the undertaking of it and carrying it through, and that, more than we could ever have dared to hope."

In April, de Brébeuf went to Teanaustayaé to explore the possibilities of settling in the town. The negotiations lasted through May. At last Echon was accorded the favor of being allowed to address the council of chiefs. He adduced his arguments, and spread before the council the presents of wampum, axes, and such-like riches. After consultation in secret councils, the chiefs accepted the presents of the Blackrobes. Not only did they permit the palefaces to live in their village, but they offered them a cabin.

Jogues and Chastellain were the last to abandon Ihonatiria. They stripped the ruined cabin and chapel of all that was of worth, and, with the help of some friendly Hurons, carried their possessions on their backs along the twenty-five-mile trail that wound through the forests and dipped through innumerable gulleys. Teanaustayaé lay inland, to the southeast of the peninsula, about fifteen miles from Ossossané. It was located on the spur of a hill whose sides had been carved into deep gorges by the twist of a turbulent stream. Appropriately, it was named "The Guardian of the Beautiful Little River."

The cabin given to the Blackrobes was not much better than the one abandoned at Ihonatiria: "It is a fact that this cabin is so poor and so mean that, if the Saviour of this world, once upon a time in His necessity, had not Himself sought a lodging in the stable of Bethlehem, we would be ashamed to offer Him each day at Mass a new sort of birth in this place, which is covered only with paltry pieces of bark through which the wind enters on all sides." It was with high elation, nevertheless, that Father Jogues began his apostolate in the second St. Joseph's at Teanaustayaé, and said there his first Mass on June 25. He and the others were amazed: "they could hardly believe what they saw, so terrifically had this village abominated the Blackrobes just a little time before." Now, Ondessonk, Echon, and the other French were actually welcome.

II

That summer of 1638 the war fever gripped the Hurons. Peace negotiations with the Iroquois were shattered. War parties formed in Ossossané, in Teanaustayaé, in all the villages of the four Huron nations. The red hatchet was raised by the arms of the chiefs, the war hymns chanted, the war dance pounded out, fiery speeches delivered. With war-whoops, brandishing their tomahawks and javelins, the bands of warriors took the trails to the south, to the Great Lakes, to the rivers, to the dense forests. Through the warm summer they returned. Never had the Hurons been more victorious. Everywhere they had slaughtered and captured the Iroquois. All the Huron villages resounded with the songs of victory, and all were red with the fires of the tortures.

At Teanaustayaé, Jogues witnessed a torture and a conversion that surpassed anything human. A chief belonging to the Oneida nation of the Iroquois Confederacy, together with eleven warriors, was to be executed. The chief listened to the Blackrobes, Ondessonk and Echon, declared he wished to be baptized, and urged his followers to follow his lead. After the ordinary cruelties had been inflicted, just prior to the killings, the chief was baptized Peter. One by one, his companions, also baptized, succumbed to the fire and knives. Peter remained alone on the platform. He was scalped, mutilated, and scorched over his entire body. Suddenly, as if inspired, he attacked his Huron persecutors. With firebrands that he snatched from them, with red-hot irons, alone, he fought the mob of villagers. He slipped, fell from the platform to the earth, and was bound.

The Hurons threw him into a huge bonfire. He rose out of the flames, with flaring torches in his hands, and rushed on his enemies. They retreated as he ran toward the palisades to set the village on fire. They felled him with a club, and cut off his feet and hands. Then, they held him over nine different fires, turning him over and over, his blood almost extinguishing the blazes. Finally they crushed him under an overturned tree trunk, all on fire. Extricating himself, he crawled on elbows and knees, pulling himself a space of ten steps toward his persecutors. They fled before him as before a fiend. One, finally, struck him down and slashed off his head.

"Happy stroke which gave him his freedom," de Brébeuf exclaimed, "for we have reason to believe that this brave spirit is now enjoying the freedom of the children of Heaven, since even his enemies exclaimed that there was something more than human in him, and that, without doubt, baptism had given him strength and courage which surpassed all that they had ever seen." The Hurons, however, bitterly resented the granting of baptism and the happiness of heaven to their Iroquois enemies. They feasted that night on the flesh of Peter and their other roasted victims. To show their disdain, they threw the bones, and notably the pierced hands of a Mohawk Iroquois, who had been baptized Francis Xavier, into the Blackrobes' cabin. These the Fathers buried in their chapel, as the bones of Christians.

While the Hurons were torturing their prisoners that summer, they were opening their cabins in charity. The Wenrohronon nation, a people of the Huron-Iroquois stock, which inhabited the far eastern shore of Lake Erie, had appealed to the Hurons for help. They had suffered much during the two epidemics of influenza, and were being exterminated by the Neutral nation which was waging terrible war on them. The Hurons agreed to accept the Wenrohronons among them. The six hundred left of them, mostly women and children, started on the two-hundred-and-fifty-mile journey, carrying with them on their backs all of their possessions. The Hurons volunteered a large number of squaws to help carry the burdens, and of braves to act as a guard and an escort.

Nearly all the Wenrohronons were still infected with the influenza. Many of them died during the migration, and those who survived were weak from sickness and fatigue. They were received with the utmost kindness, distributed throughout the various villages; "wherever they were received, the best places in the cabins were given them, the granaries or chests of corn were opened, and they were given liberty to dispose of the stores as if they owned them." Jogues and the missioners poured out their own charity, likewise, on this unfortunate people. They traveled to the villages where the Wenrohronon families were lodged, ministered to their physical needs, and missed no opportunity of instructing and baptizing those who were dying.

Early in July, Father Antoine Daniel returned to labor among the Hurons. On August 26, arrived Father Jérôme Lalemant, and in September two other newcomers, Fathers Simon Le Moyne and François Du Peron. Upon his arrival, Lalemant presented the document whereby he was appointed the Superior of the Huron Mission in succession to de Brébeuf. Willingly Jean de Brébeuf relinquished his authority. For years he had been requesting his Superiors to replace him, alleging that he lacked the spiritual qualities and the human prudence necessary to govern others. No one ever agreed with his self-estimate, not his Superiors at Quebec or in France, not his fellow missioners, not the Hurons. He was spiritual and zealous, gentle, patient, prudent, strong of purpose and of will. Of all the missioners, not one was so respected and so loved. To the natives, Echon was a demi-god, their equal in physical prowess, their master in mind. One of the Fathers truly punned when he remarked that de Brébeuf was *vrais Bœuf a l'ouvrage.*

Lalemant was of the same age as de Brébeuf, about forty-five. He had been a distinguished professor of philosophy and theology, and had showed rare executive ability as Rector of the College of Blois. The missionary zeal ran strong in his blood, for his elder brother, Charles, had been a pioneer at Quebec. Unlike de Brébeuf, he was imperious, rigid as a disciplinarian, "tolerably irascible," as one of the priests remarked. He was the leader needed at that time. Whereas de Brébeuf had that tact required for making the first introductions, Lalemant had the inflexibility of the administrator. The one was the clearer of the soil, the other was the architect, the dreamer of tremendous projects. Almost his first statement was the declaration: "Our initial step will be to travel all over the country which was the first to receive us, and make a census. Then we shall push farther on, and always on and on, until we have accomplished our task, which is only bounded by the setting sun."

That autumn of 1638, Lalemant assigned their posts to the missioners. He lived at Ossossané with Daniel, Le Mercier, Chastellain, Garnier, and Du Peron. At St. Joseph's, in Teanaustayaé, he stationed de Brébeuf, Jogues, and the two younger men, Ragueneau and Le Moyne. He elaborated a regular order for the day. All rose with the ringing of the bell at four o'clock. From then, till eight, the Fathers meditated and said their Masses. At that hour, the doors were unbarred. Formerly, the natives were allowed to enter the cabin freely, but Lalemant decided that, since "the importunity of these barbarians, lazy to the last degree, was unbearable, none were admitted except those who might be profited, or from whom profit might be gained." During the day, one Father was on duty in the cabin, and held instructions for the children. The others visited the cabins and surrounding villages, each one having the care of specified families. Dinner was at two. Grace was said in Huron, for the benefit of any savages present, and a chapter of the Bible was read. At five in summer, and four in winter, the doors were barred, but Christian Hurons might gain admittance. The evening was devoted to the study of the language, to conferences on the work of the day, to consultations on the general status and the future prospects of the Mission. Supper was at six-thirty, during which a spiritual book was read while the Fathers ate, "around the fire, seated on a log, without plates, on the ground." At eight, night prayers were said, the examen of conscience made, and points prepared for the morning meditation. By nine, they were at rest on their mats under the shelves.

Jogues was now the veteran missioner beginning his third winter. He had mastered the Huron tongue sufficiently well to converse easily. He was habituated to the courtesies and the customs of the natives, had witnessed their ruthless cruelties and their degraded vices, had been amazed by their gentleness and their intelligence. He had had the ecstatic joy that came through salvaging their souls as well as that which flowed over him at the expectation of martyrdom and heaven for himself. His zeal was intensified the more it was practically applied. More than willing was he to spend all the remaining days of his life amid these hazards, living in the midst of these peoples. It satisfied him that he was in the more dilapidated of the residences at Teanaustayaé, among savages more treacherous and vindictive than the inhabitants of Ossossané. He was the more energized in that he was in the forefront of the conflict, at the side of the heroic Jean de Brébeuf.

When they came to Teanaustayaé in June, the Blackrobes were not received in too friendly a spirit. About October began the murmurings of another wave of the persecution. A few cases of seasonal sicknesses were mistaken for another influenza epidemic. "All their complaints and clamors were renewed," the chronicler wrote. "They repeated that, since we came to the country and sown our doctrine there, one saw no longer anything but misfortune and misery. No old men were ever seen any more. The whole country was falling into decay and ruin. They complained that, after having caused the death of all those in the village of Ihonatiria, where we had first settled, we went through all the other villages to create the same destruction. They told themselves that, if the cause of all these evils were not suppressed, they would soon see their entire nation annihilated."

Such were the speeches made in the councils and at the feasts, and such the common talk about the cabin fires. If a Blackrobe went through the village ringing a bell to call the people to instruction, a brave followed him, warning the people to keep away from these Blackrobe sorcerers. He would suggest that they should be murdering the Blackrobes instead of listening to them. During the public instructions, some of the more hostile would interrupt and argue maliciously and blaspheme. "The insolence of such persons of authority," remarks Lalemant, "greatly increases the boldness of the children and common people, from whom, consequently, one has to suffer not a little. Snowballs, clubs, cornstalks, and other rubbish, for lack of stones, which are not always found when they are wanted in this country, have been seen flying over the Fathers' heads, even during the catechism classes, and during the day, through the holes of the cabin which serve as window and chimney, to say nothing of many other indignities that occur every day, living among a barbarous people against whom we have, and can have, no defense."

Lalemant, unlike Jogues and de Brébeuf, found it difficult to control his temper with the savages. Irately he declares: "Considering from anear as well as from afar this country of the Hurons and other neighboring people, it has always seemed to me one of the principal fortresses and, as it were, a donjon of the demons." He was not in despair, however, for he writes a little later: "You see clearly the spirit of God and of the devil struggling in their minds and hearts. One day you see them all killing themselves to say that they believe and that they wish to be baptized. Another day, everything is overthrown and hopeless. This contrast is a manifest sign of combat and battle. But it must be confessed that we do not yet see to which side the complete victory leans. If we had no other principle to guide us except that which appears to our eyes, we would have reason to think that the end is still very far away. However, since nothing is impossible to God, and since His blessing often depends upon certain times and moments and upon certain resources that are unknown to us, we must await with patience and courage all that it may please Him to ordain."

Despite the petty persecution of that year, the missioners made some notable conquests. They progressed with extreme caution and, almost with reluctance, they chanced baptism on healthy adults. In Teanaustayaé, Jogues and de Brébeuf laid the foundation of the Church with a chief of high repute, Aochiati by name. He was about seventy years of age. He had attended the instructions faithfully, was ready to make all the promises required of him, and publicly announced that he abandoned all diabolic seances, dances, and superstitions. He repudiated, especially, the Dance of the Naked Ones, of which he was the leader and master. His sincerity was evident. "Would he be obliged to give up the use of tobacco if he were baptized?" he inquired; and declared that he would do even this, if it were not allowed to him. "This resolution," some one remarked, "may be regarded as one of the most heroic acts of which a savage is capable; for he would as soon dispense with eating as with smoking."

Even then, they put him off from baptism, though he begged for it. On the recommendation of Joseph Chihwatenhwa they received the old man, Aochiati, into the Church on December 20, and gave him the name of Mathias, "as the one to whose lot it had fallen to be the first Christian of this village, as well as the first catechumen baptized in good health and with solemnity." With him were baptized two of his little granddaughters, his special favorites. This gave proof positive of his sincerity, since it was commonly believed that baptism was especially deadly to children. A day or two before Christmas, de Brébeuf and Jogues admitted to baptism eleven other inhabitants, selected from a greater number of catechumens because of their intelligence and fervor. And thus, "these twelve or fifteen being all present at Mass on the first day of the year 1639, this is the day which we shall always observe and recognize as that of the birth of this new Church of Teanaustayaé."

Over in Ossossané, the infant church was growing apace. Under the influence of the example of Joseph Chihwatenhwa, the Christian, "three heads of families, among the oldest and most prominent of the village," were baptized on November 11. On December 8 "occurred the second group of baptisms, of sixteen persons, among whom were four heads of families, with their wives and children." Altogether, says the chronicler, the converts "make a company of thirty persons. On the Feast of the Immaculate Conception they attended Holy Mass in a body and those who were of an age received Communion. It seems that we have every reason to acknowledge and to observe this Holy Day, devoted to the honor and memory of the first dignity of this Holy Virgin, as that of the birth of this new Church, and of the beginning of happiness and blessing for this country."

That same month the *engagés*, and Fathers assisting, finished the magnificent church of Ossossané. It was thirty feet in length, sixteen in width, and twenty-four feet high. While it was being built Le Mercier wrote: "If God grant us the favor to see this work finished, it will not be one of the largest but will be one of the prettiest which have yet been built in New France." Du Peron attests: "This chapel is very neatly built of timber-work, almost similar in style and size to our chapel of St. Julien." And Jogues, after a visit to it, exclaims: "We have built at Ossossané a chapel, all of planks, which attracts the eyes and the admiration of all the villagers." Mass was celebrated there on December 12, and on Christmas night was solemnized the first great Feast. The chapel was gorgeously adorned with pictures, tinsel and evergreen, it glowed with torches and candles, and was warmed by fires and hot plates. All the Christians from all the country, numbering upwards of sixty, attended the High Mass at midnight.

In addition to the sermons of the Blackrobes, Joseph Chihwatenhwa, broke out into discourses. "He has intelligence, eloquence, integrity, prestige, the knowledge of our mysteries and a love for them, in an eminent degree," the Fathers stated. "And so we are beginning to regard him as an apostle of these countries, rather than as a barbarian." That Christmas night Joseph heard five Masses in succession, "during most of them on his knees, and this, for a barbarian who is not accustomed to that posture, might well pass for a petty martyrdom." The Huron Christians were deeply impressed. They often asked "when that night would return, or rather, as they said, that kind of a beautiful day. These people are not familiar with the use of candles, and when they saw so many lights shining and sparkling in the chapel, they had good reason to question whether it were night or day."

Meanwhile, the missioners were restless for greater expansion. They had two permanent establishments among two of the Huron nations. They had ten missioners, of whom seven were more or less competent in the native language. Hence they looked about for the next objective they might attack. Obviously it was Scanonaenrat, The Village of the Single White Cabin, the capital place of the Tohontaenrat nation, a people adopted by the Huron Confederacy at the beginning of the century. This populous town lay some four or five miles northeast of Teanaustayaé, on a detour from the trail to Ossossané. It held a strong position on an eminence above a precipitous gorge. Though the Fathers knew that "the barbarians of that village pass, in the common talk of these regions, for the demons of the country," being the leaders in witchcraft and diabolical seances, they were daunted neither by the hostility of this nation nor by their evil reputation. With humor, they dedicated the Mission of Scanonaenrat to the arch-enemy of Satan, St. Michael.

In the early winter they marched on this new donjon of demons. They had one friend, Totiri, later baptized Stephen, a chief who lived in a small cabin of a single fire. Through him they presented their gifts of tobacco and beads to the twelve chiefs of the Tohontaenrats and announced the meaning of the presents to be their desire "to give to the chiefs and to the entire village the knowledge of the one and only God, and of Jesus Christ, Our Lord and Redeemer." Beyond all their hopes and expectations, the council of chiefs accepted their proposition and welcomed the Blackrobes with the most dignified of ceremonial courtesies. Whereupon, they lodged in the cabin of Totiri, and in one corner of it set up an altar.

Scanonaenrat was under the special care of de Brébeuf and Jogues. So successful was the foundation that, on January 1, four heads of families were solemnly baptized; their host, Stephen Totiri, two other chiefs, and a lesser, but dependable, brave. Their squaws were in fear and terror of the consequences, for they could not shake off their superstitious dread of baptism as a precursor of evil and death. The four pioneer Christians in the presence of Christian visitors from Teanaustayaé and Ossossané attended Mass on January 2,

1639, the Feast of St. Stephen, and that day was set down for perpetual memory as the birthday of the Mission of St. Michael.

All through the bleak winter and in the early spring of 1639, the missioners were traversing the entire Huron peninsula. They brought spiritual aid and gave evidence of their good-will and friendship. Their principal object in these journeys, however, was that of familiarizing themselves with the trails and the locations of the villages, of making a complete census of the population and a survey of the attitudes of the people. Back in their residences, they drew maps of the region, noted the directions and the landmarks, fixed the sites of the villages, and compiled the figures. They discovered thirty-two villages, large and small. These contained a total of seven hundred cabins, in which were two thousand fires. The number of families they computed to be more than three thousand, and the number of souls to be upwards of twelve thousand. They learned that the villages and population had decreased considerably during the past few years because of the epidemics and the losses in war.

Now they consulted on fresh strategies and further developments. Two possible plans were proposed. The one was a continuation of their present procedure, whereby they would establish residences in the more distant centers of population similar to those of Ossossané and Teanaustayaé and would attach permanent missioners to these villages. The second was that of erecting a central residence which would serve as the permanent headquarters of all the missioners. This residence would be located away from the villages of the savages and would be independent of them. From it, the missioners would go off on excursions, of shorter and longer periods, to all the districts throughout the entire country. The former plan was presumably that of de Brébeuf, the latter that of Lalemant, who records: "Now of the two methods by which one could proceed farther toward the conversion of these peoples—either by the plan of residences or by that of missions—that of the residences having appeared to us full of inconveniences and much less efficacious, we have decided upon that of the missions, although much more vexatious and more laborious, especially in these regions."

Of advantages, there were many. They could free themselves of the semi-nomadic moves, every decade or so, when the Hurons would abandon a village and build on a new site. They would be saved from the annoyances of the savages as close neighbors, from the curious-minded poking into their cabins and spying on their every move, and from the malicious-minded committing their petty depredations and more serious sabotage. They would be away from the raucous turmoil, the outcries and groans and shouts of the feasts and rituals and incantations, the filth of the village and the shamelessness of the inhabitants. They could build a permanent stronghold, like a fortress, where they would have security and privacy. Round about them, in the course of a few years, they might build up a community of Christian Hurons, a reduction such as had been established for the Algonquins at Sillery, near Quebec.

III

On the eastern side of the Huron peninsula the missioners discovered the perfect location for their proposed central house. It was some ten miles across country from Ossossané, about fifteen miles north of Teanaustayaé, and a little more than two leagues below Ihonatiria. A sluggish little river, less than a mile long and a few strokes of a paddle wide, flowed between the shallow, swampy Lake of Isaragui and the heaving level of the five-fingered bay that terminated this corner of Lake Huron. To the left, a canoe could dart across Isaragui and the emptying streams for some distance into the interior, almost across to Nottawasaga Bay. Toward the right was the route to the open waters, out northward along Lake Huron on the way to the St. Lawrence, or around the projecting spears of land to the several rivers that emptied into the bay.

Authority to plant their residence in this territory had needs be sought from the Ataronchronons, the third principal Huron nation. This people had shown itself inimical to the Blackrobes, and they, in turn, had made little effort to evangelize the villages in this area. Now they were prepared to attempt the conquest of this people by securing a site in their land. They held council with the chiefs. "There was ground for apprehension in making our proposal and opening negotiations with the communities of savages who were masters of this area," Lalemant affirms. "But it pleased God to assist us in this, for the proposition was at once accepted and immediately carried out, and the presents necessary thereto delivered at the proper time. If we had delayed two hours, I know not whether the affair could ever have succeeded."

The permission was granted in March, 1639, and the Blackrobes straightway blessed the site and dedicated it to Our Lady. "We have given to this new residence the name of Sainte Marie, or Nostre Dame de la Conception," announces Lalemant. "The general and special obligations that we are under to this great Princess of heaven and earth make it one of our keenest disappointments that we are not able to show her sufficient gratitude. At least, we claim this consolation henceforth, that, as often as people shall speak of the principal abode of this Mission of the Hurons and call it by the name of Sainte Marie, they will be rendering so many homages to her, for what we are to her, and what we wish to be to her forever."

Their choice of place settled upon a heavily wooded tract along the right fringe of the stream. It was valley land, elevated but a few yards higher than the water level. The plain spread out many miles toward Lake Isaragui, beyond which, in a hazy distance, the highlands reared broadly upwards. A half-league to the rear rose an encircling ridge of hills, and in the direction of the bay a dominating hill humped up a few hundred yards away. Sainte Marie was thus in a spacious hollow, well-protected and giving easy access to all parts of the peninsula and to the most traveled waterways. The soil was rich and virgin, the woods abundant.

Through the spring and summer, the French workmen made a clearance of a few acres in the forests and the entangled underbrush. They built a good-sized cabin of logs and planed boards, laid out small patches for cultivation, and dug an inlet for the landing and tying of the canoes. Toward the end of the summer, some of the missioners removed to Sainte Marie, from Ossossané, and transported from there the bulk of their possessions. The cabin and chapel, however, were not abandoned, but were left under the charge of Joseph, the Christian.

Jogues and de Brébeuf did not at once remove themselves from Teanaustayaé to the new headquarters at Sainte Marie. But the insolence, and then the malice of the villagers increased that early autumn to such an extent that they were practically forced to abandon their cabin. About that time the Huron flotillas were returning from their summer expeditions down to the St. Lawrence. Le Mercier had made the journey that year and returned in September with the winter supplies. Pierre Pijart, who had spent the preceding winter in Quebec, also came back to the Hurons. Two new recruits, Fathers Pierre Joseph Marie Chaumonot and Joseph Antoine Poncet de la Rivière, were added to the forces. Additional workmen, also, and some elder lads arrived, so that, Lalemant enumerates, "in the beginning of the month of October in the year 1639, in the midst of this barbarism, we were twenty-seven Frenchmen, among whom were thirteen of our Fathers. The good-will, the zeal and the courage which I remark in all of them alike, causes me to hope much this year for the service of God."

Great numbers of the Hurons had flocked down to Three Rivers that summer. On their return up along the Ottawa River they fraternized, as usual, with the Algonquins of the Islands. They lived in the Algonquin cabins and deeply sympathized with their hosts because many of them were sick and afflicted with sores and pustules. They continued homeward, and many stopped en route at the new camp of the Blackrobes at Sainte Marie. One party of the Ataronchronons, especially, found the landing-place of the Blackrobes most convenient. Their village was only a short three miles distant.

They carried with them one of the braves who had become sick a few days before. His skin was inflamed with sores. The Frenchmen knew it was the small-pox. His companions carried him from Sainte Marie to his cabin, and sat him on the mat by his own fire. He rested there, with his knees hunched up to his chin. All his family, all the neighbors gathered about him, and ministered to him. Their care availed nothing, for he died within a few hours.

A day or two later, some of the people in his cabin grew sick. Some in the other cabins also took to their mats. The small-pox infected the village. It spread to the neighboring villages, then to the villages beyond. It spread rapidly, fiercely, through all the land. By the middle of October it was everywhere. The people watched it in terror. They were frenzied. A demon was afflicting their bodies with sores and killing them. A witch was weaving evil and destruction for their ruin. They consulted the sorcerers. These prescribed games, feasts, chants, dances. They underwent sweats and supervised incantations. They watched their dreams for enlightenment and called on the demons for relief and guidance. The plague enveloped the cabins and villages so that few escaped it. It gripped the young, the old, the warriors, the squaws. They fought against it with all their ancient practices. They called for help from their oki. They pleaded with the sorcerers to defend them.

It was a universal calamity come upon the country. The chiefs and ancients consulted in council. The first man to die of the small-pox landed at the new cabin of the Blackrobes. The first village to be stricken was that nearest the Blackrobes. The next were villages in which the Blackrobes were seen most frequently. These Blackrobes did not pay much attention to any cabin except those in which lived the sick. It was quite clear, the council decided, that the Blackrobes had something to do with this disease. They recalled that Ihonatiria, where the Blackrobes first lived, had practically been destroyed by the influenza epidemic. Ossossané was not so seriously affected, until the Blackrobes went there to live. As soon as these French demons went to Teanaustayaé, the number of sick and dying increased. Now, the orators howled with rage, these evil sorcerers build their cabin in the midst of the Ataronchronons in the summer. Within a few moons they begin to kill this nation.

While these suspicions and accusations multiplied, Robert Le Coq, one of the French *engagés* who had voyaged to Quebec that summer, was deposited at the door of Sainte Marie. "The small-pox covered his whole body in a manner so extraordinary that on all his members there appeared but one crust of foulness," Lalemant exclaims. "I do not suppose that one could imagine a human body more covered with miseries. Not one of us could ever have recognized him." Le Coq had contracted the disease on the journey up the Ottawa. So horrible a sight was he, so terrible the stench from him, that his Huron voyagers were tempted to kill or abandon him. He pleaded with them, and bribed them with gifts. But though they promised to bring him home to the Blackrobes, they stole his food and canoe and left him on the shore of Lake Huron to die. Another party came upon him, but passed him by.

He was a festering mass of sores and his eyes were blinded. Nevertheless, he crawled into the woods and kept from starving by feeling about for berries. A furious storm lashed down upon him and swarms of insects fed on his foulness. He was discovered by another band of Hurons who first promised to take him with them, and then deserted him, after relieving him of the few little possessions he still retained. Finally a Huron whom Le Coq had rescued the year before repaid the debt by bundling him into his canoe and bringing him to Sainte Marie. The Fathers immediately administered the last sacraments to him. They waited for him to die. He lingered for a day or two, then slowly he began to recover.

Robert Le Coq was a final argument against the Blackrobes. That he was stricken by the disease was only a clever blind. He was given up for dead, he himself believed that he would die; nevertheless, the Blackrobes and their demon prevented him from dying. He was reported to have made a confession to his Huron friends: he himself loved the Hurons, but the Blackrobes hated them. He had lived with these Blackrobes for several years and had discovered their secret. According to one account, Le Coq revealed that the disease was a serpent which the Blackrobes nourished in a hidden corner of their cabin. Another version was that the disease was a toad, marked with pits; this toad, several testified, they had actually seen. A third variation declared that the disease was a crafty demon kept concealed in the barrel of an arquebus. Whenever the Blackrobes wished to spread the plague, they fired off this arquebus and shot the demon in that direction in which they wanted him to do harm. These confessions, so it was said, were extracted from the lips of a dying Frenchman. They were whispered from village to village.

While everyone believed these revelations, no one would credit the denial of his reputed confession which Le Coq made upon his recovery. He had returned to friendship with the Blackrobes, they slyly argued; he was again under the protection of their demon. All this tissue of lies, the priests had to admit, bore the semblance of truth. Lalemant confesses: "It has happened very often, and has been remarked more than a hundred times, that in those places where we were most welcome, where we baptized most people, there it was, in fact, where they died most. On the contrary, in the cabins to which we were denied entrance, although they were sick to extremity, at the end of a few days one saw every person prosperously cured. We shall find in Heaven the secret but ever adorable judgments of God therein."

The Hurons became more demented as the small-pox devoured their families and as the case against the Blackrobes became more certain. Their councils concluded with the affirmation that the Blackrobes must be put to death. A few Christian chiefs pleaded for clemency and suggested that they be spared death, but sent back to the St. Lawrence. This advice was rejected. The Blackrobes must die; anyone who wished was at liberty to massacre them. The braves knocked down the crosses over the cabins; some rushed into the midst of the Fathers, brandishing their hatchets; others declared they would waylay the Blackrobes along the road.

The missioners knew very clearly of their danger, so clearly that they received Communion at their Masses as if it were Viaticum. Their attitude was expressed by Lalemant when he wrote: "The greatest favor that we hope to receive from the great Master who employs us, is to die for His Holy Name after having suffered so much. Not that I do not forever praise this great God of Goodness for having thus far protected us with so much love. For it is truly an unspeakable happiness for us, in the midst of this barbarism, to hear the roarings of the demons and to see all hell and almost all men animated and furious against a little handful of people who would not defend themselves, to see ourselves shut up in a place fifteen hundred leagues from our native land, in a place where all the powers of earth could not protect us against the anger of the weakest man who might have designs on our lives, and where we have not even a bag of corn which has not been furnished us by those who incessantly hold council about killing us; and to feel at the same time so special a confidence in the goodness of God, so firm an assurance in the midst of dangers, a zeal so active and a courage so resolute to do all and to suffer all for the glory of our Master, so tireless a constancy in the labors which increase from day to day. So that it is easy to conceive that God is the One who espouses our cause; that it is He alone who protects us; and that His Providence takes pleasure in manifesting itself where we see least of the human."

Under the spell of such belief, they continued to wander about to the cabins of the sick and to the villages far and near. They were not cowed by the threats of the savages nor were they afraid of the diabolical manifestations so evident about them. They unanimously agreed that they would carry out this winter, when the Hurons were wildly incensed against them, the plans they had formed in the summer, when the Hurons seemed to be so fond of them. By the establishment of the residence at Sainte Marie they had effected the first step of centralization. Now they were preparing for the second stage, that of dispersion.

Based on their census, they projected five missionary enterprises for the winter. The first of these was in the home area about Sainte Marie. Fathers Lalemant, Le Mercier, Pijart, and Poncet were to minister to the nation of the Ataronchronons dwelling in the near-by villages which were dedicated to Ste. Anne, St. Louys, St. Denys, and St. Jean. The number of souls in their charge was estimated at 1,400.

The second mission, that among the Attigneenongnahac, was tended by Fathers de Brébeuf and Chastellain. Their main residence would be that of St. Joseph's in Teanaustayaé, and from there they would visit the villages of St. Michael and St. Ignace. The third mission was to the nation of the Attignawantan, with headquarters at Ossossané and with the care attached of twelve hamlets in the district. To this were assigned Fathers Ragueneau, Du Peron and Chaumonot. The fourth mission was to the Arendarhonons, the nation to the south, among whom no settlements had been thus far attempted. Fathers Daniel and Le Moyne were the pioneers to this people. They planned to live at Cahiagué, the village of St. Jean Baptiste, and from there to evangelize the smaller villages of St. Joachim and Ste. Elizabeth.

Fathers Jogues and Garnier were chosen to go on the most distant and dangerous of all the missions, that to the Khionontateronons, "the nation of the mountainous country," called by the French the Petun, or Tobacco, nation. This people derived from the Huron-Iroquois stock and spoke a dialect of the same root language. But it had been at war with both the Hurons and Iroquois for many years. Latterly, the Petuns and Hurons buried the hatchet and united in an alliance against the Iroquois. This treaty of peace, formally renewed that summer of 1639, made it possible for the missioners to press on their apostolate to this non-Huron people. The Petun territory bordered that of the Hurons to the west, and in its nearest limits was some forty miles distant from Sainte Marie. It extended through the Blue Mountains and the long peninsula which wedged out into Lake Huron.

In 1624, in the first abortive attempt to Christianize the Hurons, de Brébeuf had penetrated among the Petuns. No further visits were made until 1637, when de Brébeuf, accompanied by Garnier, spent a short time surveying the land. In 1639, the time had come for a missionary drive to the west, to the first of the foreign nations beyond the Hurons. There, says Lalemant, "we shall announce the Gospel to the Petuns, and plant, if we can, the standard of Jesus Christ. This, which we have named the Mission of the Apostles, has been the fifth of our missions. The lot for it fell to Father Charles Garnier and to Father Isaac Jogues."

The date for the dispersion of the missioners was November 1, the Feast of All Saints. Winter was setting in and would soon lock the land. But this was the season when the braves would be at home with their families. The small-pox epidemic festered in all the villages, and the Hurons, terrorized by it, were everywhere threatening to murder the Blackrobes. Nevertheless, the Fathers put their trust in God and on this Tuesday morning, assembled in the chapel of Sainte Marie, they recited in unison the prayers of the *itinerarium*. With these finished, with farewells said, they tucked up their black robes about them, bound on their buckskin leggings and heavy boots, and donned their skin coats and fur caps. About their shoulders they strapped their blankets and clothes, their equipment for Mass, their bags of presents of beads, knives, and awls, and strung by their side their snowshoes, breviary, and food-bags. With light spirits they went forth confidently and gleefully from Sainte Marie on their winter hunt for God.

Jogues and Garnier struck across the trail by Lake Isaragui for Ossossané. It was a dull, sodden November day, and the narrow path was slippery and rain soaked. Their travel became more difficult when they began the ascent from the level swamp-land to the rolling hills that rose up to Ossossané. They reached the village before nightfall, but found little welcome save from Joseph, the Christian, and a few faithful families. The small-pox was in Ossossané and the blame for it was fixed on the Blackrobes.

They had thought that they might secure some friendly Huron to act as guide for them to the Petun country, for the trails had not been carefully explored. But everyone in Ossossané was loath to undertake the journey, especially at that time of the year, when heavy rains were falling and the streams were swollen, when the trails were soft with mud and the prospects for a hard winter were already evident. "We were not able to find any savage at the village of la Conception to come with us," they wrote, "the roads being then too bad for people who are not seeking God. And so we were forced to start alone, taking our good angels for guides."

CHAPTER VI

Driving Ever Westward

I

WHEN Jogues and Garnier, their packs strapped to their shoulders, their staffs in their hands, trudged out of the gates of Ossossané on that lowering November morning they had but vague information about the country and the people they were to visit, and but scant information as to the route they were to follow. Their goal was the village of Ehwae, the most important of the Petun towns. There they expected to hold council with the chiefs and exchange presents that would be a pledge of friendship and hospitality. The trail, they understood, pointed south along the headlands above Nottawasaga Bay, then west through the valley country to the foothills of the mountains.

Joseph, the Christian, had informed them that there was a detour some fifteen miles from Ossossané which led to a hamlet where they would find food and lodging for the first night. The path was slimy and treacherous, especially in the hollows dug out by the hill streams. In the middle of the afternoon there fell the first sprinkles of snow. They slid their boots along the muddy trail high spiritedly, momentarily expecting to find the branching detour. The snow fell thickly, blinding them and shrouding their road through the forests. Night enveloped them. They were caught in a swampy grove of fir trees. There they camped, for they feared to wander farther in the storm. With difficulty they found enough dry wood to light their fire, and then could scarcely get it blazing. After a supper of bread they wrapped themselves in their blankets and stretched themselves on a bed of twigs. "God be blessed, we spent the night very comfortably," they reported.

When dawn trickled through the firs, they struck out along the trail, now blanketed with snow. Some distance on, beyond a cleared field, they noticed a few cabins. The families, they found, were just abandoning their huts and were going to the nearest Petun village, for they had neither corn nor any other food. Jogues and Garnier deemed the chance meeting most fortunate. They attached themselves to the band and traveled all the day, "by many bad roads at a very bad season," they related. "We made, at least, a league by the sole light of the snow and arrived about eight o'clock in the evening, with a good appetite, for we had not eaten all day, save each a morsel of bread." They walked into this first village of the Petuns, to which they gave the name of St. Thomas, and entered a cabin. The people of the cabin, with no word spoken, offered them bowls of sagamité and mats before the fire.

"We had no special plan to go to this village of St. Thomas rather than to any other," they remarked, "but since we had accepted what company the savages offered, and since we followed them thither, there is no doubt but that we arrived where God was leading us for the salvation of a predestined soul which awaited nothing but our arrival in order to die to all its earthly miseries." They had finished their supper and were conversing with their hosts, when a young man entered and asked the Blackrobes to visit his mother who was sick. "We go thither," they exclaim, "and find the poor woman in the last extremities. She was instructed, and happily received, with the Faith, the grace of Baptism. Shortly after that, she beheld herself in the glory of heaven. In that whole village there was only that one who had need of our help."

From St. Thomas, the deep-dug trails led to the farther Petun towns. They did not linger long in these places except to visit any who were ill. They had the joy of baptizing some few children and some adults who were near death. Everywhere they were received with kindness. Being adopted brothers of the Hurons, they were also regarded as brothers to the Petuns. Most of the villagers had seldom seen the palefaces. They flocked about the two Blackrobes, Ondessonk and Ouracha, staring fixedly at them, fingering their flesh and costumes and baggage.

In the second week of November they came to Ehwae, the capital village, which they dedicated to Sts. Pierre et Paul. They pushed through the stockade and into one of the cabins. There they found a child of five years sick unto death. His parents, of the Neutral nation, were forced by starvation to come to Ehwae and beg food. When Jogues and Garnier learned that the life of the child had been despaired of for several days, they exclaimed: "Out of 45 or 50 cabins, without intending it, we first visited the cabin in which this little stranger was. We baptized him, and straightway he was freed from his exile and was happy in the land of his new nativity. Here are the first fruits of this nation of the Neutrals, and this child was the first one of them to be sprinkled by the blood of Jesus Christ."

Their prime courtesy on arrival was to present themselves to the great chief. He received them amiably and offered them hospitality; but he did not summon a council to listen to their proposals and accept their presents. Thus, they had none but personal guarantees of protection. They were too much engaged to think about holding a council. For there was going on, then, a migration of the Attiwandaron, or Neutral nation, to the Petun villages. The Neutral territory bordered the Petuns' on the south, along the strip of land between Lakes Ontario and Erie. On one side they were flanked by the Iroquois, and on the other neighbored the Petuns and Hurons. Since they had preserved peace in the midst of these enemies, the French dubbed them Neutrals. Their corn crops failed that autumn and when they faced a winter of starvation, they sought salvation from their allies, the Petuns.

"There is hardly any corn in this village of Ehwae," the missioners reported, "and nevertheless, almost every day some Attiwandarons arrive, bands of men, women, and children, all pale and disfigured, whom the famine drives hither. Fleeing from the famine, they here find death; rather, here they find a blessed life, for we see to it that not one dies without baptism. Among these people was a little child about one year old, which looked more like a monster than a human being. It was happily baptized. God preserved its life only by a miracle, it would seem, so that it might be washed in the blood of Jesus Christ and might bless His mercies forever."

No less persevering were they in trying to instruct the healthy. They visited the cabins incessantly, and sat before the fires. In the Huron dialect, which the Petuns could understand, they explained the existence of God and the certainty of a future life, with happiness for the good and evil tortures for the wicked. They were content if they could but get a hearing. "We have met some persons who at first relished the gospel," they stated triumphantly. "May God grant them the grace to embrace it. We received consolation two or three days ago. A girl who was going to pledge herself to a young man heard us speak of God and the pains of hell. She went away to sleep alone, saying, 'God sees us, even at night.' "

The stock of corn in the Petun villages began to be exhausted, and there was some anxiety about food for the winter months. With lack of nourishment, many of the people fell easy preys to the influenza and the small-pox. The Petuns began to recall what the Hurons recounted about the Blackrobes, wherever they went they brought disease and ruin. Then, in late November, came some Huron traders. These inflamed the minds of the Petuns by relating the details of the latest crime of the Blackrobes, that of killing the nation through the small-pox. They announced, as a certainty, that the Huron councils had decreed death to the Blackrobes. They urged the Petuns to save their nation by slaughtering Ondessonk and Ouracha.

All at once the kindliness of the Petuns soured into bitter hate. They could find no rational reason why these two Blackrobes came into their midst, except to weave sorceries and thus destroy them through starvation and disease. In their official report, Jogues and Garnier related:

This whole country is filled with evil reports which are current about us. The children, when they see us arrive at any place, cry out that famine and disease are coming. Some women flee, others hide their children from us. Almost all refuse us the hospitality which they grant even to the most unknown tribes. We have not been able to find a house for our Lord, not any place where we can say Mass. Our host, who is the chief captain of this country, and who has appeared quite peaceable, through a natural prudence, on seeing us pray to God on our knees mornings and evenings, finally could not refrain, on one occasion, to speak in a council voice, that is to say, loud and distinct: "Truly, it is now that I fear and now that I speak. What, now, are these but powerful demons who cause us to die and to finish what the disease has left over, in our cabins? They had told me, indeed, that these were sorcerers, but all too late do I believe it. This is a thing that is beyond belief, that persons who come to lodge at one's house pass the night in postures to which our eyes are in no way accustomed."

Judge for yourself with what looks they regard us in a cabin where they can have such fine ideas of us! We could hardly quiet the mind of this chief again. They treat us very wretchedly, in order to oblige us to leave. Truly we have nothing more than what suffices to keep us alive; our hunger usually accompanies us from morning till night. But these poor people do not understand that what keeps us here is more precious than all that they can conceive in the way of the pleasures of this world.

While we try to render some honor to God, the devil continues to be adored; even yesterday, they made a solemn sacrifice for him in our cabin. All the people assembled there. They kept throwing tobacco and fat in the fire, the while they were making their invocations. All of this was to effect the cure of a wretch whom his private demon afflicts with a certain disease because he has not obeyed his demon in regard to some feasts which were commanded him.

Is it a wonder that we are held in abomination at a place where the devils are acknowledged as masters? Our host has given orders that his doors be barricaded every evening, for he fears that they might commit some violence on us during the night. If they killed us in his house, he would have to bear the reproach of it, even from those who desire nothing so much as our death. It is not this which gives us assurance. We have a more powerful protection, although it is less visible to these poor infidels.

Jogues and Garnier concluded that they could make no headway in Ehwae against these human and diabolical enemies. They left, accordingly, for a tour of the smaller villages, much to the satisfaction of the chief, their unwilling host. They battled their way against a biting December wind to the next village. None of the Petuns happened to be out-of-doors when they reached the gates, and they pushed unobserved into the door of the first cabin. They were admitted, for the law of hospitality was sacred. But bad reports had preceded them. The families in the cabins served them food and allowed them near the fire; but they upbraided Ondessonk and Ouracha, and screamed and growled at them. When the two went outdoors, the villagers surrounded them like a pack of dogs, snarling at them, threatening to kill them. After a day or two they realized that here, neither, was there any hope of exercising their ministry.

While they shouldered their packs to leave, the braves watched them sullenly and threateningly. As they stepped through the street to the gate, the villagers yelled reproaches at them and pelted them with snow and rubbish and stones. They took the trail toward another hamlet. Some young men, who had been watching to see which direction they were tending, ran ahead to give warning. By the time they came up to the stockade of the next village, they saw the chiefs and warriors ranged before the gates. These forbade the Blackrobe sorcerers, Ondessonk and Ouracha, to enter the village. Undaunted, they made as if to approach the gates. The chief flared into anger. He shouted that he would split their heads open if they came one step nearer the gate. They turned back along the trail to where it branched toward another village.

They were outcast. Some nights they slept in the forests and dug their beds in the hollow of the snow. Some days they passed entirely without food. When they were received into a cabin, they exposed themselves to even greater dangers. It happened one night that a man of the hut in which they lodged had a terrifying dream. He rose in the middle of the night and stood over them menacingly. With his face distorted like a maniac and his fingers clutching wildly, he ordered them to leave his fire at once. On another occasion, in the dead of night when all the village was asleep, they were roused by a brave pounding on the door and bellowing out threats against them, warning them that they would be murdered if they showed themselves in the village the next morning.

Thus wandering about from place to place, and everywhere meeting with blows and threats and hatred, Jogues and Garnier came to a little cluster of cabins in the heart of the hills. They were both exhausted by the terrible exposure to the cold and by the lack of food. They forced themselves upon one of the cabins and were grudgingly received. Jogues felt feverish and sick through all his body. He could not move from his mat. Here they hoped to rest for a few days in comparative quiet. Then came a messenger from one of the villages in which they had been welcomed on their entry into the Petun land. The runner told them that some of the people who were sick were begging them to return.

It was a call from God. They could not but heed it. In order to complete the journey of thirty-five miles by daylight, they started out about three o'clock in the morning. All the country was pale with snow in the dawn, and the mountain air was painfully cold. Jogues was still gripped by the fever and unsteady on his legs. They slid their snowshoes laboriously over the crackling crust of the icy snow. Frequently, they stopped for breath in deadly exhaustion.

But they had to shorten their rests, for fear lest they die of the cold. Their only food, a lump of corn-bread about the size of the fist, was hard as ice. They arrived at the village late at night, covered with sweat and yet half-frozen, they said. The sick persons were still alive. They were baptized. "Some souls gone astray here and there, who are placed on the road to heaven when they are just about to be swallowed up in hell," was their comment, "deserve a thousand times more than these labors, since these souls have cost the Saviour of the world much more than that."

While they rested at this village, they were amazed and overjoyed. Joseph Chihwatenhwa, the Christian of Ossossané, walked into their cabin. He came, they explained, "in the midst of weather that was frightful, while the cold was cracking the trees and a furious wind was blowing in his face. The fire of his charity was greater than all these inclemencies." He had heard of their danger, how they were expelled from some villages and refused entry into others, how they were starving, how their death was decreed. He thought that he might persuade the Petuns to cease this persecution, as a month earlier he had helped Daniel and Le Moyne, who were being frightfully assailed by the Arendarhonon Hurons.

At this apostolic zeal, at this fidelity, Jogues and Garnier felt their blood run cold. They admired him the more, and thanked God more fervently for him, as they listened to his story. The small-pox still raged in Ossossané, he said, but his cabin was spared by God. When he resolved to come to the Petuns to rescue Ondessonk and Ouracha, his wife, Marie Aonetta, implored him not to leave her, for she feared that his daughter Theresa and his sons would be stricken by the disease. One of the Blackrobes tried to console her by saying that Joseph would be back in two weeks. "Alas," she answered, "our children could die in that time, without his ever hearing they were sick." She would not be consoled.

Joseph reasoned with her: "My wife, whom do you take me for? I am nothing at all, and what would be the benefit of my presence here? Should our children be sick, all I could do would be to feel distressed for them, and grieve my spirit trying in some way to relieve them; to do that and to do nothing amount to the same thing. It rests with God alone to preserve or to restore health to whomsoever He pleases. As for us, we have only to try to please Him in all our actions. That is what forces me to leave you now. It is enough for me that it is God's will. As for our family, God will take care of it, if He please. And then, here are my brothers, the Jesuits, who will remain with you. Even if I were here, the best I could do would be to follow their advice. Now, just keep your mind at rest."

Joseph appeared to the two young priests as a blessing sent directly from God. They were strengthened by his courage and confidence, they felt bolder under his expert guidance. The three of them ventured forth from the shelter of the cabin and, in the teeth of the piercing cold wind, they made their way on snowshoes to a village nearly a day's journey onward. Weary and frozen, at nightfall, they entered the stockade and came to a cabin. As they pulled back the skin before the door, the people within rushed to prevent their entrance. They tried to enter another cabin, but it was barred against them. The village flared into a turmoil. Joseph faced it calmly. He found that he had kinsmen in the village, and persuaded them to take the Blackrobes into their cabin for the night. They could not refuse without incurring reproach, for the bonds of blood were strong; but they exacted a promise that Ondessonk and Ouracha must leave their cabin on the morrow.

In the village to which they next came, the chief barricaded his door against them and warned them not to attempt to enter. Here, again, Joseph discovered relatives who were obliged to furnish shelter. They had no need, however, to restrain their tongues against Joseph, whom they accused of protecting the greatest sorcerers and evildoers on earth. He answered them word for word, in counsel and in reproach. The argument dwindled off into the night, and all retired. An hour or two later a demoniac yell pierced the cabin. A man, shrieking madly, leaped to the center aisle of the cabin where the fires were glowing, and flung the burning brands recklessly in every direction. Seizing the mats, the pots, the robes, food, wood, everything within reach, he hurled them about. Finally, brandishing a flaming torch in his hand, he whirled about the cabin.

With a blasphemous curse, he leaped to the place where Jogues and Garnier had been asleep. Not finding them, he raged the more and threatened to burn down the cabin and murder all within it. He searched in and out among the savages, demanding to know where the Blackrobes were concealed. To turn away his anger from themselves, some one whispered to him the corner where they were hid. He bounded to the spot and thought to pounce on his victims.

But a moment before, Jogues had left the nook and slipped out of the cabin. The savage, fair exhausted by now, allowed himself to be soothed and placated. "God knows what were this crazy man's designs," Garnier remarked. "Either he was possessed by the devil or he pretended to be."

They left this danger spot and came to a village where they had formerly been well received. Calumny had unloosed hate of them. Not one person would allow them within a cabin. It was raining and cold and night was near. They were despairing of any shelter that night when they chanced on an old man who, they remembered, had seemed interested in their instruction. "Hello," they called out to him. "Will your door also be closed against us?"

"Come, and be welcome," he answered simply.

They followed him to his cabin, and found a place by his fire. He was a Petun by adoption. His nation was that of the Mascoutins, or Fire People, who lived on the far side of Lake Michigan. As a boy, the Petuns had captured him and made him one of their own. No one was found, they remarked, to give glory to God except this stranger of the land.

Even under Joseph's influence and tutelage, the Blackrobes continued to be treated as public enemies who were working mysterious ills on the Petun people. The three apostles decided to return to Ehwae and hold council with the chiefs of the nation. On their arrival, they were treated more cruelly than they were on their first visit. The doors to all the cabins were slammed in their faces or held closed to them. When they went from door to door, the mob milled about them, screaming insults and threats, and hurling missiles upon them. "Where are those who boasted they would split the heads of the Blackrobes if ever they returned to the village!" the women taunted. Joseph and Jogues and Garnier remained placid and unmoved under the riot. They continued their round of the cabins as if the savages were nowhere about. Any show of fear, they realized, any break in their deportment, and they would be straightway murdered. Not one door opened to them. As night was falling, they walked out from Ehwae toward a cluster of huts a few miles away, where they hoped to find a place to rest for the night.

In Ehwae, meanwhile, all the chiefs and principal warriors were holding a feast. Talk of the Blackrobes and of their insolence in trying to force themselves on the Petuns seethed heatedly, for the reappearance of Ondessonk and Ouracha had mightily aroused the village. Orators vehemently denounced these French demons as dangerous sorcerers, as carriers of disease and famine, as enemies secretly working through unnatural means to destroy utterly the Petuns, the Hurons, and all the nations of the country. The head chief publicly declared that anyone who killed these murderers would be doing a good service to the people.

A clique of young braves noted his declaration. They had authority to do what they had talked among themselves of doing. With their tomahawks in their hands, they hurried out of the gates and ran along the trail which the Blackrobes and Joseph had taken. Silently and swiftly, they coursed through the moonlit woods, racing to overtake their victims. But the Blackrobes were already within the cabins and so under the protection of the families that lodged them. Disappointed, the braves returned to Ehwae. Of this, Lalemant remarks: "I know not whether it was a good or an evil fortune for us that these barbarians set forth a little too late and could not overtake them; perhaps our blood would do more for the conversion of these peoples than all our sweat."

On the day following, the chief who had delivered the violent speech against the Blackrobes came to clear himself of any connection with the murder premeditated by the young braves. He apologized for the unfortunate occurrence, and excused the rashness and discourtesy of the young men. He was suave and gracious. Joseph, however, was in no way taken in by the chief's honeyed words. He expressed plainly his opinion of the Petuns. The Blackrobes, he argued, came to the Petuns to announce matters of the greatest importance; but the Petuns had no sense, they closed their ears to these matters. The chief replied that he was astonished that anyone with any sense could believe that these matters of which the Blackrobes spoke were matters of importance. This roused Joseph. He answered the chief:

> It is truly you chiefs who are ignorant as to what are matters of importance. It is you chiefs who have bemuddled the country and have deprived us of the maxims and good rules of our ancestors. It is these Blackrobes here, whom you despise, who know things that are important for us, and who come to teach us these things. I wish you to understand very clearly that I am the one who, in derision, am every-

where called "The Believer." They think they are speaking evilly of me; but that name is my greatest glory. I am that man. I have kinsmen in your village, and you know them. I make public profession of following the good instructions which these Blackrobes, my teachers, have given me. We have no sense, as many as there are of us. Our thoughts do not extend farther than this life. Those of us who believe place our hopes upon an eternity of good things which are surely prepared for us hereafter. As for you, who are unbelievers, you do not expect miseries after your death; nevertheless, these miseries are surely waiting for you, unless you open your eyes to your present sinfulness. You drive out from you those who love you more than they love themselves, since they count their lives less precious to them than your salvation. They come here from a very great distance and with very many labors to procure your salvation. Our ancestors were excusable in some sort if they did not adore this great Master who made the world; for no one taught them. But you will be punished a hundred thousand times more severely than they are, since you choose of your own free will to remain in your sinfulness, although these Blackrobes try to draw you out of it.

The chief and the villagers who had assembled listened to Joseph with courtesy and also respect. Some even interrupted to say, "That is true." But they regarded it only as a speech, and lightly turned to talk of other things. They would not be convinced that the Blackrobes spoke a message of importance. They believed Ondessonk and Ouracha were dangerous sorcerers, secret murderers, omens of evil. Joseph understood that it was useless, for the present, to talk to the Petuns. He advised Jogues and Garnier to return home.

They were content. They had spent the three months they had intended to remain in this country. They had gathered exact information and sketched maps of the trails, the distances, the directions. They located nine major habitations which they charted under the names of the Apostles: "sainct Pierre & sainct Paul, sainct André, sainct Jacques, sainct Thomas, sainct Jean, sainct Jacques & sainct Philippe, sainct Barthelemy, sainct Matthieu, sainct Simon & sainct Jude." They estimated the population to be more than a thousand families who lodged in about three hundred cabins. They were not at all discouraged. They had saved many by baptism and had announced the Faith to thousands. Next year they would come again, and then the next year they or other missioners would begin to reap the harvest of souls. The Petuns, like the Hurons, would finally accept the true God.

There was no cramping stress on them when, in February, they started back along the trail to the Huron country. They left the faithful Joseph Chihwatenhwa at Ossossané. He was exultant when Marie Aonetta told him that God had spared their children from the small-pox. Jogues and Garnier struck across the trail to Sainte Marie, where they were received with heart-felt rejoicing. All had suffered much in the various missions during the winter, and had been frequently under the shadow of death. But none had endured so much as Jogues and Garnier, attested Lalemant when he wrote to France: "This mission to the Petuns has been the richest of all, since the crosses and the sufferings have been the most abundant in it."

II

They had survived the winter of the small-pox. Not one of the Blackrobes had contracted the disease. Nor did one of them drop killed by the murderous frenzy of the savages, though in every village through the Huron and Petun lands the hatchet hung above their heads. Assembled, that spring of 1640, in their quiet retreat at Sainte Marie, they marveled at their miraculous preservation. The murder of the Blackrobes was the theme of every council held throughout the winter. Talk of slaughtering them was the common gossip about the cabin fires. If any brave had split open their heads, he would have been honored for his deed. Why did not the savages refuse to supply them with food, and thus starve them to death? Why did they not mix poison with the food, since they were expert in its use? Why did the warriors not waylay them on the lonely trails? In amazement, the Fathers asked themselves these questions, and with truth they also asked: "Is it not God who protects us? Is it not He who wills that we shall not doubt the care that He has for us, and that He alone is our fortress, our cannons, our armies, our provider, our all?"

They were still in danger, they knew. About March, the Hurons held their general council of all the nations at the village of St. Louis, about five miles from Sainte Marie. Of this the chronicler relates: "Our lives were roughly tossed about there for the space of a whole night (for this is the time of their councils; is it a wonder that the spirits of darkness preside there?). Most of them resolved upon our death, and, they said 'the more promptly, the better it will be.' A single nation voted against the motion, pointing out the consequences of this resolution which tended to the ruin of the country. The others flared up against this opposition. Those who were on our side, realizing that they were a minority, answer: 'Let us put the French to death, then, since you wish it so. But let those who are eager to do this, begin the execution of it themselves. We can very well clear ourselves of the guilt.' Thereupon they all send the ball back and forth to one another, pretending that it is not for them to begin."

Meanwhile, the Fathers were holding their own councils, counting up the results of their spiritual labors and planning new conquests. During the past winter they had preached before or conversed with ten thousand barbarians. They baptized more than a thousand, almost all of whom were dying with the small-pox. Among these were three hundred and sixty children under seven years of age; in addition, they counted "more than a hundred other little children who were baptized in the preceding years, but who were harvested by this same disease and were gathered by the angels like flowers of Paradise."

Consoling as these results were, they were more than balanced by the heartbreaks. In the preceding summer there had flourished a numerous church of Christian Hurons in Ossossané, a strong body of Christians in Teanaustayaé, and a nucleus in Scanonaenrat. Besides, many of the more devoted had followed the Blackrobes to Sainte Marie and were intending to settle there permanently in the Christian village that was projected.

Then the small-pox crazed them with fear and terror. They had recourse again to their superstitions, they put their faith in dreams and their oki, they joined in the diabolical seances and incantations, in the barbarous chants and dances and feasts. Another fear possessed their minds: the Blackrobes were to be murdered, without a doubt; and if the Blackrobes were killed, then, too, all who were believers in the Blackrobes' words might also be killed. As a result, many who had publicly embraced the Faith more publicly renounced it and joined with the more blood-thirsty enemies. Twenty or thirty souls scattered here and there alone remained Christians in the early summer of 1640.

Then fell a most disastrous blow. Joseph Chihwatenhwa was to be one of a party taking Ragueneau and Poncet down to Three Rivers. He had gone to the woods to cut cedar boughs for the canoe he was building. Some hours later he was found murdered. The Ossossané chiefs investigated, and judged that he was felled by the javelins of two Iroquois who were lurking in the forests; they had split open his head, scalped him, and then fled away mysteriously.

Joseph was the foundation stone of the Huron Church. He lived sinlessly, he practiced heroic virtue, he prayed with inspired fervor. He had dedicated himself wholly to the Blackrobes, and championed them in the cabins and in the councils. All through the terrible winter he had gone as an apostle to the villages where the hostility against the Blackrobes raged strongest, down to rescue Daniel, off to the Petuns to defend Jogues and Garnier. He it was on whom the Fathers had based their hopes for the conversion of the Hurons. He was snatched away from them, and, as Lalemant expressed it, his death might be "put in the number of the profound secrets and of the adorable dispensations of the Divine Providence, a thing we cannot think upon without astonishment."

A serene summer brooded over Sainte Marie. Jogues and his companion priests engaged in the making of their annual retreats, held their classes and consultations on the Huron language, strove to reduce the complexities of the inflections and syntax to rules, added new words to the dictionary they were compiling, worked manually in the construction of the cabins and in the clearance and cultivation of the fields, and from time to time went off to visit the villages up and down the country.

With September, the lethargy of the heat lifted. The flotilla of voyaging canoes trickled back. Two new missioners came up with the fleet that summer—Father Claude Pijart, the elder brother of Father Pierre, and Father Charles Raymbault. Their mission was to the nomadic Algonquin peoples who usually wintered in the vicinity of the Hurons. While the number of priests for the coming year was thus maintained at thirteen, only eleven were deputed for work among the Hurons, since Ragueneau and Poncet did not return. There came the first lay brother to assist the missioners, Dominique Scot, a young man of twenty-one, who had not yet pronounced his first vows in the Society of Jesus. The religious element at Sainte Marie was further increased by the creation of a new class of lay helpers to whom was given the name of *donati*, or *donnés*.

From the first beginnings of the settlement of the missioners among the Hurons, French workmen, or *engagés*, were hired to perform the domestic duties, to carry on building operations, to hunt and fish and farm, to act as an armed defense, in need, to accompany the missioners in their journeys, to help instruct the savages. They were not bound by any permanent agreement, however, and were free to trade and hunt for their own gain. They were, since the establishment in 1634, men of exceptional morality and courage, and were wholeheartedly faithful. Father Lalemant, in conjunction with the other missioners, conceived of a plan to unite men of this type into an auxiliary class, something between that of lay brother and *engagé*.

On his side, the *donatus*, or *donné*, bound himself by contract and by a private, not a religious, vow for life "to serve and assist the Fathers who work for the salvation and conversion of souls" in the Huron Mission; to put himself at the disposal of these said Fathers, and not only himself but all that belonged to him, "wishing to give up all for God, without any reserve or any resource except God Himself." He promised, in addition to obedience and the abjuration of possessions, to observe chastity and not to marry.

On its side, the Mission of the Hurons, with the Mission of New France as a guarantor, pledged itself by contract to support the *donné* in the same state as to food, clothing, lodging, and other necessities, as that of the missioners; to care for him in sickness and age until death; and to make him a participator in the spiritualities and privileges of the Society of Jesus. Robert Le Coq, called Robert the Good, who had been an *engagé* since 1638, was the first to sign the contract and to pronounce the vows of the *donné*. Five others came up from Quebec and Three Rivers, among whom was Guillaume Coûture, a brawny, intelligent, pious young man.

When winter closed in, thirteen priests and a lay brother, six *donnés*, six *engagés*, and two boys formed the French outpost in the Huron country. With the increase in numbers, and with the cargo of tools, building materials, and general equipment that was dragged up from the St. Lawrence, work on the building of Sainte

Marie was pushed vigorously. A solid residence of logs and planks was put together on the cleared space above the river. Beginnings were made of a goodly sized church off to the side of the residence. A cabin in the native style of beams and bark was constructed for the housing of visiting Christian Hurons and as a hospital; and further removed, another cabin for itinerant savages of all conditions who might be passing along the way. The flat, rich fields along the placid, little stream were prepared for tillage. A trench was dug from the river to the residence, and a basin excavated as a harbor for the canoes. Sainte Marie was taking on the air of a truly French civilized habitation.

In the assignment of labors for the winter of 1640, Jogues and Du Peron were deputed to look after the needs of the Ataronchronons, all of whose villages lay in the neighborhood of Sainte Marie. They were thus to remain at home, together with Chastellain, who had general care of the cabin, and with Raymbault and Claude Pijart, who were caring for the Algonquins who camped in the vicinity. The others dispersed for more distant missions on November 2. Lalemant and Le Mercier took charge of Ossossané and the surrounding district; Daniel and Le Moyne tended the central areas from Teanaustayaé down to Cahiague; Pijart and Garnier returned to the Petuns for a second assault. De Brébeuf and Chaumonot pioneered in a new field. They traveled farthest, to the land of the Neutrals who bordered the territory of the Iroquois. Their mission was dedicated as that of the Angels.

Jogues had no easy task with his Ataronchronons, despite the general prevalence of good-will and peace that blessed the country. This nation remained uniformly hostile and egregiously treacherous. They were deeper sunk in their superstitions than the other Hurons, and gave lesser signs of intelligence. They bore the reputation of being crude and inhospitable. However, they opened their doors to Ondessonk and Anonchiara, as Father Du Peron was called, and accepted them, if not in a friendly way, with some sort of tolerance.

Jogues padded the familiar trails through the damp season of the early winter, through the clear biting colds of December, the blizzards of January, the inclemencies and thaws of February, making the circuit of the five main villages three or four times each week. The route to Ste. Anne, the nearest of these habitations, traced back across the meadows from Sainte Marie, through the close-set forests, to the brow of the rising hills some three miles beyond. This was the village to which the man with the small-pox had been carried from Sainte Marie. It was particularly malevolent, for it blamed its woes on the Blackrobes. Father Jogues accepted its coldness and its animosity with a gentle kindness, and strayed through its streets and about its palisades making friendly advances to the elders and to the fierce-looking braves who lolled about. He pushed into its thirty or forty cabins with a calm assurance, and, squatted before the fires, tried to win the confidence of the children and the squaws.

Beyond Ste. Anne, some three miles across the elevated plateau ridged with ravines dug out by swollen creeks, was the village of St. Denis. It held a bold position on a level acre that spread back from a precipitous gulley excavated by a tumbling little torrent. Near the mouth of this stream, three or four miles to the east, on a bluff above the lowlands that fringed the shore of the bay, sprawled the village of St. Louis. And some six miles beyond, on another promontory overlooking the bay, perched the village of St. Jean. This, like the others, was on a narrow-topped hill whose loamy sides had been torn away into a gorge by the floods of another rapid little stream. Other villages lay to the west, across Isaragui Lake, and to the north across the river of Sainte Marie. The total number of souls in all the territory assigned that winter to Jogues and Du Peron was upwards of 1,400.

There was consolation for Father Jogues over a Sunday when he had returned to Sainte Marie to assist Father Chastellain. The Christians from Ossossané, Teanaustayaé, and other localities travelled the six or ten or fifteen miles to spend there a holy Sunday. Some of the Algonquin families who wintered in the vicinity were also turned Christians, and these united with the Hurons in their devotions. "It was a sweet anthem to hear, at the same time, in three or four languages, the praises of God," the chronicler relates. "In a word, I can say that Sainte Marie is the house of peace; so much so, that the very savages who are most hostile and insolent toward us elsewhere, take on an appearance of feeling and disposition totally different when we see them in our house."

Preëminent in this congregation was Teondechoren, the elder brother of the well-mourned apostle, Joseph Chihwatenhwa. He was a powerful man of some forty-five years, respected in Ossossané for his prowess and his eloquence. Ever since he was twenty he had been an associate and then the leader of the Aoutaerohi, the Festival of the Fire, one of the most diabolical of the Huron ceremonies. By his own account, he could handle flaming fagots without being burned, he could stuff his mouth full of live coals and not be scorched, he could plunge his arm into boiling water and feel only coolness. He was always bitterly opposed to the Blackrobes, and when Joseph Chihwatenhwa became a Christian he had objurgated him and practically disowned him as a member of the family.

Three days after Joseph was murdered, Teondechoren felt within himself a curiosity about the Blackrobes whom Joseph loved. He conceived a respect for their teaching, the more he knew of it, and slowly was convinced. He asked to be baptized. But the Fathers put him off, and tested him severely, for his past was evil in their estimation and his sincerity was questionable. However, he proved himself worthy to be the brother of Joseph, the Believer. Teondechoren was baptized and, after the Huron custom, was raised up to the name of Joseph, as the successor of his brother. Father Jogues got to know Joseph Teondechoren intimately that winter at Sainte Marie and found in him a rock as solid as Joseph Chihwatenhwa and an apostle as zealous.

When all the missioners were assembled once more at Sainte Marie in March, they totaled the results of the winter of 1640 and 1641. They had announced the Gospel to sixteen or seventeen thousand barbarians of four distinct peoples, the Hurons, the Algonquins, the Petuns, and the Neutrals. They had been able to baptize only about one hundred in sickness. They dared to chance baptism on not more than a dozen in good health, for they understood better, during the small-pox epidemic, how easy was perversion and what an heroic struggle was fidelity. The Huron church, in its totality, seven years after its inception and five years after Jogues' arrival, numbered sixty dependable Christians.

It was to be a summer of war, that of 1641. The Iroquois had launched into a violent offensive against the Algonquins, their immemorial enemies, against their kindred stock, the Hurons, and against the French palefaces. They had sought peace with the French earlier that year, but on the terms that the French would ally with them against the Algonquins and Hurons. The negotiations were abruptly terminated by an exchange of musket-shots. All winter, Iroquois marauders had lurked in the woods that fringed the Huron country. Parties painted for war paraded through the Neutral lands. Rumors were thick that the Ottawa River in its lower stretches, the St. Lawrence in its full length, the fishing-haunts, were occupied by Iroquois of the Five Nations.

With some trepidation, then, the Huron traders approached the season for their journey down to Three Rivers. One small party that left early in the summer was under the leadership of Joseph Teondechoren and Sondatsaa, the son of the old chief of Ossossané. Sondatsaa had sought baptism on many occasions, but had not been received, though his children were admitted among the faithful. He contented himself with proclaiming that he was a Christian in heart and desire. Four other Christian Hurons joined the party. With them went the great Echon, ordered to Quebec for rest and treatment of a broken collar-bone, Du Peron and some *donnés* who were deputed to bring back the supplies for the winter.

A few weeks after they had skimmed out of the river before Sainte Marie, there was rumored everywhere a nasty insinuation. Echon was in league with the Iroquois, and plotted with these enemies against the Hurons. He went to meet the Iroquois in the land of the Neutrals last winter. He was allowed to pass down the Ottawa with his Christians that summer, but gave the Iroquois whom he met along the road exact information as to how they could ambush a party that followed. All the old suspicions were linked with this new revelation, and another storm roared about the heads of the Blackrobes at Sainte Marie.

For protection against these sporadic outbursts of insanity, no less than for defense against the Iroquois who prowled secretly through the surrounding wildernesses, the Fathers hurried their plans of erecting a strong fort at Sainte Marie. Thus far there had been built only two log cabins and frail lodges of bark. A stronghold, to repel all possible attacks, was thought essential. Accordingly, the Fathers marked off a space about 150 feet from the river bank to the rear of the cleared fields and log houses.

The fort was planned to be an oblong, slightly irregular, about ninety feet in width and nearly twice that in length. Two of the walls were to be of solid masonry—that of the long side which looked to the east over the forests and meadowlands rising toward the inland ridges, and that of the short side which faced the north and the sloping hill some few hundred yards beyond. The four corners were also to be solidly built of stone. These bastions were to be of uneven dimensions and of variant shapes; those of the north stone wall were to be triangular projections, like arrow heads, and those toward the south were plotted to be four-sided towers. The westerly wall, which almost paralleled the river, and the shorter wall, facing the south and the open area under cultivation, were to be curtains of wood. These two sides were further guarded by the river and inlet and a deep moat, by the outhouses, and by a redan pointing south and extending from the stream to the inland tower.

Father Jogues was appointed the executor of these plans. Charles Boivin, a *donné*, acted as superintendent of the building operations, with Guillaume Coûture as his assistant and chief carpenter. All the summer of 1641 they were engaged busily in the work of excavation and in the assembly of the material. Jogues, the *donnés*, and the workmen rolled down rocks and stones from the hill on the north, and trundled these for hundreds of yards across the flats. They felled the trees on the hillside and meadow, and dragged them laboriously through the entangled underbrush. When the autumn came, they had practically finished the digging of the foundations and were preparing to lay the base stones.

A missionary opportunity of tremendous importance interrupted Jogues' work in the construction of Sainte Marie. That year was signalized as the one in which the Algonquin held their solemn Feast of the Dead. The Nipissings, who inhabited to the north of the Hurons along the shore of the great Bay held their ceremonial during the first week of September. The two Algonquin missioners, Raymbault and Claude Pijart, together with the Superior, Father Lalemant, accompanied the Huron delegation to the feast. On the day appointed, there assembled upwards of two thousand mourners, many of whom had traveled hundreds of miles out from the dark interior and the northlands. "In this gathering of so many assembled nations," Lalemant remarks, "we strove to win the affections of the chief personages by means of feasts and presents."

An immediate response resulted from these overtures. The visiting chiefs of the Pauoitigoueieuhak, a powerful Algonquin nation of the west, gave a most cordial invitation to the Blackrobes to visit them in their country on the occasion of their Feast of the Dead. This people, known to the French as the Gens du Sault, or Sauteurs, and identified with the Ojibwas or Chippewas, had its villages some

350 miles to the northwest, in the vicinity of the rapids which joined Lake Superior to Lake Huron.

The Blackrobes avidly accepted the invitation. They had always aspired to penetrate beyond the Hurons into the mysterious heart of the continent and to establish missions among the unknown nations about and beyond the Great Lakes. By God's guidance, now, was opened a path into this shrouded country. "We selected Father Charles Raymbault to undertake this journey," writes Lalemant, "and at the same time, since some Hurons were to be of the party, Father Isaac Jogues was chosen so that he might act in conjunction with them."

III

On a mellow day in the last week of September, Jogues and Raymbault joined themselves to the Huron and Algonquin flotillas that were pilgrimaging to the Ojibwas' Feast of the Dead. Both the Blackrobes were men inured to the savage way of life and travel. Jogues was now beginning his sixth successive winter among the Hurons. His fair skin was roughened and creased, his bones and muscles were hard as iron, he could digest any kind of food and could bear up under long fasts. He was a veteran voyageur who could equal the Hurons at the paddle and walk as easily as they under a burden of baggage. Raymbault was also seasoned by five years of experience with the Algonquins along the St. Lawrence and about Lake Huron. He was tall and rangy, expert in handling a canoe, and undaunted by any dangers. Both of these Blackrobes had a good command, the one of the Huron, the other of the Algonquin, tongues, and both knew how to conciliate and how to be stern with the natives.

Through the first few days the canoes pointed up between the innumerable islands that mottled the surface of the west bay of Lake Huron. Jogues and Raymbault had traveled this route before. About the sixth day of steady paddling they crossed the mouth of the French River, the opening which led toward the Ottawa and thence to the St. Lawrence. Beyond this were strange, unfamiliar shore lines. Nicolet, they understood, had once penetrated this wilderness and had brought back some information. They observed closely, for either they or other missioners would be following this route in the years to come. During the second week they saw the low line of the Manitoulin Islands rise out of the lake. They progressed through a mass of islands in tortuous windings, and emerged into the clear, fairly broad stretch of the North Channel. Some days later, they reached the peaked extremity of the channel and picked their route about more large and small islands, until they entered against the flowing current of a river and followed up its crooked course.

On the seventeenth day of their journey they beached their canoes in the cove beneath the rapids called Sault Sainte Marie, where was located the village of the Ojibwas. They had journeyed more than 350 miles beyond the Hurons. Jean Nicolet had reached this point in 1634, when he was seeking the route to China. He had not gone beyond it, but had returned to follow another trail through Lake Michigan. Jogues and Raymbault had opportunity to adventure just a little farther on beyond the Sault, and, after Nicolet, be the first white men to gaze over the horizon-rimmed surface of Lake Superior.

Upon their arrival, swarms of copper-skinned natives rushed to give them welcome. Jogues and Raymbault found more than two thousand natives assembled for the festival of the Ojibwas. In the opening session of the great council of the nations, they were assigned to places of honor. They presented their gifts to the chiefs of this Gens du Sault and gave assurance that the Blackrobes and the French were happy in their friendship and alliance. The orator of the Ojibwas formally accepted the gifts, and gave presents in exchange, one intended to heal them after the fatigues of their long journey, one to inform them that there waited a mat in every cabin for them to sleep upon, others to indicate that always a fire burned to warm them comfortably and that pots were filled with delicacies for their refreshment. Now that the Blackrobes had come so long and dangerous a journey from their home and friends, the orator continued, he feared for their safe return; it would be better, he urged, that the Blackrobes should not think of undertaking the journey to their French cabins, but should remain and make their home among the Pauoitigoueieuhak nation, which loved and cherished them tenderly.

Jogues, speaking in Huron, and Raymbault in Algonquin, assured the council that they were not unwilling to listen to the words of the orators, and were not displeased with the invitation offered to them to dwell permanently in these cabins. They must point out, however, that the chiefs and the people must keep their ears open, so that they could listen to the words of wisdom spoken by the Blackrobes; they must also open their minds and their hearts so as to believe in and honor the God of the Blackrobes; and they must drive out of their lives all things that were sinful and displeasing to the God who made the world.

Courteously, and with deep interest, the council listened to their discourses and promised to consult among themselves as to the propositions. In a later council, the chiefs reported that all the nations eagerly desired the good fortune of learning about the God in whom the Blackrobes believed, that the people would profit by their words and follow their instructions. They loved the Blackrobes as brothers, they protested, and wished more than ever to have them share their fires and food. Jogues and Raymbault, in response, promised to carry back the good word to their chief at Sainte Marie, and told the Ojibwas that they might expect to see the Blackrobes soon settled among them.

The Blackrobes and all the visiting nations, in the first session of the council, presented offerings to dry the tears of the Pauoitigoueieuhaks whose relatives had died during the ten years since the last Festival of the Dead. This tribute was succeeded by chants and dances, by pantomimes and games of skill and endurance and chance, by feasts and smaller assemblies. Then followed another council in which the chiefs who had died were resurrected, and their memories perpetuated by giving their names to worthy successors.

The second day was one of mourning. A large cabin, erected for the purpose, had been sumptuously hung with skins and furs. Thither, the women carried the bones of their dead and placed them upon the earth. They sat before the bones all day, and wept and lamented. At nightfall a choir of men entered the cabin and raised a lugubrious chant, tender and sad. The women joined the refrain, and alternately through the night, in the gloom of the cabin, lighted only by the flickering flames of the fire at each end, they poured out their song of grief. All the people remained in deep silence while the ceremony continued until the light of morning. Then, the women gathered the bones and carried them with elaborate ritual to the pit in which they were to be finally interred. This third day was given over to further councils, the forging of alliances, the waging of wars, the communal business of the clans and tribes and nations, to games and sports and festivities.

In the course of their visit, Jogues and Raymbault gathered much information of the nations of the west and the unexplored regions beyond Sault Sainte Marie. Some Huron clans had located in the territory of the Ojibwas, and other Algonquin clans occupied the lands about the tremendous fresh-water lakes. Beyond these dwelt nations who were of different stock from either the Huron-Iroquois or the Algonquin, who spoke a totally distinct language, who were, for the most part, sedentary.

These peoples, Jogues learned, "have never known Europeans and have never heard of God. Among others was a certain nation, the Nadouessi, or Sioux, who were situated to the northwest or west of the Sault, eighteen days journey farther away. The first nine days are occupied in crossing the great Lake Superior, which commences above the Sault. During the last nine days, one has to ascend a river that traverses these lands. These peoples till the soil in the manner of our Hurons, and harvest Indian corn and tobacco. Their villages are larger than the Huron, and in a better state of defense, owing to their continual wars with the Kiristinons (the Crees), the Irinions (the Illinois), and other great nations who inhabit the same country."

The urgent invitations offered by these far nations to visit them had to be laid aside by Jogues and Raymbault for the present, and the deep desires of their hearts to follow into the wilderness had need be curbed. Their mission, that autumn, was merely to scout the unknown lands and peoples. Another year and they might return to the Ojibwas about Sault Sainte Marie; and another year they or their successors might paddle beyond the great lake to the rivers of the Nadouessioux, and in the years to come, the Blackrobes would follow the still unknown trails and waterways farther and farther to the west; and there might come a year in which all of these nations, buried in paganism and savagery might be taught the sweet doctrine of Christ and brought under His yoke.

Hopes and visions misted their eyes as they gazed over the limitless waters of Lake Superior. Reluctantly they joined the Hurons who were restless to be on their homeward journey before the October storms and frosts should come to increase the difficulties of the route. With mutual protestations of friendship, the two Blackrobes departed from the nations of the west. Nearly three weeks later they were fondly embraced by their brethren at Sainte Marie.

In the consultations that followed the report of their mission

Fathers Jogues and Raymbault urgently contended that missioners should be sent to evangelize these western nations who were so hospitable and seemed so receptive to the Gospel. Father Lalemant and the others were unanimous in their agreement, for each one of them could be satisfied with nothing less than the Christianization of the continent. "But we need laborers for that purpose," Lalemant protested. "We must first try to win the peoples that are nearest to us, and meanwhile pray heaven to hasten the moment of their conversion." That winter, even, due to the determined drive that was to be made among the Hurons and the neighboring Algonquins, they thought it better to abandon the Mission of the Apostles, begun by Jogues and Garnier among the Petuns, and the Mission of the Angels among the Neutrals which de Brébeuf had founded the preceding year. The first endeavor must be the conversion, totally or in a major part, of the Hurons. Thereafter, in God's good time, would they advance and spread to other peoples.

Upon his return from the Ojibwas Father Jogues resumed his ministership of the residence of Sainte Marie. On him devolved the duty of housekeeping for the fourteen priests, the lay brother, the seven *donnés* and the nine workmen and boys. He saw to the provision of food and fuel and clothing, to the material necessities and the sparse comforts, to the maintenance and improvement of the buildings and fields. He directed the *donnés* and workmen in their manual employments as well as, for the most part, in their spiritual welfare. To him fell the care of the sick, and his first patient was his companion in the recent journey to Sault Sainte Marie.

Charles Raymbault, about the middle of November, started with René Menard on a tour of the winter encampments of the Nipissings. They were caught by furious gales in the great Bay. Snowstorms and the stoppage of forming ice drove them back to Sainte Marie. Raymbault was gripped by a heavy cold which settled in his lungs and rapidly developed into tuberculosis. During the dark months of the winter he was tended with brotherly care by Father Isaac.

Never had the Hurons been more friendly than they were that autumn. No epidemics, no misfortunes afflicted them. They were, furthermore, deeply impressed by the reports their braves brought back to them from the St. Lawrence. The French were a powerful people and prosperous. They loved the Blackrobes and obeyed their commands as they would those of their fathers. The great chief of the French, Onontio, as they named Montmagny, listened to the Blackrobes in silence and with deep respect. Moreover, in the council held that summer at Three Rivers, Onontio made a surprising proposition. In former years he offered gifts to pledge friendship and alliance. But this year he explained that his presents were a token that the truths which the Blackrobes preached were most certain and of the utmost importance. He told the Hurons that if they accepted his gifts they bound themselves to listen to the Blackrobes, to accept and obey all their directions.

The Hurons accepted the presents and the pledge. The results were astounding, Lalemant exclaimed. "Never have gifts been of such advantage to the Faith. For, when the canoes returned, the whole country learned what had transpired down there at Three Rivers. The people conceived the idea that the matters which we had come to tell them are received throughout the world as well-established truths (a thing which some frequently doubted, because, as they said, the first Frenchmen whom they had known said nothing to them about God). We have derived from these presents this further benefit, that never before have we had larger audiences in all the villages and cabins where we have gone to teach these peoples."

Sainte Marie became a rendezvous to the natives, and Ondessonk was their gracious host. Father Du Peron was specifically in charge of the chapel, but he needed Father Jogues' assistance in these spiritual affairs which became more arduous with the advance of winter. For Sainte Marie was verily turned into the center of Christendom in these far regions. The Fathers had agreed on the procedure that "if, in the missions, some adult in good health is deemed worthy of baptism after all the trials to which he is subjected, he be sent to Sainte Marie to be examined again, and then, with solemnity, to receive the Sacrament which makes him a child of the Church. We reserve the majority of these baptisms for the festivals of Christmas, of Easter, and of Pentecost, from which our Christians who have assembled at Sainte Marie from all parts have always departed with a marked increase in their Faith."

The missions near Sainte Marie which had been under the care of Father Jogues during the winter of 1640 and 1641, were divided between Fathers Chastellain and Pierre Pijart. The chronicler states of the latter that "in the beginning, he met with very stubborn-minded persons, who closed their ears and their cabins to him, and refused to listen to what they heard, except in a spirit of blasphemy. However, in the end, his patience tamed the majority of them and influenced some of them to such an extent that they know the truth, and complain of themselves that they have not strength enough to embrace so great a blessing." As for the former, in the villages of St. Louis and St. Denis "he was welcomed everywhere. He was able to instruct and impress many. But this fruit is not ripe, and the Faith of this people is not strong enough at present to regard them as persons won over to God."

La Conception, at Ossossané, under the charge this winter of Le Mercier and Ragueneau, yielded "the richest fruits of the Faith that we have seen in this country since we have sown the seed of the gospel here," attests the chronicler. "I may say that here is seen, through the grace of God, a Church established, and Christians who not only live in the practice of the Faith, but who, in the midst of Satan's reign, triumph over impiety itself." The spirit of the greatest and first Huron apostle, Joseph Chihwatenhwa, hovered over the village. His widow, Maria Aonetta, remained a bulwark of belief. His young daughter, Theresa, who was being educated by the Ursuline nuns at Quebec, gave promise through her intelligence and fidelity of becoming the shining female saint of the Hurons.

His brother, Joseph Teondechoren, who, the Fathers remark, "before his baptism, was a mass of flesh that covered a soul as gross as his body," had assumed the mantle of his brother and "after taking his name of Joseph, inherited his Faith, his spirit, and his zeal to such an extent that one can easily see that his conversion is a stroke from heaven." Joseph Teondechoren, in his own confession, declared that "the Blackrobes have drawn out all the evil that was in my soul." Of his spiritual processes, he asserts: "It seems to me that we are one, God and me. Either He follows me or I find Him wherever I go."

Sondatsaa, who had paddled Father de Brébeuf down to Quebec, also became a light of the church of Ossossané. The Fathers among the Hurons had refused him baptism until he had been further tested, since he was a leader of the superstitious, immoral rites. Down at Quebec, so sincere and vehement were his petitions that the Fathers not only baptized him with all possible solemnity, but Governor Montmagny became his godfather. He was named Charles.

Upon his return to Ossossané almost his first act was to spread a feast for all his fellow chiefs. In the harangue which he delivered he declared: "My brothers, you see here a Christian who would rather die than abandon his Faith. It is to the great Master of our lives that I have pledged myself by promise. Never shall the devil, or anything that comes from him, have power over me. Let no one in the future tempt me to commit any sin whatever, unless he be prepared for a refusal. I wish to save you, and myself also, from trouble, by giving you all this notice."

In Teanaustayaé, flourished a small but heroic body of believers. From this village arose the most outstanding convert of the year. Ahatsistari was honored as the greatest war chief of all the Huron nations. So amazing were his deeds that he had already become a hero of legend. "This man's life is but a series of battles," the missioners asserted. In the past summer, Ahatsistari with fifty Huron braves attacked 300 Iroquois, and brought back a large number of scalps and prisoners. A short time later, scouting about Lake Ontario, he was surprised by a strong Iroquois war band. His few followers, terrified, were for darting off in flight. "No, no, comrades," Ahatsistari shouted. "Follow me. We'll start the attack." He drove his canoe headlong into the Iroquois fleet. Alone, he leaped into the foremost enemy canoe. He split the skulls of the two Iroquois nearest him, hurled two others into the water, leaped after them, and upset the boat. Swimming with one hand, he wielded his tomahawk with the other, and smashed the heads of the floundering enemies. Hurons and Iroquois watched the single-handed battle as if entranced. Then, Ahatsistari, shrilling the war-whoop, stroked out against the other Iroquois canoes. Demoralized, they fled.

Ahatsistari had listened to Echon and Ondessonk when they first went to Teanaustayaé in 1638. He was keenly interested in their doctrines, but he refused to abandon his tribal ceremonies. He asked for baptism, later, but would not accept the conditions which the Blackrobes imposed. It was not until the winter of 1641 that he made his subjection and professed himself willing to abjure his savage practices and abide by the precepts of the Blackrobes. They tested him further, and then sent him up to Sainte Marie, where he was to be baptized on Holy Saturday, 1642. Father Jogues and the other missioners received him and the neophytes from the various communities of the Hurons. They held council, in the Huron fashion, and each of the natives who sought baptism was called upon to argue his petition.

Ahatsistari addressed them thus: "I have the Faith deep down in my heart, and my actions during the past winter have proved it sufficiently. In two days I am departing on the warpath. If I am killed in the battle, tell me: where will my soul go if you refuse me baptism? If you saw into my heart as clearly as the great Master of our lives, I would already be numbered among the Christians; and the fear of the flames of hell would not accompany me, now that I am about to face death. I cannot baptize myself. All that I can do is to declare with utmost honesty the desire that I have for it. After I do that, if my soul be burned in hell, you will bear the guilt of it. Whatever you may decide to do, however, I will always pray to God, since I know Him. Perhaps He will have mercy on me, for you say that He is wiser than you are."

"What made you first think of believing in God?" one of the Fathers questioned him.

"Even before you came into this country," Ahatsistari responded, "I had escaped from a great many perils in which my comrades were killed. I saw very clearly that it was not I who saved myself from these dangers. I had the thought that some spirit, most powerful and unknown to me, was favorable to me and aided me. We peoples attribute all of our good fortune to dreams. But I was convinced that all that was only nonsense. Still, I did not know much about it. When I heard of the greatness of the God whom you preach, and of what Jesus Christ had done when He was on earth, I recognized Him as the being who had preserved me. I was resolved to honor Him all my life. When I went to war I recommended myself to Him night and morning. It is to Him that all my victories are due. He it is in whom I believe. I ask you for baptism, so that He may have pity on me after my death."

No one could further doubt the sincerity and nobility of the man. And so Ahatsistari was solemnly baptized in the chapel of Sainte Marie on March 30, and was given the name of Eustace. He and the other Christians received communion on Easter Sunday, and later in the day Eustace led his Huron warriors out on the warpath against the Iroquois. Before his departure he, Joseph, Charles, Stephen, René, and the other Christian chiefs and braves held a council in the cabin of Sainte Marie and pledged themselves as follows:

Let us hereafter be but one body and one mind, since we all serve the same Master. Whenever any one of us passes by a village in which a Christian dwells, let him not lodge elsewhere. Whenever anyone is afflicted, let him seek consolation among the other Christians. Let us not reveal one another's faults to the infidels; but let it be recognized, through the friendship that we shall have for one another, that the name of Christian is a tie more binding than the bonds of nature. Let us inform our relatives who are not of the same Faith as we, even if they be our fathers and our children, that we do not wish our bones mingled together after our death, since our souls will be eternally separated and our affection will not continue beyond this life.

About Easter time, the missioners returned from their stations to Sainte Marie. In the total, they baptized 120 adult Hurons in good health. These all had been carefully instructed and tested most rigorously. They could be depended on to withstand persecution and remain loyal, even though disease and death should overwhelm them. In his official report of that year Lalemant declared: "As to the state of Christianity in these countries, I may truly say that the Church is gaining strength in numbers and still more in sanctity; that the Holy Spirit is working as visibly here as in any place in this New World; and that one would admire such faith, such piety, such courage that we witness here among some of the barbarians, even though it was manifested in persons brought up from the cradle amid examples of virtue and religion."

Evidences of this change of heart among the Hurons were apparent to Father Jogues at Sainte Marie. In his quiet retreat, he witnessed nothing but the gentleness and the childlike simplicity of these new believers. But his zeal made him restless. At Sainte Marie, he garnered the fruits of the harvest. He wanted to suffer for God, to battle the dark powers, to struggle with the pagans, to fight in the offensive. This was his prayer in the long vigils he spent before the Blessed Sacrament in the stillness of Sainte Marie. During the day, in the midst of his duties about the settlement, he made almost hourly visits to the chapel. At night, when the others slept, he prostrated himself for long hours in the Divine Presence. His love for God thrilled through his soul and inspired him to seek greater and greater means of manifesting it.

One afternoon—it was in the spring—when the chapel was deserted, he was kneeling before the altar in adoration. He felt surge up within him an overwhelming desire to suffer for God, to endure pain, to undergo fatigues, to face dangers, to be subjected to extraordinary trials. He bent his head low, so that it touched the wood of the altar step. There, he begged and demanded of God that he would be immolated, would be sacrificed as a victim of Divine love. He offered himself, body, soul, will, mind, memory to God, that God might do with him as He pleased.

He burned as if with fever. Then the emotion relaxed, and as he came to himself he was conscious of thought forming in his mind. Something was being told him, but at first obscurely, vaguely. He waited, passively and expectant. Then he heard drumming in his ears, as clear and resonant as speech, the words: *Exaudita est oratio tua; fiet tibi sicut a me petisti. Comfortare et esto robustus.* The message was repeated, again and again: "Thy prayer is heard. Be it done to thee as thou hast asked. Be comforted, be of strong heart."

That God had spoken to him Father Jogues had no doubt. He believed, as he said, that "these words had issued from the lips of Him with whom saying and doing are only one and the same thing." He had offered himself completely to God. God had accepted his oblation. The words were a revelation and a prophecy, he told himself. He must wait for the time of their fulfillment. In the chapel that spring day he accepted that outcome, no matter what it might be.

CHAPTER VII

Ambushed by the Mohawks

I

DREAD of the Iroquois hung like a black cloud over the Huron land. Never before had this enemy been so bold as in 1642, never more persistent in attack, never so completely victorious. The Hurons were stung into action. They were a softer people than the Iroquois, less warlike, less spirited. But they could not refuse the challenge of the Iroquois, for if they sought peace it would be as a nation of squaws and slaves. They had to fight back.

War chiefs in all the villages coursed through the streets, calling on the warriors to follow them on the warpath. They planted the war pole, flaming with red paint, and lighted fires about it. The chief, his face and body streaked with crimson, flourished his tomahawk and circled about the pole and the fires. Painted braves followed after him, lustily brawling their war-songs, pounding their heels in the earth, fighting invisible enemies, killing shadows, pantomiming war. With a blood-curdling war-whoop, the chief and the braves leaped on the war pole, and buried their hatchets in it. Orators harangued the young men to be brave. Chiefs boasted of their prowess and shouted their defiance of the Iroquois. Old men pleaded that the nation be saved. The hysteria rose, the blood lust boiled, and in wild tumult the parties burst from the village and coursed off along the trails through the forests.

Most of the Huron war bands slunk back into the villages. They could discover no traces of the enemy, some reported. The forces of the enemy were too powerful for them to attack, others admitted. And those who did have courage to fight were nearly always worsted. A great number were killed, many were captured and carried off as war victims to the Iroquois country, the remainder were put ignominiously to flight. Scarcely one of the Huron expeditions but ended in rout and disaster. For, added to their superior numbers and their indomitable courage and ingenuity, the Iroquois had the advantage of muskets and powder. The Hurons, despite their defeats, were not broken in spirit. Party followed party, all through the spring and summer, along the trail of war.

In June other Huron leaders were preparing for their trading expeditions down to the settlements of the French. They were aware that all the route was infested with roaming bands of Iroquois. Never before, in all their years, had the rumors been so frightening. They heard of Iroquois penetrating to the land of the Nipissings, of ambushes in the lower Ottawa, of enemy flotillas scouting along the St. Lawrence, of Iroquois war parties skulking in the hidden waterways and along the shores of Lake St. Peter. Nevertheless, they chose to dare the journey, for their beaver furs and skins could be exchanged for the valuable merchandise of the French. They hoped to slip through the blockade.

It was necessary that some one of the priests at Sainte Marie should attempt the journey to Quebec. Reports and letters had to be delivered, letters and instructions had to be brought back, supplies had to be gathered for the winter, tools and building equipment for the new residence and the fort had to be transported. The Superior, Father Lalemant, was in a quandary. At all times a harrowing experience, the trip that summer, because of the Iroquois, was particularly hazardous. Lalemant felt that he was almost condemning whomsoever he chose. He needed a man of experience, one who would not flinch. He decided to ask Father Isaac.

Lalemant made his position clear: he was not giving a command, he was not exerting any pressure; he was merely presenting a proposition, which Isaac was free to reject. Jogues did not hesitate a moment in accepting the proposition. Immediately the words he had heard in the chapel a month or two back sounded in his brain: *"Exaudita est oratio tua; fiet tibi sicut a me petisti. Comfortare et esto robustus."* This might be the beginning of the fulfillment of his prayer.

Though he smiled bravely at Lalemant, and assured him how happy he was to be chosen, he had no illusions. In his narrative, he recounted the fact "that the journey was of itself a most difficult one, both on account of many other dangers, and then especially, because in forty places the canoes and other baggage must be carried on the shoulders." He recalled the almost miraculous escape of de Brébeuf the preceding year, the increased numbers of Iroquois prowling about that present summer, and "that these Iroquois swore if they ever took another Frenchman captive, they would burn him alive over a slow fire, in the same way that they inflict the direst tortures on their other prisoners." He confessed later that, as soon as he received the suggestion that he go to Quebec, he judged that God was preparing some extraordinary trial or suffering for him.

He relieved his Superiors of all responsibility, for he himself asserted: "Obedience laid before me a simple proposition, not a command to go down to Kébec, in such a way that I would not have to accept it if I were unwilling. I did not say a word against it, nor did I try to escape from it. Gladly and willingly did I accept this charge laid before me by obedience and charity. I offered myself with all my heart; and that the more willingly, because the necessity of undertaking this journey might have cast some one else of the Fathers, much more valuable than I, into the perils and hazards of which we were all aware."

It was decided that Father Charles Raymbault should also be carried down to Quebec. He had been growing more weak and emaciated, and he could not be properly cared for in a rough outpost like Sainte Marie. There was a glimmer of hope that, if he survived the descent, he might be nursed back to health in the hospital at Quebec. The proposition of making the journey was also laid before the *donné*, Guillaume Coûture, in much the same fashion that it had been presented to Father Jogues. Coûture responded also in the same fashion. He was willing to take the chance, most willing to accompany Father Isaac, with whom he had been so closely associated during the past year in the upbuilding of Sainte Marie. Two other French workmen, on their own interests as well as those of the mission, also elected to accompany Jogues.

The five Frenchmen were invited to join a party made up of the Christian leaders of Ossossané and Teanaustayaé. By common consent, the leadership was given to the famous war-chief, Eustace Ahatsistari. Stephen Totiri, from the same village, led another canoe. Charles Sondatsaa and Joseph Teondechoren, accompanied by his brother Peter Saoekbata and another brother, brought two canoes from Ossossané. They carefully selected their companions from among the baptized Christians and the neophytes. There were, in all, twenty-five Hurons and French in the four canoes. These set Friday, June 13, as the date for their departure from Sainte Marie.

While the night still held, Fathers Jogues and Raymbault said their Masses in the murky chapel. Guillaume Coûture, the two workmen, and the Christians, having confessed, received Holy Communion. When the morning was breaking, they loaded their baggage, furs, and skins into the canoes, and then lit the council fire. The swarthy warriors, wrapped in their blankets, and the Blackrobes, crouched in a circle about the fire. The pipe of brotherhood was lit and was passed from mouth to mouth. Each one spoke his farewell message. Joseph Teondechoren exhorted them:

My brothers, here I am about to depart. Perhaps we shall never have the happiness of seeing one another again here on earth. This makes me desire to speak to you—just as if I were now about to die—with the most honest expressions that I have in my heart. Whatever misfortunes may come upon us, let us remember that we are Christians; that the object of our hopes is in heaven; that earth contains nothing worthy of us and nothing capable of satisfying a soul that has given itself over to God. Eternity will give us every leisure to experience that truth. For the present, it is sufficient that Faith teaches it to us, even if the sentiments that God gives us were not proofs of it. My brothers, let us never lose that grace which you and I have received in the sacred waters of Baptism. It is the pledge of our salvation, the beauty of our souls; it is that which has removed from our souls the deformities of sin, which has driven from them the demons, and has made us children of God. Let that be our treasure, let that be our riches. If the devil and all hell should try to ravish this from us, let us more love our welfare than they desire us evil. Let us be on our guard night and day. Let us pray for help from heaven, and for aid from the angels. Let us devote ourselves to prayer whenever we feel our hearts attacked. In one word, let us esteem the gift of Faith, loving the God who has loved us first; and let all our hatred be directed against sin alone. Let us make up our minds to die and to endure the pain and sorrow of this life. Let us, here and now, offer the whole to God, in order that He may turn it to His glory and that, in exchange for the moment that remains to us to suffer on earth, we may receive an eternal reward in heaven.

Joseph finished speaking, and all his comrades emitted from their groins their approval. He conjured them: "My brothers, let us place ourselves upon our knees, and all together offer ourselves to God, both for life and for death. Let all of you follow my words, so that, having but one heart, we may also have but one tongue and the same prayer in our mouths." In the tenuous glow of the fresh June morning, Joseph and the Hurons, Jogues and the French, knelt together on the damp sod. Joseph led the prayer, and all piously repeated his words. When he had finished, the Superior, Father Lalemant uttered the benediction over their bowed heads. Expeditiously they floated the canoes and climbed into their places. The hushed silence was broken as the four boats slid out of the inlet and turned right along the river and farewells and God's blessings were shouted back and forth until Jogues and his comrades had passed far down through the arching trees.

Within half an hour they were bounding in the swells and troughs of the rough waters of Matchedash Bay. They came up to the looming mainland and followed its line through the cluster of islands. By evening they had paddled some thirty miles. After a few days, they reached the recession at the mouth of the French River. Beyond, recollected Jogues and Raymbault, was the route to the Ojibwas which they had followed last October. The passage through the river and across Lake Nipissing, through more sedgy streams and black little lakes, was smooth. Then they began the drop into the Ottawa. It was turbulent with the remnants of the spring floods, yellow with the soil it had gouged out of the soft banks. For some miles it would flow majestically between wide banks. Then it would roll into a barrier of rocks and be lashed into a frothy madness, or treacherously swell up before it poured over a precipice.

Expert as they were in the manipulation of the nervous barks, vigilant as they were of the currents, the Hurons could not avoid all mishaps. On two or three occasions, when a rush of water lifted them from the shore toward a waterfall, they had to use every brawny muscle to swing the canoe out of the swirl. Another time, when they were shooting one of the rapids, Jogues' canoe was hurled amid the crags and overturned. They fastened themselves to the rocks and held a firm grip on the boat. They were able to recover most of the bundles of furs, but some small pieces of baggage were carried away. Many of the forty portages were no less treacherous than the tawny river, and some of them were more fatiguing than a day of paddling. All the while, for Jogues and Guillaume, was the added care of Raymbault, who suffered dreadfully in the dampness and exposure.

As they progressed, the danger of an Iroquois ambush increased. They knew that the enemy bands were lurking among the trees that bordered the water route. They were but four canoes, of twenty-three fighters, freighted down with baggage; they would have small chance against an unimpeded war party laying a surprise trap. They proceeded cautiously, scanning every inch of the bank, tensely alert at each turn of the river, fearful of the landings and the portages when they would be strung out and burdened, jumpy during the night camps. At any moment the dead silence might be raucous with the war-whoop. These were days of dread anticipation, of alarms. No one could know if hostile eyes were not peering at them from the forests, if Iroquois braves were not crouching low along the shore to leap on them. At many a point along the route they could remember the ambushes and massacres that had occurred within the past few years. Anywhere there might be another eruption of the Iroquois.

The last two weeks of June and the first week of July were passed amid these continual struggles and frights along the course of the Ottawa River. They emerged safely into the lake where the muddy floods of the Ottawa streak the green St. Lawrence, and struggled over the waste of waters to the passage behind the islands of Montreal. Here again were rapids and portages, here, too, were favorite stalking-places for the Iroquois. They crept stealthily through the wooded defiles, questioning each call of a bird or an animal, examining each bank and bush and tree. They debouched into the broad breast of the St. Lawrence. The river lay quiet and peaceful. They floated unmolested along its deserted banks until they came to the dangerous, narrow channel that cuts between the islands above Lake St. Peter. This alleyway, fringed with swamplands and overhung with trees, was an immemorial location for traps. They paddled prepared; but sighted no enemy. From the channel, much relieved, they emerged into the spaciousness of Lake St. Peter.

On July 17 the four canoes exultantly rounded the bend of the St. Lawrence and beached on the strand beneath Three Rivers. "At last, thirty-five days after our departure from the Hurons," wrote Jogues, "after continuous fears of attack by the enemy, after divers dangers, accidents, and shipwrecks, we arrived safely but very much fatigued at Three Rivers. Thence we went down to Kébec. We blessed God everywhere, in that His Goodness had preserved us." During the two or three days they remained at Three Rivers Jogues and Coûture were ordering the supplies and equipment they would take back to Sainte Marie, while the Hurons were trading their furs and skins for hatchets, cloth, blankets, and other French accessories. Embarked once more, refreshed in body and easy in mind, they paddled to Quebec and landed beneath the rock on the St. Charles side, not far from the residence of Notre Dame des Anges.

There was much for Jogues to do and to learn and to report while at Quebec. He delivered the written narrative of the Huron Relation and the other documents and letters to Father Vimont, the Superior of New France. He gave his oral report, the story of his comrades' heroic labors, of their notable converts, of the amazing change for the better among the Huron peoples, of the ceremonies at Sainte Marie, of the structure of the residence and the planning of the fort, of the obstacles still to be beaten down and the dangers still to be incurred, of his missionary expedition to Sault Sainte Marie and the hopes for the conversion of the western nations, of the crying need for more and more missionaries to carry through the glorious apostolate, more priests, more *donnés*, more workmen to go up into the Huron and the far Algonquin regions to spread the Gospel. Humbly he apologized for himself and his own imperfections, but begged, nevertheless, that he might be permitted to go back to Sainte Marie and spend all his life there in the service of God.

About his return, Vimont assured him, there was no doubt. But no other missioners could be spared for the Hurons that summer; not even Father de Brébeuf, who had recovered from his injuries and was on fire to go back to the Hurons. All the available priests were needed along the St. Lawrence. Vimont pointed out that no missioners came from France in 1641, and only one, an Italian, Father Francesco-Gioseppe Bressani, was expected that present summer. If this one arrived in time, Vimont conceded, he might be dispatched, but absolutely no one else. Besides, it was foolhardy to expose any of the Fathers to the danger of capture by the Iroquois. If it were not altogether necessary for Father Isaac himself to return, the Superior said, meaningly, he would be held at Quebec.

One other concession, Vimont agreed to make. After the cases of de Brébeuf and Raymbault, he deemed it necessary that a person skilled in surgery and medicine should be sent to Sainte Marie. There was a young *donné* named René Goupil, who had come over from France two years before with Guillaume Coûture, but who had been retained for work in the hospital at Quebec. Goupil was from Anjou, Vimont related, thirty-four years old. As a young man he had spent several months in the Novitiate of the Society in Paris, preparing for the priesthood, but had been forced to leave on account of ill-health, much to his own regret and that of the Jesuits. He turned to surgery as a career, and had some success in France. But he always longed to be a Jesuit, or to serve God in some spiritual capacity.

Goupil saw an opportunity in 1639, when the new class of *donnés* were being aggregated to the Society. His health was recovered by then, and he was accepted as a *donné* for the Huron mission. He was an invaluable man, Vimont confided. During two years he had labored tirelessly ministering to the French in their illnesses, and had devoted himself without stint to the care of the natives in the hospital in Quebec and in the near-by Algonquin reduction of Sillery. He was humble enough to perform the most menial tasks, and charitable beyond words. His zeal knew no bounds. He was always affable, perpetually good-humored, was simple and frank and generous, and pure-minded as an angel. All the Fathers and the French loved and esteemed him, while the savages trusted him implicitly.

With such a glowing recommendation, Jogues was eager to take René Goupil back with him to the Hurons. But he and Vimont agreed that René must be left totally free in his choice, to go or not to go. They held a conference with him, offered the proposition, and magnified rather than concealed the hazards of the journey, the danger of capture and death at the hands of the Iroquois, the hardships and terrible trials among the Hurons. René refused to be frightened by the recital. He answered that he had left France precisely for the purpose of laboring among the Hurons, that during the past two years he had been longing to be sent among them, that he was willing to face any dangers that Father Jogues and Coûture might encounter.

His face sparkled with the happiness of it and he accepted the proposal enthusiastically. As Vimont related: "When we spoke to him of going to the Hurons, his heart almost burst with joy at the thought of the dangers he was about to incur for the Master." And Jogues stated: "I cannot express the joy which this good young man felt when the Superior told him that he might prepare for the journey. Nevertheless, he well knew the dangers that await one upon the river; he knew how the Iroquois were enraged against the French. Yet, that could not prevent him, at the least sign of the will of Him to whom he had voluntarily committed all his concerns, from setting forth from Three Rivers."

Guillaume Coûture, likewise, was given his choice of remaining at Quebec or of returning. His heart was set on going back with Father Isaac. There were some complications, however, that had to be settled. When he left France in 1640 to become a *donné*, he was possessed of some property and income in Rouen. He had not been permitted to make a final disposition of this, even when he pledged himself to the Society. He was resolved, if he could secure the right, to make a full renunciation of his property and all his worldly possessions, to strip himself of everything for the service of God. A number of legal difficulties were in the way, and the Superiors of the Society were somewhat unwilling to be entangled in any controversies that might arise later. However, Coûture insisted on the renunciation and willed all that he possessed, without any provisos, to his mother in France. The matter was referred to Governor Montmagny, who gave his approval and legal sanction. Whereupon, Guillaume signed a further contract as a *donné*, by which he promised to labor without compensation and without seeking any gain in the Huron Mission, to be obedient to his Jesuit Superiors, to preserve chastity. He asked only in return his support and care by the Society, and a share in its spiritual riches.

Coûture and Goupil, in the words of Vimont, were *incomparables in leur genre.* They were a pride and a joy to Father Isaac, who appreciated deeply their zeal and piety and loyalty, their courage and their dependence in any emergency. All three, then, busied themselves at Quebec in preparing the supplies, in addition to those ordered at Three Rivers, that would be needed by the thirty-five residents at Sainte Marie for the coming year. There were rolls of cloth and blankets and wearing-apparel; there were essential foodstuffs and seeds for planting; medicines, salves, dried fruits, and sugar; axes, hatchets, saws, nails, awls, cement, and other building equipment; farm tools, muskets and ammunition for the *donnés* and workmen; sacks of wheat and barrels of wine for Mass, vestments, chalices, cruets, missals, wax, statues, and pictures for the chapel; bags of porcelain beads and trinkets, rings, pendants, ribbons, and such-like things to delight the savages; books, letters, and writing material. All these and a hundred other things had to be assembled and made ready to pack away into the tiny canoes and carried up the thousand-mile journey to Sainte Marie.

II

That July, Quebec was in a ferment over the good news which the ships from France had brought in regard to defense against the Iroquois. Jogues could relate how the Hurons were terrorized by this dreaded enemy, how powerless they were, how close was the danger of their total extermination. Vimont could tell the story of woe, as it affected the St. Lawrence. These incarnate fiends, he asserted, bitterly, were the scourge of the French and all the Algonquin nations up and down the River. So persistently and so brazenly had the Iroquois been carrying on the war, that they had driven whole families and tribes away from the French settlements. They had pursued the Algonquins far into the northern forests and into the mountains, so that they were rapidly decimating these peoples.

These Iroquois, Vimont reported, had become so insolent that they were raging about the newly established colony at Montreal. They were threatening to attack Three Rivers and then to make an onslaught on Quebec. They boasted that the Dutch, with whom they were allied, had pledged to help them in their war against the French. Whether that were true or false, affirmed Vimont, it was a fact that the Dutch were finally responsible for the supremacy of the Iroquois, since they supplied the Iroquois with muskets and ammunition. It was an outrage to put firearms in the hands of these barbarians, and those who did so, he declared, "deserve the punishment due to all the crimes which the avarice of the one party and the fury of the other have engendered."

Now, at last, the old country was beginning to understand the plight of New France. Two years before, Governor Montmagny had commissioned Father Charles Lalemant to represent the Iroquois menace to Cardinal Richelieu and the Company of One Hundred Associates. He suggested an ambitious plan whereby the Iroquois might be attacked in their own villages, and the Dutch, their abettors and allies, might be driven out of their settlements along the Hudson, on the basis that the area they occupied rightfully belonged to France. The Cardinal and the Company paid little heed to the appeal.

Last year, again, Governor Montmagny deputed Father Le Jeune to go to France and make further representations. He was to argue that, unless the Iroquois were effectually curbed, they would totally destroy the trade in furs; for they were preventing the Hurons from bringing down their peltries and were driving the Algonquins away from the French settlements, thus cutting off all the supplies. In addition, he was to insist that the Iroquois were so powerful that they could make it almost impossible for the French to remain in the New World.

Cardinal Richelieu was impressed. He appropriated the sum of 10,000 ecus for the erection of fortifications against the Iroquois, for vessels to patrol the St. Lawrence, and for offensive expeditions into the enemy lands. He made further donations for the building of the fort at Sainte Marie among the Hurons. In this he was visioning a new empire of France in the interior of the continent. So enthusiastic was he that he promised to contribute personally from his own funds, and to secure further grants from the public treasury. He assured Le Jeune and wrote to Governor Montmagny that he would dispatch, within a year or two, an adequate force of soldiers to garrison the forts and habitations along the St. Lawrence, to defend Sainte Marie, and to convoy the Huron traders the full length of their journey.

Governor Montmagny made ready to execute his plans of defense immediately that summer. Quebec was tolerably free from any incursions. Three Rivers, eighty-four miles up the St. Lawrence, was strong enough to repel attacks. Montreal, ninety miles beyond, then in the process of settlement, would soon be able to take care of itself. The Governor saw clearly that the primary defense for these three habitations and the effective method of keeping the St. Lawrence free of the Iroquois was the erection of a fortress halfway between Three Rivers and Montreal, on the south bank of the river, at the point where the River of the Iroquois empties into the St. Lawrence. This River of the Iroquois gave the enemy a direct water route from their villages into the French and Algonquin territory. A fort commanding its mouth would prevent the passage of Iroquois war parties and would cut off their retreat.

That spring of 1642, Montmagny and his engineers visited the location. They marked off a site for the proposed fort on the hill at the juncture of the two rivers. The name of Richelieu was bestowed on the fort and on the River of the Iroquois which flowed beneath it. Returned to Quebec, the Governor set his carpenters to work preparing the lumber for the first building and assembling the materials. In July, when the ships arrived, bringing the assurance of the Cardinal's appropriation, and more laborers and soldiers, and new equipment and guns, Montmagny resolved to begin building the fort that August so that it would be ready for occupancy by a detachment of soldiers before the winter set in.

Of this, Vimont wrote: "As soon as news came that fortifications were to be erected on the roads by which the Iroquois came, all fears were dispelled. Every one took courage once more and walked about with head erect and with as much assurance as if the Fort were already built. It is true that these fortifications will have an excellent effect. But, since they do not strike at the root of the evil, and since these barbarians carry on war in the fashion of the Scythians and Parthians, the door will not be fully opened to Jesus Christ and danger will not be warded off from our colony, until the Iroquois are either pacified or exterminated."

Jogues, obsessed singly by the welfare of the Hurons, rejoiced more heartily in the promise of aid for Sainte Marie and of soldiers to keep open the route to their country. His interests at Quebec, likewise, were those aspects which affected the natives rather than the progress of the French colonists. He spent as much time as he could at Sillery, the Christian village of St. Joseph, established some four or five miles from Quebec. This experiment was made possible by the generosity of the wealthy nobleman, Father Noël Brulard, Chevalier de Sillery, who had donated, three years previously, a sum sufficient for the formation of a Christian "reduction."

When Jogues visited it, he found thirty Algonquin and Montagnais families residing there, comfortably and contentedly. Their cabins were substantial, their fields were laid out and cultivated quite as well as those of the French. These Christian natives enjoyed equal privileges and rights with the French colonists. They were independent in the conduct of their own affairs, and free to follow their own tribal laws and customs. The Hospital nuns occupied a large cabin in the village and tended to the ailments of all, whether Christian or pagan. The Blackrobes had a residence and a roomy chapel in their midst. Under these religious influences, the natives advanced rapidly in the knowledge and exercise of the Faith. They thronged the services and faithfully confessed and received frequent Communion. They abandoned their superstitions, their spiritistic and diabolic rites; they accepted monogamy and sexual regularity. Such a community, Jogues reflected, could be established, within a year or two, nearby to Sainte Marie. With such Christians as Joseph, Charles, Eustace, Stephen, René, the foundation stones were ready at hand. Then, verily, would the Huron church flourish.

Father Jogues was keenly interested in two other establishments in Quebec, the Hôtel-Dieu of the Hospital Sisters and the school of the Ursuline nuns who had arrived three years before. The former were supported by the niece of Cardinal Richelieu, the Duchess d'Aiguillon. From the moment the three Sisters landed and took possession of their house near the fort, their services were in constant demand. The influenza epidemic was wearing itself out and the plague of small-pox was beginning to rage along the St. Lawrence. In the emergency, they slaved tirelessly for the French and natives alike. Their arrival at that time seemed to the French to be a miracle. By the natives they were revered as angels, and marvelous were the legends spread about them through all the nations.

The Ursulines owed their support to Madame Marie Madeleine de la Peltrie, a wealthy widow who devoted not only her goods but her life to the conversion of the natives. She brought with her to New France, Mère Marie de l'Incarnation, Mère Marie de St. Joseph, and Mère Cecile de Sainte Croix. They occupied a small, two-room dwelling at the base of the cliff, near the wharf and warehouses. In one room they lived, and in the other they housed and taught the native girls and instructed the daughters of the French. At first, the natives were loath to intrust their children to the nuns. Soon, they were fascinated by these white virgins; such virtue passed their comprehension; they concluded that the Mothers were more than human. Braves and squaws flocked to talk to them. The olive-skinned children loved them.

In 1642 the Ursuline school was crowded to capacity with fifty French and native girls. The new monastery near the summit of the rock was nearing completion. Father Jogues paid several visits to the little parlor down near the dock, and talked at length with Mother St. Joseph. She had special charge over the Huron girls, and spoke their language fluently. Within three years she had become famed and was generally referred to as the Mother of the Hurons. Under her care, during the past two years, was Theresa, the daughter of the saintly Joseph Chihwatenhwa and niece of Teondechoren.

Theresa was about thirteen years old. She was extraordinarily intelligent and spoke French easily. She had a gentility and a sweetness, yet a fire and determination that marked her off as an amazing personality. In her piety and good behavior the Ursulines saw in her a chosen spirit of God. Mother St. Joseph loved her dearly and treasured her. Laughingly, for she was almost always laughing, she told Father Jogues innumerable stories of Theresa's exploits. For example, she related, last winter Theresa was trying to persuade Paul Atondo and John Baptist Okhukwandoron to become Christians. "Theresa told them of God and the greatness of our mysteries with such gentle, natural eloquence inspired by the affection of her heart," said Mother St. Joseph, "that these good men were greatly touched by it, and one of their pleasures was to visit her from time to time." One of them, to tease her, on the eve of his baptism pretended that he could not believe what she told him and no longer intended to be baptized.

Theresa flamed out with a holy anger, Mother St. Joseph narrated, and berated him: "What are you thinking of doing, you wretch? What has muddled your brains? Do you wish to go to hell with the demons? Perhaps you will die tonight, and then you will find yourself with them before the day breaks. The devil has turned your head." The Huron remained apparently unmoved. Theresa ran disconsolate to Mother St. Joseph, crying: "He is lost. I am terribly sad. He will no longer believe in God. The devil has deceived him. He does not wish to go to heaven any more." Then, tossing her head back, she exclaimed: "If I could have broken through the grating I would have beaten him." The Huron confessed his deception, but Theresa had no confidence in him until Father de Brébeuf assured her that he was only joking.

Father Jogues could well affirm Mother St. Joseph's assertion that "no Huron came to Kébec without this young girl preaching to him."

He could relate what some of the Christians remarked: they did not know which to admire the most, a little Huron girl who preached to them about God and heaven and hell, or the holy virgins who had taught her and turned her thoughts toward heaven. Others had told him: "Theresa is so steadfast, so well taught, so beloved, so fervent in the Faith, that when one sees her, one would not imagine that she is a Huron. She will be the greatest mind among the Hurons when she shall return. The Mother who taught her is doubtless one of the greatest minds of France."

Theresa, it was decided, was to be brought back to her home in Ossossané that summer, in company with Father Jogues and her uncle, Joseph Teondechoren. She was disconsolate and the Ursuline Mothers were heartbroken. But all agreed that she was destined by God to be the successor of her father in the apostolate among the Hurons, and that now, when she was adolescent and still virginal, she should become the female confessor of the Faith.

Ten days had elapsed since Jogues arrived in Quebec. He and the Hurons were eager to be on their way homeward, especially since reports had come in that the Iroquois had, for some unknown reason, withdrawn from the upper St. Lawrence. He held his final conferences with Vimont and de Brébeuf, with Governor Montmagny and the French officials. Then he paid his last visit to Father Charles Raymbault. Together they had journeyed as far to the northwest of the continent as any white man. They had lived in closest intimacy for the winter at Sainte Marie. They had faced death together in their travel to Quebec. Raymbault was but a skeleton now. Within three months Father Vimont would be writing of his death: "Father Charles Raymbault, who had a heart greater than all his body, though he was of a great stature, had been ambitioning to find the way to China through the routes of our barbarous land; and God has now put him along the road to heaven." Death was in his eyes when Isaac said the last farewells; but both comrades knew that Isaac might meet death sooner.

They left Quebec on July 28. The original party was increased, in addition to Theresa, by Joseph Teondechoren's son, a lad of fourteen or fifteen, and another Huron boy, who had spent the winter at Quebec in the school conducted by Father de Brébeuf. René Goupil and another young Frenchman were having their first experience in the savage mode of travel. A few other Huron canoes attached themselves to the little flotilla. They beached at Three Rivers on Wednesday, July 30, much to the gratification of Father Jogues, who wished to celebrate the Feast of St. Ignatius in the chapel of the Immaculate Conception. There was deeper contentment in the soul of Isaac, after he had confessed to and counseled with Father Buteux. He revealed the warning and the pledge he believed he had received from God. Thus far, it had not been fulfilled; would there be some extraordinary trial besetting him on his homeward journey? He professed himself weak and fearful. Father Buteux listened, and strengthened him. All would be well, no matter what God sent.

The latest reports on July 31 counseled an immediate departure. The Iroquois were fled from the river. They feared the shallops and soldiers that were daily expected to begin the fortifications at Richelieu, so the rumors stated; they had seen some large ships sailing up beyond to the new French settlement at Ville Marie on the Island of Montreal; and so they had retreated and left the routes free for passage. Jogues hurried his preparations and the Hurons made ready their canoes and baggage.

Theresa, also, was deeply occupied, much to everyone's amusement and edification. She was lonely for her dear Mothers at Quebec, and insisted on writing a farewell letter. The Blackrobes supplied her with paper and ink. Joseph, Charles, and the other Hurons gazed at her in admiration; actually, she could paint talk and hear with her eyes, just like the Blackrobes and the Virgin Mothers at Quebec. Theresa spelled out in Huron words her letter: "My good mother, I am about to leave. I thank you for having taken such good care of me and for having taught me to serve God well. Is it for a little thing that I thank you? Never shall I forget it." She signed her name and made Father Du Peron swear that he would be sure to hand it to Mother St. Joseph.

About four in the morning, on August 1, Father Jogues said the Mass of St. Peter in Chains, with a commemoration of the Apostle St. Paul, and of the seven Machibee brothers, martyrs. In the oration he begged God to free him from the chains of sin, to exclude from him all evil, as Peter freed from his chains went forth free from harm. In the Epistle he read of Peter being cast into the dungeon, of having the chains stricken from him while he slept, and of the angel speaking to him and leading him forth from the prison. He passed to the Gospel side, and vibrantly proclaimed Peter's profession of Faith: "You are Christ, the son of the living God." He went on with the Mass, deeply moved, for it was the last that he would be able to celebrate for some weeks to come. Guillaume Coûture and René Goupil were the servers; Joseph, Charles, Eustace, Theresa and the other Christians were the congregation. Father Jogues fed himself the Blood of Christ and gave the Communion to those who were starting with him on the journey. After Mass, they prayed together that God might guard over them in all their ways.

The gray-blue of the dawn brooded over Three Rivers as they stepped from the Blackrobes' residence and turned to the left, along the road by the dark bulk of the fort, and descended the hill to the basin by the river bank. Twelve canoes were tied there, for some more Hurons had begged to be allowed to join themselves to the party of Eustace. There were now forty persons in the band: Father Jogues, Coûture, Goupil, and another Frenchman; Eustace Ahatsistari and his nephew Paul Onnonhoaraton; Charles Sondatsaa, Stephen Totiri, and another Stephen; Joseph Teondechoren, his son, his niece Theresa, his brother Peter Saoekbata, and another brother; a boy, an old man named Ondouterraon, two other old men, a young brave named Atieronhonk, and other warriors of various ages. Jogues and Coûture, with the help of their Christian friends, saw to the stowing away of their twenty and more bundles in the canoes. The Hurons made their last examinations of the canoes, balanced and floated them, and were ready for the start.

In accordance with immemorial custom, they haunched on the strand for their final council. They pledged to follow their chieftain, Eustace, decided on their route and their next camping-place, and roused one another to vigilance and courage should they be attacked. Ondessonk and Father Buteux, crouching in native fashion, exhorted them to trust in God and to be faithful to Him in everything that might befall. Ondouterraon, well over eighty years of age, but vigorous and influential in the councils, took up the thought and exclaimed: "What! I say, my brothers! Could there be any one of us who would cease from believing in God even though that one were burned by the enemies? We have embraced the Faith in order to be happy above, not here below on earth." All grunted and croaked in approval.

Each of the Christians spoke in turn, and pledged fidelity. One asserted that the thought of Paradise and the happiness promised him there would sweeten all the sufferings of torture. Another affirmed that the burning firebrands and the axes, heated red hot and hung about his neck or applied to his body, would remind him of the fire of hell in which sinners burn forever. At last Eustace Ahatsistari rose, towering above them. They looked up to him with pride, as their greatest chieftain and the terror of the Iroquois. He began:

My brothers, if I fall into the hands of the Iroquois, I cannot hope for life. But before I die I shall taunt them. I will ask them what the white-faced Europeans bring into their country? Some axes, some kettles, some blankets, some arquebuses; that is all. I will say to the Iroquois that these Europeans do not love them, for they conceal from them the most precious merchandise of all, that which the French palefaces give to us, but do not sell to us. I will tell them that the French come to us to tell us of a life eternal; of a God who has made all things; of a fire that is under the earth and is prepared for all those who do not honor God; of a place of happiness in heaven, a secure abode for our souls and for our bodies which will rise once more free from suffering. After that I will boast to them that this is my consolation, and I will dare them to inflict on me all their cruelties. I will tell them that they may apply all their tortures to me, that they may try to tear my soul out of my body, but that they cannot tear from my heart this hope and consolation that, after my death, I shall be supremely happy. That is what I shall preach to them while they are burning me.

Eustace paused, and then turned to his friend, Charles Sondatsaa:

My brother, if God should decree that I be captured by the enemy and that you should escape, when you shall return home to our country, go and visit my brothers and my kinsmen on my behalf. You will tell them that if they have any love for me, and still more for themselves, they must accept the Faith and must adore this Divine Majesty which is invisible to our eyes but which makes itself felt in the very depths of our souls, when we do not refuse to see its light and when we submit our wills to its commands. You will tell them that I am convinced of the truth of our Faith, and you will warn them that we shall be separated from each other forever if they do not become followers of God, of Him Who alone is my hope, and in Whom, wherever I may be, I wish to live and die.

It was the final word. Father Jogues and the other Frenchmen were thrilled almost to tears at the sincerity and the constant Faith of this man, the bravest of the Hurons, yet saintly beyond belief. The other warriors felt themselves aroused to newer courage and stronger fidelity. Then, concluding the council, they climbed into the canoes. Eustace led the way out of the inlet into the lapping waters of the St. Lawrence. The other eleven canoes rode after him and turned to the right. The morning was still cool and fresh as they rounded the arc of land that bellies out between Three Rivers and Lake St. Peter.

Along the shores of Lake St. Peter, despite the rumors that no Iroquois enemies were about, they were most vigilant and alert. They scanned, without the interlude of one moment, the wrinkling waters which sparkled to their left and the shrouded shore-line that stretched to their right. All through the day they paddled steadily on past the green hillocks and the sandy beaches and the mouths of the streams and little rivers and the tiny waterfalls, until, in the early evening, when the warm August sun was sinking before them, they turned in among the sedges at the far end of the lake, near to the marshy islands that spread out from the north bank. They had covered upwards of twenty-eight miles. Jogues narrated: "The first day has been favorable to us."

They held council that evening. Two routes lay open for the morrow, one around the islands of Lake St. Peter, in the open waters of the St. Lawrence; the other through the defile of the north channel between the mainland and the islands. The former was longer and brought them into clear view of the Iroquois bank of the river and the mouth of the Richelieu River; but it was secure against ambush. The latter was direct and easier to paddle but it was extremely dangerous, for it lent itself to traps. Nevertheless, the Hurons decided to chance it. They were fairly certain that no large Iroquois forces were in the vicinity. And so, with some sense of security, Jogues and his comrades laid themselves on the turf and slept through the night.

III

Dawn filtered through the leaves. The Hurons awoke and, as stealthily as the dawn itself, moved about preparing the corn-mush of their breakfast and readying the canoes for the day's journey.

Father Jogues gathered them about him, and in hushed voices they commended themselves to God. A golden sun flooded over Lake St. Peter and set the clouds on fire. It presaged a day of heat. Eustace Ahatsistari gave the signal, the twelve canoes crept out of the inlet and, bunched closely together, cautiously paddled through the spears of water-reed that almost netted the surface of the lake near the shore. They struck out more rapidly across the deeper waters of the open spaces and made toward the mouth of the channel through the islands. A mile beyond, they doubled a finger of land that protruded from the mainland and cut through the marsh grass that fringed it about.

A brave growled a low warning. Eustace twisted the paddle and halted the canoe. The others stopped dead. Every brave seized his bow and arrow. All eyes searched the shores and the inlet. Eustace nosed his canoe toward a patch of greenish clay, and was followed by two or three other canoes. Guardedly they slipped over the rim of the boats, holding their bows and tomahawks gripped for fight. Where the water lapped along the mire they saw the lines left in the soft mud by the ridges of a few canoes. They found the imprints of naked feet in the clay beyond. They noted the weeds trampled down, and near by some broken twigs. All agreed that these were fresh tracks, made that morning, even. Were they made by friends, Algonquins or Hurons? Or were they the footprints of Iroquois?

Some of the braves pointed out the distinguishing marks of the toes and heels; they were Iroquois. Others said no. They turned to Eustace, who stood staring at the tracks. "My brothers," he said, finally, "as far as I can judge them, these footprints are those of our enemies. But there are not more than three canoes of them. Be they friends or enemies, it does not matter. We are sufficient in number; we need have no fear of such a band of our enemies. Let us advance, and not be frightened by them."

They accepted his verdict and climbed back into the canoes. Eustace led the way with slow, deliberate strokes, toward the point where the banks closed in on the channel. The twelve canoes were forced to string out in a file in the narrowing stream. The shores were heavily wooded and bushy. Beyond was a projecting peak of the mainland, a treacherous spot, which forced Eustace to swerve over toward the island. They rounded it cautiously, then swung back toward the right shore.

For half a mile or so this was an open swamp land, from which a line of trees circled back in an arc. The marsh was green with weeds and flat, broad leaves and spears of tall grass. Along its fringe the water was stagnant and covered with scum; over to the left, toward the island, the current bucked down strongly. Eustace steered his canoe over close to the swamp, out of the current; Joseph, Charles, and Stephen guided their boats after him; the others strung out more loosely to the rear. They felt safe abreast of the marsh, but they were apprehensive of a spot to the left, half a mile on, where there was a little cross-channel between the first and second islands.

War-whoops split the air. Grotesque faces, bodies streaked with blood-red paint, erupted from the cover of the swamp. Thirty Iroquois stood among the waist-high weeds, took aim, blazed with their muskets. Balls whistled through the air, cracked against the canoes, spit in the water. Eustace and the Hurons shrilled the battle-cry of defiance. In an instant they let fly a volley of arrows, then shot the canoes toward the swamp. War-whoops from both bands mingled and rang and trebled in blood-curdling uproar. Above the din rose the mighty voice of Eustace: "Great God, to You alone do I look for help." Father Jogues lifted himself to his knees and with his arm making the sign of the cross, shouted the words of absolution over his people.

Atieronhonk, the pilot of his canoe, crouching just in front of him, was pierced in the hand by the first volley. He was the only one in the boat who was not a Christian. Jogues asked him if he wanted baptism. Yes, he answered. The Father cupped the water in his hand and sprinkled it over the head of the man, baptizing him Bernard. Another volley of shots sprinkled about them. The canoe smashed against the shore. Jogues felt himself catapulted into the weeds.

He rose to his knees and looked about. Only the five or six Huron canoes in the vanguard were caught in the fusillade. The others were still some distance downstream. They twisted about and violently paddled away from the battle, in flight, carrying with them the fourth Frenchman. They disappeared around the projecting spear of the mainland. Eustace and his close friends, Coûture and Goupil, alone were left to face the enemy. They were outnumbered two to one. They waited on the defensive among the reeds, crouched for the onslaught of the Iroquois. Undaunted, they shrieked their war-whoops. Eustace crept up the slippery marsh against the enemy.

His warriors followed his lead. The Iroquois stealthily retreated back toward the dry ground near the trees and spread out in a surrounding arc. Arrows and spears hurtled from band to band. The braves on both sides singled out opponents for a hand-to-hand clash.

Up from the river shrilled another chorus of war-whoops, ear-piercing, triumphant. Eustace and his followers looked down toward the swamp in amazement. Six, seven, eight canoes, loaded with forty Iroquois, bore down on the fringe of the shore. They had been lurking an eighth of a mile up, in the hidden passage between the two islands. With barbaric outcries they scrambled among the weeds and grass of the swamp and advanced to close in the rear of the Hurons and French. Eustace leaped at the enemies on the firmer ground before him, wielding his tomahawk fiercely at the warriors encircling him. Joseph lumbered after him, breathing heavily, warding off his attackers with difficulty. Charles was beset with enemies, as was Stephen, while Eustace's nephew, Paul, raged viciously, darting and lunging at his nearest opponent. Brawny Coûture cleared a path through the Iroqouis and gained the cover of the trees. Goupil fought clumsily against his aggressors, and was lost in the knots of fighters who by now were strewn all over the marsh and up among the trees.

Father Jogues lay concealed among the weeds where he had been dumped from the canoe. He saw the desertion of the rear boats; he watched the battle of Eustace and his comrades recede from the shore; in terror he witnessed the wild dash of the Iroquois reinforcements. He was a priest, forbidden to engage in war and bloodshed. Agonized, he prayed God to save his children from the fury of the enemy. In an anguish of soul he spied from his hiding-place. René Goupil was down, and the Iroquois were on him. A Huron fell, then another and another, and the enemies were gathered about them like ravening beasts, roaring in triumph.

All was lost. Sitting there in the soft clay, he was completely concealed by the stalks of the grass and the flat leaves of the weeds. He could escape detection if he remained motionless. All the Iroquois had passed by him and were engaged a hundred feet beyond. He could crawl through the weeds and gain the trees where they came down to the bank over by the left side. There was a chance to escape that way. He was a swift runner, and could outdistance the fleetest of the natives.

He brushed aside the thought impatiently. It could not be. "Most assuredly I could conceal myself here among the grasses and reeds," he argued within himself, "and perhaps free myself from the danger of capture. But how could I ever be able to abandon even one of our Frenchmen, or any one of the Hurons who are already captured or who might be captured, especially those who are not baptized?" He was a priest of God. The thought of escape was horrible to him. "Could I think for a moment of abandoning our French and deserting these good neophytes and catechumens, without giving them the help and consolation that the Church of my God has entrusted to me? Never, never could that be," he told himself. "It is necessary, it must be, that my body suffer the fires of this earth in order to deliver these souls from the flames of hell. It must be that my body die a death that passes in order to obtain for these a life that is eternal."

He lifted himself up and stood boldly among the reeds. Calling out to the Iroquois who was standing guard over Goupil, he walked confidently through the stalks and oozy clay. The Iroquois, fearing some trick, raised his javelin to his shoulder, ready to hurl it. Jogues halted and stretched out his arms in surrender. He called out again in Huron; but the guard stood poised, afraid that more enemies might start up from the weeds. Other Iroquois crouched for an attack. "Come on, do not be afraid!" Father Jogues shouted to them. "Take me prisoner! Put me with the Frenchman and the Hurons whom you have captured!"

Still doubtful about this amazing apparition of the Blackrobe, the Iroquois guard advanced stealthily, warily. He sprang on Jogues and bore him to the earth. Other Iroquois leaped on him, and beat him. They stripped off his black robe, pulled him to his feet, then dragged him to where the prisoners were huddled. One of them began to tie the leather thongs about his ankles. Jogues drew his legs away: "No, no," he told them. "You don't need to bind me. These French and Hurons whom you have taken, they are the bonds that will keep me captive. I won't leave them till death. I will follow them everywhere. You can be assured of my person as long as any one of them remains among you as a prisoner."

So emphatically did he speak, and so much as a master, that the Iroquois refrained from binding his feet and hands. Jogues, thus free, leaned over to René Goupil who lay stretched on the ground, tied so tightly he could not move. He threw his arms about René and whispered: "My dear brother, God has acted strangely toward us. But He is the Lord and Master. What is good in His eyes, that has He done. As it has pleased Him, so be it. Blessed be His Holy Name forever."

"O my Father," answered René. "God indeed be blessed. He has permitted it. He has willed it. His holy Will be done. I love it, I cherish it, I embrace it with all the strength of my heart."

Ondessonk spoke to the Hurons lying stolidly and silently bound. Joseph and Charles and Stephen and Paul and the newly baptized Bernard were among them. He spoke to them all kindly, urging them to take courage, to be of good faith. God was still with them. The old men, Theresa, and the two boys had been corralled from the canoes and marsh, and were joined to the other captives. They sat near by in terror. Jogues mingled with them and spoke words of consolation. He counseled the few captives who were pagans that they should be baptized, for it was likely that the Iroquois might strike them down. They consented, and he squeezed a few drops of water from his wet garments while he pronounced the sacred words. Meanwhile the Iroquois were leading in more prisoners who had tried to escape through the thicket of the forests.

A hubbub came from the woods; it grew louder; it swelled to a tumult of screams and shouts. A large band burst into the open, wildly exultant, leading Eustace. He was covered with blood, his bulging arms and shoulders were circled round with leather straps. The Iroquois had recognized him: Ahatsistari, the great war chief of the Hurons, the one Huron above all others they sought to capture. Eustace walked undaunted among the rabble of his foes, contemptuous of them, as if they did not exist.

Father Jogues almost swooned with grief when he recognized Eustace. This great warrior, this leader of the Christians, now a prisoner, would certainly be slaughtered though all the others were spared. So overwhelming was his sorrow, that Jogues could never remember what he said as he rushed to Eustace and embraced him. Even thus, Eustace was stolid. "Ah, my Father," he said to Ondessonk, "I swore to you a holy oath, and protested to you that I would remain faithful to you whether I lived or whether I died." They tore Ondessonk away and cast Ahatsistari to the earth, where they further secured him, for he was a dreaded foe, even though bound by a dozen thongs.

In the early stages of the battle, Guillaume Coûture had fought his way, step by step, through the enemy. The Iroquois wanted to take their prisoners alive, but so dexterously did Coûture ward them off that he reached the cover of the forests. He looked about him. The Hurons were routed and fleeing in all directions. He had better fend for himself. He darted, suddenly, down an open trail through the trees. The Iroquois ran after him, and hurled their hatchets and javelins; but he zigzagged through the shrubs and soon had outdistanced them. He was free. In the silence of the woods, he paused in his flight for breath. He had cast off his pursuers. It would not be difficult to make his way back to Three Rivers.

He was free, but what about Father Isaac and Goupil? They were certainly captured. They would probably be tortured and burned to death. A terrible thought struck Guillaume, like a firebrand: "I, am I to be a deserter? Shall I abandon my dear Father who has been captured by the Iroquois? Shall I escape without him? No! never in this world! What, could I ever be such a coward as to continue in flight and desert my Father in his need? How would I ever have the courage to show myself without him either at Three Rivers or up among the Hurons? Shall I be so in love with this life that I should prefer to preserve it and thus lose this wonderful occasion which God offers me, to give it back to Him, for His glory? No, a thousand times no! I must retrace my steps. I must face the same risks as Father Jogues and my good comrade, René Goupil. I cannot abandon my Father. I wish to die with him. I am willing and glad to suffer the fire and the rage of these tigers for the love of Jesus Christ, in the company of Father Jogues."

Coûture loaded his arquebus, then started back. He spotted the five Iroquois who had pursued him. They saw him at the same moment. The chief raised his musket; Coûture instinctively threw up his. The gun of the Iroquois missed fire; but Coûture's barked, and his bullet pierced the heart of his assailant. Before he could move a step, the other four enemies were on him and pinned him to the earth. Like maniacs they pounded him and stripped off his clothes, kicked and stamped on him, beat him with their fists and the butts of their muskets. They knocked him senseless, then revived him by pulling out his finger nails with their teeth. One of them jammed a long knife through the palm of his hand. When they had satisfied their first rage, they bound his arms to his body and hobbled his feet, and thus hurried him to the camp.

Jogues heard the heraldings of this new triumph joined with the wails of lamentation. The four Iroquois, carrying the limp body of their chief, and dragging a new prisoner, emerged from the woods. He looked closely at the victim but so covered with blood was he that he could not be recognized. Then he knew it to be Guillaume. He broke through the guard and, rushing out, threw his arms about Coûture's neck. "Have courage, my dear Guillaume, have courage, my dear brother and friend," he sobbed. "It is now that I cherish you, now that I love you more than ever before; for the Divine Goodness has done you the favor of suffering for God's holy Name. Let not this beginning of pain and anguish shake your constancy. The torments will be terrible; but they will soon be over; and the glory which follows will never end."

"Have no fear, Father dear," Guillaume answered. "God in His mercy has given me too much of His favors and grace. I never deserved them, and I do not now deserve the strength and the consolation that I feel within me. But I believe that He who has helped me thus far will continue to help me. Pray for that grace for me, Father."

The Iroquois stood about bewildered when they saw Ondessonk throw his arms about their captive and kiss him. Then, of a sudden, they understood; the Blackrobe was praising Ihandich for killing their chief. The impudence of it maddened them. They tore Ondessonk away and beat him with insane fury, with clubs and muskets, about the head and shoulders, until he sank to the earth. They kicked him and jumped on him till he was insensible. The four Iroquois passed on, but others took up the bloody revenge. Two younger men, especially, grasped his arms and clenched the nails of his forefingers in their teeth. They tugged and yanked till they drew the finger nails from their sockets. They took each of his forefingers in their mouths, and ground and crushed them with their teeth until the fingers were a jelly of blood and flesh and splinters of bone.

Others did the same with Goupil. It was the French whom they hated, they kept shrieking in this new frenzy that was on them. It was the French who were their greatest enemies. They offered peace to the French, and the French had answered by firing guns at them. They had been waiting a full year to capture some French. Now they had French prisoners. They would burn and torture them, they would eat their white flesh.

Two hours and more had thus passed since the first attack. The Iroquois who had been pursuing the Hurons through the woods were all re-assembling. They rejoiced and exulted over their great victory. They had taken three Frenchmen alive, one of them Ondessonk, the Blackrobe. They had captured Ahatsistari, the Huron chief, who was feared everywhere in the Iroquois villages. They had been forced to kill only two Hurons. They held twenty-three captives, most of whom could be tortured and burned. In addition, they had the canoes, all of them heavily loaded with baggage. It was a great victory, and they were swollen with the pride of it.

The Iroquois were eager to flee away from the battle scene. Algonquin war parties might be scouting in the neighborhood and be attracted by the musket shots and war-whoops. The fugitives might mass and plan a counter attack, or they might spread the alarm. Hurriedly, then, the victors assembled the Huron canoes, some of which they manned, distributed the booty, and packed in among them the prisoners. About nine in the morning, they were embarked. They fired a volley of shots over the marsh, in honor of their great deity, the sun, and chanting their song of triumph, swung their flotilla up the channel. A few hundred yards beyond, they swerved to the left through the covert between the islands in which the eight canoes of the reinforcements had lain concealed. Their route was a tortuous succession of windings through reedy swamps, fields of marsh grass, and green-scummed waters that stagnated in the maze of islands. Sometime after midday, they shot from the narrow alleys into the open, wide sweep of the St. Lawrence. Here they were free from attack and pursuit.

They beached their twenty canoes in a shallow lagoon and camped in a grove on the rising bank of the island. There the seventy Iroquois held council and each boasted of his prowess in the morning's battle. They awarded the captives to the chiefs and distributed the plunder. Their eyes sparkled avariciously, for never before had they captured such a rich prize. Twenty sacks, belonging to the French, of muskets and ammunition, of hatchets and axes and kettles, of blankets and cloths, of firewater and sweets, of wampum beads and jewelry, and of nameless other articles. And then, as many more sacks containing the baggage of the Hurons. They rejoiced with great shouts and ringing laughter as they slit open the bags and fought for their shares of the spoils.

Father Jogues, while the Iroquois were so engrossed, went to and fro among the captives, for he was left untrammeled, though all the other men were bound tightly and pinioned to the earth. He was still quivering with the pain of his mangled fingers and bruises, but his thought was of the others. He carried water to them, to slake their thirst and wash away the blood. He eased them in their minds by his words of encouragement. Goupil suffered, but showed no signs of it. Rather, he was elated that he was chosen to bear pain for his Lord, and kept muttering ejaculations of praise and thanksgiving to God. Coûture was quieter and more stolid. Jogues could not restrain his regrets; Guillaume should have escaped; he should not have returned to add himself to the miserable victims; it was an unneeded sacrifice. But Coûture was stubborn; he could not be a deserter, a coward; his duty was to remain with Father Isaac and René; he had pledged himself to fidelity till death. Father Jogues blessed Guillaume, and thanked God for him.

René called Father Jogues' attention to one of the old men, a jovial, sharp-tongued fellow who would likely irritate the Mohawks. The man had not yet been baptized, and it might possibly happen that he would be the victim chosen by the Iroquois as a blood sacrifice before they left their camp. Ondessonk persuaded the old man to accept baptism, and with it the promise of a happy life after death.

Eustace and his comrades remained motionless and stoical. To show any slightest sign of feeling, to be fearful of the Iroquois, to betray that they suffered, that was to be a squaw and a poltroon. They recognized the Iroquois, they told Ondessonk, as belonging to the Mohawk nation, the most savage of the five confederated peoples, and the strongest, since they dwelt nearest the Dutch and were well supplied with firearms. They were bitter especially against one of the leaders of the band, an ex-Huron, whom Jogues also remembered. He was known as Mathurin's man, for he had served that *engagé* in some capacity or other. About the time Mathurin left the Huron country to return to France, his man was captured by the Iroquois and was adopted by them. He it was who had plotted the trap for his own people that morning. He gloated over his former friends with the bitterness of the pervert, and roused the other Iroquois especially against Ondessonk and the French, whom he hated vindictively.

The Mohawks finished their council and the division of the booty. They herded the unbound captives to the boats and lugged down the braves. The old man whom Father Jogues had just before baptized refused to stir from where he was sitting. The Mohawks prodded and dragged him, but he protested and fought back at them, all the while deriding them. "Why should an old man like myself go visiting lands that are foreign and distant?" he asked them. "I intend to stay here just where I am. I'm too old to change my home and accustom myself to life among you Iroquois. If you don't want to spare my life, I am willing to find my death here. It won't be much of a disadvantage to lose my life, anyway." They took him at his word. Scarcely had he finished speaking when one of the braves smashed his skull and scalped him. Father Jogues rejoiced in the sorrow, for the waters of baptism had scarce dried on his head.

The twenty canoes struck across the St. Lawrence toward the headlands of the south bank. They slid up to the lip of land that stretched out at the mouth of their river, turned it, and with a few more strokes came to the strand on the left bank. They were now altogether safe from pursuit, for they were in their own undisputed territory and in one of their strongholds. They mounted the steep hill from the river, driving the prisoners before them. Here they would rest for the night.

A hundred paces from their fires, toward the brow of the hill, were the marks left by the French engineers as the site of the proposed Fort Richelieu. The Mohawks were affronted at the impudence of the French. They would leave the record of their victory and their challenge for the French to see. In the twilight, they stripped off a sheet of bark from one of the trees and on it they painted their vaunt. One of them drew in blood-red color the faces of Father Jogues, Coûture, Goupil, Eustace, Joseph, Charles, and the more distinguished prisoners. In smaller sketches, they pictured the lesser victims, and Theresa and the boys. All of these twenty-two heads were in crimson to indicate that they were still alive and destined for the fires. Three heads were in black, to show the number of those killed. They chose a huge tree on the brink of the hill on which to hang their placard, so that all who passed might read of the Iroquois victory, and tremble.

CHAPTER VIII

Along the Trail of Torture

I

BLACKER than the night was the grief within the soul of Father Jogues. He lay among the captive Hurons, under the watchful eyes of the Iroquois guard. He could not sleep. His head was bursting. God, in His mysterious designs, had once more permitted the Church among the Hurons to be destroyed. All the Christian leaders were stricken, Eustace, Joseph, Charles, Stephen, Peter, Paul, little Theresa. He had hoped so much; they were to be the apostles in the coming winter. They were captured, they would be murdered. Scarcely one Christian chief was left among the Hurons. Coûture and Goupil, who were needed so much at Sainte Marie, they were captives, too. All the supplies for the mission, the clothing, the food, the tools, the books and letters, all were taken by the Iroquois.

Everything was gone. It was ruin. Jogues stared dully at the branches above him and the patches of dark sky. Oftentimes tears flooded his eyes and he sobbed. This day was a day of doom for the Huron Mission. His Hurons and his two French comrades must suffer more, must be tortured and burned to death. No power on earth could save them, only God. He was in anguish because of them. He prayed God to give them strength, to keep them faithful. He begged strength for himself, that, being strong, he might help and console them. He knew he himself must suffer, but he cared not for that. Willingly would he accept all the tortures and any death if he could but free them. He had asked God to take him and do what He wished with him. He had had his prayer answered. *Esto robustus,* the Lord told him in the chapel at Sainte Marie. But his comrades, he had not asked pain for them.

Thus shaken with grief and shivering from the ache in his fingers, he waited for the dawn. The Mohawks roused the camp with shouts, and soon were driving the caravan down the hill to the canoes. On the river they wakened far echoes with their lusty chants of victory. It was a narrow stream, as wide as a musket-shot across, and glassy and straight-flowing. About midday, they portaged across a rapids, and then rowed past the tree-laden banks for another few hours till they came to a green-clad island on which they pitched their camp. The dull monotony of the river and the steady pull of the boats continued through the next day. A mountain towered up and was left behind. Smaller rapids forced them to carry the baggage and canoes over the slippery rocks. A wide lake, of cascades and frothing foam, was circled. The third day dawned and the fourth, and still they were inclosed in the alleyway of the river, progressing mile by mile to the south, nearer and nearer to the Mohawk lands.

The heat stifled them. The wounded fingers of Jogues and Goupil and Coûture festered and bred worms and attracted flies and insects. They had no remedies, no cloth for bandages, nothing for relieving the pain but the tepid waters of the river. All day long they were cramped in the little boats; at night they had no rest from the mosquitoes and bugs that stung them all over their naked skin. Even more unendurable were the petty torments perpetrated by the young braves. Sometimes in sudden fury, then again in cold blood, and then, laughingly, in sport, they would seize the palefaces by their hair or beard and drag them about the camp. They would deliberately pluck out their whiskers and the hair on the body, and would scratch the white flesh with their finger nails, and pinch the body in the most delicate parts, and scrape the scabs from the wounds.

To Father Jogues, such persecutions were not the most harrowing. "Much more was I shaken by the interior anguish," he laments, "when I saw this funereal procession of our Christians led before my very eyes, this cortège of death in which were the five tried Christians, the sustaining columns of the Church among the Hurons. Indeed, and I confess it honestly, time and time again I could not restrain my tears, grieving over the lot of these poor Hurons and of my French comrades, and worrying terribly about the things that might happen in the future. I had before my eyes continually the sight of the door of the Christian Faith among the Hurons and other innumerable nations closed by these Iroquois, unless it might be opened by a most extraordinary dispensation of Divine Providence. This thought made me die every hour, in the depth of my soul. It is a hard thing, more, it is a cruel thing, to bear, that of seeing the triumph of the demons over whole nations redeemed with so much love, and paid for in the money of a Blood so adorable."

From the time of their capture, Father Jogues urged the Hurons and French to watch their chances to escape. The Hurons needed no advice, for that was their law and way. Coûture and Goupil would not hear of it, unless Father Isaac made the attempt with them. Coûture flatly refused; he was bound under obedience to Father Jogues, he admitted; but his duty was just as clear to him as when he decided to surrender himself after the battle. He would not desert. Goupil was equally emphatic. He told Father Isaac "he would commit himself in everything to the will of Our Lord; and Our Lord inspired him with no thought of doing what Father Jogues proposed."

Jogues and Goupil had the consolation of being together in the same canoe, for they had been assigned to the same master. "Upon the road," Jogues relates, "René was always occupied with God. His words and the discourses that he held were all expressive of submission to the commands of Divine Providence, and showed a willing acceptance of the death which God was sending him. He gave himself to God as a sacrifice, to be reduced to ashes by the fires of the Iroquois, which that good Father's hand would kindle. He sought the means to bless Him in all things and everywhere." Goupil was the soul of gentleness, continues Father Jogues, whose love and admiration grew, for "covered with wounds as he himself was, he dressed the wounds of other persons, of the enemies who had received some blows in the fight as well as those of the prisoners. He opened the vein for a sick Iroquois. And he did it all with as much charity as if he had done it to persons who were his best friends."

About the third or fourth day on the river, as they sat huddled together in the canoe, René said, hesitatingly: "My Father, God has always inspired me with a burning desire to consecrate myself to His holy service by the vows of religion in His holy Society. All the time up to this hour, my sins have made me unworthy of this grace. Nevertheless, I hope that Our Lord will be pleased with the offering which I wish to make to Him. My Father, I wish to pronounce now, in the best sentiments that I can have, the vows of the Society of Jesus, in the presence of my God and before you."

Father Jogues felt like weeping with joy. No one was worthier than Goupil to be his brother in the Society of Jesus. René had been a novice, and would have long ago recited his vows except for his ill-health. That disability was cured, now, and there was no possible reason to prevent him from entering the Society. Every reason approved of René's request. And so, in the name of the Father Provincial of France, Father Jogues gave René permission to pronounce the vows of the Temporal Coadjutor in the Society of Jesus. René knew the formula well, for oftentimes in anticipation he had repeated it in the secrecy of his heart. On this day of grace, while he sat almost naked in the canoe, surrounded by the Mohawk savages, in a low tense voice he pronounced the words which bound him:

Almighty everlasting God, I, René Goupil, altogether most unworthy in The Divine Sight, yet trusting in Thy Goodness and Infinite Mercy, and moved with a desire of serving Thee, vow before the most sacred Virgin Mary, and the whole court of heaven, to Thy Divine Majesty, perpetual Poverty, Chastity and Obedience, in the Society of Jesus, and promise that I will enter into the same Society, forever to lead my life therein, understanding all things according to the Constitutions of the same Society. Therefore, I most humbly beseech Thee, by Thy Infinite Goodness and Mercy, that thou wilt vouchsafe to admit this holocaust in an odor of sweetness, and that as Thou hast already given me grace to desire and offer it, so Thou wilt bestow plentiful grace on me to fulfill it, Amen.

Father Jogues accepted Brother Goupil's vows in the name of the Society, and blessed him. Most truly now were they brothers in God, linked closely by the vows of religion until death, and then beyond in the life in heaven.

Thus far, the Huron captives had not been molested by the Mohawks. Between them brooded a cold, sullen hatred which occasionally flared up into threats on one side and defiance on the other. Eustace, as befitted his dignity, was especially arrogant and supercilious. He boasted of the Iroquois he had massacred; the Iroquois, in furious rages, piled up the list of horrors they would do to him when they began his torture. Jogues was fearful lest some one of the Mohawks might strike Eustace down. He arranged a sign for such a crisis: if Eustace felt himself in danger of being killed, he was to raise his hand to his breast, or lift his eyes heavenward; that would mean he was sorry for his sins, and Father Jogues would give him absolution.

All the Hurons grew fonder of Ondessonk day by day. Stripped of his black robe, he was a true Huron, not the evil sorcerer such as they had once accused him of being. The most devoted of all was Atieronhonk, whom Jogues had baptized at the first volley. The man could not get over his astonishment: "It must be admitted that these people who come to instruct us," he argued to himself and to all who would listen, "have no doubt whatever of the truths they teach us. It must be that God alone is their reward. There is Ondessonk. He forgot himself at the moment of danger. He thought only of me, and spoke to me of becoming a Christian. The musket balls whistled past our ears, death was before our eyes. He thought only of baptizing me, and not of saving himself. He did not fear death. But he did think that I would be lost forever if I died without baptism."

On the fifth day of the journey, the flotilla burst into the expanding surface of Lake Champlain. Islands, large and small, rose irregularly around, and the shore line was ragged with bays and promontories. Since the boats were heavy with people and baggage, the Mohawks kept close within the calmer waters near the bank. The heat of the day scorched them, the ceaseless paddling hour by hour fatigued them. They ordered the Huron captives to take their places with the paddle, and tried to make Ondessonk also use the blade. Much to their amazement, he refused absolutely to paddle. Though they were enraged, he would not submit. Goupil, thinking that he might substitute for Father Isaac, began wielding the paddle. The Mohawks interpreted this in their own manner; they had forced one Frenchman to work, so they renewed their threats and blows on the other one, to make him also obedient. René was confused and wretched, for he understood that he had only brought new persecutions on Father Jogues.

In a ceaseless grind, under a blistering sun, the Mohawks drove on and on down the length of the lake. All the captives knew what was to be the end of their journey. The Hurons had tortured and burned and eaten Iroquois; they would be treated in the same manner. Father Jogues had been nauseated to death by the tortures of the Iroquois he had witnessed in Teanaustayaé and Ossossané; his own people, his Christians, would now be the holocaust, together with Coûture and Goupil. He cared nothing for his own fate, for he had asked for extraordinary sufferings for the love of God; he prayed only for the needed strength and courage. The panorama of the lake passed on before his eyes, the shores more rugged, the hills higher, the mountains far off to the right and the left like blue and purple clouds humping along the skyline. There was no release, no hope of pardon, no mercy on the part of their cruel masters. They were wholly in the power of these demons. They were doomed.

If only Coûture and Goupil would try to escape, Father Jogues thought, he could bear his own sufferings more easily. If Eustace and the others could only slip away like Atieronhonk, who managed to elude the guard one night and disappear in the forests. But his escape increased the vigilance of the Iroquois and they watched the other prisoners more narrowly. It came Saturday morning, August 9, the eighth day since the battle, and there lay before them the weariness of another day upon the lake.

A canoe appeared. It approached and brought good news. A large band of warriors, two hundred of them, were encamped on an island a day's journey along the lake. The Mohawks were overjoyed; they could exhibit their prisoners in triumph and get food, for their corn was practically gone. They spurted their strokes more rapidly and sped eagerly along the shores. In the late afternoon they spied the island and saw the spiral of smoke curling in the pale sky. The Mohawks chanted their triumphal hymn as they drew near the island which was set off about a mile from the shore. They beat time with the stroke of the paddle alternately against the water and the sides of the canoe. They prodded the Hurons and forced them to stand up in the canoes and sway and sing. The canoes came abreast of the beach on the island. They halted. They burst out into a chorus, part chant, part incantation, cocked their muskets, and fired a volley into the air, in homage to the sun.

They landed and hurled the prisoners into the shallow waters and on the sand. The Mohawks of the other band leaped on the victims, beating and pounding them, tearing them almost to shreds. This was the first caress, in a *mêlée* of shouts and war-whoops. They pushed Theresa and the boys aside, and corralled the three Frenchmen and the Huron braves. They would whet their lust for blood on these; they would offer these as a sacrifice to the god of war so that they might draw new courage from their victims and give such thanks to their deities that they would be blessed with capturing more prisoners. The welcome became organized after the first wild outburst. The victorious party rescued their prisoners from the mob. The other two hundred warriors armed themselves with clubs and switches of thorny rods, and lined in two parallel columns, a few feet apart, up along the slope of the hill that ascended from the beach.

The prisoners were stripped totally naked, and whipped into file. The old men were placed at the head, for they would set a slower pace. The stronger Hurons were interspersed with the weaker. Coûture was in the forefront; Goupil in the middle; and Jogues, as the greatest in dignity was held as the last, so that his punishment might be the greatest. The signal was given. The first of the Hurons was driven between the lines of Iroquois. He ran blindly, while the executioners pounded down blows on his head and body and legs. Another Huron was fed in; the shrieks grew diabolical; Coûture rushed into the midst of the whirling clubs; then other Hurons; then Goupil; the outcries were blood-curdling; the hill was a mass of wild passion.

Father Jogues saw it all as he waited for his own ordeal of running the gauntlet. He was shoved between the columns. Blows beat down on his head and neck and arms, thudding blows, stinging strokes of switches and thorns, on his sides, on his legs. Madly he tried to race up the hill. They tripped and impeded him. He fought forward. He stumbled, and fell to the ground ere he had gone a hundred steps. They showered more blows on him to make him rise. He tried to escape; but he was hurled back. He was numbed, paralyzed. He felt nothing. The Mohawks kicked and beat him the more; but he did not move. They dragged him unconscious to the top of the hill.

When he opened his eyes, Jogues found himself lying on the rocky ledge of the summit of the hill. In the center of the open space he saw a platform, half the height of a man, roughly strung together from branches and wattle. His comrades were being driven to mount it, while the Iroquois giddily whirled around and showered them with blows. He was discovered revived; then he, too, was lifted roughly and thrown on the stage. They hauled him up to a standing position, but he sank down to the wood, utterly unable to support himself. The savages dug into his flesh with their finger nails and thrust burning fagots against his arms and thighs. He could not move to protect himself. One of them took his thumb and bit it, crunching and macerating it until the flesh was torn to bits and the bone was exposed. Another held a live coal against his other fingers. Under the onslaught, once more he swooned off, lifeless.

He awoke to witness the similar torture of Coûture, Goupil, and the Hurons. The Mohawk mob slashed them with knives, burnt them fiendishly, and macerated and cut off their fingers. When the wounds bled too profusely, the Mohawks cauterized them with red-hot stones. Seeing that Ondessonk had again come to life, some of them leaped to wreak more vengeance on him. Paul Onnonhoaraton stood over the Father's prostrate form and beat off the Mohawk braves. He begged them to leave Ondessonk alone; they were killing him outright; if they wanted to torture some one, torture him, Paul told his enemies; they could be as savagely cruel as they wished; he would endure all the things they cared to inflict; he would take the place of Ondessonk.

The Mohawks were finished with the French and threw them off the staging. They turned with newer vigor on the Hurons. Ahatsistari was the center of their rage. Jogues watched his sufferings with growing terror. He saw them slash the flesh with their long knives, from head to feet, saw them staunch the blood with burning torches. Eustace stood unmoved, never flinching, taunting and maddening them by his words and courage. They lifted his arms, and severed both of his thumbs in revenge for the arrows he had directed into the hearts of their kinsman. He remained unmoved. One of the Mohawks took a tough stake, cleared of the bark and well pointed; he rammed it into the socket from which the thumb of the left hand had been amputated. He forced the wood up through the flesh until it protruded at the elbow. Eustace held his composure. He would not disgrace his people by twitching a muscle; he would not show himself a coward and thus give satisfaction to his enemies. He drew himself up more proudly, invincible.

Father Jogues could endure it no longer. He tottered to his feet and lunged over to the edge of the platform. Tears streamed down his cheeks, his voice was choked. He called out to Eustace, to tell him to remember God, to be faithful, that he loved him more than ever and pitied him. When the Mohawks saw Ondessonk weeping, they jeered at him. They called him a squaw and a coward, they ridiculed and despised him. Ahatsistari raised his voice louder than those of the Mohawks. He stood bravely above the mob on the platform as he roared out: "Those tears that the Father sheds, they are not womanish tears. Don't get the idea that his tears are caused by weakness. They are the tears of courage and of the love which he has for me. They are not a sign of cowardice. He weeps for me, not for himself. He never wept while you were tormenting him. His face always remained dry and cheerful. He weeps for me and not for himself. Your cruelty and my pains and his love, they are the reason for his tears."

Father Jogues lifted his voice above the din and called up to Eustace: "It is true what you say, Eustace. I do not feel my own wounds nearly so much as the sorrow which I suffer for you. Look at me all covered with blood and with wounds. I do not count that anything in comparison to the anguish I feel when I see you suffering this way. Take courage, my dear brother. Keep remembering all the time that there is another life, remember there is a God Who sees everything and Who knows well how to reward all the things which we endure now, on this occasion, for His sake."

"I am trying to do that," Eustace shouted to him. "I am remembering very well. I will remain firm, even till death."

The Mohawks thrust Father Jogues away from the platform and sent him reeling. One brave followed, brandishing a long knife and cursing him venomously. Jogues faced him. The Mohawk seized his nose. Then raised the knife menacingly, and held it balanced, as if he were about to slice off the nose. Ondessonk looked into the thin slits of the eyes of the warrior without fear or shrinking. The savage hesitated and studied the face of Ondessonk. Slowly, as if some power restrained him, lowering the knife, and letting go the nose, he walked off. Father Jogues had offered himself to God in that moment: "Lord, take not my nose only, but also my head," he prayed. He was aware that if the Mohawk had mutilated him by striking off his nose he would have been put to death on the spot. It was the custom among the savages to kill outright those notably marred. And so he realized that he had barely escaped. He attributed it to God alone.

He sank to the earth, exhausted. A quarter of an hour later, the same Mohawk stood above him, raging and wild as before. He seemed to have remorse that he had not completed his intention. Methodically, he pinched Ondessonk's nose between his thumb and forefinger and steadied it. He poised the knife and calculated his stroke. He looked piercingly at the face of Ondessonk; he discovered no fear, not the slightest tremor. He hesitated and made a motion to strike; but again he held back his arm. He wanted to strike, he seemed surprised that he could not. Finally, this second time, he relinquished his grip and went off, sullenly and reluctantly, muttering something to himself. Father Jogues was as surprised as the Mohawk. "You know, my God, what I said to you at that moment in the depth of my heart," he wrote later. "I do not know what invisible force repulsed him for this second time. It was over with my life if he had proceeded, for they are not accustomed to leave long on earth those who are horribly mutilated."

The late afternoon had turned into evening while the tortures continued. The blackness of night shrouded the platform and the victims. The prisoners were limp; the executioners were fatigued by their own passions and cruelties. Now were the Mohawks satisfied with their sacrifice. They had roused their courage and their fierceness, they now were lusting for battle and blood. They were ready, all of the two hundred of them, to proceed up their northern trail along the lake, up through their river to the place where the French were daring to build a fort. Other bands were assembling there. They would attack these Frenchmen and drive them off and kill and capture them. They were no longer afraid of the French. They had proved it, by torturing Ondessonk and the other two palefaces.

Father Jogues and his white and red brothers lay indistinguishable in the moonlight. They were all caked with blood, with dirt, with cinders, all masses of festering flesh. They were weakened before by lack of food for they had been given scarcely anything to eat for several days past. They were so worn out after the tortures, by loss of blood, by the maddening thirst, by the pains of the cuts and blisters and blows, that they hardly expected to survive. In retrospect, Father Jogues recorded: "I passed the remainder of the night, not without a terrible feeling of grief and pain."

II

The day dawned. Father Jogues looked with bloodshot eyes about the camp grounds. The fires still smoldered. The ground was littered with ashes and blackened stones and charred fagots. The platform was broken and burned. The Hurons and Goupil and Coûture lay unconscious. Their faces and bodies were caked with dull, dried blood. Their features were so swollen and distorted, the wounds and blisters were so raw. The Iroquois awoke, in strong spirit after the night's orgy. They blustered about with great clatter and uproar. Father Jogues gathered his comrades about him and quietly led them in their morning prayers, while the Iroquois held council before they parted.

They straggled down the hill to the beach, the Iroquois with outcries and commotion, the captives painfully, as if groggy from drugs. The outgoing war party set their thirty and more canoes bobbing in the lapping waves. They lusted for battle, aroused by the sight and the smell of blood. They boasted to Ondessonk of the attack they would make on the French fort, and promised to bring back more French palefaces whom they would roast and eat in their villages. With a martial chant, the two hundred red-skinned warriors, flaming with crimson paint, swung their fleet northward into the lake and soon dwindled from sight.

The Mohawks were proud of their first triumph. They were eager to parade Ondessonk and Ihandich and Ahatsistari before the rest of their nation. They loaded their captives and the baggage into the canoes and struck out around the island toward the south. It was to be another day of sweltering heat. Jogues lay cramped in the boat. Today was Sunday, he reflected, and he thought of the peace at Quebec, of the solemn quiet about Sainte Marie, of the Sundays last year when Eustace and Joseph and the others gathered in the chapel. All that was over. He and they were on their way to death. The mystery was in God's keeping. Good would come of it. He would not despair.

In the late afternoon, the Mohawks descried another war party on a point of land beyond. They drew up before them, and proudly went through the rite of salute and thanksgiving to the sun. This band of warriors was also on its way to the St. Lawrence for the mass attack on the projected Fort Richelieu and for scouting along the Huron and Algonquin routes. They demanded to be allowed to welcome and caress the prisoners. But the masters permitted them to exercise only minor cruelties, since they wished to bring their victims back alive to their villages. Still the next day, they encountered another smaller party on its way to war, and for the third time the prisoners were subjected to the petty persecution. By this time the flotilla had passed from the broad expanse of Lake Champlain into the wedge of water between the bristling mountains. The shores closed in so that the lake tapered into the breadth of a sluggish river, fringed with swamps and marshes.

About noon of August 11, the tenth day since the journey began, they arrived at the end of the lake. The Mohawks emptied the canoes in the shallows and piled the baggage on the grass. They rested awhile during the midday heat. When they were ready to start along the land-trail, the chief who owned Ondessonk ordered him to shoulder the greater part of his bundles. Jogues was so exhausted by starvation and lack of sleep and the burning heat and his wounds, that he could scarcely walk. He threw the bundles from him when the chief tried to pack them on his shoulders. The savage saw it was useless to insist. "I was treated with a sufficient amount of gentleness in this part of the journey," Jogues attested. "Only a light burden was given to me to carry, both because I was not able to carry much and because I scornfully refused to carry more, for even in my captivity and near to death, I bore with me my proud spirit."

In the middle of the afternoon they started along the trail through the forests. One after the other with the Hurons and French interspersed between the Mohawks, the ninety people stretched out in a single file and fell into a brisk trot, half-walking, half-running. They shuffled their moccasins along the narrow, dusty path, which wound through innumerable trees and circled between the mountains and rose and dropped over the hills. The leaders held to the steady, grueling pace, and the guards drove Jogues and the wearied prisoners to keep up with them. At twilight, they reached the spot selected for the camp that night. The victims threw themselves in near collapse upon the ground. But they had no sleep. The damp humidity of the woods, through which no slightest breath of air stirred, suffocated them. Clouds of insects and mosquitoes were a plague devouring them.

The eleventh day of the torture trail dawned. The Mohawks had no food, even for themselves, so they hurried their departure and increased the speed of their trot. Jogues stumbled frequently and was forced to stop for breath. The young brave who guarded him was irritated beyond endurance. He concluded that the breeches which

Ondessonk wore impeded him, and so forced the Father to divest himself. He would have liked to strip off the shredded shirt also, but refrained when Ondessonk protested with vigor. They came to the banks of a swirling river. The ford was treacherous, for the current swept violently over the slippery, unsteady stones. The young brave realized how insecure Ondessonk was in his balance, how likely it was that he would miss his footing and be whirled against the rocks. He led his prisoner to another crossing where the water was deeper but quieter. Father Jogues waded in, but in the middle he slipped and was lifted by the current. If he had not been a strong swimmer, he would have been carried down to the rapids and mangled among the rocks.

The guards over Jogues and Goupil despaired of keeping them in the file. They were in a quandary; they faced the danger of starvation if they slowed their pace; they might lose the two Frenchmen if they abandoned them along the road. They chose the latter, and let Jogues and Goupil travel as best they could in the rear of the column. When they were some distance behind, Father Jogues renewed his solicitations to Brother René to escape. It was but a day's journey back to the canoes; there remained only the passage of the lake and the river; he might survive; there was no possibility of surviving if he kept on; only death and torture awaited him. Coûture might be persuaded to go with him. Goupil answered that he would escape if Father Isaac would make the try; otherwise, not. "My Father," he said, "I will die with you. I cannot possibly desert you."

Father Jogues' suggestion was born of desperation. He wrote: "The day on which we would arrive at the village of the Iroquois had always loomed up before us, during our journey, as a day of bitterness and death. It was easy for René Goupil and for me to escape that death as well as the fires. Often, since we were left unfettered and since we were a long distance behind our guards late at night, we could slip away from the road. It might be that we could not return to our own people; but at least we could die more peacefully in the woods. But he refused to make the attempt, and I wished rather to suffer the most extreme torture than to abandon the French and the Christian Hurons in their death, and to deprive them of that consolation which a priest is able to impart."

At the end of this day, Jogues and Goupil reached the camp long after the others. They were footsore and famished, for they had had no food now for several days. They saw a pot hanging over the fire. It was food at last, they thought, and eagerly they went up to it. The Iroquois guffawed at them. There was nothing in the pot but warm water. Once more, supperless, they threw themselves wearily among their comrades. They felt that they must die. Despite their bruised and aching bodies, they had already traveled more than fifty miles overland. Twenty or thirty miles more, and they would reach the Mohawk village. A day or two more, and then would come death in reality. It would be a relief.

The Mohawks roused Ondessonk with kicks and imprecations. They were hurrying frantically to reach their homes and get food. In the tenuous light of the morning, the twelfth of the journey, the file of savages took its serpentine length along the trail. Jogues and Goupil started bravely in line and struggled to maintain the pace. Before many hours had passed they were forced to drop out of the file for frequent rests. The others shuffled along and left them to starve or crumple in death through weakness. Along the way, they found some berries. But these scarcely gave them a taste and did not at all satisfy the clawings of the craving within them. They were tempted, time and again, to give up, to let death come upon them along the trail. But Father Jogues remembered Coûture and Eustace and Joseph and the Christians who were going on to their doom. He could not abandon them in their final agonies.

With superhuman effort he forced his lagging steps forward to catch up with the band of his children. He staggered into the camp after dark. The fires burned brightly. There was food. Squaws and braves had come out from the village to meet the victorious warriors and to greet their prisoners. Only a short ten or twelve miles remained, so he was told, before they would come to Ossernenon, the first of the Mohawk habitations.

It was the last night, perhaps of life, for himself and Goupil and Coûture. Since the Iroquois were in open enmity with the French, they had no thought of future peace or of holding their captives as hostages. They would execute their cruelest revenge on the French. All along the route they had dinned into the ears of Ondessonk the terrible punishment they would inflict on him and the palefaces; how they would burn him over a slow fire; how they would roast and eat him. He commended himself and his comrades to Mary, the Virgin Mother. The next day was August 14th, the vigil of the Assumption, he computed: "I gave thanks to Our Lord Jesus Christ because on that day on which the whole world rejoices in the glory of His Mother being assumed into Heaven, He called us to some part and to companionship in His sufferings and cross."

While the light still wavered in the August morning, the captives were marshaled into line and forced along the last stages of the trail. This day, there was no lagging behind. The Mohawks arrogantly marched before and behind, and ranged up and down the path beside them. Scores of women and children and many of the men lined along the route, jeering at the prisoners, and hurling dirt and stones on them. The procession wended its way through the serried trees for an hour, and a second hour; about the third hour began the gradual mounting of an upward climb. They surmounted a ridge, and then, through the trees, Jogues saw the valley of the Mohawks green and hollowed below him. Across the valley he saw the hills, and on the right a haze of smoke in the pale blue sky.

The Iroquois roared out their chant of victory and blew raucously on their conch-shells. They hurried the prisoners pell-mell down the path which sloped along the bias of the hill. In the bottom of the valley, along the flat river banks, surged a mass of dark figures yelling and screeching their jubilation. The line of prisoners was pointed up the path by the narrow river and jammed into the excited mob. They were set upon by men and women and children, beaten with clubs and slashed with knives, scratched and torn.

Most of the fury fell upon the three Frenchmen. One brawny fellow, whom the Hurons recognized as one of their own who had been adopted by the Iroquois, leaped about like a demon, roaring: "You Frenchmen, you are dead men. They are going to burn you. Have no more hope for life. You will have no more liberty. Prepare for death." The squaws screamed their rage: "We will burn you. We will eat you." The braves poured out curses and imprecations. Ondessonk was the most detested. He was French, he was a Blackrobe, he was hideous in their eyes, for his head was almost bald. This drove them frantic. They mauled him and fought with one another to get his fingers into their mouths to grind and pinch them. Before they had finished, they had yanked out the two finger nails which remained to him.

The welcome at the river bank subsided. The prisoners, bleeding copiously, were formed into line and led across the ford. Their guard marched them up the winding path to the village of Ossernenon, set up on the headlands. Along the way the savages kept up their jeering. "Take courage, my nephew," one old man told Ondessonk, "do not be grieved. You will soon see some of your brothers here to keep you company. Our warriors desire to eat the flesh of the French. You will be able to taste it with us." Jogues was so smeared red with blood that he could not see. His guard was compassionate, and as he wiped his eyes, said: "My brother, you are being treated badly."

The prisoners were now huddled in the open fields that topped the hill and stretched out from the palisades of Ossernenon. The victorious warriors stood about them. Solemnly they offered their thanksgiving to the sun and the war demons who had delivered the French and the Hurons into their hands, to roast and eat. While they thus exulted, Father Jogues made his oblation: "Since we knew that if we would separate ourselves from the number of those who are scourged, we would separate ourselves also from the number of the sons of God, we offered ourselves with an ardent soul to our God, our God paternally cruel, in order that He might do His Will upon us, as upon his children."

The Mohawks of Ossernenon, reinforced by large numbers from the two neighboring villages of Andagaron and Tionontoguen, ranged themselves in parallel lines for the running of the gauntlet. All were armed with clubs and switches and iron rods. They shrieked like wild beasts for their prey. Ihandich, as they named Coûture, being the Frenchman who shot a Mohawk chief, was placed first in line. After him were marshaled half the Hurons. Goupil was in the middle. Then came the other Hurons. Ondessonk was saved for the last. All were stripped naked except Jogues and Goupil, who were allowed to keep a shirt tied about their loins. A warrior led the way. He walked slowly between the double file of braves, urging all to salute and caress the prisoners well. Coûture dashed after him; as he raced onward the blows rained down on him. The Hurons made wild rushes to get through the narrow barrier of enemies. The uproar was deafening. Goupil started for the shambles. He was clumsy-footed and awkward. He did not keep his head lowered, nor his arms guarding his face and neck. Jogues watched him in agony.

He saw them smash René's face and head, saw him fall, and then saw his body flung out from the double lines.

Jogues alone was left. An orator harangued the braves to treat this paleface well: he is the famous Blackrobe Ondessonk. Jogues was hurled on his way. Being agile and quick-paced, he evaded many blows; but he was also pounded down by many. One of the warriors swung a lump of iron, the size of a man's fist, on a rope. He let fly with it and struck Ondessonk on the back above the hip bone with such force that it lifted him from his feet. He fell, but fear of another such blow made him leap up, and hurtle himself forward. He bolted through crazedly until he catapulted out of the columns and up against the platform erected in the open space at the gates of the palisades.

There were his comrades huddled, a bleeding, stunned pile of bodies. Worst of all was Goupil. His face and head were smeared over with blood, so that there was left no white except that of his eyes. His features were smashed and swollen. "So pitiable was his condition," Jogues alleged, "that he would have inspired compassion in cruelty itself. I found him all the more beautiful as he had more in common with Him Who, bearing a face most worthy of the admiration and delight of the angels, appeared to us, in the midst of His anguish, like unto a leper." The prisoners were given a respite from blows, but the vicious mob gloated over them and, as Jogues recalled, "filled the air and our ears with their insults; but these did us no great harm."

The prisoners were now forcibly escorted up on the strongly built, large platform, some five feet high. The three Frenchmen were placed in the center. A chief mounted beside them, and in a sonorous tone, cried out: "It is the French whom I hold to be our greatest enemies. The Hurons do not merit my anger so much. I have compassion for them. Come, let us caress the French." He struck three lusty blows with an iron rod on the back of Jogues, and then on Coûture and Goupil. A horde of savages leaped on the platform and pounded the Frenchmen and with their knives slit the skin lengthwise along the fingers.

An old man, noted as a sorcerer, who had prophesied that this band would capture Frenchmen, ascended the platform, dragging after him an Algonquin squaw named Joan, who was known to be a Christian. He drove off the braves and gnashed the fingers of

Ondessonk in his teeth. "I hate this one most of all," he called out as he lifted the left arm of Jogues. He ordered the Algonquin woman to cut off the left thumb. She shrank away in horror, for she had loved the Blackrobes. The old man grew enraged; the braves buffeted her; but still she refused. They hedged her about, threatening to kill her on the spot. She took the knife in a trembling hand and gashed the skin, searching for the thumb joint. Her fear and horror made her unsteady and blind. She slashed and tore till she cut the tendons and pulled the thumb free.

Jogues endured the agony silently, stolidly. He saw his thumb lying at his feet where the woman had dropped it. He relates: "Picking up the severed thumb with my right hand, I offered it to You, my living and my true God, for I remembered the Holy Sacrifices which I had offered to You upon the altars of your Church through seven years. I accepted this torture, O my God, as a loving vengeance for the want of love and respect that I had shown in touching your Holy Body. You heard the cries of my soul." He was aroused by the agonizing warning of Coûture: "Throw away the thumb! Throw it away! They will force you to eat it!" Father Jogues quickly hurled the thumb from him, for it would be as Coûture warned.

The executioners chose René Goupil as the next victim. They sawed off the thumb of his right hand with an oyster shell. So much blood spurted out that they feared he would die. They stanched it with a white-hot rod, and at the same time cauterized Jogues' wound. They tore strips from his shirt, the only garment he wore, and bandaged the hands of both of them. Then they turned to Coûture. They ordered him to sing and dance. They pricked him with awls and pointed stakes, carved off shreds of his flesh, burned him with firebrands and glowing irons, until he fell lifeless under their cruelties. Even the Mohawks were by now sated with blood, but they continued to torture the Hurons for the remainder of the afternoon. They withdrew from their sport only to take their evening meal.

In the dusk the prisoners were brought down from the platform. As he descended, Jogues was halted by a squaw who demanded that he will to her his shoes and leggings, the last of his possessions. She assured him that he had no more use for them, since he was condemned to die. He was too weak to remonstrate, so she tore them away from him. He and the others were distributed among the cabins and given the usual mush of corn. It was their first taste of food since the early dawn.

After they had eaten they were bound to the earth of the cabin, stretched on their backs, with their arms and legs extended wide, and their trunks, wrists and ankles firmly tied to stakes. They were helpless under the plague of flies and vermin that swarmed upon them. Much greater to bear was the onslaught of the boys and girls who now had the privilege of tormenting the prisoners. They were like little demons in the shadows and the ruddy glow of the fires. They threw burning coals on the prostrate, naked bodies of Ondessonk and the others. They sprinkled hot ashes on them, and chortled with joy as they watched their victims twist to throw off the fires. That was only encouragement to the little savages to pour more cinders and coals and burning stones. The night was more cruel than the day. And yet, Father Jogues had peace and consolation in his soul. "In truth," he murmured to himself, "these sufferings are great, but God is infinite in His goodness."

On the next day, August 15th, the prisoners were led out early from the cabins to be deposited once more upon the blood-blackened platform as public spectacles. All who wished might torture them and wreak on them any indignity. Through the morning, when the air was fresh and invigorating, through the warm summer afternoon, until nightfall, Jogues and his comrades helplessly bore up under the long-drawn-out cruelties of the men and women and children. At nightfall they were once more tied up in the cabins. So it was, also, on Saturday, August 16, the ending of the second week since their capture. They lived, but their existence was nigh unbearable. Each hour brought new griefs and the recurrence of old anguish. Forgetful of himself, Father Jogues, by his exhortations and his prayers, kept always preaching to the Huron Christians to be faithful to the God who was chastising them.

III

Andagaron, the second village of the Mohawks, demanded that the French and Huron captives be exhibited there. Only too happily did the victorious warriors accede to this request to extend their days of triumph. On August 17, accordingly, the prisoners were marched in single file out of the stockade of Ossernenon and down the hillside to the flats along the river bank. As Father Jogues passed along in the procession, one of the Iroquois was offended that he still wore a shirt, tattered though it was. "The man stripped him of it," narrates Buteux, "and left him as naked as the hand. This was a torture more hard to bear than all the tortures he had yet endured, and it would have been still more agonizing if there had not been given to him a wretched rag, little more than twice the size of the hand, to cover that which should be concealed. He marched for some time in this condition, until he judged it opportune to complain to his guard. 'Are you not ashamed of yourself,' said Father Jogues to him, 'to see me thus wholly naked, you especially, who have charge of me, you who have stolen away the baggage which belonged to me?' This savage gave him a piece of coarse, gray canvas with which a bundle was enveloped. The cloth was not much more than half a yard. What a covering it was! Father Jogues made use of it, nevertheless, and placed it over his back to protect himself from the burning rays of the sun which beat down on his shoulders, as well as on his arms and neck. This rough sacking did not soothe even a little the suffering of the Father. On the contrary, it irritated him all the more. For the cloth glued itself tightly to his back, because of the pus which exuded from his wounds. So much so, that he had to tear off the canvas and travel thus naked to the village whither they were proceeding."

The trail to Andagaron skirted the bank of the river of the Mohawks. For the six or seven miles of its length it was exposed to the merciless glare of the sun. It turned across the meadow and then climbed up an almost perpendicular slope along the side of a cascading rivulet. At the summit of a headland higher than that of Ossernenon, the troop of victors and captives came in front of the palisades of the village. All their route had been besieged by excited squaws and children, who ran before and beside them, screeching and threatening. To make the prisoners run the gauntlet at the arrival at a new village was not customary, but such was the pride of the victors and such the hate for the French, that the little band was set off apart in the field beside the walls while the squirming lines of the braves of Andagaron formed for the welcome and caress. The chief of the village exhorted his people to show their love for the prisoners by wielding their clubs and sticks mightily. At a signal, one by one, the shattered French and Hurons stumbled through the parallel columns until they reached the goal, another stage on which they were to be placed for further torture.

The people of this village repeated the cruelties of Ossernenon. One of them discovered that two of Coûture's fingers had been left intact. Towering with rage at this oversight, he vaulted upon the platform and began to saw off the index finger of Ihandich's right hand with the ragged edge of a shell. He pressed down with all his might on the flesh, and tore it, but he could not sever the tendons or cut through the joint. Frenzied, he gripped the finger and twisted it until he tore it out, dragging with it a sinew as long as the palm. Coûture collapsed on the platform. The other savages feared for him, for the arm began to swell almost immediately. They carried him away to one of the cabins. "At the same time," says Jogues, "that his poor arm swelled, the pain from it was reflected even in the depth of my heart."

All through the rest of that day the orgy of torture continued. "From time to time," Jogues narrates, "the savages mounted the stage and cut off the fingers of my Huron comrades, and bound their clenched hands in hard cords so tightly drawn that they fainted. While each one suffered but his own pain, I suffered that of all. I was afflicted with a great anguish, great as one may believe the heart of a most loving parent is afflicted when he sees the sufferings of his own children. For, with the exception of the few older Christians, I had borne all of these in Christ through their recent baptism. During these times God gave me enough strength, even though I myself was in agony, to give consolation to the French and Hurons who were suffering their agonies. Thus, both along the road and on the platform, even when the cruel crowd of saluters (for thus they name those who rain down blows on the captives running the gauntlet) separated us, I exhorted my companions, now singly, now all together, to preserve their patience and not to lose confidence in God, which confidence would bring its own reward. I told them that they should remember that it is befitting for us through great tribulations to enter into the kingdom of heaven. The time prescribed for us by God approaches, I remind them, according to His words: 'Ye shall weep and lament, but the world shall rejoice, but your sorrow shall be turned into joy'; we are like to 'a woman who, when she is in labor, hath sorrow because her hour is come; but when she has brought forth the child, she no longer remembers her anguish for joy that a man is born into the world.' Thus, I advised them; they must persuade themselves that most surely after a few days they would exchange these momentary sorrows for a joy that is eternal. Indeed, it was a profound consolation to me, and rightly so, when I saw them so well disposed, especially the older Christians, Joseph, Eustace, and the two others, Charles and Stephen."

When they were retired from the platform at nightfall they were subjected again to the excruciating pain of being tied to the ground in the form of St. Andrew's cross. They were at the mercy of the children of Andagaron who sprinkled their naked bodies with hot ashes and embers. In particular, Goupil suffered agonizingly, as Father Jogues tells: "He had his whole breast burned by the coals and the hot cinders which the young lads threw upon our bodies at night, when we were bound flat on the earth. Nature furnished more skill to me than to him for avoiding a part of these pains. But he showed an admirable patience in it all."

In the early morning they were roused and brought again to the platform. The heat wave of the past two weeks, when the sun glared fiercely, was giving place to a cloudy, sultry day. Then a wind swept across the headlands above the valley. The air became so chill that Jogues and his comrades, feverish as they were, shivered and trembled with cold. The storm burst violently, and sheets of rain in torrents beat down on them. The prisoners were forced to remain exposed on the open stage during the downpour. "Often, shivering with cold on the stage, I would come down, unordered, and enter some cabin, but I could scarcely begin to warm myself before I was commanded to return to the platform," Jogues states.

The shock of the cold breezes and the rain intensified rather than alleviated the pain of their shattered nerves and corrupting bodies. Between the showers the Mohawks gathered about the platform and continued their merciless tormentings. So passed the day of August 18. When, at dark, they were conducted to the cabins, Jogues and Goupil were ordered to sing and dance, as was the custom with native captives. "We at last complied," says the Father, "for alas, what else could we do. But we sang *de canticis domini in terra aliena.* Torture followed the chanting, and its fury burst especially on René and myself."

Tionontoguen was the third village of the Mohawks, the most

populous and the most important. It was necessary that the French and Hurons be led thither as the climax of the triumphal celebrations. On August 19, then, the prisoners were lined in single file and marshaled out of Andagaron. Jogues had a thrill of joy, for Coûture reappeared. Guillaume had been carried from the platform the day before, more dead than alive. Father Jogues feared that he had died, for he could get no answer to the inquiries he made. Now he saw Coûture, his arm still swollen and sore, but surviving.

Jogues renewed his petition to his guard for some bit of clothing to cover his nakedness. The man found him a ragged old jacket roughly woven of heavy wool. It was something to cover his shoulders and body in order to preserve some of the decencies. But the prickly wool irritated and scratched his blistered skin and scraped off the scabs that were forming, so that he had to take it off and proceed without any covering. The journey was of two hours, along the river bank toward the west where the hills became small mountains. The trail curved finally to the left and wound gradually upwards through a wooded slope until it reached the spacious plateau on which was reared a long, rectangular stockade, ruggedly and strongly fortified.

Running the gauntlet here was little more than a formality, since the prisoners had already, exceptionally, been subjected to it three times before. But the ordeal of torture on the platform was carried through with all its fury. By now, the prisoners were so lifeless, so desperately worn out, that even the Mohawks realized they could not survive much longer if they were wounded more. They were kept on the torture-stage, however, all the day, and in the night were bound fast in the cabins. The boys and girls were free to plague them by sifting fire on them, by scratching their sores and scabs with finger nails and knives and awls, by prodding them with sticks. The children of Tionontoguen were more ingenious and shameless. "What things, what sort of things did they not do to us thus bound?" Father Jogues exclaims. "What did they not do to my Huron brothers? What things, what sort of things did they not attempt to do to me? But, again, I gave thanks to you, O my God, that always you have preserved me, your priest, pure from the impure hands of the savages."

For Ondessonk, the great Blackrobe of the French, the Mohawk young men reserved a special treatment that night. They raised him up above their shoulders to the height of a crosspiece that stretched between two sturdy poles which supported the cabin. With ropes woven from vines they bound his arms above the elbows to the crosspiece. Then they let him hang, but with no support save the thongs about his upper arms, and in such manner that his feet did not touch the earth. "At that moment," he confesses, "I believed that I was going to be burned to death, for they usually act in this way when they intend to burn a prisoner. And that I might realize that, if thus far I had endured the torments bravely and patiently, the strength and patience did not come from myself, but from Him Who gives courage to the afflicted—in this torture, being left as it were to myself, I wept. Freely I glory in my infirmity so that the virtue of Christ may reside in me. On account of the overpowering pain, I begged my tormentors to loosen, even a little bit, the tightness of my ropes. But God acted justly; the more I begged them, the tighter they bound the ropes. At length, when I was in that position for about a quarter of an hour, and just as I was feeling that I was about to pass into a swoon, they cut the ropes. I offer thanks to you, my Lord Jesus, that I was allowed to learn by some slight experience how much you deigned to suffer for me on the cross, since the whole weight of Your Most Sacred Body hung, not from ropes, but from Your Hands and Feet pierced with hard nails."

His release, as he learned later, was due to no mercy on the part of the braves of Tionontoguen. A savage of another nation from the south, who happened to be visiting the village, shouldered his way through the howling mob and defied the Mohawks by cutting the ropes. So commanding was he, and such was the law of hospitality, that the Mohawks dared not oppose him. Father Jogues passed the night semi-conscious. Aroused as soon as the day came, he was thrown again on the platform. But he and his comrades were forgotten in a fresh excitement.

A war party arrived, parading with them four Hurons whom they had captured along the St. Lawrence near Lake Erie. Father Jogues left the platform and followed the howling mob of savages who rushed to welcome and caress the new prisoners. He recognized the Hurons; they were not Christians; he must baptize them. They were already mutilated; each of them had lost some of his fingers, and the chief had had both his thumbs amputated. Jogues watched in anguish as they ran the gauntlet. He hovered over them as they lay lifeless on the platform. He spoke to them consolingly and urged them to give their consent to being baptized. Eustace and the other Christians joined him in instructing and soliciting them.

Two of the Hurons, Jogues learned, were to be burned to death that night at Tionontoguen. He stayed with them on the platform and concentrated his appeals on them. Finally they consented. About that moment, the Mohawks threw the prisoners some raw corn which had been freshly plucked. The sheaths were wet from the recent rains. Father Jogues carefully gathered the precious drops of water on a leaf and poured them over the heads of the two neophytes, baptizing them in the name of the Father and of the Son and of the Holy Ghost. The Mohawks understood that his act meant to bring happiness to these hated victims. They raged at his audacity and beat him down, threatening to slaughter him with the Hurons. He more than believed their words, for all their actions toward him pointed to his death, even though the others might be spared.

That night the two Hurons were burned over the fire. The council which condemned them decided that Ondessonk and his two French comrades and the Hurons with him should be led back to the second village of Andagaron. There the general council of the nation was to assemble and discuss the interlocked questions of the fate of the three French prisoners and of the national relations with the French, either the continuation of war or the possibility of peace.

On August 21, then, the procession wended its way back to Andagaron. The two recent Huron captives were brought with the party, for they were apportioned for death in this village. Along the way, Father Jogues kept close to them, teaching them the essentials they must know and believe for baptism. They listened humbly and gratefully, and begged to be given happiness with God after their death. They came to a little stream flowing down from the hills to the river. As they waded through, the Hurons bent their heads low; Father Jogues sprinkled the water on them and pronounced the saving words. The Mohawks, despite their sharp eyes, did not perceive his action.

At Andagaron, Ondessonk and his comrades were received peacefully. They were now immune from persecution until the chiefs of the nations should hold council about them. After midnight, the chief in whose cabin Jogues was lodged returned from the council. He announced to Ondessonk and those of the prisoners held in that cabin, that the council had come to the decision that Ondessonk and some of the others were to die by torture and fire the next night.

Father Jogues accepted the verdict calmly. He had expected no other. He left the record of his thoughts: "Now through the space of seven days we had been led from village to village and from scaffold to scaffold. We had become a spectacle to God and His angels, as we hope from His Divine Goodness, a scoff and jeer to the vilest savage. At length, we were warned that that day would see the end of our lives by fire. Surely, though that final act held something of horror, still, the good pleasure of God and the hope of a better life, of one free from sin, made this final act more a cause for joy. I addressed my French and Huron companions for the last time. I begged them to be of good courage. I told them to remember, amid their sufferings of body and soul, Him who had endured such opposition of sinners against Himself; not to be weary, fainting in their minds, so that they should not weaken when they felt their sorrow slipping from them. Let them have hope, because tomorrow would bring us to Our Lord, to reign forever and ever. Since we feared that we would be taken away one from the other, I forewarned them, and especially Eustace, as follows: since we would not be able to be close together, each one should look toward me; when he lifted his hand to his heart and raised his eyes to heaven, he would thus give testimony that he was sorry for his sins; then I would impart absolution to him, as I had often done on the road down and since our arrival."

It was Friday, just three weeks since they had celebrated the Feast of St. Ignatius at Three Rivers. Jogues spent the morning in private devotions and in prayer with his comrades. *Confortare et esto robustus*; what he had asked of God was being granted to him. He encouraged and comforted Coûture, Goupil, and his Christian savages. After midday, he heard rumors that certain of the leading chiefs demanded a reconsideration of the verdict. Toward evening he was told that his death would not take place that night; another council was being called for further debate. The chiefs and sachems gathered in the dusk, while the villagers speculated tensely on the outcome.

The war faction had prevailed the night before; this was intent on a war of extermination with the French, Hurons, and Algonquins. But a powerful group advocated the policy of temporizing.

It was possible, they contended, to wean the French away from their alliances with the Hurons and Algonquins; in that case, the Iroquois would act wisely to ally themselves with the French pale-faces. The peace negotiations with the French, they admitted, had failed thus far, but they might be resumed, and with advantage, when the mutual fears and misunderstandings were removed. If Ondessonk and the two Frenchmen were murdered, Onontio and the French would be angered. They would not listen to peace talk, then or in the future. It would be better to hold the three Frenchmen alive, as prisoners and hostages. If they were once killed, they could not be brought to life; if they were allowed to live, they could be put to death later.

The peace councilors persuaded the assembly. The three Frenchmen were summoned to the council, and an orator delivered to them the verdict: Ondessonk and his comrade, René, were delivered to the charge of the chief who had captured them and were to be slaves in his cabin in the village of Ossernenon. Ihandich was given to the family of the chief he had slain, to be treated by them as they willed in their village of Tionontoguen. In regard to the Hurons, the more moderate party also was victorious. Three Hurons were condemned to death, one in each of the three communities. Eustace Ahatsistari, the most formidable of all Hurons, would be tortured and burned in the capital town of Tionontoguen; Stephen was to be given to the people of Andagaron; Paul Onnonhoaraton, the greatest of the younger warriors, nephew to Eustace, would be offered to the demons of war in Ossernenon. All the other Hurons were granted their lives and assigned to the care of families who might adopt, enslave, or kill them.

The chiefs and the crowds of visitors dispersed. Those from Tionontoguen led Eustace off triumphantly. They took with them, also, Guillaume Coûture, Joseph Teondechoren, his son, Theresa his niece, and some others. Those from Ossernenon conducted back their victim, Paul Onnonhoaraton, and Jogues, Goupil, and other Hurons. Stephen and the rest were held at Andagaron. Father Jogues spoke his final words to his comrades, especially to Eustace and Stephen, and gave them final absolution.

At Ossernenon that night, Paul was placed upon the platform and subjected to the death tortures. They feasted him first, and then they ordered him to sing and dance, which he did arrogantly. They slashed his arms and body and legs till his flesh was in tatters, and maunched anew at his fingers. They could not force a whimper from him, could not break down his stoic calm. They butchered him, and burned him with fagots, gleaming and smoking in the dark blue night, and raged at him like demons, shouting themselves hoarse. But they could not humble his proud defiance. Finally, they bound him to a pole, and heaped up the burning bush and logs about his legs. As the flames were enveloping him, Paul looked at Ondessonk. Father Jogues pronounced the sacred words of forgiveness, and a moment later a Mohawk split Paul's head with a tomahawk.

"He was a young man of about twenty-five," Jogues relates, "full of life and courage, one of the most accomplished young men among the Hurons. It is such a one, generally, that they choose to put to death, in order to sap, as it were, the life blood of the hostile nation. He showed a noble contempt for death, for he kept crying out openly that he had hope of a better life to come. Along the road, after our capture, when the Iroquois came up to me to tear out my nails or to inflict some other injury, this generous-hearted man repeatedly offered himself to the savages in my place, telling them to leave me alone and to turn their rage on him. May the Lord return him a hundredfold, with usury, for that heroic charity which led him to give 'his life for his friend,' and 'for those who had begotten him in Christ in bondage.' "

Half a dozen miles beyond, along the headlands above the valley, the sky glowed red over Andagaron where Stephen was being burned. And the same distance beyond, at Tionontoguen, brave Eustace was enduring his last agonies. Guillaume Coûture was there to witness the end. He told Father Isaac: "Eustace was burned in almost every part of his body and was then beheaded. He bore all his tortures in a marvelously Christian manner. Other captives, when they are dying, are accustomed, as the saying is, to pray that some one rise up from their bones as an avenger of their death. Eustace, on the contrary, with a spirit that was truly Christian, with which he had been deeply imbued at his baptism, begged his Huron countrymen standing about him that no consideration of his death should ever be used as an argument, or used as an obstacle to the establishment of peace with the Iroquois."

The executions were done with for the present. The three Frenchmen and the Hurons remained at the mercy of their masters. "After the many long days spent fasting," Jogues narrates, "after so many nights, one after the other, sleepless, after enduring so many lashings and woundings, and most of all, after so many excruciating tortures of the soul and mind, then came the time, in the rest granted us, so to speak, in which we were left to feel most keenly our miseries; then we were left to drag along our souls helplessly, scarcely able to walk, scarcely able, even, to place a foot upon the ground, left never to have a bit of repose either during the day or the night. This was because of many reasons, but chiefly because of our wounds, which remained raw and unhealed thus far. All of these sufferings were made more difficult to bear because of the clouds of fleas and lice and bugs which we could not ward off, except with difficulty, because of our wounded and maimed fingers. More than this, we suffered from a lack of food; more truly here than elsewhere can it be said, *non cibus utilis aegro.* And so we were brought to the verge of starvation, since nothing but unripe squash was added as a condiment to the American corn (which in Europe you call Turkish) roughly ground between two stones. René, in particular, almost died, since he was not accustomed to this kind of food, and since he had been so badly beaten that he could scarcely see. When the savages realized that we were little by little wasting away, they sought out in the village some little fishes and some bits of meat, dried in the fire or the sun, crushed into crumbs. These bits were mixed with the sagamité."

Jogues' bed was a layer of twigs, his covering an old deerskin, greasy and lousy and not long enough to half cover his body. His wounds were open and exuding pus, so that even the Mohawks showed some compassion. Neither he nor René could drag themselves about except with the greatest difficulty, and so useless were their mutilated hands and so weak were they, that they had to be fed like helpless infants. Thus they passed the last week of August, and Father Jogues concludes: "Patience was our physician."

CHAPTER IX

Bowed beneath the Tomahawk

I

THREE RIVERS awakened uneasily. There was a pounding on the door of the priests' house, the gabble of savages, footsteps sounding heavy in the morning quiet, hollow shouts over by the fort, more pounding near the home of the Commandant, some voices in conversation. Father Buteux had been first notified. With sickening soul he listened to the story which some Hurons, breathless and terrified, told him. Ondessonk, Ihandich, the other Frenchmen, Ahatsistari, the Hurons, all were massacred by the Iroquois up among the islands beyond Lake St. Peter; only a few had escaped; all the others were killed or captured. The Commandant, Sieur de Champflour, flared into a mad anger. Something must be done. This was not to be endured. Those Iroquois devils must be caught and punished. But the Commandant and Buteux, the Hurons and the Algonquins, knew that nothing could be done. When they gathered in the chapel for Mass on that Sunday morning of August 3, they prayed fervently for the souls of those who were dead and mercy for the living.

The Frenchman who had escaped and the other Hurons brought further details when they straggled into Three Rivers later in the morning. Father Jogues, Coûture, Goupil, they were not killed outright. Neither were the majority of the Hurons. The Iroquois bands had effected the capture, and carried the French and the Hurons across the St. Lawrence in the direction of their own country. That very morning, de Champflour sent the spokesmen among the fugitives down to report to Governor Montmagny at Quebec.

Montmagny and Father Vimont were aghast. They blamed themselves. They had trusted that the party would slip through safely, as always before. This attack by the Iroquois, this capture of Father Jogues and the Frenchmen, was most serious. It was a threat, no less than a tragedy. It meant that the Iroquois were growing bolder, and now that they held French prisoners, they would stop at nothing. The Governor bitterly regretted his delay in building Fort Richelieu at the mouth of the Iroquois River. If he had only had a garrison up there, he could have prevented the passage of the Iroquois, he could have sent out a detachment to smash these marauders. He would delay no longer. He ordered out his guard and the workmen, and piled them into the ship that lay at anchor in the basin of the St. Charles. Quickly assembling the lumber, the cannon, muskets, the provisions, taking Father Vimont with him, he sailed up the St. Lawrence to Three Rivers.

De Champflour and Father Buteux had received no further news. The Governor sought information from the savages. An Algonquin chief gave his opinion: "It is on this occasion that we shall see whether or not the Iroquois fear you; whether they are afraid of your arquebuses; whether they dread your cannons; whether they hold you in contempt. As soon as your brother Ondessonk reaches their country, the chiefs will hold a council. If the name of the French holds any fear for them, they will speak as follows: 'Let us not eat the flesh of the Frenchmen. That flesh is not good food; it is a poison that will kill us if we taste it. Let us take them back to their brothers and countrymen.' That is what they will say if they fear you, and in the spring they will bring back your brother and the two Frenchmen whom they hold captive. If they despise you, on the contrary, on the arrival of your brother and the two Frenchmen, they will call out: 'Now, let us eat. Let us see how the flesh of the French tastes. Let us swallow them all whole.' Thereupon, they will burn them; they will make them suffer a thousand torments; they will cut them in pieces and throw them by quarters into great kettles; they will eat them as delicacies; everyone will want to taste them. And when they are full up with them, they will say: 'That is good meat. That flesh is delicate. We must eat more.' Then a chief will make a speech and incite the young men to go and hunt the Frenchmen, so as to have similar feasts throughout the country. Then there will not be any French settlement near which they will not lie in ambush to surprise the French and carry them off to their butchery."

"That is what may be called speaking and acting like a savage," commented Vimont. "Alas! can it be possible that the Father and the Frenchmen have been treated in like manner by these barbarians? I see but few among us who are not in danger of having the stomachs of these barbarians for a sepulcher, if God do not protect us from the High Mightinesses of the Dutch." In his report to France for that year of 1642, Vimont took a happier view: "God be forever blessed for the courage that He has given to Father Jogues, and for the piety that He has bestowed upon these two young Frenchmen. If these tigers burn them, if they roast them, if they boil them, if they eat them, they will procure for them sweeter refreshment in the house of the great God, for love of Whom they exposed themselves to such dangers. Such is the price and such the coin with which Jesus Christ has bought the salvation of Greeks and Barbarians; it is with the same coin that the application of His blood must be procured for these savages. A portion of the Hurons who were made prisoners are Christians. Perhaps they will convey a good impression of the Faith of the great God to these Iroquois, who would be won over to heaven as easily as others if the Dutch, who have settled on the coast of Acadia, which belongs to the King, did not prevent the preachers of the Gospel from approach and access to them."

Governor Montmagny lost no time in speculation. He started from Three Rivers for the site of Fort Richelieu. Father Vimont again accompanied him. On August 13, they came to the Iroquois River, which they had christened the Richelieu. There they discovered the melancholy evidence left by the Iroquois a week and a half before. High on the bank was the placard; twenty-two heads in flaming scarlet paint; and distinguishable among them the faces of Father Jogues, Coûture, Goupil, Eustace, and the prominent Hurons; three heads in black. Scattered here and there about the camp were pieces of canvas, in which the supplies had been wrapped, and articles which had been thrown away. Amid the cinders and along the river banks were scraps and remnants of letters, and the torn pages of the books destined for the Fathers among the Hurons.

The French occupied the promontory overlooking the juncture of the Richelieu and the St. Lawrence Rivers, and set to work on the building of the fort. "Axes were wielded in the great forests, trees were hewn down and cut to pieces, the stumps were pulled out," Vimont narrated. "The spot was indicated, and the first Mass said there. After the Benediction, the cannon thundered, and a salvo of musketry did honor to this first beginning under the auspices of our great King and the favor of his Eminence." At the end of a week, the soldiers and workmen had raised the low walls of a redoubt across the cleared space. They were starting to erect the sturdy poles of the palisades and, within the leveled plot, were fitting together the walls of the barracks.

One morning, just when the French workmen were scattering about the cleared space, blood-curdling war-whoops paralyzed them. Red-painted savages erupted from the trees, with no warning save their piercing tremolos. They poured out from the forests on three sides, and spread in lines about the encampment. There were at least three hundred of them, naked and crimson, barking with their muskets, shrieking, rousing their courage for an attack. The workmen leaped to the shelter of the redoubt. The soldiers fired their arquebuses at the leaders. The cannon boomed.

Montmagny, who was still on board his boat, came rushing up the hill with a detachment of soldiers. He and his men took position behind the piles of lumber along the lines of the palisades, the while the men behind the redoubt kept up a steady fire against the enemy. The Iroquois leaped zigzag across the open space, desperately trying to reach the mound of the redoubt, but the volley of the French guns bewildered and repulsed them. Montmagny ordered a sortie; the soldiers sprang from their cover and, in open formation, drove determinedly against the enemy. The fight ranged forward; the Iroquois retreated, then assaulted; the French pushed out and stretched along the three sides of the redoubt. Stubbornly, the Iroquois, maintaining their position before and among the wall of the woods, kept up a steady fusillade. They slunk back, finally, among the trees. Quite as suddenly as they had appeared they vanished almost imperceptibly into the forests.

This boldness of attack by the Iroquois was unprecedented. Governor Montmagny realized keener than ever that this enemy must be crushed if New France were to survive. If the Iroquois had taken the fort, if, even, they had had any success in their surprise attack, they would have been encouraged to make an assault on the new settlement established that week at Montreal, thirty miles up the river, and would next be threatening Three Rivers. These Iroquois were an enemy to be reckoned with. "Our Frenchmen were greatly astonished," Vimont states, "at seeing the courage and resolution of enemies who, in the minds of those who do not know them, pass for being cowardly, but who perform deeds of the utmost hardihood. . . . Our soldiers learned that they must be on their guard constantly against an enemy who pounces like a bird on its prey, who wars like a robber, and who attacks like a brave man. Our soldiers praised the bravery of the Iroquois, for they had not thought that people who are called savages could use their arms so well."

Fort Richelieu was saved. After a few days, Governor Montmagny and Father Vimont returned to Quebec. They were disturbed and worried. True, the Iroquois were dangerous foes. But the Iroquois, they reflected, would be as powerless as the other savage nations if it were not for the Dutch, their neighbors, who supplied them with muskets and powder. That gave the Iroquois an immeasurable advantage over the native allies of the French; it made them the equal of the French. More than that, Montmagny and his Council were quite convinced that the Dutch were instigating the Iroquois to wage war against the French colonies. Early that summer, the Iroquois had boasted to some Algonquins: "The Dutch with whom we trade have promised to assist us against the French. We shall go well armed to see them."

The French were more incensed than ever against the Dutch, whom they held to be squatters. The territory that these Netherlanders had settled belonged to the French King, for Verrazano, sailing under the flag of France, had discovered and explored the entire region in 1524, and French traders not many years afterwards had established a post at the mouth of the river, where the Dutch now lived, and had built a fort on an island one hundred and forty miles northward along the river. Thus, they contended, France held a prior claim, for it was not until 1609 that Henry Hudson sailed into the bay and river and declared the territory contiguous to belong to the States General of the Netherlands.

In Europe, the Lords of the Netherlands avoided all dispute with Cardinal Richelieu, whom they suspected and feared; and Richelieu did not find it convenient, at the time, to make an issue of the Dutch settlements in the New World. The Dutch, who had built their homes and fort at New Amsterdam, on the seacoast, and at Rensselaerswyck, near the site of the old French fort, went on calmly possessing the land, with no curiosity about the prior claims urged by both France and England. They wanted only peace with their white neighbors to the north and to the south. They were satisfied with their portion of the unknown continent. They sought to be at peace, also, with the copper-skinned natives. In the lower settlement about Fort Amsterdam, unfortunately, they had sporadic troubles with the Algonquin nations. Up the river at Fort Orange, through the good tact of Arendt Van Corlaer, they were closely allied to and fraternized with the nations of the Iroquois confederacy, and especially with their nearest neighbors, the Mohawks. These brought in furs and peltries; they gave the savages axes and cloth and other merchandise, and, though it was against the law, smuggled muskets and powder and brandy to them.

Rensselaerswyck was not more than forty miles distant from the Mohawk village of Ossernenon. Within a few days of Jogues' arrival there, the Mohawks were down at the Dutch settlement, boasting of their great victory over the French. They gleefully described to the Dutch how they had tortured the three Frenchmen and were intending to burn them to death. They were amazed when the Dutch pleaded with them not to kill the French palefaces. They could not understand the horror of Cora, as they named Van Corlaer, nor his request that they release Ondessonk and the two French prisoners. They assured the Dutch that they would surely roast and eat all the French they could capture.

Van Corlaer and the burghers of Rensselaerswyck were deeply disturbed. After much argument, they extracted a promise from the chiefs of Ossernenon to hold council with them about the French prisoners. Meanwhile, Van Corlaer had hurriedly sent a ship down the river to report the capture to the Director-General of New Netherlands, Willem Kieft, at New Amsterdam. Kieft ordered Van Corlaer to ransom the three Frenchmen, to take every possible step except that which might precipitate an Iroquois war. Van Corlaer knew well the ferocity and treachery of the Mohawks, but he had also experienced their friendship and hospitality. He was trusted and liked by them, ever since his first visit to their villages in 1634. Accordingly, he had no fear when, toward the end of the first week in September, he and the interpreter, Jan Labatie, a French Huguenot, and the burgher, Jacob Jansen, set out from Rensselaerswyck along the trail to the Mohawks.

At Ossernenon, meanwhile, Father Jogues and René Goupil languished in captivity. Their mutilated fingers were healing, pink skin was closing over their wounds, the orange and purple stains of their bruises were clearing. About the end of August they were able to drag themselves out of the gloomy cabins into the sunlight and the freshening vigor of the early autumn. Though they found little friendliness from the people, though they were despised as outcasts, ridiculed and kicked about like cowed dogs, though they had no assurance whatsoever that they would not be killed by order of the chiefs or at the whim of a fanatic or a madman obsessed by a dream, they were, nevertheless, permitted to live.

Then, about the 5th or 6th of September, the Mohawk warriors who had been repulsed at Fort Richelieu returned to Ossernenon in a nasty, vengeful humor. These were the braves who had tortured Jogues on the island in Lake Champlain. They had gone north, after they left him, in high courage, confident of victory. They had the assurance of the sorcerers, they had offered suitable offerings to the demons. Smaller bands had united with them, so that they felt they were strong enough in numbers; they were well armed with muskets; they had devised a skillful strategy; they thought they were invincible. They were, at the first attack, amazed by the resistance of the French. Then, when the small band of Frenchmen actually rushed out against them like demons, they lost courage. Three of their chiefs were killed, and a number of warriors were wounded. Since they had failed of success in the surprise onslaught and the French were on guard, and since their food was exhausted, they decided to take the trail homeward. They were bitter and resentful, and more than all, puzzled.

At Ossernenon, they found Ondessonk and the other two Frenchmen alive. They understood. Ondessonk had cast an evil spell over them; he it was who caused their defeat. Father Jogues remarked: "We were sought out for death. This war party returned to the village furious with anger and disappointment. They acted as if they had been greatly wronged by us, even though they had gone out to commit wrong. 'It is a shameful thing,' the returned warriors cried out, 'that these three Frenchmen should be permitted to live quietly in our midst, when three of our Iroquois brothers have been slain so recently by the French.'" They demanded that unless a new council of the nation be held, they would take the matter in their own hands. They swore that Ondessonk and his comrades must be tortured to death. "Amid their outcries, René's safety, especially, and my own, were brought to the very extreme of jeopardy," says Jogues. "He alone warded off the blow Who, as He is the giver of life, so also is He the protector."

Scouts brought in the message that Cora and two Dutchmen were on the trail, approaching Ossernenon. A welcoming party was sent out to meet them. Van Corlaer was escorted grandiosely across the flats and was ushered up the hill to the village in grand ceremony. The Dutch ambassadors were halted without the gates of the palisades while the Mohawks danced, chanted, and fired a volley of musket-shots. Then, with elaborate courtesy, they were brought to the cabin of the chief. Young men scoured the forests for wild fowl, and delicacies were sought from all the cabins.

While waiting for the assembly of chiefs at Tionontoguen, Van Corlaer and Labatie held some conversation with Father Jogues. They listened with nausea and compassion to the story he told them of his capture and of the tortures. They rejoiced that they had arrived so providentially, just when the council that would absolutely decree death was being assembled. Van Corlaer had no doubt but that his words and his presents would appeal to the Mohawks. But Jogues, who knew them better, was not optimistic.

The Dutch ambassadors went on to Tionontoguen. In the grand council there convoked, in the second week of September, they renewed their pledges of alliance. Cora then suggested to the chiefs and elders that they should warn their young men to do no harm to the people of his village when they came on visit, and not to molest the cattle. He went on to say that he wished to buy from them the three Frenchmen whom he understood were dwelling in their cabins. He offered them presents of goods costing 600 florins, an infinite amount to them. The sachems listened in silence, and answered that they must consult on this weighty matter among themselves.

The next day, in solemn council, they replied. They were pleased and honored by their alliance with the Dutch palefaces. They would warn their young men against committing depredations or annoying their white brothers. They would grant all that their Dutch brothers asked, except in one regard. They could not accept the munificent gifts offered for the release of Ondessonk, Ihandich, and René. In a masterly speech they told Cora: "We shall show you every kindness in our power, but on this subject you must be silent. Besides, you know well how they treat our people when they fall into their hands."

Despite their considered refusal, Van Corlaer renewed his solicitations. The Mohawks, diplomatically, assured him that they did not intend to torture the three Frenchmen any more, and had no mind to put them to death, for the time being. They went further, and mentioned that they would present the matter to the council of all the five Iroquois nations. They were inclined to believe that the sachems would order the Frenchmen to be brought back to their people at Three Rivers within a short time, though some of the chiefs would be offended. Van Corlaer had to rest satisfied with this reply. He was escorted back to Rensselaerswyck by an armed guard of Mohawk warriors.

In his record of Director Van Corlaer's intervention, Jogues states that he "remained among the Mohawks several days, offered much, promised more, obtained nothing. Truly, this is a most artful and cunning race of savages. In order that they might seem to grant some favor to a friend making a request and not to refuse all that he desired, they lied by saying that they would return us to our people within a few days." He admits that this was, undoubtedly, the wish of some of them, but that others more powerful would never consent to their release. The Hurons, who understood better the mood of the Mohawks, assured Ondessonk that the chiefs were acting deceitfully and had no intention of acceding to the request of the Dutch. The results, however, were favorable to Jogues, who was thereafter treated with slightly more respect.

Jogues and Goupil remained as public prisoners, not under the protection of the nation and not under the guardianship of any specific family, but as derelicts. The master of the cabin in which they lived could command them as slaves, but he had no responsibility for their welfare and safety. Guillaume Coûture, at Tionontoguen, enjoyed a happier status, for he had been adopted into a family which treated him as one of its members. If he were killed or injured, his family would demand vengeance or recompense. Coûture, then, was removed from public discussion. The council could treat only of the disposition to be made of Jogues and Goupil.

The Mohawks, in the final analysis, were not acting treacherously, nor were they dissimulating. They were torn by indecision and by dissension. The Mohawk nation, like the other four allied nations of the Oneidas, Onondagas, Cayugas, and Senecas, was divided into clans or tribes dedicated to and descended from some symbolic animal, the Bear, the Turtle, the Wolf, the Beaver and in a lower status, the Deer, the Snipe, the Heron, and the Hawk. While the five nations were separate and independent entities, the clans of one nation were bound closely to the clans of another. Thus, a Bear of the Senecas was held to be the kinsman of a Bear of the Mohawks. Thus, too, the Bear and the Wolf and the Turtle clans aggregated themselves as distinct elements in the Mohawk as in the Seneca and other nations.

Three dominant tribes, then, were in conflict within the Mohawk councils. The Wolf and the Turtle clans favored peace with the French, if these could be separated from their alliance with the Hurons and Algonquins. The Bears were convinced that the French would never consent to a separate peace, and therefore emphatically declared for a war to the extermination of the French no less than of the Hurons and Algonquins. It was their clan which had suffered mostly in the battles with the French, and they demanded revenge. The case of Ondessonk and René brought the conflict to a new head. The Wolf and Turtle urged that they be released, as a gesture looking toward future peace. The Bear demanded they be executed, as a gesture of defiance against the French.

The supreme council of the five Iroquois nations was scheduled to be held in the week after the Dutch ambassadors had paid their visit. But a series of violent storms which occurred during the second and third weeks of September caused the postponement of the council until the last week of the month. The concourse of chiefs and sachems gathered in Ossernenon. The Wolfs of the Mohawks felt confident of victory. They had examined the prisoners to determine whether or not they were strong enough to make the journey up to the St. Lawrence. They had chosen the warriors who would act as escort, and the orators who would address Onontio and the French. They had even prepared the provisions for the party.

The council convened. The Wolf and Turtle orators spoke their thoughts. Their proposal was received in dead silence. The national council broke up into clans and families for private discussion. Each smaller division came to a unanimous decision, for or against the proposal. They gathered in general council once more. The Bears announced their opposition; they did not fear the French; they would wage war on the French; they would kill Ondessonk and René; if the Wolf and Turtle brothers attempted to steal away the Frenchmen, they would kill their brothers. Since every proposal must be accepted unanimously, the council adjourned and named the next day for the holding of another session in which the debate could be prosecuted.

Jogues and Goupil were in a more precarious position than ever. The Wolf and Turtle chiefs discussed secretly a plan to kidnap the three French and return them to Three Rivers. The Bears suspected their intention and counseled about forestalling the plan by murdering Ondessonk and René, at least. Squaws of the Bears came to taunt the Frenchmen and to tell them they were already dead men. Bear warriors, as Jogues relates, "tomahawk in hand, prowled about the cabins to find and murder us."

When night came, the council again convened. Every man, woman, and child crowded about the assembly. Jogues, Coûture, and Goupil, under the cloak of the night, concealed themselves near the cabin where the council was held and listened to the speeches. The orators raised their voices vehemently. The presiding officers forgot the calm which ordinarily governed their procedure. The tumult of angry voices increased. Jogues feared the outcome. The Bears were insolently crying out that they would murder the Frenchmen that night. Inspired by God, as he says, Father Isaac snatched the arms of René and Guillaume and hurried them through the deserted moonlit streets of the village, out through the gate of the palisade to a shack belonging to his master in a cornfield some distance away. There the three of them lay concealed all the night.

When they entered Ossernenon the next morning, their friends told them they had barely escaped death. A band of fiery young men of the Bear clan had burst out of the council, determined to end the debate by murdering the Frenchmen. These braves had searched through all the cabins. Nothing could have stopped them, at that time. By morning the elders and chiefs had the young men under partial control. But the leaders of the council were more than ever split apart. So bitter were they, that they were on the verge of fighting. Further talk would but increase the antagonism. And so, in wisdom, they departed hurriedly, Jogues relates, as if in flight. Coûture's family carried him back to Tionontoguen. Jogues and Goupil remained at Ossernenon, not knowing when the tomahawk would split their skulls. "We lost the hope," he says, "which I had not considered very great, of again seeing Three Rivers that year."

II

Recovered to a great extent from the wreckage of their tortures, Father Jogues and René Goupil were left in comparative freedom to wander about Ossernenon. It was all strange to René, whose only experience among the savages was in the Frenchified Christian village of Sillery. Jogues, on the contrary, found the place but little different from the Huron villages of Ihonatiria and Ossossané. The cabins of the Iroquois were of the same pattern as those of the Hurons, long houses of bark, from fifty to one hundred paces in length and some twenty feet in width and in height. Down the central aisle smoldered the line of fires, and along the sides were the heapings of twigs, covered with hides and furs, that served as beds. The poles of the framework of the shed and the rafters were littered with innumerable accessories and possessions. The earthen floor was filthy with rubbish and refuse, crawling with vermin, thick with brown dust. The air was stale and stinking with the nauseating odors of bodies and decaying foods and excrement and dogs and furs and clothes. And now, with September far advanced, and with the heavy rains, the flimsy houses were damp and cold.

Ossernenon was a village of forty or more cabins, of varying sizes, located more or less regularly in plots with paths intersecting. Most of the cabins were situated within the walls of the palisades, which stretched nearly three hundred paces from east to west and half that distance across. The stockade was strongly built of rough tree trunks, closely knitted together, inclining slightly outward. On the inner side of the wall was a hanging platform on which the warriors might perch in defense. Along the outside base of the lines of poles was a deep trench, and beyond this another wall for an outer defense. To the east and west, narrow gates, three or four feet broad, opened toward the cleared fields that extended along the ridge of the hill above the valley, and another rear gate led out toward the south, to a spring and a tiny rivulet which trickled along the base of a ridge which, a musket-shot distant, sloped up gently away from the village.

Jogues and René were at liberty to stroll up this pleasant hillside to the pines and oaks and beeches that crowded its summit, or to walk along the trampled spaces of the fields which commanded the valley. They were sent, at times, down the hollowed road between the trees to the flatlands along the river bank where were the rows of cornstalks and the maturing vegetables. Here they cultivated the soil and gathered the harvest of corn under the command of the squaws. Oftentimes they looked at the hills which reared up across to the north of the valley, beyond which lay the trail to the St. Lawrence. They remembered the six weeks back, when they had descended the slanting path into this vale of slavery, the torture by the ford of the rippling river, the climb up the road to the village, the running of the gauntlet to the gates of the palisades. That tribulation was passed. There remained for them the long, dreary winter of captivity.

Because of his six years of residence among the Hurons, Father Jogues was not only inured to the hardships of the savage mode of life, but was skillful in dealing with the savage mind. Goupil, however, was sickened by the food and the filth. He was unable to comprehend the effect of his conscious and unconscious actions on the Mohawks. In the hospitals at Sillery and Quebec, he had won the affections of the Algonquins by his gentleness and his piety and his kindness; but these virtues enraged the Mohawks. Being a sensitive-souled man who had always been treated courteously, he cowered under the rage of the savages and their open hate and maliciousness. Accordingly, he was despised by them as spiritless and no better than a cringing squaw. He was awkward in his gait, and, though strong, clumsy in the odd duties they ordered him to perform. So mutilated was he in his features because of the batterings he received in running the gauntlet, and so scarred was he in his body by the cuts and burnings, that he created a feeling of disgust in the Iroquois.

René was incapable of realizing the extent or the depth of the suspicions of the savages, and the violent extremes to which their suspicions would fling them. He had not learned the caution which was habitual to Jogues and Coûture in avoiding small irritations. He did not comprehend the charge of being a sorcerer, and how easy it was to act like one, in the estimation of the savages. When he prayed, René would move his lips and occasionally break out into sighs and heavy breaths and exclamations. He would raise his eyes to heaven, or lower his head in deep veneration. He would strike his breast in repentance, or nod his head in reverence at the sacred Name, or make the sign of the cross. He knelt, a posture painful to the savages, for long spells of time, and clasped his hands on his breast. Father Isaac warned him time and again to avoid these and similar manifestations of his devotion, and explained to him the misinterpretations which the Mohawks would deduce, that he was weaving spells against them and invoking hostile demons to come and ruin them.

The virulence of the Mohawks' hatred concentrated on Goupil. Even the chiefs who championed peace with the French were quite willing to allow him to be killed. If he died, but Ondessonk and Ihandich were preserved, that could be explained to the French as the unfortunate act of a senseless young brave. Due apologies and presents could be made. Ondessonk was a Blackrobe, the Mohawks reasoned, and thus a man of importance and repute at Three Rivers and Quebec. It would be difficult to quiet the indignation of the French if he were murdered.

As a precaution, then, the council ordered that Ondessonk and René be separated. They had been under the charge of a chief of the Bear clan, a bitter enemy of the French. He was impelled to greater rage and resentment latterly, because one of his family, a promising young warrior, was slain by the French at the attack on Fort Richelieu. This chief had power of death over his French prisoners. The other chiefs feared he might exercise it and slay both Ondessonk and René. After the great council, therefore, they ordered that Ondessonk be removed to another cabin and given in charge to a less rabid master. This change foreboded no good, Jogues concluded. While they were together, Father Jogues could shield Goupil and could instruct him how to behave, for he relates: "René did not quite realize the danger in which we were. I saw it better than he; and this often led me to tell him that we should hold ourselves in readiness."

Jogues' fears were further intensified by an incident which happened in René's cabin. The young man, in his gentleness and simplicity, had made friends with the very little children. He was playing with a toddling boy of three or four years, the son, probably, of the warrior slain at Fort Richelieu. He lifted the little fellow in his arms and made him chuckle and chortle by putting the old cap he was wearing on the child's head. Then, as he used to do at

Sillery with the children of the Algonquins, he guided the tiny hand of the child to the forehead and breast and shoulders in the sign of a cross.

A scream of anger slashed through the cabin. The grandfather of the baby had been sitting in the dark, watching Goupil and the child. He took a leap at the Frenchman and tore the baby out of his arms, yelling curses and threats. His features were twisted with rage, he trembled with his anger. The Frenchman had made the evil sign on the boy, with the intention of killing him. The Dutch had warned against this sign; it was an invocation to the devils, a diabolical superstition; it always brought ruin and death. The old man put the child aside, and beat and kicked Goupil out of his sight.

When Jogues learned of this, he sought Goupil and led him off, away from the cabin, and outside the palisades. They went out of the south gate, across the rivulet, and ascended the ridge of higher ground to a grove of fir trees. They had discovered this spot some days before. It was quiet there, rather screened from the spying eyes of the savages. They were able to talk and pray in comparative privacy.

Father Isaac spoke plainly: they were in great danger of death because of the insane attitude of the old man; it was not impossible that the old master might cause René to be killed. René protested that he feared nothing the Mohawks could do to him, as long as he was in God's good grace. He then went to confession, which he did every other day, and Father Jogues gave him absolution. They had talked about death and its imminence before, but that afternoon in the fir-grove they renewed their intention that, "mindful of the indulgence at the moment of death, the sacred Name of Jesus would be the last word of our lives." They knelt together on the soft brown needles and prayed: "We offered ourselves to Our Lord with great devotion," Jogues related, "beseeching Him to receive our lives and our blood, and to unite them with His life and His Blood for the salvation of these poor peoples."

The afternoon was growing late when they lifted themselves from their knees and walked out from the grove. As was their custom, they began to say their beads on their way to the cabin. Two savages were coming up the path toward them. One of them was from René's cabin. He was one of the tallest, and claimed to be the strongest, man of the Mohawk nation. He was the brother of the tall chief who had been killed at Fort Richelieu and the son of the old chief whom René had especially angered. Both the savages wore rough, woolen blankets wrapped about their shoulders and covering their folded arms. They awaited Ondessonk and René. The big brave scowled down ferociously on them. "Go back to the village," he curtly commanded.

Jogues read a portent of danger in the face and tone of the man. He whispered to René: "My dear brother, we don't know what these men intend to do. There is very much disturbance going on about us. These men have some evil design. Let us commend ourselves to God and to the Most Blessed Virgin, our good Mother, now, more earnestly than ever." They walked briskly down the hill path, murmuring the Hail Mary. They were now nearing the open space at the foot of the hill, and were in full sight of the palisades, about which loitered the men and squaws and children in the sun of the September afternoon. "Hail Mary, full of grace, the Lord is with thee, blessed art thou among women, and blessed is the fruit of thy womb, Jesus," Father Jogues repeated. Goupil took it up: "Holy Mary, mother of God, pray for us sinners now and at the hour of our death. Amen." They finished the fourth decade.

"You walk ahead," the giant Mohawk commanded Ondessonk. "You wait behind," he said to Goupil. Jogues searched the man's face and eyes for an explanation, but the savage merely glared at him with a masked expression, motionless, and with the blanket held tightly over his arms and hands. Jogues turned and took five or six steps toward the brook. He heard a rustle behind him and wheeled around. He saw the tall Mohawk throw back his blanket, swing the tomahawk he held concealed, raise it, and crash it down on René's head. As the blow fell, he heard René call out: "Jesus, Jesus, Jesus." René staggered a step or two under the impact of the blow, then fell.

In that instant Father Jogues said the words of absolution over Goupil. Then he dropped to his knees, facing the two Mohawks. He looked up at them, and said, hoarsely: "Give me just a moment or two." He removed his cap, bent his head, said an act of contrition, and commended himself to God before he died. He waited; he lifted his head. The Mohawks towering above René watched him. Father Jogues spoke to them: "Do whatever you please. I do not fear death." The savage who struck René answered: "Get up. You are not going to be killed this time. I have no power over you. You belong to another family."

Father Jogues bounded to his feet, to René, who lay face downward in the dust, his hair soaked with blood. He lifted René, and saw that he still breathed. With his right hand, he made the sign of the cross over the split head and again spoke the words of final absolution. The Mohawks also saw that their victim still lived. They tore Ondessonk from the body, and crashed two more sharp, thudding blows on the skull.

The savages squatting about the gate and the palisades came racing across to the spot of the murder, shouting raucously, some in protest, some in alarm, some cheering. They mobbed about the body and the two braves, and trampled over Ondessonk. He tried to force his way to René, but a man of his cabin restrained him and bade him rise. "Go back to the cabin immediately," the man ordered, tense with apprehension. "Remain there. Do not leave it." The mob milled and pushed about him, talking and shouting around his ears. All the hundreds of people of the village swarmed densely before his dazed eyes. They closed in about René's body. The man of his cabin shoved him roughly toward the gate. Blinded with his tears, though clear in mind, he marched back to the cabin.

At the door, the old chief, his master, welcomed him. The man scrutinized him; he was surprised that Ondessonk was so calm. He placed a hand on his heart. It beat steadily, it did not pound with fear or emotion of any sort. Amazed, he called others in the cabin to witness. They felt about his ribs and marveled greatly that Ondessonk's heart was not agitated. The old man was kindly and warned him: "Do not go out from the cabin or out of the village, unless you are accompanied by some one of our family. They intend to strike you to death. Watch out for yourself."

They left him alone, in the gloom of the cabin, sitting before the flickering fire. René was dead. He was free from all his sufferings, from the dreads and anxieties, free at last and happy with God. René's soul went straight to God. He was pure as an angel, innocent, sinless, brave; he loved God so much. His last words were "Jesus, Jesus." He was rescued by Jesus and the Blessed Mother. This day was Monday, September 29; it was the feast of St. Michael the Archangel, most fitting a day for this angel of innocence to shed his blood. René, poor René; it was better for him to die. Now he was happy. He was so steadfast, so loyal, so pious, so simple, so beautiful a soul. René seemed to be close, united to him, as he sat there looking into the flames. René was dead. The grief of it overwhelmed his soul and wracked him.

They came to him, after a little while, and told him that he must leave this family and cabin and go to another cabin. That meant his death, he thought to himself. The people with whom he lived were friendly and sympathetic. He knew the man who now ordered him; he knew him as being hostile. The man spoke roughly and menacingly. Father Jogues cared not; he commended himself to God and to René; he was ready for the death stroke.

He followed the man out of the cabin, into the gloaming September evening. Outside the stockade was great excitement. He could hear a crowd running up and down and shouting. He came to a cabin and entered with his guide. It was the house of one of the great sachems, a man of influence as an elder and as a soothsayer. He was the old chief who had spoken so bitterly against the French, the one who had ordered the Algonquin woman to cut off his thumb. Jogues knew with certainty that he was doomed.

The long cabin was filled with turbulent men and women and children of all ages. Their voices shrilled and grunted, their faces looked fierce in the fretful flames of the fires. They mobbed about him, taunting and threatening him. Stoic as a savage, he remained silent and unafraid. He sat motionless before a fireplace. The crowd raged about him. He is a dead man, they told him. He will follow his comrade. A former Huron, who had been kind enough to give him a pair of old moccasins, asked them back, explaining: "Very soon you will have no more use for them. Some one else would be taking them away from you if I didn't." Jogues stripped off the shoes and handed them back to the savage.

The tumult of the evening died down, the cabin settled to quiet. Jogues stretched himself on a skin and tried to sleep. He did not know what the night would bring. He might be called out to death; some madman might strike him where he lay. He thought of René, and the spirit of his brother hovered over him and consoled him. He would be happy to be with René. Truly, he thought, "René proved that he was no unworthy son of the Society of Jesus. I love him and I venerate him, not only as a brother, but as a martyr; not only as a martyr of obedience, but a martyr of faith and of the cross."

What had happened to the body of René? He must go out to find it, Jogues decided, and give it decent burial. This must be his first duty. He watched for the dawn through a slit in the bark side of the cabin. While it was still tenuous and gray, he went out into the morning. Some dim figures moved about. They recognized him; some were amazed that he still lived, some were surprised at his foolhardiness in showing himself openly. He padded in his bare feet toward the south gate beyond which René was murdered.

He saw standing there the old chief from whose charge he had been taken. The man was troubled at this apparition of Ondessonk, for he wished him well. To Jogues' inquiries, he related that the young men and a troop of children had stripped the body and tied a rope around the neck, and dragged it hither and thither about the stockade and through the streets. They had pulled it out toward the west field, later in the evening, and across to the rim of the ravine where they threw the refuse. The old chief believed that they had tumbled the body down the side of the ravine toward the little stream which flowed to the river.

Jogues thanked him and turned to go out of the gate. The old man called him back in alarm. "You have no sense," he burst out at Ondessonk. "Where are you hurrying to? You are no more than alive yourself. You are liable to be killed at any moment. Don't you see that they are seeking you, to murder you. And yet you want to go out to find the body of a dead man who is already half corrupted and which has been dragged away, far from the village. You have no sense at all. Look, don't you see those young braves going out of the gate and how fierce they look? They will kill you as soon as you step out of the stockade."

Father Jogues stood for a moment undecided. He must go. "An overwhelming care and anxiety possessed me," he revealed, "to discover what had been done with the body of my beloved friend and companion. I made up my mind to seek out the body, no matter what the danger to myself, and, if I could possibly do so, to bury it in the earth. Our Lord gave me courage enough to wish to die in this act of charity. I had no fear of anything that might happen to me. For truly it was a pain to live in such bitter anguish, and it was a profit to die in doing such a work of charity." Under the compulsion of these thoughts, despite the warning of his friend, he strode off toward the west gate. The kindly old man no longer had authority over Ondessonk, but he had a care for his safety, and so ordered an Algonquin whom he had adopted, to follow and protect him.

Jogues, with the Algonquin plodding after him, passed beyond the stockade. In the soft dust of the field he noted the swaths crossing and crisscrossing where René had been dragged. Sullen, surly men and squaws watched him; they waited to see if any of the braves would follow and strike him down. He walked fearless, as if unconscious of the enemies all about. He came to the edge of the field fringed with trees, and the dark, sharp declivity that fell down almost straight to the bottom of the ravine. Buzzards circled in the heavens above, and dogs prowled about amid the shrubs. Jogues and the Algonquin slid down the precipitous clay, from tree to tree. Some fifty or sixty feet below they came on the naked, rigid, dirt-smeared body of René. It lay stark on the damp grass by the stream. Dogs and rodents had been at it and had torn a part of the loins. The rope was still tight about the throat.

Stricken with grief, appalled, Father Jogues folded the sacred remains in his arms. He wept bitter tears over the gashed head. He must hurry. He looked about, fearful that he was being spied upon. No one was visible save the silent Algonquin. He had no tool with him to dig a grave. He must hide the body somewhere, and come back with a spade to bury it. The bed of the stream would be a good place for concealment. Only a shallow trickle of water flowed down, and the hollow was strewn with gray cobblestones. With the help of the Algonquin, he lifted the body over the crumbling bank and lowered it five or six feet to the bottom of the rivulet. He bent the stiff arms and legs straight and laid René on the rocky bed of the stream. Then he lined the body about with rounded stones, and piled other stones in a mound over it, so that it was completely concealed from the eye and safe from the clawing of animals.

Quiet in soul, he ascended from the gloom of the ravine and strode across the field to his cabin. As he entered, two youngish warriors confronted him. He recognized them; they were two brothers who had been with the band which captured him and who had been especially cruel to him. They announced that they had orders to lead him with them to the next village of Andagaron. He perceived at once that they were lying, that they had evil intentions against him.

He betrayed no trepidation, no surprise. Casually he told them: "I am not my own master. Ask those who have charge over me. If they send me, or tell me to go, I will accompany you willingly." They were abashed at his attitude and his answer. They had hoped to trick him out of sight of the village, without letting the chief who was his master know of their designs.

His former master heard of the attempt and tried to dissuade the two braves from committing the murder. He also warned the present master, and insisted that he protect Ondessonk. The old chief agreed, protesting, nevertheless, that he had no love for the French and not much affection for Ondessonk. But his sister, an old squaw of power among her people, pitied the Frenchman. She called him "Nephew," and he addressed her as "Aunt." She took it on herself to watch over his safety, and for the rest of that day harbored him safely in the cabin.

He was restless, feverish to escape from her surveillance and to go bury René. He could find no chance all the day. Night came on. He planned to rise before the village awoke, steal out alone, and inter the body secretly, where none of the savages could find and dishonor it. She divined his anxiety and kept him in her sight. The next day she thought it might be safer to get him out of the cabin where a continual rabble was about him, threatening and cursing him. She put him under guard of two of her sons, who were bound by honor to preserve his life, and sent him down to work in the plot of ground she cultivated in the flat by the river.

While he worked, he happened to look up. The two braves who had tried to lure him off the day before were dashing across the field toward him. One of them flourished his hatchet. Father Jogues prepared for death. The old chief, his master, also saw the two men. He sprang to interpose himself. He howled out at the man, shouting a torrent of abuse and waving his arms. The fellow halted, then brazenly turned away. Again Jogues felt himself saved by the power of God. "Through such occurrences did the Almighty teach me," he stated, "that I should cast all my anxiety on Him, knowing that He has care over me and that I should not fear the face of man, knowing that, since the Almighty is the protector of my life, not a hair could fall from my head without His willing it."

That afternoon a violent storm burst over the village. Blasts of rain beat down torrentially on the bark of the cabin, thunder cracked and rumbled over the valley and the hills. Jogues sat alone in the damp gloom of the lodge, and planned. Night came on and the storm continued intermittently. He dozed a bit, but waited for the first lifting of the morning. In the haze of the dawn he crawled out of the door of the cabin, taking with him a spade which he had borrowed from another hut, the better to conceal his purpose. He slunk out of the western gates of the palisades. Seeing himself free, he dashed across the wet stubble of the open field toward the ravine. He was a fleet runner and agile; recklessly he cast himself over the edge of the ravine and slid down the steep muddy banks. At the bottom of the gorge he found the rivulet swollen into a torrent by the rains. The water swirled by turbulently, up to the level of the banks.

He shivered in the raw October morning. He waded in the stream to the place where he had concealed Goupil under the stones. He toppled in the rush of the waters. He sounded the bed with his naked feet, searching for the mound of stones. Strange, he could not locate it. He calculated anew, and stepped about in the stream, and poked around the bottom with a rod, and peered down into the water, which beat waist-high about him. At last, he traced out the line of rocks with his feet. They were scattered. He bent over and felt with his hands; the cold water splashed about his face and shoulders. The mound was torn apart. The body was gone. René was not there.

"They have carried off René, my brother," he cried aloud in his first anguish. Then he thought: "No, the swollen waters might have tumbled the stones loose and carried the body downstream toward the river." He followed down the current for some yards, feeling with his feet and the stick. Climbing to the bank, he walked along it, scanning the stream and the bush. He descended to the flats over which the stream flowed into the Mohawk River, then crossed to the far bank, and up to the spot where he had left the body. He waded into the freezing water, and fought against its force, and stumbled over the ragged stones and slipped on the cobbles. "What groans did I not utter then? What tears did I not shed, mingling them with the waters of the stream? All the while, I chanted to Thee, O my God, the psalms that are recited by Holy Church in the service of the dead."

Again returned his first thought. The Mohawks had stolen away the body to spite him and to dishonor René the more. He clambered to the soggy grass along the banks, searching among the weeds and undergrowth. He scoured all the bottom of the ravine, seeking some trace of where the body had been dragged, among the trees, in the tall grass, under the vines. He was chilled to the bone. Nevertheless, he trudged up the course of the stream, along the two forks, of which one led to the village and the other into a deep gorge, on both banks, darting hither and thither, everywhere looking, always praying and weeping in his agony. Nowhere could he discover René in all the ravine.

Desolated in soul and numbed in body, he slowly dragged himself up the steep ascent toward the village. It made no difference now that the light of the morning was about him. He cared not who saw him, whether he was killed or let live. He must find out what they did with René's body. About the palisades, some braves were lounging. He asked them about René. They jeered at him and mimicked his words. He pleaded with all he met, but no one would answer his questions until he found an Algonquin squaw who was friendly. She told him that it was useless for him to search any more. The young men discovered where he had laid the corpse, she related, and had carried it off and thrown it in a river a mile or two below the village. This was a river, she explained, which he had never seen and which he could reach only with difficulty. It was useless for him to try to go there, for the corpse was already washed away. He suspected that she lied. But he could learn no more and could do no more for René.

III

Alone now, Father Jogues waited for his death stroke. He was certain that what had happened to René was fated for him. The faction hostile to the French was dominant. No punishment was meted out to the murderer of Goupil; rather, this brave was the more honored. The Bear clan hated Ondessonk rabidly, and sought an occasion to strike him down. That he still lived was a daily surprise to him. "In the midst of many other dangers," he noted, "some of which I knew and others of which I did not know, the Lord preserved me, despite the fact that the Iroquois were unwilling that I be preserved and were furious thereby. I passed several days on which they came to kill me. But Our Lord did not permit this, in ways which it would be tedious to explain."

He was at the mercy of the rabble and was not under the protection of the governing chiefs of the nation. He was not a hostage, nor an adopted member of any family. His only shield against violence was the old squaw whom he called his "aunt." She exercised greater influence than other women in the village, because of her lineage and the chiefs who belonged to her cabin. Her aged husband looked kindly on Ondessonk and sought to guard him against attack. Her brother, who technically had charge over Ondessonk, was hostile to the French, but was honorable enough to fend off harm from his slave, as a matter of strict duty as well as to comply with his sister's wishes. From September 29, when Goupil was slain, till the middle of October, Father Jogues survived. He lived, however, from hour to hour.

His single garment was a piece of cloth, about seven hand-breadths wide and long enough only to wrap about his middle. On an afternoon, when he was entering the cabin, a half-wit lad belonging to one of the families of the lodge, demanded that Ondessonk give him part of this cloth, and indicated a strip about two hand-breadths wide. Jogues followed his usual procedure of taking every request seriously and quietly. He reasoned with the simpleton: "My brother, I would gladly give it to you, but the cloth is already so narrow that it shelters only the half of my body. If you cut off even a little, you will reduce me to a nakedness that is indecent in the sight of everyone. Besides, it is my only covering at night; and you see me shivering with cold every night, for I have only this short, thin cloth. However, do as you please."

The simpleton flew into a rage. He was insulted beyond endurance by this dog, Ondessonk, who had the insolence to refuse him a strip of cloth. He went out gibbering and crying, swearing he would bring back somebody to kill Ondessonk. A short time after, Father Jogues went to a cabin where some of the Huron Christians lived, for he visited them daily and instructed them, and, as he states, "bore them again till Christ should be formed in them." The idiot burst into the cabin in high dudgeon, and fiercely ordered Ondessonk back to his home. Jogues obeyed, and marched off with the wild savage following him. Some of the women in the cabin, sympathizing with the lad, went off at his suggestion to look for the brave who had struck down René. They searched for the man all through the village, but in vain. Father Jogues waited patiently under the guard of the simpleton, and was released only in the evening when his "aunt" returned.

About the time of this incident, the only son of Jogues' "aunt" died. Two of his kinswomen held Ondessonk responsible for the death. They claimed that he cast evil spells about the man. They resolved to sacrifice Ondessonk to the shade and memory of the warrior. Plotting with the simpleton, they persuaded the man who guarded Ondessonk to allow him to go with them down to the cornfield by the river and help them carry back a load of corn. They set out the next morning, very early. Jogues noticed that the two women carried ears of corn, heads of squash, and other articles. He concluded, as he relates, "that these things were the fee for my execution. But I 'like a deaf man heard not' the vain things they devised, and 'like a dumb man opened not my mouth, and I was made like a man who did not hear nor had a reply in his mouth.' Because in Thee, O Lord, have I hoped. But mindful of His weakness, 'who was led like a lamb to the slaughter,' I went to my death, begging the Lord with David, 'that he might turn away evil from my enemies and scatter them in His truth.' "

Father Jogues followed the women out of the gate and down the road toward the river. At the foot of the hill, he saw René's murderer coming across the flats from the river trail. "Seeing him at a distance," says Jogues, "I commended myself for the last time to God, and begged Him to receive my soul, broken with care and anguish. But my sins did not yet allow me to merit that blessing." The women ran forward to accost the man, to make their request. He listened to them, and glared wickedly at Ondessonk. Praying desperately to God within him, Father Jogues looked back at the man with steady eyes. Thus they stood facing each other for some moments. Then, without a word, the warrior strode past Ondessonk and up the path to the village. At the same moment the man's mother came hurrying along. She was on her way back from her field, with a pack of corn on her back. Understanding the situation immediately, she let loose a volume of excited scoldings against the two women. They shrank from her and ran off in fright, leaving Jogues alone in the road.

Of his existence among the Mohawks from the time of his arrival on August 14 to mid-October, Jogues says: "Amid these dreads and alarms, these recurring deaths, while every day I die, or rather live a life harder to bear than any death, there passed two months. During these two months, I made no effort to study the Iroquois tongue; for why should I learn it, since I believed I was about to die at any moment? The village was a prison to me. I avoided being seen. I loved the quiet, lonely places, in the solitude of which I begged God that He should not disdain to speak to His servant, that He should give me strength in the midst of these fearful trials. In these trials, let me add, if I am regarded as a prodigy by many people, God was my strong helper, God, Who, by His overabundant goodness, often held up the soul of me in my anguish. I had recourse to the help of Holy Scriptures, my only refuge 'in my tribulations which had come upon me exceedingly.' These Scriptures I venerated, and with them I wished to die. Among all the books which we were carrying with us, at the time of our capture, for the use of the French living among the Hurons, by chance only one had fallen into my hands. It was the Epistle of St. Paul to the Hebrews, paraphrased by the Most Reverend Anthony Godeau, Lord Bishop of Gratz. This little book, with a picture in it of St. Bruno, the illustrious founder of the Carthusian Order, to which some indulgences were attached, I always carried with me. And in addition, I carried a cross which I had made for myself, rudely enough, out of wood. So that, no matter where the death which I had always present before my eyes should overwhelm me, I should die, and die most willingly, with the Sacred Scriptures, which had always been my greatest consolation; and with the graces and indulgences of our Holy Mother the Church, which always I had loved greatly, but at that time more tenderly than ever; and with the cross of my Lord and Saviour."

It happened, about two weeks after the death of René, that God manifested Himself to Father Jogues by way of a vision during his sleep, as He did, Lalemant remarks, "of old to the Patriarchs of the Old Testament." The inspiration and the strength that he drew from this occurrence made easy all his travail. He described the experience as follows:

After the death of my dearest companion, René Goupil of happy memory, at a time when I was being sought out daily for slaughter and when I was overwhelmed with anguish of soul, these things which I shall relate occurred to me in my sleep:

I had gone forth from our village, as was my habit, in order that I might groan more freely to You, my God, that I might pour out my prayers to You in Your sight, that I might pronounce before You my tribulations. When I returned to the village, behold, I find that all is new. I see the double row of palisades which enclose our village as if they were changed into towers and bulwarks and walls of amazing beauty. But I see them in such a manner that they did not bear the appearance of a city newly constructed, but of a city built for a long time, of a city venerable with age. I doubted that this was our village. But then, some Iroquois whom I knew very well, came out from the city. They assured me that it was, indeed, our same village.

And so, marvelling in amazement, I walked up toward this new city and passed through the first gate. I see on the post of the second gate, on the right-hand side as I enter, the letters L.N. cut in large capitals, and below them the picture of a lamb as though it were slaughtered. A wonder it was to me, at first, to imagine how savages, entirely ignorant of our letters, should have been able to sculpture out these characters. Then, still wondering, when I seek to find an explanation of this, I see on a chart, that seemed to be rolled out above the letters, these words fully expressed and corresponding to each of the letters placed below:

Laudent nomen ejus
L. N. (lamb)

Then, as though a light was borne in the depth of my soul, it seemed to me that there could be no doubt whatsoever but that they most especially praised the name of the Lamb who in distress and tribulations strove to imitate the meekness of Him who like a lamb made Himself mute before those who sheared Him and Who was led as a lamb to slaughter. Encouraged by these thoughts, I enter within the gate of that new city. This gate was built of square and polished stone, most beautiful to gaze upon, and was in the form of a portico with a deep vault.

In the middle of this portico, on the opposite side of the road I was following, I see a military guardhouse built there. Within it were arquebuses, arrows, and arms of every pattern. However, I saw no one at all. Then there came into my mind the thought that even if I saw no one at all, I ought, nevertheless, to salute the arms in the accustomed manner. While, therefore, I turned in that direction and lifted my hat, a soldier stationed on the same side of the road whither I was approaching, warned me that I must halt.

Whether it was because I was facing in another direction, or whether the novelty of the things which I was beholding gripped my mind so completely, I neither saw the soldier, nor understood him. For the second time, then, in a louder voice, he repeats: "Halt, there, I tell you." Thereupon, as if recalled to myself, I withheld my steps. He spoke to me again: "What do you mean? Is that the way you show yourself obedient to the sentinel stationed on guard before the palace of the kings that it is necessary to tell you the second time, 'Halt there'? Right now I shall lead you to our judge and leader (those two words, judge and leader, were very clear to me, of which one was juridical and the other was military) who will inflict on you the penalty worthy of your temerity."

I answered him: "My dear friend, as soon as I heard your voice, in that very spot I halted; and I did not advance beyond."

He was in no way moved by my excuse, but hurried me away to stand in judgment. Along that same side of the roadway up which I was advancing, a little before the guardhouse, which was on the opposite side, there was a gate which opened into the palace. This palace appeared to me like to those chambers which we call in France the Gold Rooms, where justice is dispensed; or like to those rooms in the more ancient and celebrated monasteries which are called Chapter Rooms. (The appearance and idea of each kind of place remained in my mind). It was a room magnificently beautiful. In that Chamber was an old man, venerable indeed and most majestic, like to the Ancient of Days. He was clothed in a robe of royal purple, of dazzling beauty. On his head he did not wear the four-sided Doctor's hat, but a cap. Nor was he seated on a throne, but walked about quietly and benignly rendering justice to the people, from whom he was separated by a great railing. About this palace, I saw a great concourse of people, of all ranks, as we see them in Europe before the palace doors. And I saw some whom I recognized. They asked me how things were among the Hurons. Then I said to myself: "Good! They know who I am and how innocent I am, being brought before this judge. I shall be treated more leniently."

Nevertheless, my judge listened to the charge made by the soldier. Without questioning me at all, he drew a rod out from the bundle of rods near him (this bundle seemed to me to be like the fascis which used to be carried by the lictors before the Roman Consuls in the old days).

He drew out a rod, I say, and beat me long and severely, at first on the shoulders, and then on the neck, and finally about the head. I felt the pain intensely; although it was a single hand that scourged me, I seemed, nevertheless, to experience a suffering as great as that which I had endured when, at my entrance into the first village, the warriors from all the Iroquois country rushed out of the gates at us and with most savage cruelty beat us down with their clubs. Not a single complaint, not a single groan did I utter under these strokes. I endured the pain of all that was visited on me, and I found patient endurance in the thought of my own unworthiness.

Finally, my judge, almost as if he were in admiration of my patience, laid aside the rod with which he had been striking me; he clasped his arms about my neck most sweetly, and soothed my grief, and imparted to me a feeling of happiness wholly divine and entirely inexplicable. And then, overwhelmed by that heavenly consolation, I kissed the hand which had been smiting me, and, exalted as it were into an ecstasy of soul, I exclaimed: "Thy rod, O God, my King, and thy staff, they have comforted me." When I had said this, he conducted me back to the door of the palace and left me there on the threshold.

When I awoke from sleep, therefore, and began to think deeply on what I had seen, I could not doubt that God had wrought wonders in my soul—not only because of the wonderfully apt connection there was between the things which I had seen, the appearance of which I had never had in my mind before, but also and especially because of the great fire of love which my Judge had kindled in the depth of my soul when he embraced me and I burst forth into those words: "Thy rod," etc. The remembrance of this was so poignantly sweet that it drew tears of the most wonderful consolation from my eyes for many months thereafter.

And so, I considered that the city placed newly there where our village had been, was the mansion of the Blessed, which heretofore I had not merited to enter, but which I might enter sometime if I should persevere in patience and in faithfulness to the end; and I could hope that some day it might happen that that village in which I had suffered, and indeed was still suffering such cruel torments, might be converted for me into that holy city. In that city which I was regarding as our village (at least it was superimposed almost on the same spot on which a little before our village had been) I saw not one of our savages; some of them, indeed, I saw going out when I was entering the gate, but none of them within. For in that city, nothing will enter that is defiled; outside are the despicable, outside are the impure. That guardhouse (in which I saw no one) I believed to be the station of the angels, whose faces were turned toward Paradise rather than to earthly sights. And finally, that tribunal and that judge, before whom I was dragged and by whom I was welcomed with blows, I believed to be the Divine Judgment, through which those who are to be admitted are "purified"; in which workmen by the salutary strokes of sharp-pointed instruments and by much buffeting with the mallet, polish the stones and place them in their position and thus build that holy city.

Finally, I was led back to the threshold and left there, and I did not enter into that holy city. I lifted up my eyes, however, that at least I might see that holy city which I was not entering. I saw streets similar to the streets of the city which St. John describes in the Apocalypse, pure streets, clean streets, streets breathing forth holiness itself. The blows which were landed upon my back, they were all the external torments which I had gone through among the savages. Those implanted on my neck, I interpreted as the insults, mockeries, and taunts and the yoke of the slavery among the barbarians. The blows upon my head I interpreted as the tomahawk or the fire, death itself. In truth, I wondered about one thing, namely, though I had received the strokes of the judge, I was not admitted. I asked myself whether it might be that I will live amid this terrible cruelty of the savages who sought me out daily for death, and that I might not die? I was not admitted; I was sent back; and I began to believe that I would not die, at least, not so very soon. And the strokes which I had received on the head I began to interpret as the most interior anguishes and griefs of my soul.

A thing which led me to believe all the more that I would not die was the fact that often in my dreams I seemed to be following after some one who went before me, but not to be catching up to him. I was believing that this one was my dear companion whom the eternal happiness of the blessed had enfolded. And while I followed after him from afar, I mourned him when he was snatched from before my eyes by the turnings and twisting of the roads. And then sometimes when I followed after him, I was attracted by the beauty of the churches which stood along the road and I entered into them in order to pray. But then, since I lingered longer than I should, fascinated by the magnificence of them or distracted by the sweetness of the singing, in the same way, I grieved afterwards for having lost him.

From this revelation, Father Jogues understood that it was not appointed for him to die in this flurry of hate which followed the murder of René. He realized that there was no possibility of his being released and returned to Three Rivers or ransomed to the Dutch. He believed that God had ordained that he should continue in his daily slavery in Ossernenon, and that he should be subjected to the living martyrdom, at least through the autumn that was then burnishing the hills and the valley of the Mohawks. His death might occur at any moment during the winter, from natural causes, from some new burst of fury, for no reason whatsoever. If he died, if he were murdered, that would be less hard a trial than the anguish and the sufferings of his slavery; there would be the joy of heaven, for eternity, after death. If he lived, and were forced to live through many months, that would be a bitter, long-drawn-out martyrdom.

This living death of slavery, he concluded, was his lot. And so he brushed aside the shadows that had seemed to portend his death. He confidently faced life. He was energized by the sweetness of the consolation and the flood of powerful grace imparted to him by God during his sleep. He began to interest himself in the language of the Iroquois, and conceived the hope of instructing some of them in the Faith. He came to regard them not as savages plotting his death, but as brothers whom he might lead to God.

CHAPTER X

Through Months of Slavery

I

OSSERNENON tingled with the crisp, bracing air of the autumn. The grass and underbrush were withering; the trees, stripped of their leaves of russet and red and tan, were black and gaunt; the first frosts were whitening the fields. It was the time for the Mohawks to fare forth to the hunting-grounds. Second only to war was the joy of the chase. Warriors conditioned their muskets and carefully packed their powder, primed their bows and fitted flints to their arrows, sharpened their knives and daggers, fashioned their spears, twisted strands of the elm into ropes, sliced thongs from the hides, wove the network of the traps, contrived litters from the tough hickory wood. Squaws packed cornmeal into the bark sacks and the bags, bundled together their pots and kettles, rolled the layers of birch bark for the building of the huts, gathered the twines of tendrils and the animal threads, tied together the axes and hatchets and knives, and assembled all the things needed for the shelter in the mountains.

Chiefs paraded the streets of Ossernenon lustily announcing their intention to leave for the hunt. Braves and young men, families, squaws, attached themselves to the chiefs. Some were following the trails to the mountains that lay directly south; some were heading to the highlands of the southwest, to the headwaters of the two rivers; but the majority were resolving to ascend straight to the gigantic mountains and the deep valleys of the northland. They formed their parties, they held their feasts and offered their sacrifices to Areskoui, the demon of the chase, the holder of the heavens; they chanted and danced and boasted their prowess; and in great parade, they marched out of the gates of the stockade, the warriors leading the way, the squaws plodding after with the baggage and babies.

Father Jogues followed with the squaws in one of the hunting-parties going toward the mountains of the north. He had been loaned by his master to another family than his own, in order to help carry the burdens. For clothing, he had only a thin shirt and torn breeches and a cloak. His stockings were shreds and his moccasins were worn into holes. Already he had suffered so from the October cold that he had begged for garments to protect him. The rags they gave him were not sufficient to warm him along the trail and amid the snows of the mountains.

Even though he was emaciated and still shattered by the torments he had endured, he had to bear up under the heavy load they strapped on his shoulders and the bundles they shoved under his arms. The men strode on in advance, unencumbered save for their muskets and other implements of war and the chase. The squaws and Ondessonk padded stolidly in single file to the rear. The trail coursed across the valley and up the hills along which he had approached Ossernenon in the torrid heats of August. Some miles on, it cut through to the left and wound among the foothills of the mountains.

All day long, the caravan maintained its grinding, dogged pace along the narrow path. At nightfall, they camped within the shelter of a grove or on the lee of a hill. Jogues could then lay aside his burdens, but he had to forage for firewood and water, under the shrill commands of the women. He snatched what portions of mushed corn he could get out of the pots, despite the blows and kicks of the Mohawks, who treated him as they would one of the dogs. His legs and feet were torn and bloodied by the swordgrass and rushes and thorny stubble over which the trail led, so that, after only one day of travel he could scarcely walk from the pain. But he had to stumble along, the next day and the next.

Always, they were climbing to higher altitudes, into the towering mountains white with snow. The air and the winds were piercingly cold. About the fifth or sixth day they had progressed about ninety miles and reached their hunting-station in the region of the lakes that were cupped in the valleys between the peaks of the mountains. There the squaws, under the direction of the men, threw up the three slanting poles of the hunting-huts and tied them at the top and sewed the bark and skins firmly about the triangular frame.

"This season, which is one of joy and relaxation of spirit to the savages," Jogues recorded, "was a season of increase of new sorrow for me." At first, the family to whom he had been loaned treated him kindly, for he was a help to them. They granted him little privileges, saw that he secured some food, and shared some of their blankets with him. In the night camps, while they sat about their fire, they talked to him and put questions for him to answer. He himself tells: "As I was mindful that I should uphold the character and office given to me by God, I began to teach them unostentatiously, as much as I was able, about the adoration due to the one God, about the observance of the Commandments, about heaven and hell and other mysteries of our Faith."

Tracking along the journey, he was something of an entertainment for them, something of a novelty, with his attempts to speak their language, with his earnestness to make them understand him. He was docile and eager to help, and that they appreciated. But in the zest of their arrival at the hunting-grounds, they lost interest in his talk, and for the greater part, in his existence. When he tried to press himself on them, they became irritated by his repetition of the elements of Faith, by his condemnation of their beliefs. They turned against him, ridiculing and mocking him and driving him out of their sight.

Upon their arrival at the mountain lakes, the Mohawks offered their sacrifices to Areskoui, the deity of the hunt, who was most powerful to lead into their traps the deer and the elk and the moose, and equally powerful to prevent them from having any success in the chase. Assembled about the huge fire, the head of the party held up before him the choicest portion of the first animal they killed, while he exhorted the elder or the sorcerer to offer supplication. The disciple of Areskoui, then, in a vibrant, clear voice, pleaded: "O demon Areskoui! Behold! We offer to thee these meats and from them we prepare for thee a banquet, so that thou mayest eat of the meats, and show us where the deer lurk, and drive them into our traps." Each day the sacrifice was repeated, and the meat was thus dedicated to Areskoui, the great god of the Mohawks.

Father Jogues, when he understood the significance of this ceremony, was troubled in conscience. "I was filled with a deep detestation of this superstition of the savages," he declared, "and I firmly resolved to abstain forever from the meat offered in this way." There was an abundance of game. The savages gorged themselves with feasting and were generous in offering the venison to Ondessonk. He needed the sustenance sorely, for he was still weakly and the cool air of the mountains created a ravenous appetite in him. He craved for the flesh, but he refused to permit himself to touch it. He ate only the corn which had been brought as fare along the road.

For the first week or two the hunters were successful. They beat up the stags and the elks from their coverts, and drove them headlong toward the fences stretched between the trees and into the narrowing alleys of the traps, where they could be easily slaughtered. They tracked the animals over the rise and fall of the mountains, and had the zest of dropping them with musket or arrow or javelin. At the day's end they returned jubilant, and made the forests ring with their chants of thanksgiving to Areskoui and the other demons.

Their luck changed. The animals grew scarce. The hunters ranged all the territory for miles about the camp. They found few tracks, and could scare up no game anywhere. They traveled farther into the ridges and the glens, but with little success. Back at the camp, they sought reason for the change in fortune. Areskoui was offended and was angry with them. Why? They debated. A sorcerer revealed the cause. Ondessonk had refused to eat the venison; he had spoken contemptuously of Areskoui; he wove charms by his prayers and gestures so that the animals were commanded to leave their haunts and go to another part of the mountains. The hunters, believing what the sorcerer said to be true, turned their rage on Ondessonk. They berated and beat him, and hated him more than ever.

He tells of himself: "The savages interpreted my abstinence from meat and my contempt of their demon as the cause of their taking little game: 'the wicked have hated me without cause.' And so, since they hated me so much that they were not willing to listen to my instructions, or to answer my questions about their language, by means of which I could refute their fables, I decided to devote myself to spiritual exercises. Accordingly, every morning during these days, I set forth from the midst of Babylon, that is, our hut, where there was constant worship paid to the demon and to dreams, and I 'was saving myself in the mountains,' that is, on a neighboring hill."

In the retreat of a spruce grove he erected for himself a cross of shaggy wood, and, he relates: "at the foot of this cross I spent almost the whole day with my God, whom I alone, in these vast regions, worshiped and loved. Sometimes I meditated, sometimes I prayed, sometimes I read from an *Imitation of Christ* which I had recently recovered." To coördinate his prayer better, he followed the order of prayer laid down by Saint Ignatius in the *Spiritual Exercises.*

Not for long was he permitted to pray in peace. The savages spied upon him in his wooded oratory. At times they were sportive. They crept silently on him while he knelt, oblivious of all but God, and rose suddenly with whoops and yells. They stood concealed some distance away, and sent their arrows whizzing dangerously near him. They lurked along his path and lopped off branches or toppled trees over to fall on him. As he walked they leaped from hiding-places and brandished their tomahawks about his head, as if they would strike him dead. Since their petty tricks did not seem to frighten him overmuch, nor disturb his composure, they became more enraged. Besides, the game was utterly failing.

They believed that his silence and his disregard for them was his way of showing his triumph, for they were certain, now, that he had snatched the animals from them by his charms and incantations. In particular, they attacked him because of the cross he had built for himself. They tore it down and broke the wood into splinters: "We hate the wood crossed," they shrieked at him. "It is not a good omen. We have nothing to do with it. The white men who are our neighbors and friends they do not have it. They hate it. They have warned us to beware of it."

Since it was made impossible for him to enjoy any peace in his spruce grove, he went farther into the forests and varied his place of prayer. He found a hidden recess into which he could slip unobserved. It was at the base of a majestic tree, round which the undergrowth was thick and matted with vines. He skinned the bark off the trunk of the tree in the shape of a cross, and there again he knelt in prayer. The keen-eyed savages soon discovered his new haunt, and the white cross cut into the tree. They stripped the bark off the tree, defacing the sacred image, and beat him unmercifully.

"Upon this, I changed my way of acting," he affirmed. "Before this happened, with set purpose, I had avoided praying openly and aloud, and kneeling in their cabins. I did not wish to give them even the slightest pretext for complaint on this score, for we must act most prudently at all times when we are among barbarians who are not accustomed to our practices. Now, I decided that I should no longer refrain from these exercises of devotion, for by them the spiritual life is built up, a life which I prized more than the temporal. Moreover, I believed this manner of acting would be profitable to them in the future, at such time as their conversion would be brought about, a thing 'which the Father had put in His own power.' "

They regarded Ondessonk all the more as an abomination. They said he was an evil demon, that all he touched became contaminated. They forbade him to lay a finger on anything in the cabins, and drove him out of the camp on many occasions. He describes his condition: "Indeed, under the influence of that terrific hate of the savages, I suffered beyond telling from the cold, the hunger, from the contempt of the basest of them, from the furious ill-temper of the women; since the hunt furnished them almost everything that counts for wealth, they hated me as the cause of their want and poverty. Great hunger, also, I had to endure. Since nearly all the venison, and on the hunt they eat scarcely anything else, was offered in sacrifice to the demons, I spent many days without eating. It happened day after day that when I came in about nightfall, fasting, I would see our Egyptians seated about their fleshpot which I had forbidden to myself by my own rigid law. Although reasons occurred to me why I should not act in this way, and although these reasons were persuasive, nevertheless, by the grace of God, I never once permitted myself to be swayed from my resolution. As a starving man, I said to my Lord: 'We shall be filled with the good things of thy house.' 'I shall be satisfied when thy glory shall appear,' 'when truly you will fill the desire of thy servant's hungering, in the holy city, Jerusalem,' 'which thou wilt fill forever with the fat of the corn.' I suffered greatly from the cold, in the midst of the deep snows, with nothing to wear but a short and threadbare cloak. Especially at night did I suffer, since I was forced to sleep on the bare ground, or on the rough bark of trees. Though they had plenty of deerskins, many of which they were not using, they would give me none. Sometimes, on an extremely bitter night, shivering from the cold, I would take one of the skins secretly; as soon as they discovered it, they would rise up and take it away from me. That shows how terribly much they hated me. My skin was now in such a state that I could say with David: 'It had withered with the filth of the dust.' It was split open with the cold, all over my body, and caused me intense pain."

A greater anguish than that of being naked and cold and hungry and despised was his. He was assailed by a terrifying desolation, an almost unendurable sadness of soul. God seemed to have forgotten and rejected him. The powers of hell seemed to swarm about him and to oppress him. He could derive no sensible consolation from the prayers he offered to God; he was borne down by a hopelessness that bordered on despair. At times, a gleam from God came to dissolve the blackness that enveloped him. He narrates in this regard:

It seemed to me on a certain day, that I was present at a consultation with several Fathers of our Society whom I had known when they were alive and whose virtue and merit I esteemed most highly. I have not a distinct recollection of any of them, however, except of Father Jacques Bertric; I have some recollection of Father Estienne Binet, and more vaguely of Father Pierre Coton. I begged them, with all the most intense ardor of love, to secure favor for me from the Holy Cross, to the end that it might receive me as a disciple of Him who had been fastened upon its arms, that it might not cast me off. I remember that I adduced an argument which had never come into my mind before, even while I was praying or meditating before the Cross; I alleged that I was a fellow-citizen of the Cross, since I had been born in a city whose principal and metropolitan church was dedicated to the Holy Cross.

A similar instance, which affected him deeply, he recorded as follows:

At another time, when I was in the grove where I prayed, I seemed to myself to be in the city of my birth, in the cloister of the Cathedral of the Holy Cross. From the cloister, I entered the shop of a bookseller whom I knew well. I asked him if he did not have some new book that was pious and edifying. He answered that he had one which he valued very highly; it was a book about illustrious men. At his answer, I felt an overwhelming desire to examine the book, and so I asked him if he would lend it to me for a few days. I assured him that I would return it very promptly, just as soon as I had read it in my own room with two or three of my closest friends. The bookseller showed some unwillingness; he told me that the book was very valuable in his estimation.

Meanwhile, some people who were in the shop were talking about tribulations and misfortunes; each one was relating what he had suffered. And I dared to say that I had suffered something for God. After some time, since I could not see the book which I was desiring so earnestly, I undertook to ask one of the servants to look for it and fetch it to me. The servant, acting as if he were concealing the matter from his master, brought me this book which I wished so much to acquire. When he placed it in my hands I heard a voice saying: "This book contains the lives of men illustrious for their sanctity and of hearts brave in war." These are the very words which I heard; they stamped this truth upon my soul, that it is always necessary for us through many tribulations to enter into the kingdom of heaven. Now, as I was leaving the shop, full of happiness in the possession of the book, I saw the whole place covered, as it were, with crosses. I told the master of the shop that I would return, as I wished to buy some of the crosses which he had in great quantities and of all patterns.

About this time—it was December and the snow lay deep on the mountains—a further danger beset him. A family came up from the village of Tionontoguen bearing the news that Ihandich had been exquisitely tortured and burned to death. Father Jogues was stabbed with pain when he heard that his dear comrade and spiritual son, Guillaume Coûture, was killed, without his being able to give him spiritual aid. He had been with René, and had absolved him. He had not seen Guillaume now for many weeks. He was desolated with grief.

Then came men from Ossernenon, ordering that he should return to his village. He was as good as a dead man, they told him. He would be killed just as soon as he arrived, for the people were enraged against him, and were waiting to slaughter him; nothing would stop them this time. "At this news," he states, "arose the remembrance of my past life, stained with so many sins, so unfaithful to God. I was cast into the depths of grief that I, in the middle course of my life, as it were, with no good works sent on before, rejected by God, should be snatched out of life without any of the Sacraments. Yes, I was in that frame of mind in which I did not wish to live and in which I feared to die. I uttered many a cry of misery. I said unto my God: 'When, oh, when shall there be an end to my miseries and my griefs? How long wilt thou forget our needs and our tribulations? When, O my God, when wilt thou give peace after the tempest, and when wilt thou pour out joy and exultation after the tears?' 'Unless those days had been shortened, my flesh would not have been saved.' In this sadness I had recourse to the help of the Scriptures, my accustomed refuge. The passages that I recalled in memory taught me how I should think of God in His Infinite Goodness. Although I was not upheld by sensible consolation, nevertheless, I would know 'that the just man lives by Faith.' I searched the Scriptures; I followed their streamlets, desiring, as it were, to quench my daily thirst. 'In the law of God I was meditating day and night,' and indeed, 'unless the law of God had been my meditation, I would then, perhaps, have perished, in my abjection.' "

God did not abandon him entirely to his dreads and despairs, but sent into his consciousness, while he was swooning into quietude, an understanding which he thus describes:

While I was in my hidden retreat in the forests, when the snows were deep about me and I was half dead through hunger and cold and nakedness, when I was reputed a vile thing among those vilest savages, and was the mud and the mire of those barbarians, an offense and a sport to these men, I had to endure to a terrible degree the inner anguishes of soul; the realization that my life had been marred by many negligences and had been made hateful through sin; the bitter anticipation of the sorrows that would fall upon me when I should be killed by the savages, as they forewarned me; the perils of hell that surrounded me on all sides. To quiet me, these things occurred. I heard very distinctly a voice which condemned me for my anguish of soul, and which advised me to think of God only in His goodness, and to cast myself entirely upon Him. I heard, I repeat, those words which I understood to be from Saint Bernard writing to his monks: "Serve God in that charity and love which casts out fear; such love does not regard merit." These two counsels were given to me very opportunely, for my soul was being burdened down with an excessive fear, and this, not a filial but a servile fear; then I did not have sufficient confidence in God; besides, I was sorrowing because I was being hurried to judgment, as it were, in the middle of my life, without having sent before me any good works, whereas I should rather have sorrowed because of my offenses and my many negligences toward God. Now these words bolstered up and strengthened my soul in its sorrowings, and roused it to love toward God. That fire of love was so vehement that in the fervor of my soul, even before I had returned to myself, I added to what had been told me, the following words, also from St. Bernard: "Not without reason does He ask our life, Who has given up His own for us." After this, God so greatly enlarged the soul of His servant that I returned even with joy to our village, at the entrance to which I firmly believed I would be beaten to death.

Father Jogues, strengthened anew in soul, was now prepared to leave the winter hunt and return to his doom at Ossernenon. The family with whom he lived was eager to be rid of him, for he was too weak to be of any use to them. They abominated him as the cause of their failure in the chase and they feared him for the other evils his incantations might bring on them. They would have killed him outright if they dared; they did not dare because they would be held responsible by the chief who had loaned Ondessonk to them. The opportunity came when some old men decided that they had had enough of the hunt and the hardships of the camp, and were returning home. Jogues begged that he might be sent back with them, and to this his masters readily assented.

Since they wished to make recompense for his services to the family whose slave he was, they loaded on him the head and neck of a moose, and the four quarters which had been smoked and dried. This, he was to carry back as a present to his master. He staggered under the burden, as he followed the old men along the route down from the mountains. They went easily before on their snowshoes, but he had to stumble and slip as best he could in the crackling snow. The trail lay through the tangled underbrush and the thorny vines, so that his arms and legs, already frostbitten and cracked by the cold, were a mass of scratches and blood. The camps at night were in the open, in a hollow of the snow. He had no furs, as the others, to protect him, and could not move the hearts of any of the party to lend him any covering, though they carried several skins back as their spoils of the chase. The travel was slower and more painful than on the upward trail.

Along the way, they had to cross a gorge of a swift mountain stream. The bridge was a tree trunk stretched a few feet above the swirling, deep waters. It was unsteady, and slippery with moss. One of the party was a pregnant woman, who also carried a baby in the basket on her back and was otherwise burdened with the camp utensils. The strap of the cradle was across her forehead, and the bundles were fastened to her shoulders. The squaw started to climb across the tree, while Father Jogues waited to follow her. She lost her balance and toppled over into the tumbling rapids. The baggage strapped to her shoulders weighed her to the bottom, the thong that held the cradle slipped from her forehead to her neck and was strangling her.

In an instant, Father Jogues leaped into the gorge and the icy current. Wading and swimming, he fought his way to the woman, unstrapped the bundles and the cradle, and dragged her and the baby to the bank. He took good care to baptize the baby before he lifted it out of the water. The Mohawks made a roaring fire, and revived the woman, who was numbed almost to death. They allowed Ondessonk to warm and dry himself, and even commended him, for they realized that the woman would have been drowned except for his aid. She recovered, but the newly baptized child died within a few days.

Further on, the party came upon the winter huts of other hunters. Among these was the old chief who had ordered the braves to kill René. He now showed himself cordial, and invited Ondessonk to eat with him. Jogues accepted the invitation, and squatted with the old man before the fire. When food was placed before him, Father Jogues blessed the food and himself with the sign of the cross. "Stop that," the old chief snapped at him. "That gesture is no good. The Dutchmen have told us of it. They are not like you, they do not practice this thing. They hate these ceremonies of yours, and we hate them also. It is the making of that sign which caused the death of your comrade; and it will be the cause of your death if you continue to form it among us."

"That doesn't make any difference to me," Jogues answered. "I shall continue to form this sign of the cross, since the Author of our lives commands it. Let the people do whatever they please about it." The response silenced the old man. He could not understand this Ondessonk, and kept staring at him all during the rest of the meal. As for Father Jogues, the words of the chief gave him confirmation of his belief, that René Goupil was a martyr and had been put to death for this profession of his faith. He received final proof that

René had been killed for making the sign of the cross, from the mother of the little child with whom he had played. She was in the camp with the old man, and was serving food to Ondessonk and the chief. She told Father Jogues that the old man had commanded the murder because of this single reason.

After they left this camp, a blizzard came sweeping across the hills. They were blinded and blanketed by the swirling flakes of the snow, and buffeted by the high winds. For two days they had to battle through the storm, trusting only to their instinct that they were advancing in the true direction. At times they despaired ever of reaching their village. Father Jogues especially felt that he could force his legs to carry him not another step. Death in the snow was pleasant to his soul. It would be easier far to lie down along the road, to be numbed and frozen, than to march on and on to the village where the savages were waiting to torture and murder him. But his only thought was God's will. "I was always striving to be united to God during this journey," he relates, "for I did not know what was going to happen to me in the village."

II

On the eighth day of their travel down from the mountains Father Jogues and his party cut their path through the deep snow that shrouded the hills above the Mohawk Valley. He expected death when he would cross that valley and would ascend the hill to the stockade. He would welcome the stroke of the tomahawk. Not many people were about the gate. The streets within the walls were quiet. His cabin was deserted. No one molested him, no one threatened him. What the people who had last come from Ossernenon to the hunting-grounds had told him, he learned, were lies. He was not wanted for execution in the village. His murder had not even been discussed. Moreover, Guillaume Coûture had not been killed. He was in good health, except for a frozen foot.

His "aunt" and her family had gone to the hunting-lands toward the west. The very day of Jogues' return, a messenger had come back from them to report that they were in need of corn. Their friends, to whom they made appeal, judged it most convenient to send Ondessonk with the food. Accordingly, the morning after his arrival they piled two large sacks of crushed corn on his shoulders and ordered him off to the camp, which was a distance of several days' journey from the village. Jogues objected. He protested that he was so exhausted that he could not enter on another journey. He showed them his arms and legs, his hands and face, pitiably swollen and cracked by the cold. He could scarcely walk, and, burdened by the sacks of meal, he told them that he must surely die along the way.

They would not listen to his pleadings or protestations, but strapped the bags on him and drove him out of the cabin. His legs wabbled under the load. Without, the streets of the village were a sheet of ice. He was unable to hold his footing, and slipped and sprawled. The savages still drove him on, out through the gates, and along the trail down the hill to the river road. Cautiously he picked his steps and tried to preserve his balance, but to no avail. The path was heavily iced, and rendered more slippery by the waters from the melting snow. For a little while he struggled to make some progress. He could not go on. He cared not what might happen. He turned back to the village and reached it, crawling on his hands and knees, and laboriously dragging the bags after him. When they saw him the savages raged furiously at him, naming him a dog, a monstrosity, a misshapen cripple, a loafer who would do nothing but eat, hurling on him a thousand curses. They kicked and pounded him where he lay helpless in the cabin. He was too far gone to mind anything. Finally, the savages themselves realized that he was half dead.

A day or two later they found another occupation for him. There was a man in the village who was dying of a vile and loathsome disease. He was putrid with sores, and so nauseating was the stench of him that no one wished to go near him. He was left in a little cabin by himself, utterly abandoned, and with scarcely enough food to keep him from starving. Ondessonk was ordered to live with this sick man, to feed and nurse him. He knew the man well, for this was the brave who had beaten him over the shoulders thrice when he was first put on the torture platform at Ossernenon, the same one who had torn out two of his finger nails. Though his soul revolted at the sight and the smell of the sick man, he nursed the man for fifteen days.

Jogues was almost naked when he arrived back from the hunt. He had the good fortune of picking up some rags and scraps of cloth to wrap about his shivering body. Then a chief gave him an old cloak that had once been a brilliant red, but was now stained and filthy and foul. Soon he managed to secure a worn-out skin to tie over the cloak. "In this wretched guise," he recounts, "I went about the streets of the village. I begged the Lord that He would one day join me to the company of the Saints who had served Him 'wandering about in sheepskins and goatskins, distressed and afflicted, of whom the world was not worthy.' All the while, day after day, I saw the savages well dressed in the cloths and the garments of which they obtained a plentiful supply from our baggage which they had captured. And meanwhile I was shivering day and night in the cold. That did not sadden me so much. I was more incensed to see these utter heathens unworthily abusing the sacred vestments which they found among the spoils. One of them had made leggings for himself out of the two veils destined to be used at Mass. *Non hos servatum munus in usus*. Of all that period up to the middle of January, I can say honestly before God: 'Even unto this hour we hunger and thirst, and are naked, and buffeted, and have no fixed abode. And we labor, working with our hands; we are reviled and we bless; we are persecuted and we suffer it; we are blasphemed and we entreat; we are made as the refuse of this world, the offscouring of all, even until now.' "

About the first week of January, in 1643, he was recalled from the care of the diseased man to his own cabin. His "aunt" and his master were still away, but a young squaw and an adolescent girl, related to his "aunt," demanded that he come back. They were most sympathetic and compassionate toward him. They wished to render him those services which squaws do for their husbands and daughters for their fathers, cooking and serving his food, preparing his cot, tending to his comforts. Jogues took good care not to accept their attentions nor to admit their help. He was extremely wary and suspicious, and more so since none of the men of the family were at home.

He understood the situation better when he observed that a Mohawk brave was visiting the younger girl at night, and then practically lived in the cabin, openly. Father Jogues thought of leaving the place and seeking a lodgment elsewhere, but he could not very well commit such an affront to his family. He could not prevent the sin which he painfully realized was being committed in his presence. He could and did rebuff the older squaw, and he did not refrain from rebuking both women and showing his distaste for them. His confessor, Father Buteux, records that "never once during all that time, and in such dangerous occasions of sin, did Father Jogues experience any emotion or any imagination or any thought against purity. Still, it is true that such thought should have been far removed from him, since he was feeling anew the rigors of the wintry weather, having only a wretched old blanket as all his clothes, and that barely long enough to cover half his body, and living day and night in a cabin open to all the winds and ordinarily without a fire." The women felt grievously insulted. They treated him with a sharp resentment.

His "aunt" arrived a week or two later, much to his gratification. She saw to it that he was better fed and nursed, and gave him one of the new deerskins she had brought back from the chase for wear in the day, and another skin to cover him at night. She came to look on him as the one to replace, in the Mohawk fashion, the son who had died shortly after René's murder. Since she was a woman of notable ancestry, and was, besides, influential in her own right and one of the few women councilors admitted to the conferences of the sachems, she could do much to guard him from petty malices. At first she had pitied and tolerated him; then she was shrewd enough to discern his intelligence and his gentleness of soul; finally she respected and admired him and grew very fond of him. "She took care of me," he attests, "and 'the Lord gave me grace in her eyes.' Yet all this was but a slight solace in such overwhelming woes."

In due time, also, the chief who was his official master began to relent in his attitude toward Ondessonk. He had signalized himself as one of the most rabid leaders of the war faction, one who demanded the death of the three Frenchmen. During the autumn and early winter he treated his prisoner with personal disdain. Later, he came to look on Ondessonk as a member of his family, came to enjoy talking with him and showing him off. Since he was a powerful chief in Ossernenon, his cabin was the gathering-place for the elders and the braves on these wintry nights when the hunters luxuriated in idleness and feasted on venison.

Father Jogues now breathed more freely. He had no longer the daily hazard of death; he was spared, in great part, the continued show of spite and hate. He began to study in earnest the intricacies of the Iroquois dialect. Though it was a kindred language to the

Huron, which he could speak fluently, he found notable variations in vocabulary, in inflections and in pronunciation. "But what kind of progress can one make without any material for writing," he complained. Nevertheless, through the opportunities he had for listening to the discourses and conversations of the men gathered in his cabin, from the answers the Mohawks now deigned to give to his queries, he acquired the ability to understand the savages and to communicate his thought to them.

This season of idleness, when all coveted the warmth and security of the cabin, was a resurrection for Jogues. He found chance, he says, "to instruct the ancients on the articles of our Faith. They inquired of me, with much curiosity, about the sun and the moon, and the faces that seem to appear on its disc, and about the size of the earth, and the vastness of the ocean, and the tides coming in and going out, and about whether at any point the earth and the sky met together, as they had heard was the case, and about such-like things. I managed to satisfy them in these inquiries, adapting from philosophy what was within their comprehension. Then, indeed, they began to wonder, and would say: 'Truly, we would have made a great mistake if we had put this man to death as we had so often been on the point of doing.' After that I tried to lead their minds from creatures to a knowledge of the Creator. I argued against their old-wives' tales about the creation of the world, which, they say, was built by a tortoise. I explained to them that the sun was not endowed with intelligence, that it was without any life whatever, and that it was in no sense a god. The sun, 'if they were delighted by the beauty of it, and took it to be a god, let them know how much the Lord of it is more beautiful than it is.' I told them that Areskoui was not a god, but a demon; that it was a lie to say that he was the author and conserver of life, and the giver of all the good things they enjoyed."

Though Father Jogues was given a hearing, he was discouraged of results. "If they believed as easily as they were easily convinced," he remarked, "the matter would be quickly settled. But 'the prince of this world,' driven out from almost every quarter of the globe by the power of the Cross, seems to have fled into these regions as his best fortified stronghold. So that, the kingdom which 'this strong man armed' has possessed for so many thousands of years cannot be overthrown except by the process of time and by the constant attacks of the soldiers of Christ." He carried his apostolate out to the bleak streets of the village and to the wind-swept gates and wherever he could attract a listener. "Some refused to listen to me," he narrates, "others drove me off, others assented merely with the lips, from a kind of polite convention which makes them consider it rude to contradict you; this manner would deceive anyone who did not understand the ways of the savages."

With his new-found freedom he visited the cabins of Ossernenon in search for the sick and dying, much as he had done in the first terrible years among the Hurons. Some few adults who listened to his words of promise and warning consented to receive baptism. Many infants, in a critical state, he also contrived to baptize. He confesses: "This was my only solace in the bitterest mental pangs." These ministrations were not adverted to by the savages, or, when noticed, were rather approved. They even sought his help on one particular occasion. A sick man had a dream. He was told by his friendly demon that a dance and chant should be enacted ceremoniously by his cot and that Ondessonk must hold his book in his hand and must behave as the French do when they pray to their God.

This word was brought to Father Jogues, and, according to the law of the natives, it was veritably a command. He refused to accede to the request. He judged that he would be coöperating with and encouraging the savages in their superstitions. The friends of the sick man heard him with surprise. To obey the dreams of a sick man, that was a rule never violated under any circumstances, they pointed out. They impressed him with the fact that the man's health was in his keeping: if he obeyed the dream, the man would surely recover; if he refused, the demon would be angry and the man would die. He still refused. They pointed out to him that the sick man would most certainly get well, and that Ondessonk would be blessed with his gratitude and would have renown as a powerful medicine-man.

Father Jogues smiled at their arguments and rebuked them for their superstition in putting such implicit faith in dreams. They urged him more, but he would not relent. Other messengers came and pleaded with him that it was cruelty, even a species of murder, to refuse to cure the sick man. When they had finally exhausted their patience and found he would not come willingly, they dispatched some strong braves to seize and carry him by force to the cabin. He was agile and adroit, Lalemant, who knew him well, comments, and was little burdened with flesh. He eluded the savages, took to his heels, out of the cabin, into the street, down to the gate. They pursued him at full speed, with hue and cry; but "he had the legs of a deer," and, on the open path of the trail, he far outstripped the fleetest of the savages. Later, when night came on, he returned to the village, resolved to die rather than to connive in the smallest way in their superstitions.

On various occasions, Jogues was taken, or was allowed to travel by himself, to the villages of Andagaron and Tionontoguen. Thus, in February he walked the six miles to the nearer town where the Mohawks were holding their winter festival and games. Since he was not much interested in the sports, he wandered through the cabins, searching for the sick and for those affably inclined. In one lodge he discovered five babies, all dangerously ill. He baptized them, without attracting any notice, and three days later, says Lalemant, "he heard that these little innocents were no longer in the land of the dying. What an admirable stroke of predestination for those little angels."

In these visits, Jogues ministered to the spiritual welfare of the Huron and Algonquin prisoners. All remained loyal and steadfast. In later years, Joseph Teondechoren used to say to Father Ragueneau: "Oh, how I love the crown, or rosary, of the Holy Virgin! Never do I tire of reciting it; and she has granted to me all that I have asked of her when offering her this prayer. It was good Father Jogues who gave me this devotion when we were both captives in the country of the Iroquois. We often used to recite our rosary together, in the very streets of Anniene, the Mohawk village, without those infidels perceiving us." To Father de Brébeuf he related: "I talked incessantly with God and spoke to him in my heart as if we had been two who carried on a conversation; and thus I was not discouraged. As soon as I thought I had sinned, I went to find Father Jogues, in order to confess. As regards the Father, he offers his prayers quite openly. But as for us, he told us that we should pray under our breath, since the Iroquois had no sense, as yet. The Father, he speaks to the Iroquois of God, but they do not listen to him."

Theresa, the niece of Joseph, was tenderly under the care of Father Jogues. She had been so carefully nurtured by her pious parents and by the Ursuline nuns that she was virginal at the time of her capture. Jogues feared for her amid the licentiousness of the Mohawks. Her uncle, however, reported that "Theresa is not ashamed of her baptism. She prays publicly to God. She says that she believes. She often confesses herself to Father Jogues. . . . She speaks to Father Jogues whenever she sees him. But these things do not prevent her from being exceedingly sad, living among our cruel enemies. She has well endured the cold and inclemencies of the winter. She was very sick, but God restored her to health. . . . She has no rosary; she uses her fingers to recite it, or little pebbles which she lays on the ground at each Hail Mary that she says. She often said to me: "Alas, if the virgin sisters should see me in this condition among these wicked Iroquois who do not know God! How they would pity me!"

The Huron Christians revered Father Jogues during this winter. Based on their remarks, Father Lalemant asserts: "It was a profound affliction for these devoted Christians to see their good Father in such misery and inconvenience throughout a very severe winter, when his sole covering consisted of a piece of blanket which barely covered one half of his body; and when the ardor of his charity impelled him, even in the worst of the coldest weather, to drag himself from village to village to visit the children he had begotten in our Lord. 'But it must be confessed,' adds Joseph Teondechoren, 'that his discourses animated by such charity in the midst of all those sufferings, inflamed the hearts of all the Christians and made them prize this blessing that they enjoyed in their captivity; that God had given them a man who was to them a father, a mother, a consoler, indeed everything, in a place where all consolation failed them, except what God gave them through Father Jogues' mouth.' "

Guillaume Coûture and Father Jogues were now, in the changed circumstances, enabled to see each other more frequently. Guillaume had always enjoyed a comparative freedom, and in the autumn, before and after René's death, he came down from Tionontoguen to visit Father Jogues. In January and February, Jogues was permitted to travel the twelve miles to Tionontoguen. He knew that Coûture had need of him, for this intimate contact with the loose pagan life could easily spoil the virtues of a weaker man. But Guillaume, with a strength that surpassed nature, held exactly to the more perfect service of God that he had promised as a *donné*.

He and Father Isaac prayed together, and kept alive in one another the religious spirit.

Often their talk turned on René Goupil. He was a saint, they both agreed, and a martyr of Christ. Coûture had heard, on his side, that René was killed for making the sign of the cross. And Father Jogues had found proof positive of that from the lips of the old chief who had ordered René's execution and from the mother of the child on whose account he was slain. Both of them were aware that, despite the period of safety in which they lived, they, too, might be murdered for like reason. The Mohawks had a fiendish, diabolic hatred of the Cross, engendered in them by the powers of darkness and by the warnings of the Dutch Calvinists with whom they traded at Fort Orange. Revering René as a martyr, both Father Jogues and Guillaume Coûture prayed that they might discover his sacred bones and carry them back some day to an honorable grave at Quebec.

Jogues had always doubted the word of the Algonquin woman who told him that René's body was thrown into the distant river. Hence, throughout the winter he made further inquiries. He could glean no information, however, until a day in early March. Some children declared to Ondessonk that they had chanced upon the bones of the other Frenchman down in the ravine below the village. Immediately, Jogues hurried across the field and over the side of the glen which he had searched so heartbrokenly in October. He stamped up and down the banks of the stream and about the woods. He could find no trace of the sacred remains. Doubting whether or not the children were liars, he returned to the village to question them more closely. They mocked at him, now that they saw him so excited and eager, and told him fantastic tales, but they gave him no more definite clues.

Once more he went to search the ravine, scouring the underbrush, pouring out his soul in a prayer of anguish, straining his eyes for tracks and marks. All the day he searched and searched through the gloomy hollow, but at the end of the day he had to return, sore in heart and despairing. It was then some of the older boys pitied him. They confided that the body lay concealed higher on the bank, in a little depression where there was a clump of closely knitted trees. Following their directions, he hurried once more to the ravine. This was his fourth attempt; he could not be sure that he was not being made sport of anew. He slid and trod down the steep, muddy decline, to a hollow where the trees and underbrush were thick. He tore away the branches and vines.

There lay the yellow skull and bones. The skull was cracked in several places, where it had been smashed in by the blows of the tomahawk. The bones were marked by the teeth of the dogs and foxes which had stripped off the flesh from them. Some of them were half-gnawed. Father Jogues crouched on his knees. He took the skull reverently in his hands and kissed it. He wept and rejoiced. Still kneeling, he lifted up each piece of bone to his lips and deposited it near the skull. He gathered all the smallest fragments scattered about the damp mold of the hollow. They were precious. They were the relics of a true martyr of Jesus Christ.

What now to do with them? First, he must preserve them from the touch of the savages, who would dishonor and contaminate, even destroy them. He must bury them somewhere, where they would be safe, where he could get them easily, if he should escape from the Mohawks, if he should be released. He searched for a place to bury them. He found a spot, in the soft loam and dust in the hollow at the base of a giant tree. He dug out the hole and smoothed the brown dust. There he deposited the skull and the bones, as in an urn. He sprinkled the loam over them, and packed the tiny sepulcher with earth, the while he quietly intoned the *De Profundis* and the *Benedictus*. As he picked his way up the hillside to the village, he felt himself not so much alone.

III

Ossernenon expanded in the balm of the spring which spread over the Mohawk land that March in the year of 1643. Now was the time to make ready the nets and traps and weirs, to spin the cords for the lines and bend the hooks, to pack meal into the sacks and gather the kettles and other utensils for the journey to the fishing-grounds. With some anxiety, Father Jogues watched the families bundling out of the village. He remembered the horrors of the winter hunt. He hoped he might be allowed to remain in peace in Ossernenon.

His fears were somewhat eased when his "aunt" told him that she was taking him with her and her husband and their young grandson, just the four of them. They left the cabin about March 15, and traveled by canoe down the river of the Mohawks toward the settlement of the Dutch. It was not a hazardous passage, though the river was still swollen and the rapids, around which they had to portage, were many. The paddling was easy, for the current ran strong. The next day they reached the waterfall where the Mohawk emptied into Oiogué, the river of the Dutch. Only a few hours away, Ondessonk learned from his "aunt," were the cabins of the white men. They turned away from these, however, up against the flow of the river of the Dutch. Two days after, they came to the creek which empties the water of Lake Ossaragué into the river. A few miles up its winding course they landed on the sedgy shore at the outlet of the lake.

Their first concern was the choice of a place to plant their tent, somewhere on the low banks that rimmed Lake Ossaragué to the east. Other families lodged here and there on the nearby hillocks and along the strand. Most of them clustered near this narrowing part of the rounded lake, for perch and bass and smaller fish abounded hereabouts. The savages all were in holiday mood, for next to war and next to hunting, fishing was the favorite diversion. For the squaws it was sport as well as useful occupation; the store of dried, smoked fish that they would pack away would be a staple of food and a delicacy for months to come.

Off here in the private little hut on the shore of the lake, Father Jogues found peace and tranquillity such as he had not experienced since his capture. He was away from the closeness of the Mohawk village, from the packed cabins and the noisy streets, from the rout of savages always about him, from the continuous tumult, from the sneers and curses and blows which beset him. Here was the solitude of the forests, the silence of the waters, the freshness of nature. He was not called upon to do many chores; in the morning and the late afternoon he gathered twigs and logs for the fire and helped split and smoke the fish. "The entrails of the fish," he relates, "generally served as seasoning for our sagamité. The fish were laid aside to be carried back to the village. This food, and other like it—such as the intestines of the deer, full of blood and half-putrified excrement, fungus growths boiled in water, decayed oysters, frogs eaten whole, head and feet, not even skinned or cleaned—custom, hunger, lack of better had made such food not only tolerable, but I might even say pleasant."

Thus left to himself, Father Jogues sought solace in the woods, where he would be free from the intrusions of the savages. He built a little cabin of bark in a grove of evergreens, and in this, his oratory, he erected a Cross. As in the mountains, during the winter, he carved another Cross upon the broad trunk of a tree. There he knelt before it, for long hours of prayer. He exclaims: "How often in those journeys and in that lonely retreat 'did we sit by the rivers of Babylon and weep, when we remembered thee, O Sion,' not only exulting in heaven, but even on earth praising thy God. How often, though in a strange land, have we sung the canticle of the Lord; and the woods and the mountains about resounded with the praises of their Creator, which never, from their creation, had they heard. How often on the stately trees of the forests did I carve the most Sacred Name of Jesus, so that, seeing it, the demons might take to flight, and hearing it, they might tremble with fear? How often did I strip off the bark from those trees, and fashion on them the most holy Cross of the Lord, so that, at its sight, the enemy might flee before it, and that through it, O Lord, my King, thou 'might rule in the midst of thy enemies,' the enemies of the Cross, the unbelievers, the pagans who dwell in these lands and the demons who rule far and wide through all these regions? I rejoiced, moreover, that I had been led by God into this wilderness at that very time in which the Church recalls the Passion of Our Lord, so that I might be free from interruptions in remembering the course He followed, its bitterness and gall, and that, thus recalling, 'my soul might pine away.' "

His ecstasies were rudely shattered after a single week. On Monday of Holy Week, March 30, some young braves burst into the fishing-camp. They had hurried all the route from Ossernenon, they announced, to give warning that the Algonquins of the Mohican nation, who lived not very far to the east, were on the warpath; parties of them had been detected prowling about in the country nearby. The braves advised earnestly that the old couple and their grandson and Ondessonk should return to the village, if they had any care for their lives. They might be attacked and massacred. There was no moment to lose.

At this terrifying report, Jogues' people hastily gathered their bundles and fled homeward, charitably escorted and helped by the young braves. All of Tuesday, all through Wednesday and Thursday, they paddled tensely, affrightedly. On Thursday they shoved their canoe along the river bank at the landing-place below the hill of Ossernenon. They were overjoyed that they had escaped safely from the Algonquins. Almost at that same moment of their arrival they learned the truth. The scare about the Algonquins being in the vicinity of Lake Ossaragué was a ruse to get Ondessonk back to the village as quickly as possible. It had been decided that he was to be tortured and burned to death.

The details, as far as Father Jogues could gather them, were these. About six months before, in the latter part of September, ten warriors had taken the warpath against the Abenakis, an Algonquin nation which inhabited the regions along the seashore above the place where the English were settled. Since the band did not return before winter set in, as they had expected, and sent no word about their welfare, their relatives grew fearful as to their fate. Then rumors began to trickle back to Ossernenon. It was reported that the ten Mohawks had been captured by the Abenakis and tortured to death. In mid-March, a few days after Jogues left the village for Lake Ossaragué, a war party returned with an Abenaki prisoner. He boasted that his people had captured the Mohawk band, and, after torturing them, had burned them at the stake.

One of the warriors thus reported killed was the son of the old and influential chief who had charge of Ondessonk. He loved this son dearly. He sorrowed unconsolably, and ordered that the Abenaki prisoner should be tortured and burned as a sacrifice to the spirit of his dead son. On further thought, he decided that this wretched man was too mean and too cheap a sacrifice. Abetted by the two women of his cabin who hated Ondessonk, he resolved to offer up his Frenchman as a further, more honorable sacrifice to the spirit of his son.

It was on the evening of Holy Thursday that Father Jogues reached Ossernenon and learned his doom. The execution was set for the next day, Good Friday. In vain his "aunt" raged at the trickery, at the sentence, at the old chief, her brother, at the women. The chief had the power to kill Ondessonk; he refused to be moved by pleas or threats. He was inexorably set on burning his Frenchman the next day. This time, Jogues realized, death would be certain. There was no escape, there would be no change of mind. He was content. Death would be a release from this slavery that was worse than any death. Death meant joy with God in heaven. "The next day, which had closed the Saviour's life, was now to end mine," he wrote.

"But then," he continued, "it pleased Him who had given life to my spirit by dying on this day, to give life to my body also." At daybreak on that Friday morning, a herald came tearing into Ossernenon, shouting a cry of triumph. The ten warriors who had been reported dead were alive. They were but a day's journey away. They were bringing in with them twenty-two prisoners. They had joined themselves with another Iroquois band, and all through the winter had spread terror throughout the Abenaki lands. Ossernenon woke up to noisy jubilation. Men, women, children rushed through the gates and along the trail to welcome the heroes and to caress the prisoners. Ondessonk was forgotten in the excitement. "In this manner did God dissipate the evil resolutions of the savages," attests Father Jogues. "He taught me through these dispensations, and He showed me clearly that He had me under His care, and that I should cast myself wholly on Him, that I should know well that He would not withdraw His help and let me fall."

The prisoners arrived on Saturday morning, and Father Jogues hastened down the hill with the horde of howling Mohawks to welcome them by the river ford. It was there that he had been first welcomed and caressed. Now he stood by and watched the cruelties practiced on these new victims. Only six of the twenty-two were men; the remainder were squaws and children of both sexes. These latter were not harmed, for they were destined for adoption. The six men, however, stripped naked, were slashed and beaten and led in triumph up the hill. There they were forced to run the gauntlet and were placed on the platform before the gate, where they had their finger nails drawn out, their fingers slashed off, their bodies burned and cut.

Father Jogues hovered about the torture platform all that day, and mingled with them during the night when they were allowed some rest in one of the cabins. He did not know their language, but he secured the help of an Algonquin woman who was a Christian and through her instructed them and gained their consent to be baptized. He poured the saving waters over their heads on

Easter Sunday, before they were led out of the cabins once more for the final tortures. Though he was sickened that day by the cruelties that he steeled himself to witness, he could rejoice that God, in His Providence, had deigned to save the souls of the prisoners, though He permitted their bodies to die in the flames.

Once more had Father Jogues escaped. His "aunt" and other of his friends assured him that it was a narrow escape. "Although, naturally, I rejoiced not a little to be snatched from this and other dangers," he protests, "nevertheless, I grieved that I must be exposed once more to new and continual griefs, to the most acutely painful sufferings, that I must again begin to live an existence more painful than death of any kind. For every chance occurrence, whether good or ill, fell heavily on me alone. If one of them should be killed in battle, I was demanded as the victim to be offered in sacrifice to his spirit. On the other hand, as usually happened, if they brought in some prisoners, after having killed the others who were captured, a terrible grief gripped my heart; for these prisoners were either Frenchmen or allies of the French."

A few weeks passed, during which Jogues was allowed quietly to pursue his own ways. Then, toward the end of April, there arrived at Ossernenon ambassadors from the nation of the Sokokis. This people, though of Algonquin stock, was at war with the Montagnais and other Algonquin nations who were in alliance with the French. They were united in these wars with the Iroquois, and though they enjoyed all the rights of friends and allies, they were forced to pay annual tribute to the Iroquois. The Sokokis were received at Ossernenon with the elaborate ceremony accorded to friends. They were given food and mats before the fire and calumets to smoke. At length they requested that a council of the Mohawks be called, for they had words to deliver from their nation.

Accordingly, the council assembled in the cabin of the ancient where Father Jogues was lodged. The Sokoki chief arose, and in persuasive language presented his message. One of the warriors of his nation, one who was a great chief among them, had been captured and tortured by Algonquin enemies. He was led in triumph to the French settlement at Three Rivers, thence to Quebec, where he was doomed to further torture and death. But Onontio, the great chief of the French, and the Blackrobes had begged the Algonquins to deliver the chief into the hands of the French, and offered presents of great value. The Algonquins granted the request of Onontio and the Blackrobes. The Sokoki chief, thus rescued by the French, was loaded with gifts and sent back safely to his own people.

Before releasing him Onontio made a request. He asked the chief to have the Sokoki nation intercede with their good friends and allies, the Mohawks, so that the Mohawks might release the Blackrobe named Ondessonk whom they held a prisoner. The French Governor sent his greeting to Ondessonk and wished that these papers with painted speech on them be delivered to him. The ambassador announced that he came to Ossernenon to fulfill the promise of his kinsman, and begged the Mohawks to lead back Ondessonk and the other Frenchman, Ihandich, to their own people. He would console the Mohawks for the loss of their prisoners by the most valuable presents of wampum which he laid before them.

The Mohawks, in the council that followed their private deliberations, agreed to accept the presents of wampum and thus grant the request of their friends and allies, the Sokokis. They assured the ambassadors that they would lead Ondessonk back to the French; moreover, already they were making preparations to do so. The Sokokis went on their way, satisfied. Days passed. There was more talk of Ondessonk's death than of his departure. He denounced them: "These wretches had so little intention to deliver us that they committed a treachery against the law and custom of all these nations. . . . The Iroquois retained the presents offered by the Sokokis without setting one of us at liberty; and this treachery, perhaps, is unexampled among these peoples. For they inviolably observe this law, that, whoever touches or accepts the present which is made to him, is bound faithfully to fulfill what is asked of him through that present. This is why, when they are unwilling to grant what is desired, they send back the presents or make others in place of them."

It happened that the Sokoki embassy almost resulted in the unexpected death of Father Jogues. One of his enemies, who feared that he might be released, was seized with a sudden insane fury. He would settle the problem by killing Ondessonk. Rushing into the cabin, brandishing his war club and shrieking imprecations, he leaped on Jogues. Before anyone could interfere, the madman had delivered two heavy blows on the Father's head and knocked him unconscious. He was preparing to beat his victim to death when he was dragged away. Jogues' "aunt" was indignant and drove the fellow out. She was genuinely fond of her "nephew" and actually wept over him as she tended his hurts. Since many were secretly plotting to kill him, she told him that he must try to escape. Not only would she not hinder him; she would help him to liberate himself.

Of this period, he recalls: "Naturally, I loved to get away into the quiet and solitude, where, far from the village, I would not be nauseated by the usual cruelty of the savages, and where I could be with God more freely and with greater devotion. Nevertheless, I knew that Lia, though blear-eyed, was more fruitful than Rachel and bore more children. I was mindful, too, of the Institute of our Society, which places the salvation of our neighbors before our own private spiritual delight. Therefore, without reluctance, I remained about the cabin. By staying in the village, I had more opportunity to make progress in the study of the language. Also, I could better effect the baptism of children and the salvation of adults. I was greatly grieved whenever, during my absence, an adult died who had not been instructed, or a child who had not been baptized."

In the early part of May, he had his first opportunity of visiting the Dutch in their settlement at Rensselaerswyck, forty miles to the east of Ossernenon. He went under a strong guard of young braves with his "aunt," who was intent on trading furs and skins for the Dutch merchandise. Coûture, at the same time, accompanied a party from Tionontoguen. They were happy to be allowed to mingle with the white men, to talk with Arendt Van Corlaer, the Director, and with the Huguenot interpreter, Jan Labatie, who had tried and were still trying to effect his release. Jogues found a most congenial friend in the Reformed Minister of the Dutch, Dominie Johannes Megapolensis. The Dominie welcomed Isaac Jogues as a brother in the Lord, though he was a Frenchman, a papistical idolater, and a dangerous Jesuit. He had a present for Isaac—his breviary. It had been brought to the settlement by one of the Iroquois for trade, and the Dominie had salvaged it. Father Jogues was deeply touched by the charity of Megapolensis.

During the few days that his party remained at Rensselaerswyck, he was strictly guarded by the Mohawks. Even though he wished, he could find no opportunity to elude his masters. Van Corlaer and the Dutch burghers renewed their pleas to the Mohawks, and offered large ransoms to buy the Frenchman, Ondessonk. The savages were obdurate; the release of Ondessonk could be granted only by the great council of the nation; however, they said, to mollify the Dutch, it was more than probable that their people would take the Frenchman back to Three Rivers during the summer and present him to Onontio, the French Governor.

In this visit Jogues obtained writing-paper, pen, and ink. He planned to get into communication with Governor Montmagny and his Jesuit Superiors. Since early spring, war parties were almost daily taking the trail to the St. Lawrence. He hoped to find some friendly brave, or better, some Huron or Algonquin captive taken along by an expedition, who would carry a letter for him. He felt it to be an imperative duty to warn the French of the increasing violence of the Iroquois and of their determination to wage a more bloody and extensive war than ever before.

Back at Ossernenon, he wrote the letter and fortunately found a Mohawk band willing to carry it. They told him that they would fasten the paper on some pole or tree by the bank of the St. Lawrence, some place where the French would discover it. They thought of the advantage for themselves in having this paper of Ondessonk; it might be used to lay an ambush; or again, in case of their capture, it might be an evidence of their good-will and secure their release through the French. In the next few weeks Father Jogues wrote two other letters which the Mohawks swore they would carry to his friends and brothers.

While some war parties were rousing the village with the tumult of their departure, others were returning triumphant. On May 24, Jogues notes, a runner burst into Ossernenon announcing the return of a victorious band. Later in the day, writes Jogues, twelve warriors marched proudly into the village:

"On Pentecost, they brought in new prisoners, three women with their little children. The men were killed near the French settlement. The three women and children were led into the village, entirely naked, without even loin cloths. They were horribly beaten with clubs and their thumbs were cut off. One of them (and this was an act never done before) was burned all over her body and was then thrown into a roaring funeral pyre. Then I was a witness to something new, something worthy of note. When this woman was being tortured, at every burn which the Mohawks inflicted on her by applying lighted torches to various parts of her body, an old man, in a strong and vigorous voice, cried out these words: 'Great god Areskoui, we offer thee this victim whom we burn for thee, that thou mayst eat of her flesh and that thou mayst always from now on make us victors over our enemies.' Her body was cut into pieces, and these were carried to the various villages, where they were eaten. The reason was this. About the middle of winter the Mohawks grieved, as it were, that they had abstained from eating the flesh of some of their prisoners. In a solemn sacrifice they had offered two bears to their divinity and had addressed him in these words: 'Great god Areskoui, justly dost thou punish us, since now for a long time thou hast not permitted us to take any of our enemies captive.' (During the summer and autumn, their warriors had captured no Algonquins, whom they specifically name as their enemies.) 'We have sinned against thee, because we did not eat the last captives thrown by thee into our hands. But if, in the future, we capture any Algonquins, we swear to you that we will devour them in the same way that we are now about to eat these two bears.' They kept their pledge. I baptized this woman while she was on the funeral pyre, since I was unable to do it before, while I was offering a drink to her parched lips."

Again were the Mohawks victorious in their guerrilla warfare along the St. Lawrence. On June 25 the chant of triumph floated from the trail across the valley to the hill of Ossernenon. A strong detachment of warriors appeared, leading with them eleven Hurons and a Frenchman. Father Jogues fled down the path to the river to meet them. The Frenchman, named Henry, was a young man who had been living the past winter at the new settlement of Ville Marie, on the isle of Montreal. The Hurons, mostly Christians who had been baptized the preceding year, were well known to Jogues. His heart froze within him. "A new and most heavy burden was added to my many other griefs," he states.

To his amazement, the Mohawks had not tortured the prisoners at the time of their capture nor along the route homewards. Neither did they subject them to excessive cruelties at their arrival, nor slit and crush their fingers, nor did they make them run the gauntlet. Nevertheless, his soul was tortured when he beheld these increasing holocausts. "Truly, I had a feeling within myself that this was a punishment that my sins had merited," he laments, "such a punishment as was of old pronounced by God on His people when he said, 'their new moons, their solemnities and their feasts' would be turned into grief and sorrow. For, on Easter, on Pentecost, on the Feast of the Nativity of St. John the Baptist, new sorrows poured in on me. And these were afterwards most poignantly increased by a slaughter of a hundred Hurons in the neighboring villages. The greater number of these were butchered by the most dreadful torments and burned to death. 'Woe is me! Wherefore was I born to see the ruin of my people.' Truly, in these and other like tortures that anguished me deep in my soul, 'my life is wasted with griefs, and my years in sighs,' 'for the Lord hath corrected me for my iniquities and hath made my soul to waste away like a spider'; 'he hath filled me with bitterness, he hath inebriated me with wormwood'; 'because the comforter, the relief of my soul, is far from me.' But in all these things we are victorious, and by the favor of God we will be victorious 'because of Him that loved us,' unto that day when He will come 'Who is to come and will not delay.'"

Among the booty the Mohawks who captured Henry brought back to Ossernenon was a packet of papers which Father Jogues contrived to secure. Avidly he tore off the wrapper. There was a large linen envelope. The writing on it was that of Father Jérôme Lalemant: "Relation of what occurred in the Mission of the Hurons from the month of June of the year 1642, to the month of June of the year 1643." He slit the seals of the bundle of papers. There he read the account of his capture and of his being carried off to slavery among the Iroquois. He learned that Father Lalemant and his fellow priests among the Hurons believed that he, Goupil, and Coûture had all been tortured to death. And then, most eagerly, he read of the labors of his fellow missioners and of the conversions among the Hurons, of their aspirations and their fears for the future.

In the packet, also, were the letters which the Huron missioners had written to their relatives and friends in France. Among these was an envelope addressed by Father Lalemant to the Very Reverend Mutius Vitelleschi, the General of the Society of Jesus, in Rome. If Father Jogues had opened it, he would have read a glowing eulogy of himself, the official report of his death at the hands of the Iroquois savages.

CHAPTER XI

Escape through the Dutch

I

FEROCIOUS and persistent was the Iroquois offensive in the summer of 1643. In former years they had appeared from time to time in brief war expeditions. They captured and massacred what enemies they happened to surprise, and then wandered off for other diversions. This summer, they warred steadily and with a fixed determination to establish their supremacy in all the northern country. Forming smaller bands of twenty or fifty or one hundred, they stationed themselves in all the narrow passages and portages along the St. Lawrence, the Rivière des Prairies, the Ottawa and the Lakes. One party relieved another, so that at no time were the waterways left open.

The Iroquois were invincible. They had so terrorized the Algonquins and Montagnais that these peoples fled to the security of the mountains north of the St. Lawrence; but even to these haunts did the Iroquois pursue them. They had overwhelmed so many Huron flotillas that this nation scarcely dared to attempt to make the usual summer journeys down to Three Rivers. The Iroquois no longer feared the French. Parties of them were lurking continually about the new settlement on the island of Montreal, so that the people there scarcely dared to venture out of sight of their cabins. They infested all the forests and river banks in the vicinity of Fort Richelieu, and neither by day nor by night could the small garrison relax its guard. On Lake St. Peter, twelve miles above Three Rivers, and along the same bank, the Iroquois established a base camp from which they menaced the town.

Governor Montmagny strove to break the grip of the Iroquois by sailing up the St. Lawrence with four armed shallops. He located not a single enemy, for at his approach the warriors melted into the woods. As soon as he had passed, they again stationed themselves at the vantage-points and waited to pounce upon the Hurons, Algonquins, and the undefended French. Montmagny was enraged and baffled. Vimont asserts: "If Monsieur the Governor had had the soldiers from France for whom he was hoping, he would no doubt have proceeded into the country of the Iroquois, with two hundred or three hundred Algonquins and Montagnais who offered themselves to accompany him, I believe that this would have produced a very good effect; he would have constrained those proud barbarians to an honest peace, or he would have entirely subdued them."

The Iroquois supremacy was due, in large part, to the abundant equipment of muskets and ammunition supplied to them by the Dutch. It was the French policy to withhold arms from the natives. Only in exceptional circumstances and only to the faithful Christians would they entrust arquebuses. They were enraged, therefore, and placed at a disadvantage by the Dutch practice. With acerbity Vimont wrote in the preceding autumn: "We have had letters from France telling us that it is the intention of the Dutch to have the French harassed by the Iroquois, and that to such an extent that these Dutch may force the French to give up and abandon everything, even the conversion of the savages. I cannot believe that those Gentlemen of Holland, being so closely allied to France, have this evil design. But the practice of the Iroquois is so consistent with it, that they ought to apply to it a remedy in their settlement, as Monsieur the Governor has done here. He has often prevented our savages from going to kill the Dutch. It would be very easy for the Dutch to do the same. Otherwise, they will have difficulty in clearing themselves and in exculpating themselves from the wrong that is committed."

Though the Dutch at Rensselaerswyck held no enmity toward the French and were in no way envious of their possessions along the St. Lawrence, and though they passed laws against selling muskets to the Iroquois, their traders freely dealt in firearms. Every band of warriors that left the villages of the five confederated Iroquois nations carried guns and ammunition. That summer, most of the braves followed their chieftains on the warpath. The villages were quite deserted. Fearing that the Huron and Algonquin captives might rise in a revolt if they were left behind, and needing their services in paddling the canoes and carrying the stores, the war parties carried along with them their prisoners. It thus happened that Joseph Teondechoren, Charles Sondatsaa, and others captured with Father Jogues followed the trail to the St. Lawrence.

In the middle of June, Joseph and his brother slipped away from the Iroquois stockade near Three Rivers and safely reached the settlement. They gave the first authentic news of Father Jogues to Buteux and de Brébeuf. Ondessonk was still alive, Joseph reported. He had his left thumb cut off. He passed the winter with a single red cape for all his clothing. René was murdered. Ihandich had his foot frozen. The Iroquois spoke of bringing Ondessonk back; they must not be believed. With such scraps of information as these, confirmed and increased by other refugees, the Jesuits at Three Rivers and Quebec pieced together the harrowing story of Father Jogues' first year among the Mohawks.

Meanwhile, Jogues lived in any agony of despair. Helplessly he watched the fury of the Mohawks departing for war along the St. Lawrence. Sadly would he see them return triumphantly, always bringing in new victims. And each success encouraged them to greater daring. He had written to warn the French during May. On June 30, he took advantage of an opportunity offered by "Mathurin's man," the Huron who had become an Iroquis chief, the same who had captured him. Jogues distrusted the man; nevertheless, he felt in conscience bound to send a letter. He relates:

Among several bands of Iroquois who were going to war against the French, the Algonquins and the Hurons, there was one which took a resolution to go round about Richelieu, in order to spy on the French and the savages allied to them. A certain Huron of this band, who had been captured and adopted by the Iroquois, came to ask me for letters which he promised to carry to the French—hoping to surprise some one of them by this bait. I had no doubt but that our French would be on their guard. I saw, moreover, that it was important that I should give them some warning of the plans, the arms and the treachery of our enemies. I found means to secure a bit of paper in order to write to them, the Dutch according me this charity. I knew very well the dangers to which I was exposing myself. I was not ignorant that these warriors would make me responsible if any misfortune happened to them, and that they would blame my letters for any setback. I anticipated my death; but it seemed to me pleasant and agreeable, since it would be for the public good, and for the consolation of our French and of the poor savages who listen to the word of Our Lord. My heart was seized with no dread at the prospect of all that might happen therefrom, since it was a matter of the glory of God. Accordingly, I gave my letter to that young warrior.

Since he did not know what use the ex-Huron might make of the letter, nor into whose hands it might fall, he composed it in phrases of French, Latin and Huron, depending on Father de Brébeuf or some other of the Huron missioners about Three Rivers, to decipher the Huron words. Addressing the letter to Governor Montmagny, he wrote:

Monsieur: Here is the 4th that I have written since I am with the Iroquois. Time and paper fail me to repeat here what I have already given to you at great length. Coûture and I are still living. Henry (one of those two young men taken at Montreal) was brought here on the eve of St. John's day. He was not loaded with blows from clubs at the entrance to the village, like us, nor has he had his fingers cut, like us; he lives, and with him all the Hurons brought with him into the country. Be on your guard everywhere; new bands are always leaving, and we must persuade ourselves that, until the autumn, the river will not be free from the enemies. There are here nearly three hundred arquebuses, and seven hundred Iroquois; they are skilled in handling them. They can arrive at the Three Rivers by various streams; the Fort of Richelieu gives them a little more trouble, but does not hinder them altogether. The Iroquois say that if those who took and killed the French at Montreal had known what you have done—in redeeming the Sokokis whom you delivered from the hands of the Algonquins—they would not have done that; they had started in the midst of winter, and before the news of it came. Nevertheless, quite recently there has departed a band, and the "man of Mathurin" (Father de Brébeuf knows him well) is in it, and leads the band, as at our capture last year. This troop desires and purposes to take some French, as well as Algonquins. Do not let any consideration for me prevent you from doing that which is to the glory of God. The design of the Iroquois, as far as I can see, is to take, if they can, all the Hurons; and, having put to death the most considerable ones and a good part of the others, to make of them both but one people and only one land. I have a great compassion for these poor people, several of whom are Christians,—the others Catechumens, and ready for Baptism. When shall a remedy be applied to these misfortunes? When they shall all be taken? I have received many letters from the Huron mission, with the *Relations*, taken near Montreal. The Dutch have tried to ransom us, but in vain; they are still endeavoring to do so at present, but it will again be, as I believe, with the same results. I become more and more resolved to dwell here as long as it shall please Our Lord, and not to go away, even though an opportunity should present itself. My presence consoles the French, the Hurons and the Algonquins. I have baptized more than sixty persons, several of whom have gone to heaven. That is my single consolation, and the will of God, to which very gladly I unite my own. I beg you to recommend that prayers be said, and that masses be offered for us, and above all for the one who desires to be forever,

Monsieur,

Your very humble servant,

Isaac Jogues, of the Society of Jesus.

From the village of the Iroquois,
the thirtieth of June, 1643.

Knowing well the tribulations which this letter might bring upon his head, Father Jogues, nevertheless, intrusted it to the warrior. He had survived all the threats of a year, he was indifferent to death as to life. He rather believed, at this time, that he was normally secure. After the Sokoki embassy sought to ransom him, with their tale of the French courtesy, the Mohawks treated him with greater respect and kindness. Sometimes now, in good humor, the sachems would remark: "Ondessonk, it would have been an ill deed to put you to death. You act the master well, when you choose, and act the child when anything is commanded you to do." When he strove with them in trying to force them to listen to his words about God and baptism, they reproved him gently: "Ondessonk, you will yet cause your own death. You speak too boldly. If here, in our own country, where you are a prisoner and all alone in your cause, you dare to oppose us, what would you do if you were at liberty and among your own people? Never will you speak in favor of the Iroquois." Father Lalemant tells that Jogues "later on, was astonished at his own freedom of speech; but, since he expected neither life nor deliverance, in a word, since he had nothing to lose, he had, also, nothing to fear or dread. This courage caused him to be honored by those who had more judgment; but it procured him the hatred of all the common crowd who judge only by their senses, after the manner of beasts."

In the summer, while the younger warriors waged their wars, the old chiefs went on embassies to the conquered nations to collect the annual tribute of wampum. It thus happened that a day or two after Jogues had written his letter to the French, he was led off by the old chief, in whose custody he was, upon an embassy to the nation of the Susquehannocks who had their villages along the two large rivers to the south, the Delaware and the Susquehanna. Ondessonk, it would seem, was brought by the chief to impress the tributary nations with the might and power of the Iroquois who triumphed even over the white man. Jogues was forced to be the beast of burden for the chief, and to paddle for him in the canoe. It was a journey of nine or ten days, at times along the river routes and then along the winding trail through the endless forests. For food, they had but the usual sagamité, and that in limited rations. On many of the days they had naught but a little wild purslane which they gathered in the fields and cooked into a soup. They had, it is recorded, "certain seeds to eat, but these were so insipid and so dangerous—for they served as a very quick poison to those who know not how to prepare them—that Father Jogues would not touch them."

During the early and middle part of July, the Mohawk embassy progressed from village to village among their tributaries, holding feasts and councils and renewing their agreements. Everywhere, they exhibited Ondessonk as their slave. Jogues cared little for this. He was intent upon his own work. As soon as he would arrive at a village, he would boldly walk from cabin to cabin and seek out the sick. He knew enough of Huron and Iroquois to converse in the dialect of these more southernly peoples. The adults who were ill, he would try to instruct briefly and win their consent to baptism, which he would administer if they were nearing death. The children were his keenest quest; so many of them died, and these he could safely salvage.

Once when he had entered a cabin in one of the villages to inquire about the sick, he heard his name called from the darkness of a corner. Going over, he found a young man desperately ill.

"Ondessonk," the sick young man exclaimed, "do you not know me?"

"I do not remember ever having seen you before," Father Jogues replied.

"Do you not remember well the favor I did you at your entrance into the country of the Iroquois?" the man questioned.

"But what favor did you do me?" asked Jogues, puzzled.

"Don't you remember the man who cut your bonds, in the third village of the Agnieronon Iroquois, when you were at the end of your strength?" he continued.

"Of course I remember that very well. That man put me in his debt very, very much. I have never been able to thank him. I beg you, give me some news of him, if you are acquainted with him."

"It was I, myself, who did it. It was I who took pity on you and loosed you."

Father Jogues bent over the sick man and embraced him. "But oh, how sad I am to see you in this pitiable condition!" he exclaimed. "How much I regret that I am unable to help you in your sickness! I never knew who you were. Nevertheless, I have often prayed for you to the great Master of our lives. You see that I am in great poverty. Despite that, I shall do you a greater favor than you did to me."

Father Jogues told the dying man about God, of the happiness in the next life with God for those who believed, of what it was necessary to believe in order to be baptized and be made happy forever after death. The man listened with attention. With deep sincerity, he begged for baptism and for the happiness Ondessonk promised him. Father Jogues poured on his head the water of salvation. While he prayed beside the mat, a few hours later, the man died peacefully.

Jogues felt himself compensated by winning the soul of this man for God. All his labors and fasts and slavery had their reward through his spiritual conquests among these nations to the south. But he was eager to be back in Ossernenon. There were waiting for him the two Frenchmen and the native Christians. There would be new prisoners dragged to torture and death, and the opportunity of baptizing them. He was happy, then, when the embassy of chiefs pointed their steps homeward. In leisurely stages, along the streams and through the mountain trails, they finished their return journey of two hundred miles and arrived at Ossernenon in the latter part of July.

Scarcely was Jogues back in his cabin before he was required to leave again with his "aunt" for the summer fishing. The families with whom she was traveling intended to spend a few days of trading at the Dutch settlement, and from there to proceed a day's journey to the shallows amid the islands down the river. She had pity on her "nephew," Ondessonk. She let him understand that if he wished to escape through the Dutch palefaces, she would not prevent him. The thought was in his mind. But he rejected it, and records:

Although, in all probability, I could escape either through the Europeans or through other savages living around us, if I should wish it, I decided to live on this cross on which Our Lord had fixed me in company with Himself, and to die with His grace helping me. For who would be able to give solace to the French captives if I were absent? Who could absolve them after their confessions? Who could remind the baptized Hurons of their duty? Who could instruct the prisoners who were being constantly brought in? Who could baptize them when they were dying, and strengthen them in their torments? Who could pour the sacred waters on the heads of the children? Who look after the salvation of the adults who were dying, and after the instruction of those in good health? Indeed, I believe that it happened not without a singular providence of the Divine Goodness, that I should have fallen into the hands of these very savages. On the one side, the entrance of the Faith was barred from these regions by a nation fallen away from the Catholic and the true religion; on the other side, the Faith was cut off from them by a fierce war waged between the savages, and through them with the French. These savages, I must confess, unwillingly and reluctantly have thus far spared me, by the will of God, so that thus through me, although unworthy, they might be instructed, they might believe, and be baptized, as many of them as are preordained for eternal life. From the time that I was captured, I have baptized seventy children, adults and old persons, belonging to five different nations and languages, "so that from every tribe, tongue and people, they might stand in the sight of the Lord." For this reason, every day, I bend my knee to the Lord and to the Father of my Lord, and ask that, if it be for His glory, He may bring to failure all the plans of the Europeans as well as of the savages, who are thinking about ransoming me or sending me back to our French people.

Thus, definitely, Jogues repudiated the idea of escape from Ossernenon. He hid away in his cabin his few precious possessions, his breviary, which Megapolensis had returned to him, and the packet containing the Huron *Relation* and the letters, which he had salvaged from the Mohawks. He took with him the small books of *The Following of Christ* and *The Little Office of the Blessed Virgin.* On July 31, just one year since he had celebrated the Feast of St. Ignatius with Father Buteux at Three Rivers, he left Ossernenon with his "aunt." He carried down to the river the kettles and sacks of food, the bundles of peltries and the furs and skins which had been looted from the Hurons. In the canoe he took his place with the other oarsmen and paddled with the current until, on the evening of the second day, they reached the long portage of some two miles which brought them to Oiogué, the river of the Dutch. There they camped, and on the morrow they went forward to the trading-post of the Dutch at Fort Orange.

II

Rensselaerswyck spread out along the slightly elevated bank of the west side of the river. For seven or eight miles were clearings and farms and low-slung cabins and barns, with a line of hills rising as a near back-ground. The little Dutch houses clustered below the farmlands, and at the far end of the habitation was the mound of Fort Orange. To paddle down to this settlement, to meet once more and mingle with white men, to touch civilization, was an exciting interlude for Father Jogues. When he had visited the place in May, he was so closely watched and curbed that he had but the slightest contact with the Dutch. He was now left more at liberty to wander about and converse with the Europeans.

"There are two parts to this settlement," he related. "First, a wretched little fort, named Fort Orange. It is built of logs, with four or five pieces of Breteuil cannon, and as many swivel guns. The Company of the West Indies has reserved this Fort for itself, and maintains it. This Fort was formerly on an island formed by the river; it is now on the mainland, on the Iroquois side, a little above the said island. Secondly, there is a Colony sent out to this place by the merchant Rensselaer, who is its Patroon. This colony has about a hundred persons. They live in twenty-five or thirty houses built along the river, located as each has found convenient. In the principal house is lodged the Patroon's representative. The Minister has his own house apart, in which preaching is held. There is also a sort of Bailiff, whom they call Seneschal, who has charge of justice. All their houses are merely of boards, and are covered with thatch. There is as yet no masonry, except in the chimneys."

The Dutch and the Iroquois, Jogues observed, treated each other with friendly familiarity. The Mohawks wandered about the houses as they willed, and sometimes lodged in them. The Dutch, on their side, accepted the savages as if they had no fear of them. In reality, the Dutch realized that they were at the mercy of the Iroquois, if these chose to dig up the war hatchet; and the Iroquois swaggered about insolently, knowing that they had the power to massacre the whites, and without fear, whenever they might feel themselves offended.

Arendt Van Corlaer, Dominie Megapolensis, and the burghers showered their hospitality upon Isaac Jogues. They were genuinely concerned about this French Jesuit, though they did not love the French, though they detested Catholicism, and abominated, in particular, the Jesuits. They deemed it an outrage that any white man whatsoever should be enslaved by the savages. The convivial Dutchmen entertained him in their homes and invited him to sit with them in their tavern. They swigged their foamy beer jovially, and urged Isaac to join them in their drinking, for his health's sake, they admonished, because a glass of gin or a cup of mulled wine would raise his spirits. He declined their invitation with polite thanks. His reason, he revealed later, was to show good example to the savages. When the Mohawks came to Rensselaerswyck, they craved liquor and they managed to get it, though the sale was forbidden to them. They were easily and rapidly intoxicated and became beastly and wild. Jogues wanted to impress on them that the drinking of firewater was wrong, and that they should abstain from it, since it caused great evils.

Megapolensis constituted himself host to the Jesuit. The Dominie had been reared a Catholic in the Netherlands, but had given up the Faith as a young man, having found the true belief, as he explained, in the Dutch Reformed Church. He entered the ministry as his career and obtained an appointment in Rensselaer's colony under the auspices of the Dutch West India Company. Being well versed in Latin, and intellectually far superior to the burghers, he found Isaac a scholar of his own type, one who could converse wisely, who could quote the Bible at great length, who could debate the doctrines of religion, and who was altogether companionable.

The Director, Van Corlaer, acting on his own initiative as well as under instructions from Willem Kieft, the Governor at New Amsterdam, was active in securing the immediate release of Father Jogues. Once more he renewed his pledges of gifts to the savages, once more he berated them and bribed them; but, as always, they returned shifty answers. They did, however, accept some of his gifts as token that they would not maltreat their French captive. Meanwhile, Van Corlaer urged Isaac to escape, promising help and refuge. He was mystified, rather, he was irritated, by the Frenchman's attitude. Jogues thanked him cordially for his good wishes and his offer of services. He stated that he was perfectly content to remain with the Mohawks. He had made up his mind on the matter. He admitted that the life among them was repulsive, that he was in perpetual danger of death, but that, nevertheless, he was sent to them by God and would remain as long as it was God's will for him to do so.

During the few days which Jogues spent at Rensselaerswyck, in the intervals which he could steal away from the savages, he was intent on writing a report of himself to his Superior, Father Jean Filleau, the Provincial of the French Province of the Society of Jesus. He had long awaited the opportunity to acquaint his Superiors of what had happened to him since his departure from Three Rivers. And so, assured by Arendt Van Corlaer that the letter would be transmitted to Europe, Father Jogues laboriously and awkwardly, because of his crippled hands, began to write:

Reverend Father in Christ: Pax Christi.

When I sat down to write to your Reverence, the first doubt that came to me was whether I should write in Latin or in French, since I have almost forgotten both languages after so long a disuse of them. I found difficulty as much in one as in the other. However, two reasons impelled me to write in Latin, the less common language. The first is that I shall be able more freely to make my own the words of Holy Scripture which have always been my greatest consolation "amid the tribulations which have found me exceedingly." The second reason was that I wished this letter to be less easily understood by any who chanced upon it.

The very great charity of your Reverence, which, in other days overlooked the multitude of my sins, will pardon me if there be some fault against the rules of decorum or language, for they will have been committed by a man who has lived for eight years after the manner and even in the appearance and dress of the savages. Still more, I fear that, rude in language, I may be more so in knowledge, "nor know the time of my Visitation," nor remember that I sustain the character imposed on me by God, of a preacher of the Gospel, of a Jesuit and of a priest. This induced me to write to you: if, by chance, this letter should sometime come into your hands, I might be helped by your own Holy Sacrifices and the prayers of your whole Province, I who live in this dreadful region among the Iroquois and the Mohawks. I trust that this help will be given more earnestly when you read this letter and see both how much I owe to God, and how much I need the prayers of pious people, in whose prayers, I know, a powerful protection is raised up for me.

Thereafter, through some thirty and more pages of fine script he narrated in exact detail all that had transpired during the past fourteen months, from the time he left the Huron country till that moment when the Dutch were striving to effect his liberation. He concluded his letter as follows:

But now I am weary of writing so long and verbose a letter. I therefore beg your Reverence from my heart that you may ever regard me, although unworthy, as one of your own. Even though I may appear to be a savage in manner and dress, even though I might seem to be without God in such a tumultuous kind of life, nevertheless, I have always lived as a son of the most Holy Roman Church and of the Society should live; and as I have lived that way always, so also in that way I hope to die. Obtain for me from God, Reverend Father, by your Holy Sacrifices, that though heretofore I have made poor use of the many helps God has given me to attain the highest sanctity, I may, at least, make good use of these last occasions which He gives to me. Your charity assuredly owes this to your son who has recourse to you. For I live a truly wretched life, one in which all the virtues are endangered: faith, in the black darkness of paganism; hope, in trials that are so long and so harsh; charity, in the midst of so much corruption and in the lack of all the Sacraments. Chastity, indeed, is not endangered here so much by delights; but it is endangered, nevertheless, by the promiscuous and intimate manner of living together of both sexes, in the free permission for anyone to dare or to do anything whatsoever, and most of all in the complete nudity. For here you cannot help but see, whether you wish it or do not wish it, what elsewhere is hidden not only from wandering eyes, but even from spying eyes. Hence, daily, I groan to my God begging Him that He may not leave me without help amid the dead. Begging Him, I say, that amid so much foulness of the flesh, and such superstitious worship of the devil, to which He has exposed me, naked as it were and unarmed, "my heart may be undefiled in his justifications," so that, when that Good Shepherd may come, "who will gather together the dispersed of Israel," "he may gather us from among the nations to bless His Holy Name. Amen! Amen!"

Your Reverence's most humble servant in Christ and son,

Isaac Jogues.

Permit me through your Reverence to greet all my dear Fathers and Brothers, all of whom I love and cherish wholeheartedly in Christ, and to commend myself to their Holy Sacrifices and prayers.

At the Colony of Rensselaerswyck in New Netherland, August 5, 1643.

He entrusted the letter to Arendt Van Corlaer, of whose integrity and charity he had a high opinion. It might be examined, he felt, by some of the officials of the West India Company or by the High Mightinesses of the Netherlands Government. But he believed it would finally reach France and his Superior. He was ready, now, to go on with his captivity, if so it were decreed.

By this time his "aunt" was finished with her trading, and the party departed from Rensselaerswyck. They took to their canoes and paddled about twenty miles down the river till they came to a place where the waters spread out as in a shallow lake. The surface was strewn with plots of reed grass, and broken by low sandbanks that rose scarcely a few feet about the waters. They erected their hut on the slight elevation of the shore amid the pine trees. Several other parties from Ossernenon and the other Mohawk villages were camped in the vicinity. There was peace for Father Jogues, here by the water and with the forests behind. His tasks would be light and his "aunt" would let him wander off to some retired spot where he could pray uninterruptedly to God.

In the morning they were stretching their nets across the current of the river and placing their weirs in position, when some more canoes arrived. The people had come straight from Ossernenon. They carried happy news. A war party had returned in triumph. The warriors had penetrated far up around Lake Huron, where they boldly attacked a Huron encampment. They had taken five or six scalps and brought back four prisoners. The people from the village related how two of these were tortured thrillingly, more so than ordinarily, and had finally been burned to death. They said the other two were being held for the time being and would later be killed.

While the Mohawks exulted over this good news, Father Jogues records of himself: "My heart was pierced through with a most bitter and sharp pain because I had not seen, nor consoled, nor baptized these poor victims." He must forego the delights of contemplation and the peace of his retreat; he must return to the village, to its turmoil and squalor, in order to help the prisoners. Accordingly, he sought permission to return.

"My 'aunt,'" he said, "I would like very much to return to our cabin. I grow very weary staying here."

"Go, then, my nephew," she answered him, "since you are tired of this place. Take something to eat on the way."

Put under the guard of some braves who were not too kindly disposed toward him he was lead back to Rensselaerswyck. There he was stricken speechless. He was surrounded by a snarling, shrieking, raging mob, cuffing and buffeting him, calling down imprecations on him. He was a dead man, he heard. He was to be tortured and burned. They were waiting for him at Ossernenon. He was a dog, a traitor, an ingrate, a worker of evil, a sorcerer. He must be killed. Out of the bombardment of blows and words, he learned of the latest reasons for his death. It was the letter which he had given to "Mathurin's man." He had foreseen disaster for himself when he wrote it; now he knew he must bear the penalty.

The war party came back to the village without scalps or spoils. They related how the messenger had gone boldly up to the French fort and had been admitted. As soon as the French had read the letter, they fired their cannons. The Mohawks fled from the thunder, naked and unprepared as they were, and were forced to abandon one of their canoes, in which were three arquebuses and other baggage. The warriors came back to Ossernenon in a great rage. They blamed all their failure on Ondessonk. He had advised the French to fire their cannon. They demanded his death. They were supported in this by another war party, lately returned. These warriors had been setting ambushes for the French near Montreal. They were attacked, and one of the men was killed and some others were wounded. Ondessonk, they swore, was responsible also for this. He must be brought back to the village and burned.

Jogues knew that this was no ordinary threat. He believed that if he had happened to be in the village at the time this defeated troop had arrived, he would have been killed outright. There was a slight possibility, however, that their anger would quiet down. "I listened to all these rumors," he wrote, "and offered myself without reserve to Our Lord, and committed myself in all and through all to His most Holy Will." No freedom now was granted to Ondessonk. He was a man condemned absolutely to execution. He could not mingle freely with the Dutch, as but a few days ago, but must stay at the Mohawk camp, near the shore of the river above the settlement. When they went indoors for the night, they slept close about him in the barn where they lodged.

For Van Corlaer, the question of Isaac Jogues' return to the Mohawk village became critical. He knew the fury of the savages, and he knew very well that now they were terrifically aroused. There was no possible chance of warding off death from the French Jesuit once he was back at Ossernenon. To let Isaac Jogues be carried off from Rensselaerswyck seemed to him and his councilors as if they were coöperating in murder; or were, at least, negatively responsible for it. Van Corlaer sought out Jogues in the Iroquois camp. He found the Jesuit comparatively unconcerned. He asked Isaac if he would not attempt to escape from the Mohawks. The Father told him that he doubted whether that would be more in accord with God's plan, or that his remaining would be for God's service and glory. Van Corlaer argued and pleaded with him to attempt to escape.

"Yonder is a vessel at anchor," he said. "It will sail in a few days. Slip away from the savages and stow yourself away on it. It is going first to Virginia, and from there it will take you to Bordeaux, or on to La Rochelle, where it is to land."

Jogues thanked him courteously for his generous help and his charity. But, he objected, the Iroquois would be enraged. They would most certainly suspect that the Dutch, and Van Corlaer himself, had helped in the escape. And then they would turn all their rage and hate on the Dutch settlement. Who knows but what they would burn and massacre all the whites. At the least, they would hold in a grudge for the Dutch and charge them with treachery. Van Corlaer, who knew the savages as well as Jogues, realized this. Nevertheless, he cried out:

"No, no, have no fear. This is a fine opportunity for you. Get on board the vessel. You will never find a more certain or safe way to escape."

Under the kindly and persistent urgings of Van Corlaer, Jogues weakened in his resolution. "My heart was perplexed at these words," he stated. "I began to doubt if it really were expedient, for the greater glory of God, that I subject myself to the danger of the fire and to the fury of those barbarians in order to aid in the salvation of some soul. I said to the Superintendent of the Dutch, then: 'Monsieur, this matter seems to be of such grave importance that I cannot give you my answer at once. If you please, allow me the night to think upon it. I will commend it to Our Lord; I will examine the arguments on both sides. Tomorrow morning I shall tell you what I have finally resolved.' He acceded to my request, but he looked at me with astonishment."

Left to himself, Father Jogues debated what he should do. He called on God for guidance. It was within a day or two of the eve of the Assumption, almost the anniversary of his arrival at Ossernenon. He had expected death on the Feast of his Mother; he had expected it daily during the week that followed; during the next month, when René had been murdered; every month since then. He had been spared, for some reason he could not understand. Now there was a greater threat, a more certain danger. The hostile Mohawks could pin their demand down to a definite action of his. They would kill him not through a general hostility to the French, not because of hate of his religion and its practices, as with René, but because he had betrayed them by the letter he had written.

Night came on. He was brought into a barn belonging to a Dutchman who had married a Mohawk squaw. A dozen savages stretched themselves about him, and soon fell off into sleep. Of himself he writes: "I spent the night in prayers, earnestly beseeching Our Lord that He should not allow me to reach a conclusion by myself, but that He should give me light so that I might know His most holy Will. I protested to God that in all things and through all, I wished to follow His Will, even if I should be burned over a slow fire."

In the darkness and the stuffy closeness of the barn he tossed about in an agony of irresoluteness. He had wished and prayed for death so often. Now, he told himself with shame, he was seeking to escape from it. He would expose the Dutch to the revenge and vengeance of the Mohawks if he tried to free himself while in their midst. As for the latter, the Dutch themselves urged him vehemently to escape; they had no fear. As for the former, it was a weakness, approaching to sin, that had led him to seek death as a deliverance. More to the point, he had solemnly resolved just a few days previously that he would remain with the Mohawks in order to aid the two Frenchmen who were prisoners, the Christian Hurons and Algonquins already dwelling in the Mohawk villages, those savages newly brought in as captives.

That was a few days ago, he told himself. The circumstances were changed now. He must reconsider his resolution. First, as for the Frenchmen. René Goupil was dead. Guillaume Coûture was safe at Tionontoguen, for he had been adopted. Besides, Guillaume used to say very earnestly: "Father, do your best to escape. As soon as I know you are gone, I shall find the means to get away. You know well that I remain in this captivity only out of love and loyalty to you. Make an effort to escape, then. I cannot think of my own liberty and life unless I see you in safety." The third Frenchman, Henry, recently captured at Montreal, had already escaped. After he had been but a few days in Ossernenon, while he was watching the tortures of the latest Huron prisoners, he had been told that he was the next to be roasted. Henry slipped off into the woods. Seven days had now passed and he had not been heard of. Hence, Father Jogues did not have Henry as a reason for remaining among the Mohawks.

As for the savages, Jogues saw absolutely no way of helping them, even though he escaped death this time again. The best of the Huron Christians had escaped. The majority of the other Hurons and Algonquins avoided him; they knew that he was destined for the fires; they feared that, if they were known to be friends, they might also be forced to share his torments; at least the Mohawks would rage against them and hate them for being sympathetic with Ondessonk.

Jogues concluded that these Christians would not be much benefited. As for the Mohawks themselves, he realized that it was out of the question to hope to instruct them, or convert them, after this latest misfortune. They were too terribly enraged, and would no longer listen to him.

Now, he argued within himself, as he lay quietly with the Mohawks, there were three possible courses for the Mohawks—to release him, to hold him indefinitely as a prisoner, and to kill him. The chance of release was most slim; the majority of the most powerful chiefs were unalterably opposed; that was made clear by the treachery committed when the Sokoki embassy was sent off in April. The good he could do, if he were detained, was now, and would be, stopped completely. There remained only death. He was not afraid of death, he assured himself. But would it avail anything? Would it not be more for God's glory and the salvation of souls for him to escape death? He had acquired a considerable knowledge of the Iroquois language. He knew their strength in war, their habits, their intentions; he knew their country and the routes leading to it. All this information was valuable for the French and for the missioners. If he died, it would be lost with him. If he escaped now, he might return at a later date and really be an apostle respected by them.

The Mohawks were waking. The gray of the morning showed between the cracks of the barn. He had formed his resolution. "Having weighed before God, with all the impartiality in my power, the reasons which inclined me to remain among these savages and the reasons which impelled me to leave them, I believed that Our Lord would be better pleased if I should seize the opportunity to escape."

III

At the first stirring of the Mohawks, Jogues slipped out of the barn and hurried down the road to the home of Van Corlaer. He told the Director that he had decided to accept the proposal to escape. Van Corlaer was surprised; he professed himself delighted, and sent for Dominie Megapolensis and some others of his councilors. They not only agreed to the rightness of Isaac's resolve, but were determined to help him to the last extreme. Van Corlaer summoned the officers of the Dutch ship that rode at anchor in the river opposite to the Fort. When the captain arrived, the Director explained the situation and asked a pledge from him that he would guarantee safe passage to the Frenchman. The blustering captain swore his word with a seaman's oath: "If he once sets foot on our vessel, he is safe. He will not leave it till we reach Bordeaux or Rochelle."

With that settled, Van Corlaer advised Isaac: "Well, then, go back to the savages. Toward evening, or sometime during the night, steal away quietly and make for the river. You will find there a little rowboat which I will have kept ready for you, to take you secretly to the ship." Jogues thanked Van Corlaer humbly and politely, as he related, and bowed himself out of the room. He put on a casual air and sauntered back along the wagon road toward the barn where the Mohawks were gathered. The rest of the morning and the afternoon he tramped about with his guard. As evening drew near he followed the men back to the barn, which lay about a mile above the settlement and the Fort.

The owner was a Dutch farmer, a man of some substance and influence. He was married to a Mohawk woman and had several children by her. The structure in which he lived was a frame building about one hundred feet long. One end of it was his home, solidly built and consisting of several rooms. A back door opened from the house into the barn. Here the party of savages slept. Beyond, at the far end, were the stalls of the horses and the cattle. A picket fence extended around the farmyard and the building.

Father Jogues studied all the details in preparation for his flight. At dusk, when the Mohawks went into the barn, he stretched himself out on the dirt floor as if he were tired and wanted to sleep. After a while, when it was totally dark and the savages were quiet, he thought it might be well to reconnoiter and make sure of the directions. He picked his way among the prostrate figures and let himself out of the swinging doors of the barn. The night was black and he walked a few steps out into the yard. There was a growl, the rapid pad of feet. The watchdogs charged on him. A big mastiff circled about him, barking furiously and lunging at his legs. Jogues tried to beat the beast off, but the dog drove in on him and nipped him twice on his bare legs before the Dutchman could rush out of the house and drive the brute away. By this time, all the Mohawks were aroused and crowding out into the yard.

The Dutchman brought Isaac into his house, and lit the candles to examine the wounds. They were nasty gashes from which the blood was flowing freely. The Dutchman was much upset; he knew the mastiff for a vicious brute who would likely have killed the Frenchman. He applied the only remedy he could think of to prevent rabies, that of inserting the hair of the dog in the cuts made by its teeth. After he had thus tended the wounds and wrapped a rag about the injured leg, he sent Jogues back into the barn with the Mohawks. They fumed at him for waking them up. In bad humor, they barred the doors more securely against the dogs which were still barking and howling, and they made Ondessonk lie down between two of them. So closely was he wedged in that he could not move without disturbing them.

He was suffocated by the closeness of the summer night and the stench of the barn, and sweated between the hot bodies of the savages. He trembled from the fright caused by the mastiff, and suffered keen pain in his leg. "This whole night, also, I spent without sleep," he recounted. "When I saw myself surrounded with those evil creatures, and the barn well locked, and the place surrounded with dogs which would raise the alarm if I tried to go out, I almost came to the conclusion that I could not escape. With deference, I complained to my God because, after he had given me the decision to escape, 'he hath shut up my way with square stones; he hath turned my paths upside down.' He was stopping up the ways and the path of escape." The hours passed wearily and painfully. He was trapped. The cattle at the far end of the barn ruffled the straw, the cocks fluttered and crowed shrilly, the faint purple of the morning showed through the cracks of the walls.

A door creaked, the door leading from the Dutchman's house. Jogues discerned a servantman groping his way toward the barn door. Wriggling out from between the savages he stuffed into his blouse his two little books, the *Office of the Blessed Virgin* and *The Following of Christ*, and stuck his small wooden cross into his pocket. On hands and knees he crawled over to where the man was unbarring the door. He whispered and gestured to the servant to tie up the dogs. The Mohawks slept soundly. He crept out into the yard, shrouded in mist.

He darted across to the fence, and ran for the river bank. His leg pained him so horribly that he could scarcely put any weight on it. Nevertheless, running and limping, he made his way along a narrow path near the river. The trail cut across a marshy stretch, where the reeds and thorny bushes scratched his naked legs. He looked back fearfully. No one pursued him. The morning was still dim and blue. He kept on, breathlessly, under what cover he could find, past the farmlands, to the outskirts of the settlement, beyond the cluster of houses vaguely outlined on the rising ground, till he came near the fort. Fifteen minutes had passed, and as yet there was no alarm.

The ship was riding a little distance from the shore. There was the rowboat Van Corlaer had promised to have ready for him. It was aground, in the mire, for the tide had receded several feet, stranding it. He pushed it, but could not move it down to the water. He pulled at it; it was heavy and was stuck in the oozing mud. Frantically he tugged and twisted and rolled it from side to side, and lifted it; to no avail. He hallooed over the water to the ship. They did not answer. He called louder and shouted; still no one appeared. He was despairing, for now it was growing lighter.

A few hundred yards away, on the other side of the fort, were huts belonging to the Mohawks. He was in full view of them. The braves and squaws would wake with the sun. They would certainly discover him. In his extremity, he prayed to God out of the depths of his soul. Grasping the boat once more, he pushed with his full strength against the stern. It moved, just a fraction. He eased the prow, and again strained every muscle of his body superhumanly, the while he supplicated God for aid. The boat moved a bit more; then more; at last it was at the water's edge. He swung it about, wildly, feverishly. It floated.

As he rowed toward the vessel he scanned the shore which was now lit up by the first streaks of the sun. Miraculously, not a living being was anywhere visible. He bumped along the hull of the ship, clambered up the rope ladder and scrambled on deck. The captain came out. Once more he assured Jogues, now he was on board, he was safe. For greater security, since the Mohawks might come prowling and spying about the ship, the captain suggested that Jogues should hide in the hold of the vessel amid the cargo and ballast. Father Jogues lowered himself into the dark hold, and heard the captain close the trapdoor and move over it, as he said he would, a heavy chest to conceal it.

The Mohawk guard woke to fury. Ondessonk was gone. They searched the barn and the yard, they scoured the roads and the woods and the river bank, they burst into the streets of the Dutch village and looked into the barns and dwellings. Quickly they spread the alarm among all the Mohawks in the vicinity. They besieged the houses of Van Corlaer and Megapolensis, and openly accused the Dutch of stealing their prisoner. Van Corlaer allowed them to search wherever they wished. He swore to them that Ondessonk was nowhere concealed in the town. They did not believe him. They ravaged about, firing their muskets and brandishing their tomahawks, swearing they would slaughter the cattle and burn down the houses and murder all the Dutch, unless Ondessonk was given back to them.

Van Corlaer invited them to hold council that night. He gave them his word of honor that Ondessonk was not held concealed by him or the burghers. He told them that he wished to assuage their grief, to show them his friendship in their loss; he offered them presents to the amount of three hundred gulders. The Mohawks answered insolently. They had no authority from their people to barter about Ondessonk. He belonged to the Mohawk nation. He must be given back. They refused to touch Cora's presents. They would return to Ossernenon and hold council as to what action it would be needful for them to take. Meanwhile, they said pointedly, it would be well if their friends, the Dutch, returned their prisoner to them.

That the savages were in a dangerous mood Van Corlaer and his councilors well knew. They were alarmed, for never had they seen the Mohawks raging about so fiercely and threatening so openly. Stricken with a great fear as to what revenge the warriors might take, on the second day they decided that they could not, in such a crisis, allow Isaac to sail away on the ship. They had better bring him back as an emergency measure, and keep him concealed in Rensselaerswyck, at least for the time being. They commissioned Dominie Megapolensis to go out to the ship and persuade the Frenchman to return.

Meanwhile, Father Jogues lingered in the hold of the ship. The surgeon, on his arrival, applied some ointment to the wounds of the dog bites. This was a salve for the cure of scurf. Instead of relieving the pain, the ointment intensified it. The wounds became more inflamed, the leg began to swell. "I was two days and two nights in the belly of that vessel," Jogues stated, "with such discomfort that I thought I would suffocate and die from the stench. Then it was that I remembered poor Jonas, and I prayed Our Lord 'that I might not hide myself before His face,' that I might not withdraw from His wishes. I prayed, on the contrary, 'that He might overthrow all the counsels which might not tend to His glory,' that He might detain me in the country of those infidels, if He did not approve my escape and flight."

He was brought up from the hold when Megapolensis and the Commandant of the fort came on board. They related the disturbances and the wild threats of the Mohawks, and how Van Corlaer and all the people feared for their lives. The Director and his councilors, therefore, thought it better for Isaac to stay in the vicinity, at least until the fury of the savages was somewhat quieted. Megapolensis assured him that it was not their intention to give him back to the Mohawks; they would keep him well hidden and would protect him. They only wanted him to be near until they had finished holding council with the Mohawk chiefs. They pledged him safety, Megapolensis insisted, to the extreme extent of their power. To this, Father Jogues listened quietly. It seemed to be an answer from God, and he replied to the minister from the book of Jonas: "If the storm has arisen because of me, cast me into the sea."

Not so calm was the captain of the ship. He swore roundly that it was a crime to take the Frenchman back to the settlement where he would be discovered by the bloody savages. He shouted that it was a betrayal. He would not allow Jogues to be removed from the ship; he had pledged his word that Jogues would be safe if he once set foot on their vessel. Jogues had put his life in greater danger by escaping, through trust in their promises; he was being taken off the ship, now at the very time that he should be brought on, if he had not already been put on board. The captain roared out his decision: Isaac Jogues would not leave his ship.

Touched deeply by the honest indignation and the loyalty of the captain, Jogues explained that he could not imperil the whole Dutch settlement by trying to save his own life. He told the captain that he released him from the pledges. He begged to be allowed to return to the settlement, for that was his wish. He turned, then, to Megapolensis and the Commandant, and said: "Messieurs, I most assuredly do not desire that, on any account, any harm whatsoever should happen to your cattle, and much more, any harm to your persons. The thought that I have had to free myself from the hands of the Iroquois and to escape death, was suggested, first of all, by you. And so, since you now feel, or think, the same about my escape, I relinquish my desire. I am quite prepared to give myself up to the Iroquois again. Have no doubt about that."

He finished his little speech, and sagged to the floor in a dead faint. He had had no sleep for four nights, had scarcely any food, was sickened by the stench and the heat of the hold, was poisoned by the wounds of his leg. Finally, the excitement of this interview with Megapolensis was more than he could stand up under. They lifted his head and poured a strong drink of brandy down his throat. When he was revived, he got to his feet and told them he was ready to leave.

Megapolensis misattributed his swooning to fear. Interminably he tried to explain to Isaac that Van Corlaer would not abandon him to the savages. The uproar would pass, he repeated; the Mohawks would not execute their threats; they were merely putting on a bold front, in order to extract a large ransom; Van Corlaer would eventually pacify them and make them reasonable. But there was just the slightest possibility, Megapolensis argued, that the Mohawks would not be satisfied with the presents and would resort to violence; under those circumstances and only at that time, would the Dutch begin to think about surrendering Isaac to the savages. Jogues told the Dominie explicitly that he did not seek assurance of protection from the burghers. He was perfectly willing to return to Rensselaerswyck and even to Ossernenon.

In the middle of the night they rowed Jogues back to the town and conveyed him to the fort, where Van Corlaer and the principal men were awaiting him. They were profuse in their apologies and their promises. "In all these proceedings," stated Jogues, "I might have urged some arguments in my own favor. But it was not for me to speak in my own behalf; rather, it was for me to follow the orders of these others. I submitted to them cheerfully. At the end, the Commandant told me that we must yield quietly to the storm and wait till the minds of the savages were pacified. All concurred in this advice."

For the next twelve days, then, Father Jogues lay concealed in the house of the Commandant of the fort. He was now totally exhausted by the strain of the past week. Besides, the wound inflicted by the mastiff in his leg was raging with pain. Harmen Meyndertsz van den Bogaert, the surgeon of the settlement, found that the salve for scurf which was applied on the ship had gangrened the wound. The infection spread, and van den Bogaert was seriously considering whether it might not be necessary to amputate the leg.

During these days, Father Jogues wrote a long letter to Father Charles Lalemant, then in France, narrating the details of his escape. He concludes:

Here, then, I remain a voluntary prisoner in the house of the Commandant, from which I am writing to you the present letter. If you ask my thoughts in all these adventures, I will tell you, first, that that ship which had sought to save my life, sailed without me. Secondly, if Our Lord do not protect me in a manner almost miraculous, the savages will discover me, for they come and go here at every moment. If ever they suspect that I have not gone away, I must necessarily be returned to their hands. Now, if they were so enraged against me before my flight, what treatment will they inflict on me when I fall again under their power? I shall not die a common death; the fire, their anger, and the cruelties which they invent will actually tear away my life. God be blessed forever! We are always in the bosom of His Divine and ever adorable Providence. "The very hairs of your head are numbered. Fear not, therefore; better are you than many sparrows. And not one of them shall fall on the ground without your Father." He who has care for the little birds of the air does not cast us into oblivion. It is already twelve days that I have been here in concealment; it would be truly marvelous if misfortune will not come upon us. In the third place, you see the great need that we have of your prayers and of the Holy Sacrifices of all our Fathers; procure us this alms everywhere: "to the end that God may render me fit and well-disposed to love Him; that He may render me strong and courageous to suffer and to endure; and that He may give me a noble constancy to persevere in His love and His service." This is what I would desire above all—together with a little New Testament from Europe. Pray for these poor nations which burn and devour one another, that at last they may come to the knowledge of their Creator, in order to render Him the tribute of their love. "I do not forget you; my captivity cannot fetter my memory." I am heartily and with affection,

Your humble servant in Christ,

Isaac Jogues, S.J.

From Renselaerivich, this 30th of August, 1643.

A day or two later, the Commandant thought it safer and more expedient to remove Isaac from the fort and lodge him in the house of the sutler, a frame building across the courtyard from the fort. The old trader and his family occupied the rooms on the ground level; these were to the rear of the larger room used for a store and workshop. A ladder led up to a garret in which were kept skins, leather, and various utensils. A small corner was partitioned off crudely by a circular wall of wide boards, loosely spaced. Into this compartment Jogues was brought to hide.

The place was uncomfortable to an extreme. It was so low, under the slanting, thatched roof, that a man could stand up only in the center, under the ridgepole. It was a veritable oven during the day, and remained unbearably hot in the night, for there was but a tiny window under the gable for ventilation. Some rainstorms burst after the days of torrid heat and the water poured through the thatch and flooded the garret. For bed, there were only the hard planks. Always was the possibility of being discovered. The window of the garret overlooked the courtyard about which the savages lounged. Jogues could overhear their guttural talk in the street below or when they came into the shop of the sutler. He could not walk lest the creaking boards reveal him. To increase the hazard, the sutler sometimes brought the Mohawks up the ladder to the open part of the attic, where he kept some of his merchandise stored. Between them and Father Jogues were only the slats of the partition.

"I am astonished," he narrated, "that those barbarians did not discover me hundreds of times; or that they did not come searching for me, particularly when the sun was shining in such a way that my body cast a shadow against the partition; since there is nothing so natural for them than to betake themselves behind the partition to see what it was that was casting the shadow. I saw them without difficulty. And unless God had turned away their eyes, they would have perceived me a thousand times. I concealed myself behind casks, and had to crouch into a cramped, strained position for two, three or four hours in succession, and that very often; this position gave me gehenna and torture. To go down to the yard of the house, or to go to any other place, was casting myself headlong; for every place was filled with those who were seeking me to death."

The sutler was a crotchety old man who bore it ill that the Frenchman should have been lodged in his attic and that he should have to tend to the needs of the Jesuit and face the dangers of discovery. He treated his visitor with scant hospitality. For food, Lalemant states, "they gave him to eat as much as was necessary, not to live, but yet not to die." The old man took less trouble to supply Jogues with drinking-water. Every two weeks he used to make lye. He would then wash out the tub, more or less, and carry it to the loft and fill it with water. This supply was all the water that Father Jogues had. After a few days, due to the lye and the excessive heat, the water became spoiled and stinking. Jogues, nevertheless, was so parched with thirst that he had to drink it, with the result that he was poisoned and wracked with cramps.

No one visited him in his solitary confinement except the minister, Dominie Megapolensis. He could bring no assurance as to what the Mohawks would do nor as to when Isaac could be released. The savages were still searching everywhere for him, Megapolensis said. The great chiefs of the nation were holding council at Ossernenon. The Bears were boiling with fury because their victim had been snatched away from torture and death. The Wolf and Turtle clans were coldly bitter because he had escaped of his own accord or been stolen by the Dutch; they had hoped to use him as a hostage in dealing for peace with the French. What the results of the deliberations might be Dominie Megapolensis could not foretell. But he again assured Jogues that the Dutch would not surrender him unless that would be necessary to save all the lives of the settlement.

On one of his visits, the good Dominie happened to ask Isaac how he was being treated. Jogues told him that he was content, that he was long used to suffering and was pleased that God should punish him for his sins. He did say, however, now that he was asked, that they brought him very little to eat. Megapolensis shook his head understandingly. "I am not astonished," he told Isaac. "I suspected that. This old man is a terrible miser. Doubtless, he keeps for himself most of the provisions that are sent to you." Thereafter, Jogues was given half a loaf of bread and a piece of meat every day.

Many days passed one after the other. August was finished, and the greater part of September, while Father Jogues remained cooped up in the attic. "Only God and His Saints were his company," Lalemant reflected. He had with him the little copy of *The Following of Christ* and that served him for his reading and meditation. He had, also, the cross which he had made for himself. But books were not necessary for him, says Buteux, "for he was totally absorbed and intimately united to God, even in his sleep."

Once more came to him such strange visions as he had experienced before leaving the Hurons and such as he had had after René's death and during the winter hunt. These visitations of God strengthened him in his pain. They gave him courage to be prepared for all that might befall him. They consoled him, so that the more God gave him to suffer, the greater grew his love for God.

CHAPTER XII

Christmas Day and Old France

I

SHIPS from the Netherlands landing at New Amsterdam in the early summer of 1643 delivered instructions from the Noble, High and Mighty Lords of the States-General to Director-General Willem Kieft directing him to use all his good offices to aid and save the French Jesuit named Isaac Jogues who had been captured by Iroquois savages. These instructions were issued at the request of the Queen Regent of France, Anne of Austria. Then, in the latter part of August, the captain of the vessel which came down from Rensselaerswyck informed Director Kieft of the abortive attempt which Isaac Jogues had made to escape. According to the captain, Arendt Van Corlaer still held the Jesuit in custody. Whereupon, Kieft sent a peremptory command to the Director and Commandant at Fort Orange. The Jesuit, Isaac Jogues, must be sent down to Fort Amsterdam at the earliest possible moment.

Director-General Kieft's orders reached Rensselaerswyck about the time the delegation of Mohawk chiefs arrived to hold council with Cora. The sachems were resentful over the treachery of their pale-face neighbors and the warriors were in an avenging mood. When they descended in great numbers upon the little settlement in the middle of September, they plainly indicated that it was only their deepest love for the Dutch that prevented them from a massacre. Van Corlaer endeavored to beguile them, in the first council; then, to bribe them through the ransom he offered. Since the Mohawks remained stubborn, Van Corlaer ceased to plead. He declared bluntly that he had taken Ondessonk under his protection. He offered them a present of three hundred gulders. If they refused this gift, he and the Dutch would refuse to trade with them. After much haggling and flowery oratory, the Mohawks touched the presents of Cora and professed themselves consoled over the loss of Ondessonk.

Fully aware of how treacherous were the Iroquois, and how easily aroused, Van Corlaer continued to keep Jogues closely concealed. Then, in the last week of September, under the cover of darkness, he smuggled Isaac from the sutler's garret to a sloop that was ready to sail with the turn of tide next morning. For Father Jogues, on that cool September evening, was the first breath of freedom after six weeks of the closest confinement, was the first moment of security. He was content. He had followed the will of God, not his own; he had sought the greater end, to escape now, but to return later and dedicate himself wholly to the conversion of the Iroquois nations.

In the morning, under the impact of the wind, the sloop rippled down the flat level of the river. Dominie Megapolensis and a goodly number of the important burghers were aboard, for they had been summoned by Director-General Kieft to New Amsterdam for a conference on the state of the Colony. Well rounded and comfortable-looking were they, with their broad-rimmed hats crowning their jovial faces, their long coats amply covering their paunches, their knickerbockers swelling out about their hips, their hose trimly showing off the bulging calves of their legs, their slippers elegantly buckled. They smoked their long-stemmed pipes and exuded an air of prosperity and well-being.

They were in dire contrast to Isaac. Though he was but thirty-six years old, his face was drawn and deeply lined with furrows. After seven years in the open weather with the savages, his skin was rough and dyed almost a copper color. His beard was graying and untrimmed; the hair of his head was sparse and scraggly. For clothes, he wore an ill-fitting, worn-out suit that had been donated to him by some one of his hosts. He was uncomfortable and self-conscious, as he stood in the midst of his Dutch friends.

That day they sailed carefully through the channels of the upper river, between the shallows and patches of green water weeds and sprawling islands. It was the path that Jogues had traveled in early August when he went to the fishing-haunts under the escort of his "aunt." The wind not being too favorable, they made on that first day not more than about twenty miles, and there they anchored for the night, in the vicinity of the place where Jogues had been with the Mohawk party.

Dominie Megapolensis, in a holiday spirit, had brought with him a number of bottles of wine. That evening he dealt them out lavishly to the burghers and crew in order fitly to celebrate the escape of his friend and fellow-minister. He wished to signalize the event, so he announced, by naming an island in honor of Isaac Jogues. What more fitting, than, that of baptizing this island near which they were anchored, seeing that it was near this island that their guest had encamped. All the ship's company loudly applauded the speech of the Dominie. They raised their tankards for a toast, while the Dominie proclaimed that for all times hereafter the island near by would be called "The Island of the Jesuit Jogues." Guns and muskets fired a salvo and set the echoes booming; the company cheered. Father Jogues laughed with them, but he was much embarrassed. Though touched by the tribute and the kindliness of his Dutch friends, he remarked deprecatingly, when he narrated the story to Buteux: "Each one manifests his love in his own fashion."

If Father Jogues thought the river of the Dutch, as he saw it about Fort Orange and some miles below, was mean and unimpressive as compared with the grandeur of the St. Lawrence, he changed his opinion as he sailed down its length. During the five or six days that followed he passed beyond the area of shoals and weedy, sandy islands, down where the shores widened out grandly and stretched before him in majestic vistas; where the banks rose up in rough and hardy magnificence, covered with the tapestry of the trees blazing in fiery color; where far off the mountains rose tier upon tier in dizzy ridges of blue and purple, bulked against the pale sky; where, again, the river narrowed to defile through precipitous mountain cones; then, where it spread out into broad expanses of lake and sea. Finally, when they had passed away from the tumbling hills and sailed around a wide-sweeping curve, Father Jogues looked curiously at the shaggy walls of rock that reared up hundreds of feet, straight and regular as if they were the walls or palisades of a town.

For Megapolensis and the Dutchmen, these palisades marked the beginning of the settlement of New Amsterdam. On the bank opposite to them, the Dominie gleefully pointed out the familiar landmarks; the little hamlet of Yonkers, the mouth of the small river called the Harlem, which made Manhattan an island; then some distance below the bouwerie of the Dutch West India Company, and the gardens and orchards; the little clearing of the cemetery; and over the shoulder of the hill the arms of the windmill. Jogues, hanging over the ship rail with the Dominie, watched the square wall of Fort Amsterdam emerge between the trees. He followed with his eyes the curve of the land about the lower tip of the island, noted the islands that dotted the far-reaching harbor toward the sea, the sweep of the river to the left. As the sloop tacked about the fort he gazed upon the cluster of gabled houses planted in rows on the lowlands beyond the fort. The ship veered to the left again and made for the wharf and strip of rock which the Dominie called Schreyers' Hoek.

Under the towage of Megapolensis, who was proud of his distinction, Father Jogues walked through the townsmen who were congregated about the landing-place. They were fascinated to see a Jesuit priest, whom they had been taught to believe was a devil in disguise. This Frenchman, this Isaac Jogues, seemed more pitiable than fearsome to them. He seemed to be a gentle, quiet man, with a kindly look in his face, who greeted them with smiles, who was rather grotesque in his poorly fitting coat and knickerbockers.

They marched a few hundred feet up the cobbled road from the dock until they came to the block of houses stretching along Parel Straet and faced the length of the Marckveldt. On the right-hand side was the intersection of Brugh Straet, and the storehouse and stone workshops of the West India Company. To the left, whither Megapolensis led Jogues, was the open space before Fort Amsterdam. This appeared as a rectangular pile, some three hundred and fifty feet in length and two hundred and fifty in width, scarcely higher than a breastwork, with curtains of earth and stone between the triangular bastions at each corner.

They passed within the gate, about which a few soldiers lolled, into the courtyard of the fort. On the west side of the inclosure were the barracks of the soldiers. On the east, in the far corner, stood the newly erected Church. Nearer was the elegant, red-brick mansion of the Director-General. A broad, smooth pavement flanked with grass and flowers led from the flagged courtyard to the mansion door, which was some twenty feet broad.

They were admitted into the spacious, low-ceilinged living-room, comfortable with its capacious fireplace. Director-General Kieft welcomed Father Jogues heartily. He was an officious, self-assertive man, most autocratic and decisive in his words and gestures. After he had inquired solicitously about Isaac's ordeals, he assured him most emphatically that now all his troubles were over and that he, the Director-General, would arrange personally for his passage either to Europe or to New France. His keen eye surveyed Isaac's costume. He emitted waspish remarks about the niggardliness of the people of Rensselaerswyck, and straightway ordered his tailor to measure and fit Master Isaac in a black suit of good material, with a heavy cloak to match, and with a beaver hat of respectable style. For the first few days the Director-General lodged Father Jogues in his own mansion. Then he arranged a suitable place for him in the Stadts Herbergh, the city tavern. This hostel had been erected just a year or two before to accommodate the growing number of visitors to New Amsterdam.

Director Kieft honored Isaac with a state dinner to which were invited Dominie Everhardus Bogardus, the chief officers of the West India Company, and all the principal burghers. The diners were most expansive in their greetings, and were most curious about the experiences and adventures of their guest. And now, one of them questioned Father Jogues, what reward would be given him by the Messieurs of the Company of France? Father Jogues could but smile at the naïveté of the inquiry. He relates that he "gave them to understand that worldly considerations had not caused him to leave his own country, that the preaching of the gospel was the sole and single good that he had in mind when he cast himself into the dangers in which he had fallen." Neither Dominie Bogardus nor the Director-General nor the rest of the company thought his answer convincing.

Two topics of conversation held sway in New Amsterdam. The first was Director-General Kieft. He was denounced as an autocrat, since he had dismissed his councilors, and was condemned as a tyrant who levied high taxes, enacted rigid regulations, and inflicted the severest penalties. The principal inhabitants, exasperated by his irascibility and imprudence, flared against him in their talk, as much as they dared. The second topic was that of the wars with the natives of the vicinity. These were Algonquins, hence, deadly enemies of the Iroquois whom the Dutch at Rensselaerswyck favored. They had previously sought friendship with the Dutch, but felt that they had been badly treated. Then, under Director Kieft, they found new grievances.

First, the Dutch were encroaching on their land along the North

River, along the Raritan, on Staten Island and across the East River on Long Island. Then, in January of 1643, a drunken savage shot a Dutch settler near Hackensack. Kieft demanded that the murderer be handed over to him; the savages refused, but professed their willingness to pay indemnities. In February, when a band of Iroquois came sweeping down the river on the warpath, an Algonquin party camped near Pavonia, across the North River, and another group settled at Corlaer's Hoek, on the East River, thinking they would be safe under the protection of the Dutch. On the night of February 25, Dutch soldiers fell on the Algonquin refugees, and slaughtered eighty of them at Pavonia and forty at Corlaer's Hoek.

Thereupon, all the Algonquin nations for fifty miles about dug up the war hatchet. They devastated the outlying Dutch hamlets, slaughtered the cattle, burned the homes and barns, attacked the settlers wherever they found them unprotected, and even menaced New Amsterdam. In May, the Dutch effected a peace. The savages, interpreting this as a sign of fear and weakness, continued to meditate the complete annihilation of the Dutch.

That summer and early autumn, New Amsterdam lived in terror. Father Jogues learned that the savages had "in various reprisals killed forty Dutch, burned many houses, and wrought damage reckoned at 200,000 livres." Farmers were bringing their families and possessions into the town, settlers in the various hamlets were fleeing to the fort. Anne Hutchinson, the Englishwoman who had settled at Pelham Neck, John Throgmorton who had built a group of houses at Throg's Neck, the Rev. Francis Doughty who had established a colony on Long Island, and many others were driven off their lands and barely escaped with their lives. The latest depredation occurred just two weeks before Father Jogues' arrival, when the colonists at Achter Col, across the North River, were almost massacred.

Jogues and most of these refugees were housed in the Stadts Herbergh, the public hostelry presided over by Philip Gerritsen. This stone house, two stories high, surmounted by a slanting roof as high again, and topped by three tall chimneys, was the pride of New Amsterdam. It was on the bank of the East River, removed less than a hundred steps from the Ditch and the bridge across it, the social promenade of the town. A few hundred steps beyond this was the fort. All of New Amsterdam, Father Jogues found, could be traversed in a quarter of an hour.

His interest in the settlement was keen, and he noted data for a report he was later to make. "New Holland, which the Dutch call in Latin, Novum Belgium, and in their own language, Nieuw Nederland, that is to say, New Netherlands, is in the latitude of forty degrees, thirty minutes," he stated. The channel of the North River, or the river Maurice or Nassau, as it is sometimes named, "is deep and navigable by the largest ships which go up to Manhattes Island, which is seven leagues in circumference. Thereon is a fort intended to serve as a nucleus for a town to be built, and to be called New Amsterdam." He continues:

This fort, which is at the point of the island, about five or six leagues from the River's mouth, is called Fort Amsterdam. It has four regular bastions, provided with several pieces of artillery. All these bastions and the curtains were merely earthworks, most of which had quite given way, and through them the Fort could be entered from all sides; there were no trenches. For the defense of this Fort, and of another which they had built further on against the incursions of the savages, their enemies, there were sixty soldiers. They were beginning to case the gates and the bastions with stone. In this Fort there was a house of worship, built of stone, which was quite spacious; the house of the Governor, whom they call the Director General, built quite neatly of brick; and the storehouses and soldiers' quarters.

There may be, on the Island of Manhate and in its environs, about four to five hundred men of various sects and nations. The Director General told me that there were men of eighteen different languages. They are scattered here and there, up and down the waterway, according as the beauty or the convenience of the sites invited each one to settle. Some artisans, however, who work at their trades, are located under cover of the Fort. While all the others are exposed to the incursions of the savages, who, in the year 1643, while I was there, had actually killed about forty Hollanders, and burned many houses, and barns full of wheat.

There is no exercise of religion except the Calvinist, and the orders declare that none but Calvinists be admitted; nevertheless, that order is not observed. For besides the Calvinists, there are in this settlement Catholics, English Puritans, Lutherans, Anabaptists, whom they call Mnistes, etc.

When anyone comes for the first time to dwell in the country, they supply him with horses, cows, etc., and give him provisions; all of which he repays when he is well settled. As for lands, at the end of ten years, he gives the Company of the West Indies a tenth of the produce that he harvests. . . . The climate there is very mild. As that region is situated at 40 and two-thirds degrees, there are plenty of European fruits, as apples, pears, cherries. I arrived there in October, and even then I found many peaches.

Of the diverse nationalities represented in the tiny settlement, Father Jogues had experience. One day, as he strolled along the country road out from Hoogh Straet toward the farm and pasture lands, he heard a man calling after him. He paused, and saw a young man, evidently a laborer indentured to one of the farmers, running breathlessly toward him. The lad fell on his knees before Father Jogues, took his mangled hands, and kissed them most fervently, exclaiming, "O Martyr! O Martyr of Jesus Christ!" Jogues gently raised the man from his knees and, in surprise, asked him if he were not a Calvinist. "Nenny, not at all," the fellow answered, trying to make himself intelligible. "Polakim. Lutheranim." Father Jogues was touched by the fervor and faith of the young Polish Lutheran, and grieved that he could not show his appreciation except by smiles and gestures.

On another occasion, while he walked along Parel Straet, near the fort, and was admiring the neat little houses banked about with vines and flower-boxes, a soldier accosted him. The man was the standard-bearer of the garrison, and in a friendly way invited him to enter the house. In the tiny room, Jogues was amazed and delighted to see two pictures hanging over the mantelpiece, one of the Blessed Virgin, the other of Blessed Aloysius Gonzaga. He looked at the soldier inquiringly. The man pointed to his wife and explained that she was a Portuguese and a Catholic. She was quite young, Father Jogues noted, "and wore an expression of Christian modesty." She had remained faithful to her religion in the midst of the Calvinists, and was proud to display her holy pictures. It was a great joy to her to meet Father Jogues, to receive his blessing and make her confession.

Still another confession he heard was that of an Irishman who came up from Virginia. The man never thought he would meet a

Catholic priest and a Jesuit among the Dutch Protestants. He was full of conversation. There were Jesuits in Virginia, too, he related, but they were English. Not long before, one of them was killed by the natives, not by the tribe he was with, the ones he had followed off to the forests to convert; these were friendly; but by their enemies, who attacked the ones he was with; they put him to death and scalped him. In answer to Jogues' questions, the Irishman related that there were about twelve thousand English in Virginia. It was going to be a very prosperous colony as time went on. It was very healthy there. The soil was fine, and yielded a good harvest of all kinds of fruits, grains, and vegetables.

In his conversations with the Irishman and the others at New Amsterdam, Father Jogues learned that, to the south, the Dutch colony of New Netherlands "has for its limits the river which they call the South River. There is also a Dutch settlement on this river. But nearer the mouth of the river, the Swedes have another settlement, which is extremely well-equipped with cannon and people. It is believed that these Swedes are maintained by Amsterdam merchants, who are incensed because the Company of the West Indies holds a monopoly of all the trade of these regions. It is somewhere down near this river that it is reported they have found a gold mine."

The Reverend Mr. Doughty, Throgmorton and the other English people who had fled the wrath of the savages and were living at the Stadts Herbergh gave Jogues information about the colonies of New England. There were 100,000 souls in all of those regions, they stated. Their land lay mostly near the ocean, situated between the country of the Iroquois and the Abenakis. Commerce was well established. The land was not fertile and the weather was not so temperate as at New Amsterdam. Jogues registered some surprise at the statement of one of the Englishmen that the farmers in the colony cultivate the earth with codfish, by first letting the cod decay and then using the mass resulting as manure. The dividing line between the English and the Dutch was a river which they called the Fresh River, or the Quinnehtukqut. But many of the English crossed over this dividing line, he reports the refugees as saying, for "they prefer to have lands among the Dutch, who do not force them to pay anything, rather than depend upon English Milords who exact rents, and who like to put on the airs of being absolute rulers."

Enlightening and interesting though he found New Amsterdam,

Father Jogues grew rather uneasy as October passed. Director-General Kieft had assured him that he would find passage to Europe. But all the regular vessels sailing for the Netherland had already departed before he reached Fort Amsterdam. The season for trade along the coast was practically over, so that no boats were clearing for New England, which was one way of returning to Quebec. Kieft began to waver in his promises as the autumn advanced. He confessed that it might not be possible to find a vessel bound across the ocean, or, in fact, an outgoing ship to anywhere. Jogues feared that he might have to remain among the Dutch for the winter.

II

In that October of 1643, Director-General Kieft and the Council of New Amsterdam were in deadly fear of new attacks by the Algonquins. The near-by nations were massing their strength and seeking allies. Their vicious guerrilla warfare begot terror on all sides. The people of New Amsterdam realized how impotent they were to strike back effectively at the savages. They were only too well aware of their weakness, even in defense of their settlement. The blame for the war, most of the people attributed to Director Kieft. They laid on him the guilt for the massacres at Pavonia and Corlaer's Hoek. He, in turn, repudiated the charge and placed the responsibility on the soldiers and the Councilors. All agreed, however, that some action must be taken to avert the calamity. It was imperative, they decided, to send full information of their plight to the Home Government and to the West India Company. About this, however, they were in a quandary, for all the seafaring ships had already departed.

Unexpectedly, toward the end of October, there arrived at New Amsterdam a small bark of less than a hundred tons. It was not in good condition, and was hardly large enough to sail the ocean at that time of the year when the autumnal storms were beginning to rage. But the need was desperate. New Amsterdam might survive the winter, but meanwhile, the Home Government must be preparing to dispatch aid at the first break of spring. Kieft, therefore, decided to take a chance on sending the little vessel across the ocean.

The Council of Eight, representing the burghers, drew up a Memorial which was authorized by Director Kieft and approved by the inhabitants. They addressed their petition, dated November 3, 1643, to the "Noble, High and Mighty Lords, the Noble Lords of the States General of the United Netherland Provinces." Most piteously they related how:

We were here pursued by these wild heathens and barbarous savages with fire and sword; daily in our houses and fields they have cruelly murdered men and women; and with hatchets and tomahawks struck little children dead in their parents' arms or before their doors; or carried them away into bondage. . . . In fine, we experience here the greatest misery, which must astonish a Christian heart to see or to hear. We turn, then, in a body, to you, Noble, High and Mighty Lords, acknowledging you as our Sovereigns and the Fathers of Fatherland. We supplicate, for God's sake, and for the love your High Mightinesses bear your poor and desolate subjects here in New Netherland, that your High Mightinesses would take pity on us, your poor people, and encourage the Company thereunto, and command them (to whom we also hereby make known our necessity) to forward us, by the earliest opportunity, such assistance as Your High Mightinesses will deem most proper, in order that we, poor, forlorn people, may not be left all at once a prey, with wives and children, to these cruel heathens. And should suitable assistance not speedily arrive (contrary to our expectations), we shall, through necessity, in order to save the lives of those who remain, be obliged to betake ourselves to the English at the East, who would like nothing better than to possess this place.

When it was settled that the little ship was to be dispatched to Amsterdam with this Memorial, Director Kieft told Father Jogues that he might board it. Kieft did not minimize the danger, nor did he urge Isaac to leave. On the part of Father Jogues, there was not a moment's hesitation in thanking the Director for the opportunity. Kieft, then, with continued kindness, supplied Isaac with an additional coat and with a warm blanket, and ordered that a supply of food, sufficient to last him for the six or more weeks of the passage, be provided. He also gave Father Jogues an official letter of passage:

We, Willem Kieft, Director General, and the Council of New Netherland, to all those who shall see these presents, greeting:

Isaac Jogues, of the Society of Jesus, for some time a prisoner among the Iroquois savages, commonly called the Maquaas, and daily persecuted by these was, when about to be burnt, snatched out of their hands, and ransomed by us for a large sum, after considerable difficulty. As he now proceeds with our permission to Holland, thence to return to France, Christian charity requires that he be humanely treated by those into whose hands he may happen to fall. Wherefore, we request all Governors, Viceroys, or their Lieutenants and Captains, that they would afford him their favor in going and returning, promising to do the same on like occasion.

Down at Schreyers' Hoek, on Thursday morning, November 5, the whole of New Amsterdam gathered to say farewell to the little vessel that was to carry the appeal for help. The Director-General, the Committee of Eight, Dominie Bogardus, all the principal burghers waited for the moment of sailing with tense nervousness. The bark would make a safe crossing, they said to encourage themselves and one another, though it was small and though it might meet with storms and high winds. It was a stout little ship. They interrupted their speculations to wish safe passage to the French Jesuit. And Father Jogues was deeply moved and grateful to them for their charity.

The decks were cleared, ropes were tossed off, anchors lifted, sails hoisted; the captain shouted his orders, the crew shouted back, the men, women, and children on the dock and the rocks cheered and waved their canes and scarfs and hats; the ship nosed forward, the masts creaked, the ship cleared the dock, was off from the land, was cutting across to the islands; the guns boomed from the fort, the last cries and shouts floated across the waters, the people on Weeper's Hook grew small, the houses and fort dwindled, the river and bay widened, a sharp breeze blew up over the deck, and Father Jogues, standing above the stern, looked back along the white wake toward his friends on Manhattan Island, and looked his last up the North River with a prayer for his Iroquois.

"He did not lack crosses in this voyage," Buteux, who heard the narrative from Jogues' lips, could testify. In the first place, he enumerates, the ship was extremely small for venturing out on such a long trip of three thousand miles and more. In the second place, Father Isaac had to make his bed on the upper deck and on the coils of ropes and riggings. Since the seas ran high for the greater part of the time, he was drenched by each wave that broke over the deck. Thirdly, he was forced to descend into the hold of the ship; here, the horde of cats infected the air with their stench, and night after night fouled all his blanket and coat. Finally, the victuals, which were at best wretched, were almost completely exhausted. Over and above that, Buteux asserts, the vessel, because it was so small, was tossed about at the mercy of the storms.

The tiny craft continued to rock its way across the Atlantic during the weary forty-eight days that followed from November 5. About the end of the third week in December it neared the entrance to the English Channel. A fierce storm burst, and a gale blew from the French coast. To buck the wind, the rain, and the tumultuous waves would be foolhardy, the captain decided. He made for the shelter of Falmouth on the lower coast of England, there to wait for better weather. They ran before the wind and sighted the headlands of Cornwall looming up black under the clouds. Out of the waves and the mist rose up a vessel, off from the stern; and then another vessel. They were obviously giving chase. They were large ships, pirates or privateers or warships. The captain crowded on sail. The two pursuers let fire with their cannon. They plowed menacingly after the little boat which was now leaping almost frantically through the waves. The Dutchman finally drew in between the hills that sheltered the Bay of Falmouth, while the pursuers faded in the storm.

At the town of Falmouth, where they docked along the quay, Father Jogues learned that Civil War was raging in England between King Charles I and Parliament. Falmouth was held by the Royalists, and the warships they had eluded belonged to the Parliamentarians, or Roundheads, who were patrolling all the ports in Cornwall and along the Channel. Jogues had had a narrow escape. There was a law in England proscribing Papish priests and, in particular, Jesuits. Just the year before, in 1642, four priests were executed, two at Tyburn in London and two at York; and that before the Parliamentarians had risen into open rebellion against King Charles. Now that Cromwell and his Roundheads were in the ascendancy, they would have even less mercy on any Papist priest who fell into their clutches.

The Parliament leaders were sworn to bitter enmity against France because of Queen Henrietta, the daughter of Henry IV, who, they claimed, was the evil genius of King Charles. They had raised the battle cry of the complete extermination of Popery in all of England. Just at that time they were hysterically afraid of the rising of the Catholics in support of Charles, and of the money and forces being raised in his behalf in France. If they had taken Father Jogues, they would have acted like the Mohawks and would have surely sentenced him to be hung and quartered.

Father Jogues remained incognito at Falmouth for pursuivants were everywhere. The Dutch captain was pleased to coöperate, for it might go ill with him if it were known he had landed and was harboring a Jesuit priest. Isaac remained on board the ship, with only a single sailor as a watchman, while the captain and the crew went on shore, as he narrates, "in order to go and refresh themselves a little from the sea and from the long voyage." In the quiet of the evening, while he sat on a coil of ropes and meditated, he became aware of a bulky figure creeping upon him. He heard the man give him an order, saw a pistol pointed at him. The man held the cold muzzle of the pistol against his throat.

Other figures clambered on deck. He and the Dutch sailor were held covered by the guns. The marauders disappeared stealthily down the hatchway to the hold. Jogues could hear them tumbling about the baggage and ballast below. They came on deck disappointed, for, as he told some one, "they expected the bark to be laden with great riches since it had come in from such a long voyage." The robbers had to content themselves with carrying off the few bundles belonging to the crew. Before they left they stripped Jogues of his hat, cloak and greatcoat, leaving him shivering with nothing on but the thin suit which Kieft had given him. But they did him and the sailor no other harm.

As soon as it was daybreak, Father Jogues went ashore to find the Dutch sailors. The Captain burst into a furious anger and rushed down to the quay, raging about the place, imprecating the robbers, seeking to discover them. One of the men whom Father Jogues met on shore gave him an overcoat, which was welcome, though it was threadbare and greasy, and brought him to a tavern where he gave him his breakfast. It was here that he met a Frenchman to whom he revealed, but very discreetly, that he was a priest and a missioner returning from the New World and seeking a passage to France. Until the storm abated, the Frenchman told Father Jogues, no boats would be leaving Falmouth. But there would be a collier sailing within a few days on which he could cross; until that time he could live aboard with the crew. The Dutch captain was satisfied and happy to be relieved of his passenger.

About dawn on Christmas Eve the lumbering French collier raised sail and, easing its way out of the inner harbor of Falmouth, pointed for the broad estuary guarded by the castles reared up on each point of the headlands. The boat was bound for Bordeaux on the lower west coast of France, and drove a straight course across the English Channel. The winds were favorable, the waters not too rough, so that the captain could predict to Father Jogues that they would be reaching the islands off Finisterre sometime early the next morning. It would be Christmas morning; there would be Christmas Masses in the churches of the fishing villages along the Breton coast; it might be that the captain could put him ashore near one of these villages, Jogues suggested. That could be done, the captain answered him, if the weather continued fair.

That night on board the collier, Father Jogues kept vigil. Seventeen months had passed since he had said his last Mass, since he had savored the Body and Blood of Christ. Seventeen months since he had made his confession to Father Buteux at Three Rivers. He could confess on the morrow and could receive Communion. While he huddled under a shelter on deck, and listened to the splash of the waves, and looked up into the starry night, he examined his conscience. He had lived in an environment where sin was difficult to avoid; he questioned himself as to the sins he had committed.

Though in his humility and self-abasement he told himself that he was a great sinner, truly he had little that was sin upon his soul. At a later date he was to make a general confession to Father Jacques Buteux, who states: "I can say in all truth, for I know it most certainly, having heard his general confession for the period between the time he departed from the Hurons until we were together in Montreal (after his return from France), one of the most remarkable things I know of has been the purity in which he kept himself among so many various vicissitudes. One of his great faults was that of having quite often wished for death in the midst of his long and continual exterior and interior sufferings."

Father Jogues did not tell of his virtues, says Buteux: "His modesty kept secret from me the principal thing, that which adorns all else: I mean his interior virtues, his charity, his patience, his conformity to the will of God through which he suffered; all of this it would be, indeed, desirable to know; and yet about this we know the least." However, Buteux revealed what impressions he gathered as to the sins and virtues of Father Jogues:

That which seems to me most to be admired in him is that, during the whole period of his sufferings caused by the cruelties of the Iroquois, he never had the slightest ill-feeling against them. On the contrary, he pitied their blindness, with the tenderness of a mother who was patient to her little son in a temper, or he looked on them as instruments of the justice of God in his regard.

2. Not only had he no ill-feeling toward them, but rather intense longings of charity to bring about their salvation, to pray for them; in addition to the joy that he had in suffering, seeing that God had heard his prayers and was chastising him here below in this world, was the satisfaction of being the first to pour out his blood for the glory of God among these savage peoples.

3. I have said that God had heard his prayer, for some time before the departure of the Hurons, while he was in prayer before the Blessed Sacrament and while he was fervently pleading with Our Lord that it would please Him to let him feel the rod and suffer here below, Our Lord let him understand and feel that this would actually happen. He did not know what he would have to endure until he saw himself a captive in the hands of the Iroquois.

4. The peace of soul that he felt during his sufferings, and the thanks that he rendered to God for them, both during that time of trial and later, only he himself could explain. He did not tell me expressly, but I gathered them from certain phrases that unwittingly he let slip in various conversations with him. Here is an example that sufficiently indicates what I am trying to tell: "I have always loved those who punished me, and even kissed the rods of my teachers. Especially was this the case with the Iroquois,. after they had spared our lives. I did not cease, for many days in succession, from kissing the uprights of the platform on which we had suffered, and the sight of this place of exquisite torture was a source of consolation and an occasion of gratitude and thanksgiving for the favors that God had given me."

5. The purity of body which he guarded during all the time of his captivity, which lasted a year and more, was not less remarkable than the rest. I knew the greater part of his trials during this time; and one of

his greatest faults, in his own judgment, was that one time, when he thought he was going to die, he rejoiced that it would be the end of his sufferings. It is wonderful to think of what he did to avoid the slightest occasions of committing smaller sins, or giving scandal, whether amongst the savages or amongst the Dutch; he did not wish to ask nor to accept what might scandalize, in order to teach the savages that we may never approve of what is against the commandments of God.

Jogues searched his memory and conscience through the night, while the collier splashed its way across the English Channel. Lying flat on the deck, he thought dreamily of Christmas Eve among the Hurons, where the little chapel of Sainte Marie was blazing with candles and glowing with the fires, where the Fathers were gathering the redskins for the Mass. He wept that he was not with his Hurons. But, he would be in France for Christmas. He could not believe it. It was so strange that he should be so near to France. Slowly the night evaporated. The faint blue of the dawn spread over the heaving waters. There, through the mist, he saw the white breakers splashing about the rocky islands off the coast of Brittany. The collier crept on, bumping and thudding on the choppy waves. The blurred coast line spread out and rose above the islands. They were making for a point of land halfway between Brest and St. Paul de Léon, the captain told Jogues. It would be easier to land him there, in a bay near one of the fishing-villages. The collier cautiously picked a way near to the shore. They let down a rowboat for him and pulled him into the dock.

He was in France. Not far from the dock, across the sand, was a little stone house. He hurried his steps toward it. Two men were standing at the doorway. They watched him with curiosity as he staggered toward them. They smiled at his appearance, for he wore a battered sailor's cap and a ragged overcoat, much too big, that hung on him like on a scarecrow. They took him to be an Irish refugee; many a one had landed on the shores of Brittany these past few years since the bloody persecution of Catholics was raging in Ireland and England.

He spoke to them in French, a queer French, they thought. He inquired if there was a church near by where he might hear Mass. They said he could; there was a monastery of the Récollets up the road a bit, and Mass would be being celebrated. Since he was going to Mass, they told him, he should look more decent. So they put a better-looking cap on his head and tied a scarf about his neck. Before they set him on the road they made him promise that he would come back to their house after Mass and have his breakfast.

Noël, Noël, the day that Christ was born. His soul sang Noël as he hurried up the road to the monastery church. It was Christmas morning; it was France. He was free, free of the Mohawks, free of the Dutch, free of the English. *Venite adoremus,* throbbed in his brain. The Christmas carols he had sung as a boy pulsed through him. He was before the monastery church. He sought out a gray-robed priest and knelt before him to make confession of all the sins he could remember since July 30, a year ago. With bowed head he listened to the priest pronouncing the words of absolution. He knelt on the flagged floor among the people near the altar. The candles, the priest in white vestments, the words he said were blurred and indistinct. It was time for Communion. He felt the Host upon his tongue. It was the Body of Christ. He knelt in adoration. The cloud cleared about him. He came to himself. "It seemed to me that it was at this moment that I began to live once more. It was then that I tasted the sweetness of my deliverance," he said.

Unobtrusively, he slipped out from the church and avoided the knots of villagers who gossiped about. He returned, light-footed with ecstasy, down the road to the cottage of the fishermen. Some neighbors were there, for they had heard of the strange visitor thrown on their shore that morning. Some others who had watched him at church also strolled down to the cottage. They still judged him to be an Irish refugee, for his speech had a queer French accent. However, glad they were to welcome him, and they sat him down at the little table and laid his breakfast before him.

His hands, they noticed, were knotted and scarred; his fingers were crooked; some were stumps; some had no fingernails; he had no left thumb. They were in pity for him, for his cheeks were sunken and his skin was roughened. With simple curiosity they asked him of himself, of who he was and where he had been. He told them, briefly and modestly. "When they learned how he had suffered that martyrdom, they were at a loss to know what welcome to give him," he related.

The two little daughters of his host listened to him with rapt attention. How they were sorry for this poor priest who had suffered so much for God; how they wanted to show him they were sorry, to help and console him. They had saved up a few pennies, which they were hoarding carefully. They whispered together; they would give these to Father Isaac, for he was in terrible need and they would get more pennies after a while. Demurely, bashfully, the young girls stood by his chair and put their pennies in his hand. He must take them, to help him on his way, they urged. Father Jogues was touched to the soul. He was reluctant to accept their precious fortune, but such was their eagerness, such their simplicity, that he must bless them and receive their gift.

News of the strange priest who had landed on the shore on Christmas morning rapidly spread through the countryside and among the fisherfolk who lived along the coast. Monsieur Berson, a merchant from Rennes, was transacting some business in a neighboring town. When he heard of Father Jogues, he hurried to the fisherman's house and offered his services. He knew the Jesuit Fathers in Rennes, he said, and would be returning to that city within a few days. He would be honored if he might escort the Father thither. This invitation, thought Father Jogues, "was not by chance, but by the Providence of God which leads everything to its issue." Accordingly, he accepted Monsieur Berson's offer of aid. On the last days of 1643 Father Jogues and Berson mounted their horses and set out, followed by the fervent prayers and good wishes of the Breton fisherfolk, on the journey of some two hundred miles along the winding roads which trailed over the Côtes du Nord.

III

Among the most popular books in France were the annual narratives written by the Jesuit missioners in New France. These, sent to the home country by the ships arriving in the middle of November, were issued in book form the following January or February. They were eagerly sought after in all the religious circles for their pious recitals; they were avidly read for their novelty and their marvelous stories of adventure by the Court and the nobility; and by the intellectuals they were admired for their charm and style. *The Relation of What Occurred in New France in the Years 1641 and 1642,* published in January 1643, contained an announcement that Father Isaac Jogues had been captured by the Iroquois enemies and carried off a prisoner to their country. Not many details were known, but Barthélmy Vimont, who wrote the account, indicated that the missioner might have been tortured and burned to death.

The ships arriving from Quebec in the autumn of 1643 brought with them *The Relation of What Occurred in New France in the Years 1642 and 1643*. This instalment carried the good tidings that Father Jogues was still alive, though he had been cruelly tortured by the Iroquois. All of France, by this time, was curiously interested in Jogues' fate, and impatient to learn the sequence. But the *Relation* could not be edited and printed before the end of January, 1644. However, the Jesuits of Paris were so joyful over the fact that Father Isaac still lived that they sent news of it to all their friends.

Shortly after the *Relation* arrived, two letters, from Father Jogues himself, were delivered from the Netherlands. One was addressed to the Provincial, Father Jean Filleau, dated August 5, 1643, at Rensselaerswyck, the settlement of the Dutch. It told of Jogues' experiences from the time he left the Hurons through the full year that followed. The other was to the Procurator of the Missions in Paris, Father Charles Lalemant, and was dated August 30. This related some of the details of the abortive attempt to escape. Though these three communications furnished confirmation that Isaac lived, they left his ultimate fate in doubt.

On Monday evening, January 4, 1644, after night had fallen, Father Jogues and Monsieur Berson drove their tired horses through the ancient gateway of Rennes. Jogues would have liked to rush straightway through the streets and up to the College of the Society of Jesus, to throw himself in the arms of his brothers. It was too late at that hour, for the doors were already barred and all had retired. Berson offered him the hospitality of his own home for the night, and Jogues contented himself to remain with his friend and host. He was wide awake long before the earliest glow of dawn, was dressed and impatient to leave Berson's house.

About five-thirty on Tuesday morning the Brother porter of the College of Rennes rang the signal bell for the community Mass. At the same time he heard a pounding on the street door. He opened it to a dilapidated man, clothed in an old greatcoat, with a scarf about his neck, and a peasant's hat perched upon his head. Brother eyed his visitor with some suspicion. The man asked if he might see Father Rector. Brother told him that Father Rector could not be seen at that hour of the morning; he was just preparing to begin Mass. However, the Brother admitted, if the man wanted to wait, the Father Rector would probably see him after Mass. He led him into the dark parlor. The man answered that he must absolutely see the Father Rector immediately, even before he began Mass. "I have something to tell Father Rector," the visitor explained. "I have some news from Canada and from the Fathers there."

Something about this poor, starved-looking man impressed the Brother. He thought he had better speak to the Father Rector, and so went over to the sacristy. He found the Rector partly vested; nevertheless, he whispered to him that there was a poor man in the parlor who wanted to see him right away because he could not wait and had news of the Fathers in Canada. The Rector said the man had to wait until after Mass, and continued vesting. The thing troubled him; Brother had said it was a "poor" man from Canada. "It may be that the man is in a hurry," he thought to himself. "He may be in want and may need some help." Taking off his alb and his amice, he went to the parlor.

The room was shrouded in darkness. Father Rector could see only the dim outline of the visitor. He greeted him kindly, and the man handed him a letter. Under the gleam of a candle, the Rector glanced at it hurriedly and read: "We, Willem Kieft, Director General, and the . . ." He did not bother to examine the paper, for he was in a hurry. He asked the visitor if he had come from Canada, as the Brother related. Yes, the man answered, he had been in Canada. Do you know the Fathers there? Very well. Father Vimont? Yes. Father de Brébeuf? Extremely well. And Father Jogues, did you know Father Isaac Jogues?

"I knew him very well indeed," Isaac answered.

"We have had word that he was captured by the Iroquois. Do you know, is he dead? Or is he still captive? Have those barbarians not murdered him?" Father Rector inquired.

"He is at liberty," he said, with a queer gulp. "Reverend Father," Isaac broke into tears, "it is he who speaks to you."

He fell on his knees, at Father Rector's feet, kissed his hand, begged his blessing. A cold shiver passed through the Father Rector. Then a burst of joy. He lifted Isaac from his knees, threw his arms about him, kissed him on both cheeks. With a loud voice, that rumbled strangely through the quiet corridor at that hour of sacred silence, he welcomed him and brought him to the community room. The Brother porter, the other Brothers, the Fathers, startled by the excited voices, came hastening into the room. They gathered about Father Isaac; they embraced him and kissed him; they were so overjoyed that they could only gasp sounds, they could scarcely find words. They stripped off his old coat and found a cassock for him. They brought him in triumph to the chapel, where Father Rector, thrilling with the joy of it all, said Mass and gave Father Jogues Communion. All the community was hushed with awe, and in every heart there was offered a prayer of thanksgiving to God for His great mercy.

Later in the morning Father Jogues, now clothed in a soutane and cloak and broad-rimmed hat, accompanied Father Rector to the house of Monsieur Berson to express their gratitude to the merchant for his generosity and courtesy. Father Rector offered to remunerate the gentleman for the expenses he had incurred in bringing Father Isaac to Rennes, but Monsieur Berson protested that he had already been too much repaid by the honor he had of escorting the Father back to his brother Jesuits.

If they were eager to hear his story, Father Jogues was starved for all the news of them and of Canada. He had read of the Fathers among the Hurons in the *Relation* which the Iroquois had captured and brought back to Ossernenon. But what of the others? They told him what they knew. Father Charles Raymbault was dead. His companion on the journey to Sault Sainte Marie, whom he had brought down to Quebec! He had died October a year ago of tuberculosis. Father Ambroise Davost was dead, too. He was on his way back to France and was carried off by scurvy. They buried him at sea. That was last September. Father Jogues had succeeded him among the Hurons in 1636. There was another death at sea, Father Jean d'Olbeau. The enemy had captured the vessel on which he was returning to France, for he was in ill-health; while they were plundering it there was an explosion in the powder-room, and Father d'Olbeau and all on board perished. Only one missioner was sent out in 1642, an Italian, Francesco Gioseppe Bressani, who had been loaned to Canada by the Roman Province. That summer four priests were assigned to the Mission. There was a rumor that no others could be spared for another year or two. Eagerly, Father Jogues absorbed all the news of home and friends and New France.

In the bit of leisure that he had that day of jubilation, he wrote to his Provincial, Father Jean Filleau, formally announcing his arrival in France. He stated:

After all, my sins have rendered me unworthy to die among the Iroquois. I still live, and God grant that it be to amend myself. At least, I acknowledge it as a great favor that He has willed that I should endure something. I say often with gratitude: "It is good for me that thou hast humbled me, that I may learn thy justifications." I departed on the fifth of November from the Dutch settlement, in a bark of fifty tons, which conveyed me to Falmouth in England, the day before Christmas. And I arrived in Lower Brittany, between Brest and St. Paul de Léon, the very day of Christmas, in time to have the blessing of hearing Mass and offering my devotions. An honest merchant, having met me, took me and paid my way to Rennes, where I have arrived this day, the eve of Epiphany. What happiness, after having dwelt so long among savages, after having conversed with Calvinists, with Lutherans, with Anabaptists, and with Puritans, to see one's self among servants of God, in the Catholic Church! To see one's self in the Society of Jesus! It is a little comparison to the happiness that we shall receive some day in Paradise, if God please, when "he will gather together the dispersed of Israel." When will God withdraw His hand from over our poor French and our poor savages? "Woe is me, wherefore was I born to see the ruin of my people!" My sins and the unfaithfulness of my past life have made very heavy the hand of the Divine Majesty, justly provoked against us. I beseech your Reverence to obtain for me from Our Lord a perfect conversion; and that this little chastisement that He has given me may avail, according to His purpose, to render me better. Father Raymbault, Father d'Olbeau, Father Davost are then dead? They were ripe for Paradise, and New France has lost in one year three persons who had accomplished great labors there. I do not know if a copy of the *Relation of the Hurons* has been received this year. The first copy was captured with the Hurons who were going down to the French in the month of June and was restored to me in the country of the Iroquois, with a large package of letters which our Fathers among the Hurons were sending to France. If I had supposed that God intended to deliver me, I would have carried it with me when I paid the visit to the Dutch. Everything was left in the cabin where I lived. Another time, I will write at greater length. This is enough for the first day of my arrival.

At Rennes, this 5th of January, 1644.

Some further details of his escape he gave the day following in a letter to Father Charles Lalemant. His next letter, dated January 6, was to his mother in Orléans. Madame Jogues was firmly convinced that her dear Isaac was dead. He knew how much she worried about him, how she must have suffered bitter pangs when she heard, as she must have heard, of the tortures to which he had been subjected. Only a phrase or two of his letter are known. But he urged her "to thank God for the peace which He had given to her son, and to thank God also because He had willed that her son should endure a few small sufferings for His love." As a bit of consolation, he added: "There is not one of our Fathers who does not envy me my lot, and who would not wish to have been in my place."

After the first glow of happiness over his homecoming, Jogues quickly became ill at ease in Rennes. His fellow Jesuits treated him with so much reverence, they looked on him with such awe, they loaded him with so many kindnesses, that his humility and common sense rebelled. In his letters he spoke always of the little he had endured and minimized as far as possible the heroism he had shown. He could not bring himself to talk much of his adventures, lest he give the impression that he was actually worthy of some consideration. He was most unwilling to show his mutilated hands or the scars on his body and arms and legs, lest people might think he was truly a martyr. He wanted to be unnoticed. He loathed praise.

Father Rector understood, and was doubtless amused, but certainly most edified. In a long letter which he wrote to the Provincial, he began: "When I begged Father Isaac Jogues to relate to us the details of his capture and his captivity, he answered me that he had written about it sufficiently at length. Since I perceive every day that he is so reserved in speaking about himself that he may have omitted many interesting particulars, I shall here record what I have drawn from his lips on sundry occasions." The Father then narrated some of the experiences and stated: "In conclusion, he is as cheerful as if he had suffered nothing. And he is as zealous to return to the Hurons, amid all those dangers, as if perils were to him securities. He certainly expects to cross the ocean once again, in order to give help to those poor peoples and to finish the sacrifice already begun."

The idea of returning to New France was frequently expressed by him, for another remarked that the community "regard him as a Lazarus raised from the dead, one who is destined to go and die for the last time in the country where he had already suffered so many deaths." To expedite this, Jogues was eager to go on to Paris. Accordingly, about January 14, he departed from the College of Rennes. The road from Rennes to Paris ran through Orléans, and, whether he wished it, or whether he wished to practice saintly abnegation by abstaining from it, he could scarcely avoid the home of his mother. It is not unlikely that he spent the Saturday and Sunday of January 16th and 17th with his family. Madame Jogues had the joy of weeping over her martyr son, of hearing from his own lips the marvelous story of God's providence over him. He would belittle the pain he had suffered and conceal the horrors. He would show only the happiness of being chosen by God to live among these poor savages.

She would accept it all, though she knew the truth. But her heart would be broken at the sight of his gnarled hands, with all the nails torn out save two, with the tips of the fingers mangled and scarred, with the left thumb gone, with the index finger not more than a stump. She would be terribly concerned about his skinniness, about the haggard look upon him. She would scold him for not taking care of his health, and beg him to stay in France nor ever to go back to those barbarous lands. Whatever she said or did, she was in bliss, now that once more her *cher Isaac* was with her. His brothers, François, Philip, Laurent and Samuel, now a Capuchin friar; his sister Françoise, his half sisters; all his numerous aunts and uncles and cousins; the Jesuits of the College of Orléans; all the townsfolk gazed on him as though he were a canonized martyr.

He endured the adulation of Orléans only as long as his duty to his mother forced him to remain. He took the stage for Paris. If he hoped to be unknown there he was doomed to disillusionment. Fathers Filleau and Lalemant were just then correcting the proofs of the *Relation of 1642 and 1643*. Therein was a rather complete narrative of his experiences, and Vimont had concluded by a glowing tribute to the courage and saintliness of "this living martyr, this suffering confessor, this man rich in extreme poverty, joyful and contented in the land of pain and sadness—in a word, this Jesuit clothed like a savage, or rather, like St. John the Baptist." And in the section devoted to the Huron Mission, Father Jérôme Lalemant testified: "We do not know when all this will end, nor how long these barbarians will allow Father Jogues to live. We know only that he expects death from day to day, and from hour to hour. We know that, while a breath of life remains within him he will employ it for the advancement of the glory of God, and will fulfill a more glorious mission than ours, for, since it is in the midst of our cruelest enemies, it is full of more crosses and it bristles with more thorns."

The editors of the *Relation* allowed the laudatory texts to remain. They added an extra chapter, dealing with his "Deliverance and Arrival." It was in the hands of the printer before Father Jogues arrived at Paris; it began: "This poor Father was no longer spoken of, save as one speaks of the dead. Some believed him burned and devoured by the Iroquois. Others regarded him as a victim who waited nothing more than the knife and the teeth of the sacrificers of Moloch. But the fact is, the God of the forsaken saved him by a wholly special Providence at the moment when he was destined for the fire and for those other cruelties which are beyond the malice of men. He is living. And if his hands are shortened, his heart is enlarged. The sufferings of his body have not diminished the strength of his mind. We are expecting him from day to day. If the printer were not so hurried, we could learn from his own lips the pleasant ways which God has taken in order to deliver him. The letter which he writes from his captivity to Father Charles Lalemant speaks to us of these quite amply. But it does not satisfy all the questions which we might put to him."

By the time Father Jogues arrived, the *Relation* was being eagerly read by all of Paris. Isaac quailed under the publicity. He could speak of himself only with the greatest reluctance. As in Rennes, so in Paris, it required the greatest cleverness to draw him out and to get him to recount his experiences. So great was his suffering that the Superiors requested his Jesuit brethren to respect his feelings and to spare him the strain of being treated like a saint. Lalemant said of him: "He was endowed with a humility altogether rare. He was not only convinced of his own lowliness, but he desired to be treated according to his nothingness. . . . Never had the Society (according to his own words) received as a member anyone so base as he was, or so unworthy of the garb he wore. It was necessary to use shrewdness and obedience upon him in order to make him tell what we have related. Not that he was restive under obedience, but because he really had so low an opinion of himself that he could not speak of himself except with contempt. To show him even the slightest bit of esteem for that which he had endured for Jesus Christ, was to afflict him."

The students of Clermont, of whom there were about two thousand, crowded about to get a glimpse of him, and besieged his coming and going. Beyond the College walls, everywhere he went, all Paris was eager and curious to look on him. They made him and his story news of the first interest, and the nouvellistes in the Gardens of the Palais Royal and the Luxembourg shouted his story to the gaping crowds. He hated and recoiled from this public attention.

Queen Anne, the Regent, was told of his arrival and listened with fascinated attention to the recital of his experiences. She was deeply moved, and remarked: "They try to invent tragic stories, and use their imagination to concoct strange adventures to surprise one and to touch one's emotion. But here is a story of great adventures which have really happened, here is a recital of the most astounding deeds joined with the truest heroism." She then expressed a royal wish that Father Jogues be brought to her presence. When the Father Confessor told him of the Queen's wish, which was a command in reality, Isaac was alarmed. He could not understand what interest Her Majesty might have in him, or that she really wished to receive him at the Palace. He tried to evade the honor by every means he could invent. It was only after a second and more imperative command was laid on him by the Queen and his religious Superiors that he did consent to appear at Court.

With the greatest reluctance and with trepidation, he allowed himself to be led to the Palais Royal, where the Queen then resided. He felt ill at ease in these magnificent halls which Cardinal Richelieu had built for himself, for he was used to a crude, savage world. He was a gentleman, nevertheless, one who had been bred to courtliness, and so could bear up under the gauntlet of noblemen and ladies who were assembled in the Grande Cabinet about the Queen. She was seated in an armchair, simply dressed, for the Court was still in mourning for Louis XIII who had died the preceding May. Seated by her knee was the little King, Louis XIV, then about five years old, and his brother, Philippe. Cardinal Mazarin stood nearby the Queen Regent, and the Princes and Princesses of the royal blood were in attendance.

Queen Anne received him with the gracious, kindly manner that was hers. She was a pious person, simple in her devotions, and was sincerely attracted to this poor missioner who had suffered as a martyr of Jesus Christ. She looked on him with deep reverence. She begged him to tell her of his capture by the Iroquois, of his tortures and his journeys, of the life he had led among them, of the threats of death, of his attempts to escape. Taking his mutilated hands in her own, she examined his mashed and twisted fingers. So tender was her pity that tears filled her eyes.

France weighed heavily on the soul of Father Jogues. He was sickened by the honors showered on him. He was not at ease amid the comforts, little as they were, of the Professed House of the Jesuits in Paris. Abroad, he felt like a hunted prisoner in the cobbled streets and thoroughfares, amid the noises and talk of the white people. Everyone revered him. He was troubled that he was doing nothing for God's service and glory. How he longed for the shores of the broad St. Lawrence, for the unending stretch of the Lake of the Hurons, for Sainte Marie, for Ossernenon and the Mohawk Valley, for the expanse of the blue skies and the fragrance of the forests, for the winding trails, for the quiet of the wilderness. How he longed to be again with the copper-skinned braves and the squaws; they were so gentle when they became Christians, so simple, so pious; to be with the little children whom he might instruct, whom he might baptize if they were dying. He did not belong in France. He was homesick for New France.

CHAPTER XIII

Peace along the St. Lawrence

I

ISAAC JOGUES lived once more. He had feared that he would be held in France. But so repeated were his requests that he be permitted to return to his Mission in New France, so insistent and convincing were the reasons he alleged, so compelling were the prayers he offered to God, that his Provincial Superior, Father Filleau, with a smile of understanding and a gleam of veneration in his eyes, ordered him to leave for Canada on the first ship sailing in the spring of 1644. Isaac was ecstatically happy, and his wrinkled features glowed. He was only thirty-seven years old, he told himself with assurance; he was strong and rugged enough to live for years more among the savages. New France was his true home.

He expedited all his business. He wrote to Director-General Kieft, thanking him for all the splendid hospitality and courtesy accorded him at New Amsterdam. He wrote to Director Arendt Van Corlaer at Rensselaerswyck and arranged through the Dutch West India Company the repayment of the 300 livres of the ransom money. Cordially he wrote to Dominie Megapolensis, but, as he stated, he could not refrain from offering some considerations on the Dominie's state of soul, and from urging him to return once more to the true Catholic religion of his childhood. In exhaustive conversations with Fathers Filleau and Charles Lalemant, he pleaded that more and more missioners be sent to New France for the conversion of the Algonquins, Hurons, Iroquois and the nations to the West. Following his audience with the Queen, he had opportunity of conferences with Cardinal Mazarin and the Directors of the Company of New France. He was a living example of the dangers to the colony of the Iroquois wars. He brought it about that Queen Anne, in the name of Louis XIV, signed an order whereby a company of soldiers would be dispatched that very spring to Canada for the specific purpose of guarding the Huron routes and garrisoning the fort that was being erected at Sainte Marie.

One blessing above all others, Father Jogues desired before he left France. He could not offer the Holy Sacrifice of the Mass canonically. His left thumb had been amputated at the root, and the index finger of that hand was only a stub; the thumb and index finger of the right hand were so shortened and distorted that he could not hold the Sacred Host in the appointed manner. As soon as he reached Paris, in January, he set about seeking a dispensation from the canonical requirements. This dispensation had to be sought from the Pope. Accordingly, he drew up his petition to His Holiness, Pope Urban VIII, instancing the reasons for his mutilated condition and begging for permission, despite that, to offer the Sacrifice of the Mass. His letter was sent with the approbation and recommendation of Father Filleau to Father Mutius Vitelleschi, the General of the Society of Jesus, in Rome. It was accompanied by letters royal from Queen Anne and her Council.

Father Vitelleschi, supported by the French Ambassador to the Papal Court, presented the petition to the Pope. His Holiness inquired with great interest about Father Isaac Jogues, about his missionary endeavors in the New World, about all that he suffered during his captivity among the Iroquois savages. He was deeply moved by the story. *"Indignum esset Christi martyrem, Christi non bibere sanguinem,"* he exclaimed: "It would be shameful, that a martyr of Christ be not allowed to drink the Blood of Christ." Straightway he granted the petition, and ruled that Father Jogues, despite the mutilation of his canonical fingers, should be permitted to offer the Holy Sacrifice.

The Pope's answer reached Father Jogues in March. It exalted him to Paradise itself. Twenty months had elapsed since he wore the sacred vestments, since that first day of August, at Three Rivers, when he said the Mass of St. Peter in Chains. Twenty months since he had pronounced the sacred words of Consecration and lifted the chalice to his lips. Now, once more, he was empowered to ascend as a priest to the altar of his God to offer the Divine Oblation. It seemed to him like his first Mass over again.

In April came the heartening news that the first ships for New France would be leaving within a few weeks from the port of La Rochelle. Toward the end of the month, Father Jogues said his farewells to his brethren in Paris and proceeded to the seaport. His route lay directly through Orléans. He was with his mother once more and had the consolation of saying Mass in her presence and of laying the Host upon her tongue. She knew that she was seeing him for the last time. Though she was more reconciled than she had been eight years before when he was newly ordained and venturing off to Canada, her heart was pierced with a sword of poignant sorrow. She fondled his twisted, knotted hands, touched her fingers to the scars on his face and neck and arms. He was returning to suffer again, and even more. Eight years before she had tried to dissuade him from going. She was braver now, and prepared to make the final renunciation of him to God. Her *cher Isaac* was a martyr of Christ; the Pope had said that, the Queen had said it, everyone in France was saying it. He had a duty, and God's will was clear. Isaac must go back to Canada.

Arrived at La Rochelle, he busied himself with the shipment of the supplies, the baggage, the books, letters, equipment that was to be transported for the Missions. To his great satisfaction, he found the company of soldiers ordered to Canada by Cardinal Mazarin waiting to sail on the same vessel. They were a rough, swaggering set, collected from the byways of Paris, and from the purlieus of the provincial towns and villages. Most of them were young adventurers, reckless, swearing, fighting. They had joined the army for fighting in Europe; foreign service in Canada was not much to their liking. Still, the prospects were good enough; after a term, they could settle down in the New World, if they liked it well enough, and grow up with the country.

The soldiers had not been long at La Rochelle before they developed a grievance about the transport. The ship assigned to them was small, too small for the voyage; and if that were not bad enough, it was old, for it had been built years before when Cardinal Richelieu first began to create his navy. They discovered that it was nothing more than a leaky old tub. They swore at their officers, at Cardinal Mazarin, at the Queen herself. The officials quelled their grumbling enough to march them on board. Father Jogues and a few civilians were the only other passengers.

The ship sailed in the first week of May. It nosed its way out of the fortified inclosure of the inner harbor, out through the narrow opening of the sea walls, past the wooden wickets of the outer defense. The vessel was slapped by the heaving, splashing waves of the Bay of Biscay. Soon it got under way, gathered itself together, and vaulted out toward the green circle of the ocean. The bold headlands of La Rochelle kept imperceptibly shrinking and the floor of water increased between them and the deck of the ship. Soon the shore was but a rim of deeper black, and soon it merged softly in the far horizon.

Scarcely was the vessel swallowed in the circle of the ocean before the soldiers returned to their grievance. They were convinced that the ship was not seaworthy. Its timbers were rotten, it leaked, it would fall apart in a heavy storm. Some of the sailors leagued with the soldiers, and soon the grumblings were mutinous. A delegation approached the captain and demanded that he turn about and bring the vessel back to La Rochelle. The captain dismissed them gruffly and swore that he never would put back to port. At this, the soldiers turned nasty. They were plotting to force the captain to return, even if they had to make him a prisoner. Father Jogues, aware of their fears, soothed them and advised the mutineers to do nothing rash. Strangely, they listened to his pleadings and gave up their demands on the captain.

The weather was blustery during the first week. The soldiers were terrified, but Father Jogues in his quiet, persuasive way pacified them. Storm followed storm, rain and wind and mighty waves rocked the little vessel. It lunged about precariously in the deep troughs, it was lifted up to the pinnacles of mountainous walls of water and slid down into the hollows, it listed to right, to left, and was beaten down upon by the sheets of rain. The old ship creaked and groaned, as if it were about to capsize, and was flooded with bilge water that flowed in from innumerable leaks. Jogues recognized the hazards, but he had no fears. He had been tumbled so much in the little Dutch vessel that he had had experience as to what a ship could stand. His confidence in God and his calmness quieted the terror of the soldiers and the sailors.

Far out, now, in midocean, the elements roused themselves in even greater fury. Following a day when the air was raw and the sky threatening, in the late dusk, there burst over them the most violent of all tempests. A gale swept down on them as if intent on grinding them in the caldrons of the water. Rain slashed against the sides of the ship in sheets and drummed on the deck. Waves reared up and broke over the masts. Wind screeched in the rigging and whistled deafeningly. The vessel lunged about like an infuriated, desperate animal. The crew, helpless under the terrific impact, stood tense and horrified as the boat quivered and creaked, from keel to masthead, from prow to stern. The soldiers and passengers huddled together in the black, beamed cabin under the deck. They felt themselves hurled helplessly from wall to wall, catapulted off their feet, twisted dizzily as the tortured vessel tumbled about.

"The ship's sinking! We're lost! We're lost!" The cry came from the deck, shrilling out above the thunder of the storm. In the cabin, the soldiers went mad. "We're lost! We're lost!" They shouted and fought, in fear, in despair, cursing, shrieking, as they churned over one another in the closed compartment. Father Jogues was on his knees in the little cubbyhole of his cabin. He was reading from a French translation of the Book of Isaias, praying God for help and preservation. "The ship's sinking. We're lost!" He heard the agonized cry. Commending himself and all on board to God, he leaped from his knees and struggled into the ship's cabin. While he clung to the doorpost, he shouted out to the raving mass of maniac men. His voice was steady and penetrating. He waved the book he held in his free hand over them in a gesture for quiet. Fascinated as if by an apparition, the soldiers for a moment forgot their fear. He was calm, masterful. Lifting his voice above the tumult, he spoke to them the words of Isaias which he had been reading. They listened. He spoke on and on. He called on them to pray to God, to trust in God, to beg mercy for their sins. He signed the cross over them in absolution.

Awakening, they noticed the ship was rolling steadily, the stridor of the wind was died down. The storm was past. They were saved. They joined with Father Jogues in a fervent prayer of thanksgiving to God for His mercy and providence over them. That night, they followed one another in kneeling at his side and making their confessions to him. Those who did not confess that night, did so and were absolved during the next few days, so that not one on board but was at peace with God before the ship sighted the shores of the New World. As for Father Jogues, they regarded him now more than ever as a saint of God. To him they attributed their preservation during the unending storms that assailed them all the way across the Atlantic.

Late in June, after seven weeks of battering, the transport struggled through the lower waters of the St. Lawrence Gulf and up toward the converging banks to the landing at Tadoussac. Already many Algonquins were assembled about this trading-post at the mouth of the Saguenay, waiting for the ships from France, and with them were one or two Blackrobes. A thrill of joy and exaltation shot through Father Jogues. He was with his own, at last, with the copper-skinned savages and their guttural grunts, with his brother missioners, in the log cabins and the huts of bark, amid the broad waters and the mysterious forests. God had brought him back safely once more, for life or for death, in New France.

Also like one risen from the dead, he was welcomed at Quebec. The Fathers along the St. Lawrence had had vague rumors during the autumn and winter that he had escaped from the Iroquois. They suspected that he had taken refuge among the Dutch in New Netherlands, but of this they had no certainty. His was the first ship that came up the river from the old country that summer. And it brought him back, himself. They embraced him and wept over him and bombarded him with a thousand questions. He was not so reluctant to talk to them, for they understood better than the people of France. They would not be so amazed, nor would they look on him with such awe and venerate him as a saint.

He was hungry for news. Almost the first he heard from the Superior, Father Vimont, was that Father Bressani, the Italian, who had come over in 1642, was captured by the Iroquois. It happened last April, the 28th, about eighteen miles above Three Rivers, on Lake St. Peter. He, six Christian Hurons and a French lad, in three canoes, were attempting to get through to the Huron country. The Fathers there had had no supplies since 1641. They were in rags, had scarcely any wheat to make hosts, were using the juice of wild grapes for Mass wine, had no medicines, nor any of the necessities. It was thought a canoe could make the journey in April, when the ice was beginning to break. No one believed that the Iroquois would be on the warpath that early. At Pointe du Lac, one of the three canoes collapsed. Then, on their first night, a snowstorm blew up. The next morning, foolishly, one of the Hurons took a shot at a buzzard. This attracted the Iroquois, and three canoes of them, carrying thirty warriors, ambushed beyond a point of land, captured Father Bressani, and led him to their own country.

One of the Hurons escaped and reported that they had tortured Bressani at Lake Ossaragué, that later they had slashed and burned him horribly in their villages. The latest news was that the Iroquois intended to kill him.

Jogues heard the tale with sinking heart. He knew the ordeal through which Bressani was passing, and that knowledge cut into his soul deeper than if he himself were in suffering and bondage. He was almost in despair, also, when he listened to the woeful story of the Iroquois warfare that spring and summer. All the Five Nations were on the warpath. Some of them had invaded the lands of the Neutrals, against whom they had recently raised the hatchet. They had attacked the Petuns beyond, whom Father Jogues had tried to evangelize in 1639. Others were penetrating to the Huron peninsula and terrorizing the villages there. Iroquois were stationed along the Ottawa River, about the Rivière des Prairies, at the Sault above Montreal, in the vicinity of Villa Marie and Fort Richelieu, all about Lake St. Peter. They were sighted near Three Rivers. They were ravaging all the land. They were invincible against the Hurons and Algonquins. They were no longer afraid of the French.

As for the Hurons, they were being destroyed bit by bit. As for the Algonquins, they were being exterminated rapidly. First, disease, plagues, epidemics, carried them off. Then, the Iroquois were slaughtering them in large numbers. Thirdly, famine was killing them; their crops were destroyed, they could neither hunt nor fish with safety. They were migrating to the north country. Around Quebec, Father Vimont related, where you would see eighty or a hundred cabins in a village just eight years ago, now there were barely five or six. Eight years ago, a chief would lead eight hundred braves out on a war expedition; now, he could muster fifty with difficulty. Then they had fleets of three hundred, four hundred canoes; now, scarcely twenty or thirty. The majority of the men were killed or captured; only squaws and children remained.

Grief and sadness were heavy on the soul of Jogues as he learned from Vimont and the other missioners at Quebec of these catastrophes wrought through the Iroquois. If God would but soften their hearts and bring about a firm and lasting peace among them. If God would but prepare the way, and send him back among them, to instruct and baptize them, to establish a mission among them. He begged his Superior to promise that, if ever there came an opportunity, he might venture once more among the Iroquois. He knew their language, somewhat; he was known to them; he was familiar with their country and their habits; he loved them and yearned for their conversion. He did not fear death by their hands.

Father Vimont gazed on this heroic soul with admiration. That he might partly satisfy Jogues' zeal and place him where he might be of most use, he assigned him to the far outpost of Montreal, which had been established just two summers ago. In the opinion of all, the foundation of Montreal was mingled with the miraculous. As far back as 1631, Jérôme le Royer de la Dauversière, of an ancient Breton family, heard a voice from heaven telling him he must build a religious haven for the natives of New France on the island of Montreal which Jacques Cartier had discovered and Samuel Champlain had explored. When he consulted his Jesuit confessor, Father Chauveau, he was told that his vision was extravagant and was not to be bothered about. De la Dauversière, however, persevered in what he considered a Divine call, and some five or six years later discovered a similar ambition in a notable ecclesiastic, Father Jean Jacque Olier de Verneuil. Together, they formed an association of wealthy, devout persons called the Société de Notre Dame de Mont-Real.

The purpose of the Société, so the prospective read, was to provide funds and offer prayers for colonists who were "to labor for the conversion of the poor savages of New France, and to endeavor to gather a goodly number of them on the Island of Mont-Real. . . . Their intention is to have houses built in which to lodge the savages; to till the soil in order to feed them; to establish schools for their instruction; and a Hôtel Dieu for succoring their sick." Not one of those engaged in the fulfillment of these intentions had ever been to Canada. Besides, the island of Montreal was the possession of Jean de Lauson, who refused to cede his rights. Father Charles Lalemant, the Procurator in France of the Jesuit Missions, became interested in the project and secured from de Lauson the deeds for the territory.

While these negotiations were progressing, Father Lalemant met a gentleman called Paul de Chomedey, Sieur de Maisonneuve, who related that he felt inspired to offer himself as a volunteer, in some capacity, to serve in Canada. He had had experience as a soldier and sailor since his thirteenth year. Lalemant introduced Maisonneuve to de la Dauversière, who straightway offered him the post of Commandant. In accepting it, Maisonneuve declared: "I have no selfish interest in view. I can support myself by my income of 2,000 livres. I shall employ my purse and my life generously in this new enterprise, without ambition of any honor save that of serving God and my King in my profession of arms."

When de la Dauversière, Maisonneuve and forty colonists assembled in the spring of 1641 at La Rochelle to take ship to New France, they learned that the Hospital Nuns of La Flèche, who had promised to accompany them, were prevented from joining the expedition. It was essential that some women should go to Montreal as nurses for the sick savages. It happened at that very time that a lady named Mademoiselle Jeanne Mance called on Father de la Place at the Jesuit residence in La Rochelle. She said she was thirty-four years of age and that she had long desired to devote her life to the care of the savages of New France. Her Jesuit confessor in Paris, Father Saint-Jure, had encouraged her in her desires. She had traveled to La Rochelle, she related, for no special reason save that God seemed to incline her to do so. She had never heard of the Société de Notre Dame de Mont-Real. Father de la Place summoned de la Dauversière. They told her of the aims of the Société, of the expedition making ready to sail, and invited her to come with them. Having taken advice with Father Saint-Jure, she left France that very spring with the first colonists.

They landed in Quebec in August. Governor Montmagny and Father Vimont escorted de la Dauversière, Maisonneuve, Mademoiselle Mance and the pioneers to the island of Montreal in October. They decided on the location of the settlement, which they named Ville Marie, and blessed the spot. But on the advice of Montmagny, they returned to Quebec for the winter. On May 17, 1642, they began to build a redoubt of strong palisades for protection against the Iroquois, and on August 15 formally dedicated the island to Our Lady on the Feast of her Assumption.

For Father Jogues, the prospect of living in such a strategic post as Ville Marie was most acceptable. During the first week of July he left Quebec and sailed up the St. Lawrence to Three Rivers. Nearly two years had passed since that fateful August 1 when he had started to paddle up to the Huron land with Goupil, Coûture and the faithful Hurons. After a few days at Three Rivers, he proceeded up along the south bank of Lake St. Peter till he came to Fort Richelieu. Here it was that he had been ferried across from the islands on the day of his capture. On the hillock above the juncture of the two rivers, where the squat fort was squared, was the place of the first night encampment of his Mohawk masters. From the Richelieu River, his sloop turned into the magnificent curve of the St. Lawrence toward the island of Montreal.

II

Ville Marie was lovely to the eyes of Father Jogues. The habitation was plotted on a slight elevation above the strand along the St. Lawrence, below the green tapestry of the trees that rose to the top of the mountain beyond. The shaggy oblong of the palisades stuck up out of the cleared space; clustering under the shadow of its walls were the few dozen thatched cabins that housed the fifty or more colonists; near by was the bark-covered chapel; a short stride to the east was the larger cabin of the Commandant, Sieur de Maisonneuve; beyond that, a small distance, was the Hôtel Dieu, over which presided Mademoiselle Mance; on the sloping hillside were scattered the log homes of Madame de la Peltrie, of Louis d'Ailleboust, and the other more prominent personages. Gardens were neatly cultured in the spaces between the cabins and flowers bloomed along the pathways. The level meadows, patched with crops and smooth pastures, stretched out to the line of the encircling forests.

More attractive than the place, however, was the exalted spiritual fervor of the people. Only those who were united and bonded to the apostolate of the Société de Notre Dame were permitted to reside at Ville Marie. Idealistic and high principled and sanctified must be their souls, religiously exact must be their performance in the daily routine of life. That, however, was not enough. They must be dedicated to the endeavor to convert the natives of all the nations from their paganism and savagery, to civilize them, to minister to their needs whether physical or spiritual.

Father Jogues was particularly pleased with his appointment to Ville Marie because there he would be able to form closer contacts with the natives. The Hurons, more and more, were finding it a convenient place to rest on their journeys between their villages and Three Rivers. Some of the Christians had already seriously considered bringing their families down to settle in the vicinity. But Ville Marie was even more advantageous for his purpose. Should the peace ever be pledged with the Iroquois nations, the island of Montreal would be the logical rendezvous for their warriors and hunters.

That Iroquois peace seemed to be shrouded in a gloomy future in this summer of 1644. Yet, it might be brought about. Rumors reached Jogues that Bressani, who had been captured by the Mohawks in April, had been released on payment of a ransom to the Dutch. True, Father Bressani had been tortured and was almost condemned to death; but the great council of Mohawks had ordered his release on June 19. That was significant, for it was an evident victory for the peace faction. The French made a pronounced gesture which might prepare the way for peace negotiations in August. A party of Hurons and Algonquins captured three Iroquois of the Oneida nation and had led them in triumph to Three Rivers. The Hurons kept two of the captives and gave the third to the Algonquins. These began the torture and mutilation of their Iroquois. Monsieur de Champflour, the Commandant at Three Rivers, intervened. He forced them to postpone the execution of their prisoner until Governor Montmagny could be summoned from Quebec.

On his arrival at Three Rivers, at the beginning of August, Montmagny demanded that the three prisoners be delivered over to him. He pointed out that such a release could be used to secure peace with the Iroquois. The Algonquins handed the Governor thirty-two straws; he spread before them thirty-two presents. They then surrendered the Iroquois, whose name was Tokhrahenehiaron, protesting that they did so not because of the gifts, but because they loved Onontio so much they would not wish to offend him, and because they sought an honorable peace with the Iroquois. They brought to him their prisoner who had been so burned and mangled that he could scarcely walk. The Iroquois, when he realized he was saved, was overcome with gratitude, and kept repeating again and again, "Onontio, Onontio."

But Montmagny failed to persuade the Hurons. Their orator declared in the council: "I am a man of war, not a trader. I have come to fight, not to barter. My glory does not consist in bringing home presents, but prisoners. Consequently, I cannot touch your axes and kettles. If you are so anxious to have our prisoners, take them.

I still have enough courage to go and capture others. But, if the enemy kill me, it will be reported throughout my country that Onontio has taken our prisoners away from us and has forced us to expose ourselves to death in order to capture others."

Then arose a Christian Huron who explained in graceful speech that the Hurons were pledged by their chiefs to bring back prisoners. They must present the two Iroquois to the council of the nation. The Hurons, he declared, were willing to negotiate for peace; for that reason they would convey their Iroquois prisoners to the Huron land without torturing or injuring them. The safety of these prisoners was a matter of importance to their nation and a point of honor with them. They would plead with their chiefs to spare the Iroquois, since that was the wish of Onontio.

The Governor professed himself satisfied, but he exacted from the Hurons a solemn pledge that they would not break faith with him. One of the Iroquois arose, and with the thongs still hobbling his legs, dramatically lifted his eyes to the sun and then lowered them upon Montmagny. He cried out: "Onontio, that sun shall bear witness to your kindness on our behalf, and shall manifest everywhere your liberality." He gazed out over the St. Lawrence and continued: "Listen, you who command in the country of the Iroquois, lend me ear, you who are the chiefs of my people. From this time, be good and courteous and strive to acknowledge by your actions what the French have offered for my deliverance. More than that, even though I should be put to death, be not ungrateful."

Jogues rejoiced when he heard of the success of Governor Montmagny in saving the lives of the Iroquois. Such an act of friendship would impress the Mohawk peoples and would strengthen the arguments of the Wolf clan who favored peace with the French. But meanwhile, the Iroquois carried on their depredations. No one could predict the moment of an onslaught. Everyone lived precariously. To venture out of sight of the palisades was to expose oneself to lurking enemies. In his letter to France that year, Vimont thus expressed the situation: "I would almost as soon be besieged by goblins as by the Iroquois; the latter are hardly more visible than the former. When they are far away, we think they are at our doors; and when they fling themselves at their prey, we imagine that they are in their own country. The people who dwelt in the forests of Richelieu and Montreal were brought in and shut up more closely than any religious or Nun in the smallest monastery of France. It is true that these Croats did not make their appearance at Montreal this year; nevertheless, there was no assurance that they were very far away from there."

A deep consolation for Jogues was the fact that Father Jacques Buteux was also to be stationed at Ville Marie that winter. He arrived late in autumn, having spent the summer with the Algonquins far down the St. Lawrence at Tadoussac. Father Isaac regarded Buteux, whom he had first met at Clermont College, as his best friend and his most trusted spiritual adviser. He admired the older priest's kindly humorous geniality, his essential seriousness, his peasant simplicity, his sanity and fine judgment. Buteux, on his side, was attracted by Jogues' piety, his self-effacement and humility, his intensity and zeal and spirited heroism and generosity. Boxed together as they would be in the close confines of their cabin within the palisades of Ville Marie through the long winter, they had needs be of aid one to the other.

At the time of his annual spiritual retreat, Jogues made to Father Buteux a general confession of all the sins, of all the serious temptations, of his past life. He was reluctant, however, to reveal any of the virtues that he practiced, and was prevailed upon to speak of the graces God had given him only at the insistent demands of Buteux. He was forced by his friend to put down in writing the visions with which God had encouraged him at certain crises in his life. Other Divine interventions, Buteux himself recorded. Thus, Buteux learned that after the vision at Sainte Marie wherein Father Jogues was told: *Exaudita est oratio tua; fiet tibi sicut a me petisti; confortare et esto robustus,* Isaac offered himself up a hundred times a day as a victim extraordinary to God. Buteux revealed:

And when he was captured by the Iroquois he was not surprised, as he had been always expecting something even worse than that which happened in fact. When he saw that he was in the hands of the savages, his first action was to bless and to thank God, with a fervent enthusiasm and in all humility; and he continued to do so among all his sufferings. In the midst of all his torments, he never had any other but the tenderest charity toward those who persecuted him. "God gave me," he confided, "from my earliest years, this pious affection in regard to those who chastised me, even more than I deserved, as a boy at school. I took the ferule, and when I could, even the hand of him who corrected me, to kiss it in token of joy and affection."

I leave it to your Reverence to think whether I ought to strive to bring out his humility by other details, that humility which is one of the virtues I have most admired in him. According to his manner of talking, never had the Society accepted a man less fitted than he was, to serve Our Lord in it. Never had he known anyone so ungrateful to God, and so little responsive to the graces of God. When he spoke of the graces God had showered on him in enduring his suffering for His Holy Name, and of the small profit that he drew from them, the tears would fall copiously from his eyes. Nevertheless, I am able to state in entire truth, for I know it with certainty, since I heard his general confession, extending from the time that he left the Hurons until we were together at Montreal. I can state that one of the most remarkable things I have ever been witness to, is the purity with which he lived among so many, so diverse temptations. One of the gravest faults was that he had, as it were, a desire for his death in the midst of his long and continued sufferings, both exterior and interior. These interior sufferings were more intense, since they were the more deeply spiritual. To my urgent inquiries what they were and how great, all that I was able to draw from his humility were these three words, *dies isti mali!* "Those terrible days!" By that he meant, on account of the interior sufferings that he had endured at that time.

We cannot doubt but that God, who is Goodness itself, accorded him sometimes sensible consolations in proportion to the anguish that He made him suffer. I have not been able to learn from him what these were. All that I have been able to draw out from him have been certain visions which I have sent to your Reverence, put down in writing in his own hand. He qualified these by the name of dreams, such was his humility. But from the effect that followed from them on him, one can easily see that they were of the same nature as the mysterious dreams which the patriarch Joseph experienced.

I am reproachful of myself that I have been so little importunate in his regard as not to have forced him to tell that which would have been for the greater glory of God and his saints. But what could a person do otherwise with a man who, in order to conceal God's graces to him, used to ask me to show him the way to pray fervently and to offer his thanksgiving after Mass. He would ask me with the deepest humility and in all sincerity, for he believed that he himself could do nothing that was worth while. Helas! it would have been well if I had learned from him the one thing and the other, the manner of praying and of making thanksgiving, and most particularly the latter, as from a soul, if I might use the phrase, glued to the Blessed Sacrament. It was before this hidden God that he performed all his spiritual exercises, his prayers, his examens, his breviary, and he did not mind the bitterness of the cold nor the annoyances of the insects.

Thus, in intimate union and peace of soul and mind, the two friends passed that winter in Montreal. Jogues, with such leisure as never before since he came to New France, spent many hours, day and night, in prayer and meditation. Always he was animated by an ideal of preparation for some greater call. He had a foresight that God had not finished in His demands of him, that God would lead him farther in the way of sacrifice, that God was giving him this time in which he might perfect himself.

Developments so miraculous that they seemed a direct answer from God began to occur in the spring of 1645. In May, a war party of Algonquins penetrated down the Richelieu River to Lake Champlain. They trapped a party of Iroquois, of whom they killed eleven and captured two. Contrary to all their ancient traditions, the Algonquins brought their prisoners back to Sillery without having tortured them in the slightest way. Pieskaret, the chief of the party, and a leading Christian, held council with Onontio and surrendered the Iroquois to him. With noble generosity, he announced: "I have seen. I have killed. I have captured. I have brought back prisoners. Here they are present. I enter into your thoughts. They are good. I penetrate into your hearts. You have but one abode and one opinion. May you be gods of the earth. Cause peace to reign everywhere. Give rest to the whole country." Stretching his hand over the heads of the prisoners who lay bound before the Governor, he proclaimed: "Here are the prisoners. They are uninjured, with no harm done to them. I deliver them to you. Do as you think best with them."

Bernard, the Christian chief of Sillery, arose and spoke: "I confirm all that has been said by him who has just spoken. To prove that his words are true, and that he and I give you these prisoners, I will cast into the fire their bonds, the knife that will cut them, and all my anger against them." As he said this, he cut the thongs, and threw them and the knife into the council fire. "I have no longer any passion, except for peace." Governor Montmagny praised their valor in war and their generosity in peace, so unusual, so unheard of in all the traditions of the Algonquins, and bestowed on them generous presents.

The two Iroquois lifted themselves to their feet. One of them was Honatteniate, the Mohawk. He was the grandson of Father Jogues' "aunt." He was a tall, well-formed brave, sullen and proud in his bearing. His companion, an older warrior, addressed the Governor confidently: "I hail you. This is done well. My body is delivered from death, I am drawn away from the fire. Onontio, you have given me my life. I thank you for it, I shall never forget this kindness. The whole of my nation will be grateful for it. The earth will all be beautiful, the river will all be calm and smooth, peace will make us all friends. No longer have I any shadows before my eyes. The souls of my ancestors killed by the Algonquins have disappeared. I have them under my feet. Onontio, it must be admitted that you are good and that we are wicked. But our anger has departed. I no longer have any ardor except for joy and peace." He swayed his body in a dance and raised a chant of exultation. Suddenly he stopped, burst into a terrific rage, seized a hatchet and slashed furiously with it. As suddenly he paused, threw the hatchet into the fire, and said: "There is my anger cast away. Farewell to war. I lay aside my arms. I am your friend forever."

In May, Governor Montmagny sent Honatteniate and the other Mohawk up to Three Rivers, with orders to the Commandant, Sieur de Champflour, to treat them well. He directed that the other Iroquois, Tokhrahenehiaron, who had been kept a prisoner at Three Rivers during the winter, be sent back to his people. He was to say to the Iroquois that Onontio was grateful for the release of the two Blackrobes, Fathers Jogues and Bressani. In token, he was set free, and the two other Iroquois held by the French would also be delivered, unharmed and healthy, after Onontio had heard from the Iroquois chiefs. He was told to announce to his people that the French believed that this was the time to bring about a universal peace.

Hearing these reports, Jogues tingled with anticipation. What would be the Iroquois answer? Would the peace advocates among the Mohawks prevail? Would the violent enemies of the French refuse to enter negotiations? Could they be restrained from treachery and violence even if some of the Mohawk leaders did give Governor Montmagny a favorable answer? In his retreat at Montreal he importuned God to soften the hearts of the Iroquois enemies whom he loved as his own children.

III

The Iroquois were seeking peace. They had responded favorably to the French invitation and sent an embassy for the purpose of holding council at Three Rivers. Governor Montmagny, his official family of councilors and soldiers, Fathers Vimont and Le Jeune hurried up the river from Quebec. Hundreds of Algonquins from many nations gathered from the forests of the entire St. Lawrence region. Hurons who had seeped through the Iroquois blockade lingered in anticipation. Father Jogues skimmed in his canoe down the St. Lawrence from Montreal, hopeful and determined, and with vigorous strokes darted his skiff among the hundreds of canoes that fringed the shore below the fort.

Guillaume Coûture greeted him, Guillaume whom he had left among the Mohawks two summers ago. He had remained at Tionontoguen and was now the interpreter and a member of the Iroquois embassy. The leader was Kiotseaeton, also from Tionontoguen, easily the most eloquent of the Mohawk orators. His associate was Aniwogan, who was recognized as the shrewdest diplomat of the nation. The third delegate was Tokhrahenehiaron, the man whom the French had rescued from the Algonquins and sent back to his people in May. Jogues knew them well, and all three of the Mohawks had guilty memories of Ondessonk, the Blackrobe. He welcomed them with an affection and sincerity that amazed them, for they had not expected such forgiveness on his part.

Jogues' chiefest welcome, however, was for Honatteniate, the grandson of his "aunt," who had been brought up with the other prisoner from Quebec. Ever since his capture, Honatteniate had been sulky and depressed. With scorn and a rigid silence, he had rebuffed any kindnesses which the French and Algonquins tried to show him. He and Ondessonk met at Three Rivers. Immediately, Honatteniate became a different man; his whole manner changed; he talked, he laughed, he danced, he shed all his fears and his arrogance.

On July 12, 1645, the council convened under a huge tent spread in the courtyard of the fort of Three Rivers. Governor Montmagny, brilliantly garbed in a brocaded coat and cloak as for an official function of state, sat in an ample armchair placed against the wall of the fort. On his right was the Commandant of Three Rivers, Sieur de Champflour, impressive in his gleaming breastplate. To the left sat Fathers Vimont, Le Jeune and Jogues, conspicuous in their black robes among the elegantly clad officials and the armored soldiers. Opposite the French were ranged the Algonquins, their faces and naked bodies streaked with white paint and the colors of peace, their heads adorned with crests of brightly colored plumage. On the shorter sides of the rectangle were lined the Hurons and the French people of the town. Kiotseaeton and the Mohawk ambassadors elected to sit on a large hemlock mat before the chair of Governor Montmagny. They loved the French so deeply, said Kiotseaeton, that they wished in no way to be separated from them. They were magnificent in their spreading head-dresses of flaming feathers, clothed in buckskin jackets decorated with beads and vari-colored quills, their necks and arms and legs hung with wampum belts and pendants.

When all were assembled, a profound silence brooded over the courtyard. The council fire flared in the center of the square. The pipe of peace was lit and passed from mouth to mouth. Kiotseaeton, the Mohawk, stood upright. He was a giant of a man, majestic, masterful. Suave he was, with a glib tongue, ready with an answer of wit and flattery. So clever was he and so urbane, that the French officials and Blackrobes distrusted him entirely. They dubbed him le Crochet, the Hook. But they were in admiration of his charm and his subtle diplomacy. Now, with superb poise, as he stood before them, he raised his eyes to heaven, then swept them over the four lines of the square, and finally fixed them intently on Governor Montmagny. In a voice deep and reverberating, he began:

"Onontio, lend me your ear. I am the mouth for the whole of my country. When you hear my words, you listen to all the Iroquois nations. My heart has nothing of evil in it. I have only good chants in my mouth. We have a great number of war songs in our country. We have thrown them all on the ground. We have now no other songs than those of jubilation."

He chanted merrily, and swayed his body. The four other Iroquois gathered about him and took up the song, now in unison, now alternately, striding in time, pounding their heels, crouching, swaying, gesturing, back, forth, creating a pantomime of joy. He finished, and faced the Governor. Ostentatiously, he drew from his wallet a collar of wampum. It was a present for Onontio, he announced, who had saved the life of his kinsman, Tokhrahenehiaron, who had drawn him out of the fire and away from the teeth of the Algonquins. He thanked Onontio for that. Then he became worried; he showed by his gestures that he was fearful of something; he put on a look of reproachfulness. He complained that Onontio had sent back his kinsman all alone, on such a long journey. "If his canoe had been upset, if the winds had overwhelmed and capsized it, if he had been drowned, you would have waited a long time for the return of this poor man who was lost. You would have accused us of a fault of which you yourselves would have been the cause." He fastened the collar on the rope that stretched between two poles in the open space of the square.

He selected another collar from his pouch, and tied it about Coûture's arm. "This is the collar that brings you back this prisoner. I would not have said to him: 'Go, my nephew, take a canoe and return to Quebec.' My mind would not have been at rest. I would always have thought to myself, over and over again: 'Is he not dead?' Truly, I would have shown that I had no sense, if I had acted that way. The prisoner that you sent back to us had all the difficulty in the world on that journey." Kiotseaeton imitated a man paddling, struggling against rapids, walking over the portages, stubbing his toes, losing his courage, being afraid in the loneliness, fighting the wild animals, forcing himself, in utter despair and weariness, to continue on the trail. "I do not know where your mind was to send a man back, all alone, in so many dangers. I did not do that with Ihandich. 'Come, my nephew,' I said to him whom you see before your eyes, 'follow me.' "

The third present, offered with flowing oratory, was in exchange for the gifts which the French had sent by Tokhrahenehiaron. The French gifts, he explained, had been distributed among the five nations of the Iroquois. The fourth belt signified that he was no longer saddened or angered by the remembrance of the Iroquois whom the Algonquins had killed that spring. The next belts signified, through vivid pantomime, how the waterways from Quebec to the Iroquois land were open, how the waves were quieted, the rapids smoothed, the winds calmed. Next, he cleared the trails of the land routes, chopped down trees, lopped off overhanging branches, tore out bushes, filled up the valleys and leveled the hills. "It is all finished," he announced triumphantly. "We can see the smoke of the villages, from Quebec to the farthest limits of the Iroquois country. All the obstacles of the journey are removed."

His tenth present was an extraordinarily beautiful belt of wampum. He took a Frenchman and, linking arms, he marched him across to the Algonquins. He clasped the arm of one of their braves, and all three strode back before the Governor. "Here is the knot that binds us inseparably. Nothing can part us. Even if lightning were to strike us, it could not separate us. For if it cut off the arm that holds us to each other, we will at once seize each other with the other arm." He next assured the French that there was fish and venison waiting in the Iroquois villages for them. "It is everywhere full of elk and deer and beaver. Give up those stinking hogs that run about among your houses and that eat nothing but filth. Come and eat good meat with us. The road is clear, there is no longer any danger," he advised them.

The twelfth collar waved off the clouds, so that the sun might shine and light up the hearts of the Iroquois and show to the French that there was nothing hidden there in malice or treachery. His next concern was with the Hurons. They were not officially the representatives of their nation, he knew; but he reprimanded them for not continuing the peace move they were contemplating. They must have no fear, nor be bashful like squaws. They must send an embassy to the Iroquois.

Adroitly, he passed to the word which the fifteenth collar spoke. The Mohawks had always desired to bring Ondessonk back safely to his French brothers, he said suavely. They regretted that Ondessonk had been stolen, as they thought, by the Dutch, for they had intended to release him of their own accord. As for Bressani, they gave him to the Dutch because he requested it. The other Frenchmen whom they had held as prisoners, if they had remained among them, they would have been adopted and married to Iroquois women, so that, "we would be but one nation, and I would be one of you."

Father Jogues listened with amazement and amusement to this discourse. He had to smile as he whispered to Father Le Jeune: "The stake was all prepared for me to be burned. They would have put me to death a hundred times if God had not preserved me. This good man twists things to suit himself."

Kiotseaeton continued unabashed. His sixteenth present was to protect the Iroquois who visited the French and the Algonquins, to silence the cannon of the one and to stay the hatchets of the other. He came to the last collar of wampum. He fondled it affectionately, tearfully. It was the very collar which Honatteniate, the young brave whom they held as prisoner, wore in his own village of Ossernenon. His mother had sent it to him. She loved her son, she feared that he might be injured by the French or the Algonquins. She had rejoiced when she had learned that Onontio had saved the life of her dear son, and so she sent this collar to the great chief Onontio, in thanksgiving. She rejoiced, too, that her "nephew," Ondessonk, was safe and well, and had returned to his own people. She had loved Ondessonk, and had been good to him, and truly treated him as one of her own family. While Kiotseaeton spoke thus tenderly, Father Jogues again smiled; his "aunt" had indeed been his friend and protector, but he saw the cleverness of the orator in his appeal to these tender emotions.

In conclusion, he sent a barb toward the Hurons. "I am going to spend the remainder of the summer in my own country, in games and dances and rejoicings over the fruits of peace. But I have a fear; while we dance, the Hurons will come to taunt and molest us." Kiotseaeton began to chant and sway. The other Iroquois joined him. The Algonquins, the Montagnais, the Attikamègues, the Hurons, the French took up the song and rhythm, and forming in a line danced about the whole courtyard of the fort.

That night, Governor Montmagny and his councillors consulted. They were in high admiration of the oratorical genius of Kiotseaeton, of his plausibility and persuasiveness, but they doubted his sincerity. They decided to continue with the negotiations, but to be watchful for any signs of treachery. The next day was given over to feasting and dancing. Montmagny was concerned lest the Algonquins or Hurons might make even a slight show of unfriendliness. He sent word to their chiefs that they must banish all distrust and suspicion, and warned them against gossip and rumors. Kiotseaeton heard of his, and delivered that day an impassioned harangue to the

Algonquins, urging them to obey their great Father, Onontio, and to accept the thought and intentions of the French.

On July 14 the French delivered their answer in another council held in the courtyard before the fort. Through an interpreter, Governor Montmagny presented the Iroquois with fourteen gifts, each carrying a message. He thanked them for the release of their French prisoners, agreed with them that the way between their two countries was now open and safe, assured them of his protection over any Iroquois who might visit him, and accepted all their proposals for peace. But he added a condition of extreme importance. Peace between the French and the Iroquois was dependent on peace between the Iroquois and the French allies, the Algonquins and Hurons. He bound the Iroquois to pledge that their people would commit no act of hostility against these nations until their chiefs had held council and had authority to make all pledges. He demanded that there be a universal truce from all warfare among all the nations represented. To each of the fourteen words of Montmagny, the Iroquois uttered their guttural affirmative; and accepted the French presents.

Pieskaret, the Christian chief of Sillery, representing the Algonquin nations, placed at the feet of Kiotseaeton bundles of furs. They were to be a stone, placed over the graves of the Iroquois killed by the Algonquins last spring. Noel Negabamat, spokesman for the Montagnais nations, laid ten great elk skins before the Iroquois. These were protection for the feet and legs of the Iroquois on their homeward journey, and shrouds for the warriors killed in battle. These presents, too, the Iroquois received as offerings preparatory for the opening of peace negotiations. The Algonquins and Montagnais, it was understood in the language of their diplomacy, would hold council among themselves, and return a final word to the Iroquois.

The council ended in perfect amity and accord. That afternoon a Huron who nursed a grudge against the French, approached Kiotseaeton secretly and warned him the French were meditating some treachery. The Iroquois listened undisturbed, and answered: "I have painted and streaked my face on one side, and I have left the other side altogether clean. I do not see very clearly on the side streaked with paint; on the other side I see very plainly. The painted side is toward the Hurons, and I do not see anything at all. The other side, which is so clean, is turned toward the French, and I see as clearly as if it were midday." He lapsed into deep meditation, while the Huron slunk away.

Kiotseaeton, on his side, sought private interview with Governor Montmagny. Coûture, alone, as interpreter, was present. The Iroquois announcing he had a great present to make, delicately hinted at its meaning: the Iroquois sought peace with the French and the Hurons, but not with the Algonquins. Montmagny repudiated the suggestion and the present furiously. He insisted that any peace with the French must include the Algonquins. Kiotseaeton stalked away in rage.

Montmagny saw all the hopes for peace crumble in this treachery. He consulted Vimont and Le Jeune; they were horrified; the Algonquins must not be sacrificed. Then, Le Jeune thought of a solution which Montmagny accepted. He called Kiotseaeton and proposed it; there were two classes of Algonquins; those who were Christians, and therefore brothers to the French; those who were pagans, and of no concern to the French; in any peace settlement, the Christian Algonquins must be included. The Iroquois accepted the distinction and agreed that all Christian Algonquins should be regarded as the French themselves, but that the pagans might be warred upon. Montmagny and Kiotseaeton pledged themselves to this agreement and swore to keep it absolutely secret.

Amid mutual expressions of good-will, the three Iroquois ambassadors, Honatteniate and the other prisoner, now officially released, departed from Three Rivers. Coûture, who was free to remain, was sent back as a peace advocate, and with him two other young Frenchmen who, Montmagny explained, would help the Iroquois carry their presents and would be proof of the French faithfulness. Father Jogues also wanted to join the party, but neither Governor Montmagny nor Father Vimont would consider such a proposal. The Iroquois were notoriously treacherous. They must be further tested before Jogues or any of the missioners could safely venture among them.

Father Jogues, disappointed in his ambitions, returned to Montreal. Still, he hoped. It had been agreed that another council should be held in September; perhaps then, he thought, God might lead him to his mission of the Mohawks. In early September, Father Jérôme Lalemant, after seven years among the Hurons, arrived at Montreal with a large Huron fleet. He announced his appointment as Superior of the New France Mission, in succession to Father Vimont. Jogues straightway, as to a friend who understood, as to a missioner who had great vision, urged that he be assigned to the work of evangelizing the Iroquois. Lalemant knew well the spirit of Jogues, knew that he would never be satisfied till he had wrecked himself for God. He promised that he would send Father Jogues to the Iroquois as soon as it could be safely arranged.

On September 8, Fathers Lalemant and Jogues traveled down from Montreal to Three Rivers. With them were the ambassadors from the Huron nations and a flotilla of sixty canoes. On the 12th, Governor Montmagny, Fathers Vimont and Le Jeune, came up from Quebec. Upwards of four hundred Algonquins assembled, from the lower St. Lawrence, from the northlands about the source of the St. Maurice, from along the Ottawa and the Great Lakes. They awaited the Iroquois with growing apprehension, fearful that no ambassadors might come. On September 15th, suddenly, as if springing from the water, an Iroquois canoe carrying five men appeared across the river, at Sainte Angele. It announced that the Iroquois orators were on their way. Two days later, with dignity, Kiotseaeton, two fellow ambassadors and Guillaume Coûture drove their canoe straight down the middle of the St. Lawrence and drew up before Three Rivers.

The great council convened on Monday, September 18, in the courtyard of the fort. Coûture was deputed by the Iroquois as their first orator: "I have no voice," said the chief who introduced him. "Do not pay attention to me. I do not speak. I hold in my hand only a paddle by which I bring back to you a Frenchman who has in his mouth the word sent you by all our country." Speaking in French, but employing the picturesque symbolism of the natives, Coûture declared that the Iroquois, at the voice of Onontio, had thrown away their muskets and hatchets, thrown them so far away beyond the skies that no arm was long enough to reach them and bring them back. Seventeen other presents, each with its meaning, he offered. Some dissolved fears that the French and their allies might have; others offered hospitality in the Iroquois country; still others were to urge the Hurons and Algonquins to express their thoughts freely and honestly.

Kiotseaeton took up the discourse of Coûture. He addressed himself primarily to the natives. In his country, he said, were many Algonquin and Huron women; they were seated on logs and stumps outside the villages, not bound, but free to return to their kinsmen; they were like the dried trees on which they sat waiting, for they had no roots which could not be easily moved. Specifically, he spoke of the Huron girl, called by the name of Theresa, who had come into their land with Ondessonk, the Blackrobe. If the Algonquins, if the Hurons sent embassies to the Iroquois, and held council, their relatives would be released.

Then Kiotseaeton gave a message to the French. He had faithfully delivered the presents which Onontio had intrusted to him to the Iroquois nations, to his own people, to the Oneidas, to the Onondagas, to the Cayugas, to the Senecas. He studied the string of beads which he held in his hands; he was perplexed; he explained the meaning of the wampum; the Oneidas were not satisfied with the worth of the present that was sent them. He excused this nation, but still delicately hinted that it would be well for Onontio to nourish it a little more.

For the Hurons, John Baptist Atironta, the brilliant young Christian chief of the Arendarhonons, was the orator. Resolutely, and enthusiastically, he exclaimed: "It is done. We are brothers. The resolution has been taken. Now we are all cousins: Iroquois, Hurons, Algonquins, French. We are all one and the same people." He turned upon the Iroquois and spoke sharply: "Do not betray any one of us. As for the Hurons, you know that we have sound hearts."

"I hear you," replied Kiotseaeton. "Your word is agreeable. You will find me a true speaker."

The Algonquin spokesman came forward: "I can no longer speak. My heart is too full of joy. I have large ears, and so many good words crowd into them that they drown me with pleasure. It is true that I am no more than a child. It is Onontio who has great words in his mouth. He will speak for me. He it is who fashions the earth and brings rejoicing to all men."

A day was given over to feasting, and on September 20th, the second council convened. At this, the Hurons returned their official answer: they wished peace and friendship with all the Iroquois nations; they had the doors of their cabins open, the mats prepared, the fires burning, the kettles filled, in preparation for the coming of the Iroquois; they promised to send ambassadors to lodge in the villages of the Iroquois. The Algonquin orators spoke similar sentiments. One of them offered gifts—to tell the rivers to wash away the blood that had been spilt in the wars; to break down the gates of the Iroquois villages, so that there might be free entry; to supply all with pipes and tobacco, so that they might speak as friends; to build a canoe in which they might travel together: "Thus, as we shall be but one people, one village, one house, one calumet, so one canoe only will be needed. The rest of our words, they will be brought to your country."

Governor Montmagny confirmed the pledged words of his allies. He guaranteed their honesty, and assured the Iroquois that they should have no fears. As for the French, they wished a lasting and a universal peace between themselves and all the nations of the land, the Iroquois, the Hurons, and all the Algonquins. Kiotseaeton, accepting the presents, cried aloud rapturously: "Onontio, you have dispersed the clouds. The air is peaceful, the sky is unclouded, the sun shines brilliantly. I see no storms anywhere. Peace has made all things calm. My heart is at rest. I go on my way well content." He announced that ambassadors from the Iroquois nations would return later in the year, and that these would be empowered to conclude all the negotiations for peace.

The Iroquois left on September 25. Coûture was once again sent back with them, and was given instructions by Governor Montmagny to be present at all their councils, and to observe and fully report what the Iroquois did. Two Frenchmen, two Hurons and two Algonquins accompanied the Iroquois as hostages, and they, in exchange, left three of their warriors with the French, Hurons and Algonquins. "Praise be to God," the French exclaimed fervently when the hundreds of savages had melted away from Three Rivers. It was all miraculous. There was to be peace, a universal lasting peace between these nations that had been slaughtering one another for generations back beyond the memory of man.

Montmagny and his advisers experienced some disquietude. Kiotseaeton spoke for the Mohawks alone, not for the other four Iroquois nations. He had, moreover, hinted that the Oneidas were not favorable to peace. Hence, these other Iroquois were not pledged to bury the war hatchet. Father Jogues pointed out, besides, that the Mohawks themselves were not united; the Wolf and Turtle clans sought peace; the Bears remained hostile. Then, Montmagny was troubled by the secret pact that he had made in July, whereby he agreed to leave the pagan Algonquins out of the peace. In attacking, the Iroquois would not inquire as to whether the Algonquins were Christians or not. In council, they could use this as a cover for treachery. He understood, moreover, that the secret understanding was published all through the Iroquois country.

Father Jogues was present at all the proceedings. He watched and weighed them keenly. He had learned that the Iroquois could not be trusted, even when they swore good faith. Yet, he favored a continuation of the negotiations. With God's help, peace was possible. If peace were established, he had assurance that he would be allowed to go back to the Mohawks. At this September council he had again and again begged that he might be chosen as one of the hostages to the Iroquois. His plea had been rejected. He told himself that the time would finally come. And with that hope in his soul, he took the canoe once more up the St. Lawrence to his station at Montreal.

CHAPTER XIV

Ambassador to the Mohawks

I

VILLE MARIE, on the island of Montreal, was again to be the home of Father Jogues for the winter of 1645 and 1646. His dear friend and confessor, Jacques Buteux, was transferred to his old post at Three Rivers, and in his place came Paul Le Jeune, who had been Superior of all the missions in New France when Jogues arrived at Quebec in 1636. Father Le Jeune had but recently returned from France, where he had spent three years, as a special representative of Governor Montmagny, trying to persuade Louis XIII and Cardinal Richelieu of the dire need of defense against the Iroquois and of supplying men and money to take the offensive against them.

Jogues missed the company and the direction of Buteux. He had, however, in Le Jeune, a friend whom he admired tremendously and in whom he had implicit confidence. He knew him as a man of will and vehement energy, generous but decisive in his judgments, hard, yet tender and humorous, and deeply spiritual. As in the preceding year with Father Buteux, so with Father Le Jeune, he sought spiritual direction. He fasted from food, and habituated himself to do without sleep, to such an extent that Le Jeune feared he was further ruining his health. When he was urged to eat more of the foods that would strengthen him, to partake of the few, occasional delicacies, to drink wine, his answer was: "That is not what I need, nor what I lack. When I get down among those Iroquois again, I do not wish my miserable nature to be turning its head toward the houses in which it has found its ease. I need only to take those things which are absolutely necessary for me."

Always, his mind and heart were fixed on a return to Ossernenon and the Iroquois land. He felt that he had the certainty almost of a divine revelation that he was destined to live and die for the sake of these nations. He foresaw the loneliness, the spiritual deprivations, the crudeness and sparseness of the food, the filth, the turmoil, the nauseating immorality and the sexual temptations, the malice and the cruelty and the superstition of the Iroquois, the hate of the sorcerers, the blood lust of the braves, the undying antagonism of the Bear clan to the French and their intensive hostility to the Blackrobes. He knew the Iroquois as a fickle, treacherous, arrogant, cruel and lawless people. Yet, he wanted nothing in life but the chance to dwell in their midst and lead them to God.

During the preceding winter of 1644, the people of Montreal lived a cloistered life of fear on account of the Iroquois. In the winter that began in 1645, all breathed freely. The truce preparatory to the final peace with the Iroquois was pledged. And so, the original purpose of the settlement, that of a haven for the savages, could be better executed. The nomadic Algonquins from half a dozen nations erected their huts of bark in the woods about and along the water courses. They appreciated the advantages of food and care if they should be sick, and of spiritual ministrations if they were baptized. Some Hurons, too, remained in the vicinity and were beginning to like the location so well that they promised to bring their families down to live there permanently. The ancient, abandoned village of Hochelaga was being resurrected.

Ever since the council held at Three Rivers in September, Montreal received many of the Iroquois braves. In other years they crept stealthily about the island, to murder and pillage. This year, drawn by curiosity, they affected friendliness. Lalemant reported: "As this island is in some sort a frontier of the Annierronnonon Iroquois, nearly all the winter there have been some young braves of those tribes who have come through curiosity to see the French and the Algonquins. It was very fortunate that Father Jogues lived in this settlement, for he encouraged them in their kindly feelings and their desire to continue the peace; and prepared them, little by little, to lend ear to him when he should go to visit them in their own country." He was gentle and affectionate toward them, and "embraced as friends those who had lacerated his body, torn out his nails, cut off his fingers, in a word, those who had treated him as tigers would." He believed "that the time of fury was passed, that those monsters would become changed into men, and from men would become the children of God."

Jogues was amused by an incident that happened to Le Jeune. One of the Iroquois, curious about the prayers of the Algonquins, would slip into the chapel with them when they came to hear Mass. Le Jeune noticed him and told him he should not attend Mass unless he were a Christian. The man protested he was a believer like the Algonquins. To prove it he drew a Rosary from his pouch. Though the Algonquins accepted this as proof, Le Jeune still doubted.

"Ask him if he is baptized and what is his Christian name," the Father told the Algonquin interpreter.

"What does it mean to be baptized?" the Mohawk asked.

"To be baptized," replied the Algonquin, "is to receive a water of great importance, which cleans away all the spots and stains from the soul."

A smile of inspiration flashed across the face of the Mohawk as he announced: "The Dutch have often given me that water of importance. I drank so much of it and became so drunk that they had to bind my hands and feet, for fear lest I should injure someone."

The poor man was crestfallen when Le Jeune and the Algonquins burst into laughter and explained that brandy was not baptismal water.

The arrogance and effrontery and insulting boasts of the Iroquois irritated the Algonquins and the French. One of them nearly caused bloodshed at Montreal by chanting before Algonquin braves: "I wished to kill some Algonquins. Onontio has arrested my anger. He has leveled the earth, he has saved the lives of many men." A band of them strolled up to an Algonquin camp from which the men were absent. All the women fled, all except an old squaw who was unable to walk. They did no harm, however, except to taunt the Algonquins about their cowardice. The Algonquins restrained themselves to answer: "We dread only the wicked. You are good, and it is not you whom we fear, but the Onnontagehronnons (Onondagas). They have no sense. They have refused to enter into the treaty of peace which you have made with us."

Disquieting reports about the observance of the truce came up to Montreal from the lower St. Lawrence. The two Algonquins who had agreed to accompany the Iroquois ambassadors as hostages were stricken with fear and abandoned the party. In October, some Christian Montagnais belonging to the Reduction at Sillery were attacked while hunting, and massacred. One escaped and reported that the murderers were Iroquois Mohawks. All the Algonquins burst into fury and rushed out in pursuit. They found two of the victims still living, though scalped. These denied that the attackers were Mohawks, but affirmed they were a nation allied to the Mohawks. The Algonquins suspected that, if the Mohawks were not the actual perpetrators, they were accomplices or instigators. To arouse suspicions further, a Huron and an Algonquin, recently escaped from the Mohawks villages, spread the report that the Iroquois had no honest intention of ratifying the peace with the Algonquin nations.

In all the lower settlements, the Iroquois passed freely about, but their truculence and contempt for the Algonquins was precipitating retaliation. They were suspected of only feigning a desire for peace, and of contriving ambushes and seeking to take the French and the natives unawares. So precarious became the situation, about the end of 1645, that the Christian chiefs of Sillery, fearing they could not protect the Iroquois hostages they held, sent them home, but with friendly messages of assurance, especially telling them to report to their chiefs that, even though the murders recently committed were done by Mohawks, the peace would not be discontinued provided satisfaction were made in other ways. The other Iroquois who were continually coming and going, tried to assure the Algonquins that the Mohawks were acting in good faith; but they did give warning, which was not conducive to good-feeling, that the Algonquins should beware of the other Iroquois nations, particularly the Oneidas and Onondagas, who had not agreed to the peace.

In January, 1646, was revealed the most startling news. A Huron named Tandihetsi reported that he had been told, under the strictest secrecy, by the Mohawks that the Iroquois would never conclude a peace with the Algonquins, and that three hundred warriors were preparing to take the warpath in February. He stated that the French had agreed, in the councils at Three Rivers, to exclude all Algonquins who were not Christians from the peace negotiations. Tandihetsi spread the report at Montreal. Then hastened down to the large Algonquin encampment near Three Rivers. All were profoundly troubled.

The chiefs sought out Sieur de la Poterie, who had succeeded de Champflour as Commandant, and Father Buteux. Both of these denied absolutely that the French had ever entered into such a treacherous agreement. But the Mohawk hostage at Three Rivers confirmed the truth of Tandihetsi's story. De la Poterie, though disbelieving the tale, warned the Hurons and Algonquins to be watchful lest the Iroquois smash the truce.

Tandihetsi traveled to Quebec, and was intrusted with letters to Father Lalemant. The letters mentioned nothing about the report, but the Huron sedulously publicized it. Lalemant was shocked and went to Governor Montmagny to acquaint him of what was being said. He was further shocked to horror when Montmagny said the report was true, and confessed that he had made a secret pact with the Iroquois at the suggestion of Fathers Vimont and Le Jeune. Montmagny and Lalemant decided it were better not to admit the truth to the Algonquins, who, by this time, were murderous. The Algonquins summoned a council of all their nations at Three Rivers. They investigated the rumors and came to the conclusion either that the Mohawks lied to Tandihetsi or that Tandihetsi lied to them.

Still, all the natives were creepy and on edge. The Iroquois hostages demanded they be sent back to their people, and the Mohawk visitors ceased to come near the settlements. Algonquins were reported to be lying in wait for the hostages or for any Iroquois hunters who might pass along the way. All were uncertain. In Montreal at daybreak on January 1, the cannons were fired in honor of the Feast. The Algonquins and Hurons rushed frantically up to the stockade. An Iroquois attack, they feared the signal meant. The French were amused by their panic, and reassured them by explaining that "on that day the Son of God had been named Jesus, that is, the Saviour, and that the noise of the cannon signified that He should be honored." The savages rebounded with good humor and said one to another: "Come, let us also give Him the same honor." They formed in line, like the French soldiers, and fired a neat salute.

Before the new year and through January, 1646, white winter had spread everywhere about Montreal. The St. Lawrence was frozen to a solid sheet of crystal, and then was coated deep with snow. The evergreens were tufted with white, the bare, black branches of the other trees were limned against the universal glare. On January 31, when the snow was already waist deep, there began to fall the soft, steady pad of another blizzard. Jogues and Le Jeune, boxed in their little hut at Ville Marie, remembered it when, a few days later, messengers came up with tragic news from Fort Richelieu, thirty miles below.

Father Anne de Nouë had set out from Three Rivers on January 30, to minister to the little garrison at Fort Richelieu on the Feast of the Purification, February 2. With him were two raw soldiers; they found difficulty walking on their snowshoes, and in dragging the sled loaded with provisions. They made only eighteen miles that day. On the following morning, Father de Nouë started about two o'clock with the intention of hurrying to the fort and sending back aid. He did not bother to take a blanket, nor a flint, nor food, except a small loaf of bread and a few prunes.

They found him on February 2, just six miles above Fort Richelieu, in a hollow that he had scooped in the snow. He was on his knees, in prayer, with his arms crossed on his breast, with his eyes open and lifted toward heaven. He froze rigid, and fell thus against the side of the snowbank. It was on the Feast of the Purification of Our Lady that he went to heaven. And when the messenger coursed up to Montreal to inform Fathers Jogues and Le Jeune, they were shocked, but happy.

Across the snow that shrouded the St. Lawrence, a few weeks later, on February 22, advanced the black figures of a party of men. The sentinel of Montreal gave the alarm, for they were discerned to be Iroquois. Sieur d'Ailleboust, the new Commandant, roused the garrison to arms, and the settlers gathered near the stockade. The oncoming Iroquois halted, and gestured they were friends. They came up the iced incline slowly, Guillaume Coûture, Kiotseaeton, six Iroquois, and the two Huron hostages. They were swallowed up in rapturous greetings and the cannons boomed from the fort in a salvo of welcome.

The nation of the Mohawks was faithful to the truce, it still sought a treaty of peace, Kiotseaeton related. Jogues listened to their every word, with tautened ears. After deliberation the council gave unanimous approval to the diplomacy of Kiotseaeton, Ihandich the Frenchman, and their associates in the embassy. It accepted the presents, ratified the agreements, and pledged the Mohawks to further efforts for peace. Kiotseaeton was empowered to return that same month to Three Rivers and to carry presents from the Mohawks. He was to express regret that the four upper Iroquois nations were not yet agreed to bury the war hatchet with the Algonquins, but to affirm that they had a mind to treat in due time with the French and the Hurons.

According to Coûture, the Mohawks were in good faith. The peace with the French was popular, that with the Hurons desirable, and peace with the Algonquins something that might be experimented with. He stated that the secret agreement of Governor Montmagny in regard to the pagan Algonquins was not broached publicly, though it was discussed privately by the chiefs. All the three villages celebrated the success of the parleys with feasts and dances for several days. About the end of October, Kiotseaeton, Coûture and the others took the trail for Three Rivers. They arrived at the lower lake, Andiatarocté, and were surprised to find that the canoes they had cachéd were some of them smashed and others stolen. They had to make the three-day journey back to Ossernenon and Tionontoguen to secure other boats.

Their chance return was timed with that of an embassy from the Sokoki nation. The visiting orator stated that he heard with regret that the Mohawks were contemplating peace with the Algonquins. "For a long time I have heard you say that the Algonquins were your irreconcilable enemies," the Sokoki spokesman harangued. "I have heard you say that you hated them to death and beyond the grave, so much so that if you could meet them in the other world, you would carry on your war eternally. As we are your allies, we enter into your passions and your interests. Look then. Here are the heads of some of the Algonquins whom we have massacred. Behold, here is a cord which we present to you for the purpose of binding—you and we together—as many of these heads as we possibly can." He held up the scalps of the five Christian Montagnais from Sillery, massacred some weeks before.

The Mohawks had already received the Algonquin protest about these murders. They remained motionless toward the Sokokis. Kiotseaeton rose to speak, with anger deepening his tones: "We are astonished at your boldness, rather, at your audacity. You cast shame on our faces. You make us out to be criminals. Onontio, with whom we have treated for peace, is not a child. If we regard you with a favorable eye, he would have reason to say: 'The Annieronnons have not killed my allies, it is true; but it was their hatchets that killed them. I thought I was dealing with honest men, but instead, I find I am dealing with liars and rogues.' This is not all. If the Algonquins learned that the heads of their brothers are in our cabins, they will cut off the heads of our people who are now in their country. See what would be the evil results of your audacity. Begone! Hide these heads, take away these bonds! As we have but one heart, we desire to speak but one language."

Coûture insisted that the Mohawks sought peace, honestly and eagerly. They had sound reasons, such as would powerfully impel them. Being superstitious to the core, they believed the warnings of the sorcerers that the demon of war, hitherto favorable, was turning away from them; their extraordinary offensive of the past two summers had not been so successful as they had anticipated. Again, the game seemed to be failing in their mountains and hunting-grounds; they understood that the deer and elk were plentiful in the Algonquin territories. They were aware that the French were supplying the Christian Algonquins and Hurons with muskets and powder; this would take away their advantage in battle. Then, they were truly grateful for the French kindness in releasing their kinsmen.

Father Jogues blessed February 22 as a day of gratitude to God. Clearly, the trail to the heart of the Mohawks was opening before his steps. He received testimonials of respect and affection from Kiotseaeton and the other Iroquois. He was assured by them that his "aunt" and his cabin at Ossernenon wished once more to receive Ondessonk, that all the villagers remembered him with affection, and regretted that he had ever stolen himself away from them. He was invited to take his place again on their mats, beside their fires. Jogues prayed, then wrote a letter to Lalemant, offering himself, in a heartrending appeal, as a missioner to the Iroquois. All the obstacles were now being removed through the infinite power of God.

His letter he intrusted to Guillaume Coûture, who left for Three Rivers and Quebec with the Mohawks. He hoped that he might have his answer at the time of the council which was announced to be held at Three Rivers in May when the ice had melted and the waterways were open for the canoes to assemble.

II

Guillaume Coûture and Father Isaac held intimate conversations about their pasts and futures. Each had come to a definite decision, and each agreed to the resolution of the other. Coûture carried

Jogues' letter petitioning to be sent down to the Iroquois country. Jogues approved Coûture's desire to be released from his obligations, and sent him on his way with a blessing. At Three Rivers, Coûture was treated handsomely. The French respected him as a hero and a patriot; the Hurons considered him as a brother; the Iroquois trusted him implicitly as an adopted son. At the request of Kiotseaeton and the other ambassadors, a feast was held in his honor, in the middle of April, for the purpose of conferring on him a new name. Ihandich, he had been called by the Hurons. This word had an evil sound and a bad connotation in the Iroquois tongue. It was resolved, therefore, that Coûture should hereafter be known as Achirra, and be raised up in place of the great explorer who held that title, Jean Nicolet.

Down at Quebec, Coûture urged Father Lalemant to grant Father Isaac's request to be sent to live in the Mohawk villages. He presented, also, the reasons for his own dispensation. In 1640, at Sainte Marie, he had pledged his religious promises as a *donné* and vowed perpetual service, obedience, chastity, and renunciation of temporal possessions as a lay helper to the Huron missioners. He had labored with generosity and self-sacrifice; his piety had been more than ordinary; his loyalty, as was proved when Father Isaac was captured in 1642, was heroic. Four years had elapsed. He had been living as an adopted son of a Mohawk family at Tionontoguen. For the greater part of that time, he was a lone white man in a native environment. Despite his efforts, he had suffered spiritually. He was now free to remain among the French and, with peace established, his presence among the Mohawks was no longer required. He asked to be released from his religious promises so that he could marry and establish a home in Quebec.

Father Lalemant took up with his advisors the two petitions. He recorded the decisions in his Journal, for April: "On the 26th, I held a Consultation with reference to father Jogues' journey to the Annieronons (Mohawks); the Advisers were father Vimont, father de quen, father Dendemar, father p. pijart; *omnium consensu approbata profectio. Item,* concerning Cousture's marriage; *approbatum item omnium consensu.*" Coûture was free, from the Iroquois, from the missionary labors, from his extraordinary bond of serving God. Father Jogues was vowed anew, by his own wish and the will of his Superiors, to a life-long service in the Iroquois villages, in poverty, in chastity, and in obedience, till death.

Up at Montreal, in the latter part of that April, Father Jogues entered upon his annual Spiritual Exercises. He was confident that his petition would be granted, and so he diligently prepared himself by renewed prayer before the Blessed Sacrament, by meditation on the sustaining truths of the spiritual life, by mortification of his flesh and its castigation, by the upbuilding of the virtues which would be assaulted by the devils and the pagans. But again, in his uncertainty that he would be chosen to go among the Iroquois, in case another Father were chosen, he prepared himself to accept his Superior's decision with generous obedience and in perfect resignation. To bear this denial of all his hopes would be more difficult than to bear death by torture or a life in slavery.

Through ten days, he secreted himself from the French and the natives, and was alone with God. He recalled the purpose of his existence: to praise, reverence and serve God, and by this means to save his soul. He affirmed, with St. Ignatius, that all creatures were created by God to help him, whether they were pleasant or whether they were hard on human nature. He thought of sins in general and in his own life, of hell, of judgment, of death. He leaped to enthusiasm in the rousing meditation on the Kingdom of Christ, and offered himself exultingly to his Divine Leader in the conquest of the world. He studied the Captain, Christ, in the mysteries of His life, and especially in those of His sufferings and death. He was finishing the series of meditations and contemplations when he was interrupted by Le Jeune, who handed him, in silence, a letter from Father Lalemant which a native courier had just brought from Quebec.

Here was the answer. Jogues prayed God for courage, that he might have strength to accept the decision either way, to go or not to go. The note was brief, kindly but curt. Lalemant advised him that he approved of the project of returning as a missioner to the Iroquois. He ordered Jogues to be prepared to leave as soon as the matter might be arranged. Meanwhile, the Governor would be consulted and would be asked to allow Jogues to join the Mohawks in their journey home to their villages, that is, provided the council to be held at Three Rivers ended in amity.

The answer to his petition coincided with the end of his Retreat, with that "Contemplation for Obtaining Love" which climaxed all his spiritual aspirations. Ten years before, when he was at Rouen making ready to sail for Canada, he had poured out his soul in the total offering of all of himself to God. Now at Ville Marie he repeated that same prayer of supreme love by which he gave himself wholly to God: "Take, O Lord, and receive all my liberty, my memory, my understanding, and all my will, whatsoever I have and possess. Thou hast given all these things to me; to Thee, O Lord, I restore them; all are Thine, dispose of them all according to Thy will. Give me Thy love and Thy grace; for this is enough for me."

Under the spell of that total oblation of himself to God, he sat in the light of the small square of the window of the log cabin and, holding the pen in his crippled fingers, wrote his answer to Father Lalemant:

Most Reverend and dear Father:

The letter which it has pleased your Reverence to take the pains to write to me, found me engaged in the exercises of my retreat, which I began after the departure of the canoe which carried my letter to you; it was a good time, for the savages are all away on the chase, and give us more silence. Would you believe me, that when I opened the letter of your Reverence, my heart at first was seized as if with dread; for I feared that that which I desired and that which my spirit would prize as the greatest of all desires, might actually come to pass. My poor nature, which remembered all that had gone before, trembled. But Our Lord, in His goodness, bestowed calm on it, and will calm it still more. Yes, Father, I desire all that Our Lord desires, and I desire it at the peril of a thousand lives. Ah, with what regret should I be filled, if I lost such a wonderful occasion, one on which it might depend only on me that some souls were not saved. I hope that God's goodness, which has never abandoned me on former occasions, will still continue to assist me, and that He and I, we together, will be able to trample under foot all the difficulties which rise up against us. It is a fearsome thing to be "in the midst of fallen peoples," alone, without Mass, without the Sacrifice, without confession, without the Sacraments. Nevertheless, God's holy Will and His sweet command on us are well worth that. He who has preserved us by His holy grace without these aids for eighteen or twenty months, will not refuse the same favor to us who do not thrust ourselves into this position but who undertake this work solely and only to please Him, and undertake it against all the instincts and inclinations of nature. The thing I would say about all these comings and goings of the Iroquois is that I see very few from the first two villages (Ossernenon and Andagaron); and yet it is with these that we must principally deal, and it was to these villages that those who were recently slain belonged. There have been scarcely any Mohawks come here except from the third village (Tionontoguen), the one where Côuture lived. And these have professed, according to themselves, that they did not ordinarily come to war in these territories. It is not among these last that we shall have to live, but among those others whom we do not see visiting us. I thank your Reverence very sincerely for sending me your Huron precepts. Join the rest to these, when it pleases you. It is principally prayers, formulas for confession, and other things, *ejusdem generis,* that I need. You will increase my debt to you, as I am already your debtor on many grounds. I owe your Reverence the account of the capture and death of our good René Goupil, which I should already have sent to your Reverence. If the bearers give me the spare time to write it, I shall join it to the present letter. If God wills that I go to the Iroquois, it is necessary that he who accompanies me must be virtuous, docile, courageous, one who would be willing to suffer anything for God, one who is able to make and handle canoes, so that independently of the savages we might be able to go and come. May your Reverence permit me to send my respects, if it so please you, to our Reverend Fathers. I am your very humble and obedient servant.

Isaac Jogues, from Montreal, the 2nd of May, 1646.

As soon as he had finished his letter to Lalemant, and while the messenger waited, for he had time since the council at Three Rivers would not begin until May 7, Jogues wrote his *Notice sur René Goupil.* In a rapid, simple narrative, he told of René's early birth in Anjou, of his entry into the Society, of his ill health, of his desire to labor for God in New France, of his ability in surgery, of his care of the sick in Quebec, of how "he left so sweet an odor of his goodness and his other virtues in that place that his memory is still held in benediction there." Jogues related his own request to Father Vimont that René might be sent with him to the Hurons, and of René's joy when the offer to go was laid before him. He told of the attack by the Iroquois, of René's conformity to God's will when he was captured, of his help in preparing the Hurons for baptism, of his spiritual conversation along the route, of his willingness to die if God so ordered, of his request to be allowed to pronounce the vows of a coadjutor in the Society and of the acceptance of them, of his charity to the Iroquois in dressing their wounds, of his loyalty in refusing to escape, of his courage and sweetness under the cruel tortures, of his zeal, intemperate, perhaps, because he did not understand the savages, in praying openly and making the sign of the cross, and then, of the day when they walked from the village to pray and were ordered back, and he was struck down with the tomahawk.

"It was the 29th of September, the feast of St. Michael, when this angel in innocence, and this martyr of Jesus Christ, gave his life for Him who had given him His," Father Jogues wrote. He went on to tell how he himself was spared, how he sought out René's body to bury it, how he hid it in the rivulet from which it was stolen, how he searched for it everywhere but found it only the next spring, how he buried reverently the few bones remaining. "I kissed them very devoutly," Jogues related, "several times, as the bones of a martyr of Jesus Christ. I give him this title, not only because he was killed by the enemies of God and of His Church, and in the exercise of an ardent charity toward his neighbor, for he placed himself in evident peril for the love of God—but especially because he was killed on account of prayer, and notably, for the sake of the Holy Cross." He proved this by relating the incident of signing the cross on the little boy and of the orders given by the grandfather of the child, as well as by the testimony of the mother of the child and the grandfather who had had him executed.

His narrative was concluded in ten pages of closely-written manuscript. He felt that he should have written at greater length, with more care. But the messenger was waiting, and Lalemant was eager to incorporate the *Notice* in the *Relation* he was sending to France that summer. And so Jogues added a paragraph of apology: "I ask your Reverence's pardon for the haste with which I write this, and for the lack of courtesy of which I am guilty. Will you please excuse me, for I feared that I might lose this occasion to discharge a duty which I ought to have performed long ago." He inclosed the memories of René Goupil in the same envelope with his letter signifying his joy in being ordered to go back among the Iroquois, among those who had martyred René, those who had almost murdered him and might yet murder him.

On May 7, at Three Rivers, Governor Montmagny opened the final council for peace. In it were represented the French, the Mohawks, the Algonquins, the Montagnais and the Hurons. Kiotseaeton, suave, poised, eloquent, was the first orator. He bowed in courtesy to the Montagnais, and offered them a present to assure them that his people had no part in the massacre of last autumn. He turned to the chief of the Blackrobes, Father Lalemant, and placed before him a wampum belt in remembrance of Father de Nouë, declaring: "That is to warm again the place where the cold has caused this good Father to perish. Put this little gift in your bosom, in order to divert yourself from the thoughts which might cause you sadness."

With these preliminaries done, he turned to the business of the council. His first present was a bath to refresh the ambassadors who would come to his country, an ointment for their feet. His second stated that the war hatchet which had been held suspended from the Algonquins and Hurons was now thrown far away, at the request of Onontio. With the third, he expressed regret: that miserable child, Onnieoute (the Oneidas) was insolent and refused to listen to the word of her mother (the Mohawks), and so would not enter into peace negotiations. The remaining gifts were for Onontio, who leveled the earth, who was the father of the nations, who gave sense to the Algonquins. Kiotseaeton requested him to be the arbiter of all disputes between the peoples united in this peace.

At the second session, Montmagny named Achirra Coûture as the spokesman for the French. Onontio offered appropriate gifts to the Mohawks to congratulate them on the good faith they had shown in preserving the truce; he was delighted that all obstacles were now removed. He assured them by a necklace of a thousand beads that the council fire would be kept lighted at Three Rivers. He stated that he would like to see the young Frenchmen they were detaining in their midst, and also his Huron daughter, named Theresa, so that she might prepare corn in the Mohawk fashion when they visited the French.

Paul Teswehat, chief of the Upper Algonquins, announced that he was the mouth of all the Algonquin nations. With a present of elk skins to the Iroquois, he protested that his people would never violate the truce or the peace. With a present to Onontio, he humbly begged, but significantly because of the rumors current, that he and the French should not walk all alone in safety over the earth he had leveled, but that the French should also share this happiness with the Hurons and Algonquins. Turning to the Iroquois again, he announced that the Algonquins had thrown their war hatchets beyond the sky; and then, with another present, requested that there be no false alarms. He opened the lands of the Algonquins for the Iroquois to hunt there, and prepared for them a place by the fire in the Algonquin cabins. He ordered twelve more handsome elk skins to be laid before the Mohawks: these were to be divided between their three villages, for the release of all the Algonquins held captive there. Thus he concluded the Algonquin peace.

Kiotseaeton, personally, dealt with the Hurons. He offered gifts of courtesy and gratitude for their kindness to the Oneida and Seneca prisoners they held; he suggested that if they were returned to their people, the Upper Iroquois would be under obligations that would entice them to enter the peace parleys But he warned them, at the same time, that they must be on their guard against attack by these nations. As for the Mohawks, his own people, their ambassadors were soon coming to visit the Huron villages; let the Hurons fill their pots and keep them boiling, for the Iroquois hoped to be feasted well.

Father Jogues had not been called to the council at Three Rivers. But when Lalemant saw that it was progressing so favorably, he sent an urgent command to Jogues to hurry down as quickly as possible. On his arrival, Lalemant brought him to Governor Montmagny. He relates: "Monsieur our Governor, having resolved to send two Frenchmen to the country of the Annieronnons (Mohawks), in order to convey to them his word, and to assure them of his joy and satisfaction over the peace so happily concluded,—Father Isaac Jogues was presented to him to be of the party. As Father Jogues had already purchased an acquaintance with these people and their language, with a coin more precious than gold or silver, he was straightway accepted."

On Sunday, May 13, the Governor entertained the Mohawk ambassadors at a feast in an Algonquin cabin. He presented the Iroquois with two "words," each accompanied by valuable gifts. The first present declared that he thanked the Mohawks for refusing to accept the scalps of the slain Montagnais Christians, offered to them by the Sokokis. The second announced to them that he had resolved to send into their country two Frenchmen: the great Blackrobe, Ondessonk, his own dear brother, whom they already knew; and the councilor and advisor of the French, Jean Bourdon. These two ambassadors, he promulgated, would probably start for the Mohawk villages in three days.

With stolid faces but tremulous hearts, the Governor and Lalemant, and Father Jogues in the shadows of the cabin, waited for the answer. It was given spontaneously. Kiotseaeton accepted the gifts in the name of his people, thus guaranteeing safety to the ambassadors, to, from and within the Mohawk territory. Encouraged, the Algonquins offered to send two of their chiefs with the French; and these also were accepted.

Father Jogues was ready for the hazards and dangers. According to his Superior, who insisted with him that he was free to go or not to go, "Father Jogues was ready sooner than the proposition was made to him." Lalemant remarked: "The Iroquois welcomed him. He who had sustained the dangers of war was not for retreating in time of peace. He was very glad to sound out the friendship of the Iroquois after having experienced the rage of their enmity. However, he was not ignorant of the fickleness of these barbarians. The difficulty of the danger was patent to him, as a man who had experienced it. He saw the dangers into which he was throwing himself. But he who never risks for God, will never be an extensive dealer in the riches of heaven."

Three days he had to get ready, and they were all too many. He prepared not for this limited journey as an ambassador, but for his permanent residence as a missioner. Kiotseaeton left four strong Mohawks as a guard and an aid in carrying the baggage of Jogues and Bourdon. Jogues resolved to take advantage of their help and transport all the clothing and accessories that would be needful for the winter. Most important of these were the things necessary for Mass. It might be possible, he hoped, to have this consolation for himself and the native Christians who would winter among the Mohawks. Accordingly, he packed the vestments, a small chalice, a tiny Missal, candles, hosts and a bottle of wine into a solid trunk that was small enough to be fitted neatly into a canoe. He filled it with heavy clothes and leggings and wampum and trinkets he would need as presents. He was proud of his forethought in carrying this compact black box with him on this first short journey. He would leave it with his "aunt" and she would guard it faithfully so that he could claim it when he returned for the winter.

On second thought, and by the advice of a wise Algonquin, he carried his soutane in the box. This man warned Ondessonk that he must not speak too freely about hell and sin and the mysteries of the Faith. The Algonquin told him: "There is nothing so repulsive to us at the beginning as is your doctrine. For your teaching seems to destroy completely everything that men hold dear. Your long robe preaches as well as your lips. Hence, it would be better for you to walk in clothes which are shorter." Following these sagacious hints, Jogues had himself fitted out in a sober secular costume, of high-topped boots, pantaloons and coat and cloak, and broad-rimmed hat. Which procedure Lalemant countenanced while he excused it by saying: "It is considered necessary to treat the sick as sick people, and to behave among the pagan as one does among the heretics (of England) so that one must become all things to all men, in order to gain all to Jesus Christ."

Jean Bourdon had more to leave, as he had more to carry. He had come out from Normandy in those dire, pioneering days of 1634, when the French under Champlain were reconstructing the colony after the English occupation. He settled himself in a hut at the base of the Quebec rock, and was employed as an engineer and surveyor in Quebec and along the St. Lawrence. He had worked at Three Rivers when that settlement was begun. When the plans for the establishment of the fort and residences in the Upper City of Quebec were executed, he was of expert value. In 1641 he was commissioned by Governor Montmagny to draw up a map of the St. Lawrence from Cape Tourmente to Quebec.

His choice as fellow ambassador with Father Jogues was most significant. To know the route to the Iroquois country in an accurately scientific way, to plot out the waterways and land trails and to note the distinguishing signs, to compute the distances and the hazards, were an absolute necessity to the French, for trade purposes, for diplomacy, for the military above all. The Governor specifically appointed Monsieur Bourdon to these functions, while he just as specifically designated Father Jogues as the spokesman and good-will messenger to the Iroquois and to the Dutch.

Bourdon was a man of position in New France. He built a most respectable home on the grant of land he held along the Plains that stretched along the highlands overlooking the river above Quebec. There resided his wife, his four girls and two boys. He was highly respected for his integrity, his charity and piety. He was courageous and adventurous, and hardened against the travails of the wilderness. He was willing to die for King and for God. As Lalemant expressed it: "He showed his zeal for the public welfare all the more that he forsook his own family in order to throw himself into the hazards which are never small among these barbarians." Bourdon, too, filled the requirements set down in advance by Father Jogues in his letter of May 2, and went beyond them. He was, in all respects, the best choice in all the French colony for the duty that had to be performed.

Wednesday, May 16, was the day marked for the departure of the ambassadors. In one canoe were Father Jogues and Jean Bourdon, with two of the Mohawks assigned as guides and guards. Their curved, shaggy little craft was steady with the ballast of baggage, with Jogues' solid black box, with the bundles of blankets and iron goods he carried as peace offerings, with Bourdon's personal equipment and his scientific instruments. The two Algonquin ambassadors, accompanied by the other two Mohawks, traveled in a canoe that was loaded down to the rim with the twenty-four bulky elk skins which the Algonquin nations were presenting to the Mohawk villages.

It was a gala morning for Three Rivers. All the inhabitants, soldiers, officials, priests, gathered along the strand and shouted their final messages. The white flags on the ramparts above the hill stiffened in the morning breezes, the cannons intonated and rumbled into the distances. Smiling and intrepid, Isaac Jogues, Jean Bourdon and the natives dug their paddles into the water with sharp, starting strokes. The canoes spurted out of the shallows and across the river to the glades along the southern shore. They were dots, they were lost in the silver sheen of the St. Lawrence.

Prayers followed them. The diary of the Jesuits at Quebec recorded on the following Sunday, Pentecost: "The benediction of the Blessed Sacrament was held on the Day of Pentecost, and on the two following feasts, as at Easter,—in order to give thanks for the success of the journey to 3 Rivers; to recommend the journey of father Jogues and of monsieur Bourdon." Lalemant was writing his amazement in the *Relation* to be sent to France: "When I speak of a mission among the Iroquois, it seems to me that I speak of a dream, and yet, it is a truth."

III

On that same Feast of Pentecost, Jogues and his comrades rested at the ruined Fort Richelieu. After he said his Mass to the Holy Ghost, the party pointed the canoes southward. He had traveled this soft-flowing stream four years ago when he was a captive, his fingers still agonizing with the first torture, his body purple with bruises, when René was by his side. Then the whole world was tumbled in chaos and his soul was in despair about his companions and the Huron Mission. But this Sunday was a bright, alive, gleaming morning of May. The Church among the Hurons flourished, the Church among the Iroquois savages was being born, there was the glorious prospect of universal peace. God, in His Divine Omnipotence, was leading all things to His blessed ends.

Thrilled though he was with the supernal joy, Jogues kept close to the earth. He had to be familiar with every mile of this route, for he would be traveling it again, and without guides. He kept his eyes glued on every detail as he blithely swept his paddle back and forth, and consulted with the surveyor Bourdon as to distances, the lead of the river, the turns, the elevation of the banks, the portages, and all that need be recorded in a scientific narrative or specified on an accurate map. For ninety miles they traveled the hedged-in river named the Richelieu. Then they found themselves on the expanse of the upper Lake of Champlain with its widening panorama. They crept past the tree-decked islands, the crescent bays and the promontories nosing their way out, beneath precipitate crags and in the dark shadows of the mountains. To the right and to the left, they saw the land swelling up higher and higher in ridges that were white-capped in the blue sky.

About the fifth day on the lake, and the eighth since they left Fort Richelieu, they camped on a little island which Father Jogues could never forget. Ghastly had been that night of torture when he and the other prisoners had been sacrificed by the two hundred warriors. The next day they passed through a narrowing of the lake;

Monsieur Bourdon visioned a fort on the hill to his right. A little later they approached another promontory, boldly outlined against the conical mountains beyond. Here the canoes halted.

Jogues noted how the lake petered out toward the left; it was along that lower portion that he had traveled on his first journey. Now, his guides were intending to follow another route through a lake unknown to him. The Mohawks had a rite to perform, for this was a sacred spot. Mumbling incantations, they strewed tobacco strands upon the waters of the cove. They were thanksgiving offerings to a race of invisible men who dwelt at the bottom of the lake, and who were true benefactors, for they cut and fashioned the hard flints in the shape of arrow heads and cast them along the shores for the Mohawks to gather as they passed.

This sacrifice offered, the guides pointed the canoes across the cove, and wove a way through sedges and water plants to a hidden channel and into a little stream that tumbled down between the hills. They came to the terraced rocks of a rapids. Shouldering their baggage and slinging the canoes over their heads, they padded through an overgrown trail to a higher level. It was an important link in the journey. Jogues and Bourdon studied it, and calculated the portage as half a league.

They emerged from the thickets on the grassy shore of a tapering pond. From there, a new lake spread out, about the width of the St. Lawrence in the stretches below Montreal. The waters were nervous and choppy. Soon, they were bound in with rugged banks, grimly, heavily wooded, sometimes rising almost perpendicular in grayish, brownish slabs of stone, sometimes slanting to dizzy, ragged mountain elevations, sometimes hollowing ever upwards in amazing vistas. The level of the lake was interspersed with islands and jagged with reefs and bays. After two or three days' paddle along this gorge in the mountains they floated into the circular basin that terminated the lake. "Andiatarocté—There where the lake is shut in," was the Mohawk designation of the place.

Never before had the white man traversed this lake, and scarcely had its existence been known. Standing on the sand at Andiatarocté, Father Jogues was inspired to bestow a name upon it. The day was that of May 30, which was the eve of the Feast of Corpus Christi. He christened these waters Lac du Saint Sacrement. Monsieur Bourdon so inscribed it on the map he was devising.

From this point onward the trails lay overland. The eight voyageurs slung over their shoulders their boxes and bundles. The Algonquins were in an impossible state. They had brought twenty-four elk skins; each one of them could possibly carry no more than five at a time; in the portages they had to make several trips. Nothing was to be done except to cache fourteen of the skins in the woods. They took up the trail in a single file and slid their moccasins rapidly in the hollowed gutter of yellowed dust. The path rose for the most part and then turned down to where it branched, one fork turning westerly toward the Sacandaga River and cutting straight across country to Ossernenon, the other bearing in a southerly direction to the fishing-grounds at Lake Ossaragué.

Though it was a longer way, the Mohawks decided that it would be better to go toward Ossaragué, since the people would be gathered there for the spring fishing and help could be procured in carrying the heavy bundles. For some miles they wound through the damp valley that curved below the mountains and came upon a lively mountain stream. The Mohawks called it "Oiogué—The Beautiful River"; it was recognized by Jogues, and noted by Bourdon, as the upper portion of the river that flowed past the Dutch settlements. They skirted its banks till they reached another stream, along which they turned, and came up through the marshes to the place where Lake Ossaragué poured out. Father Jogues knew the spot; it was here that he had such peace for a few days with his "aunt," and from here that he was tricked back to Ossernenon to be murdered.

As they had anticipated, they found great numbers of fishing-parties camped above Ossaragué. All the people gathered noisily and curiously about the French and Algonquin ambassadors, welcoming them with hospitality and formal respect. Ondessonk, whom they all had known as a slave and a wretched outcast, now dazzled them. He was dressed in French garb, not in a black robe; he was the especially appointed ambassador of the great French father, Onontio. It was a revived and resurrected Ondessonk whom they looked on, a man of authority who acted like a great chief, not like a squaw. In all the throng that visited them, one especially was ecstatic with happiness. Theresa, the little Huron girl, the daughter of Joseph Chihwatenhwa, and niece of Joseph Teondechoren, who had been captured with Ondessonk four years before, was with her adopted family at Ossaragué.

Theresa, now fully grown into a woman of seventeen, was married to a brave of Tionontoguen. Father Jogues loved her as a daughter, and saw in this early meeting a special act of Providence: "God has a guidance full of love; His goodness caused the detour to be made in order to give some assistance to the poor Theresa, the former schoolgirl of the Ursulines." He was under definite instructions, moreover, from Governor Montmagny to secure her release, for her case was become of international moment. During the four years since her capture, the *Relation* states: "the Ursuline Mothers were not able to endure the thought that this poor little creature should remain in that captivity, removed from all the help which could open for her the gates of heaven; and so, they spared no pains, and moved heaven and earth to procure her liberty. Monsieur the Governor, approving this great zeal and this great charity, lost no opportunity for releasing her from that slavery, and of coöperating in the matter with all his power."

She was unspoiled despite her life among the Iroquois. Though she had been forced by her adopted family to marriage with a Mohawk brave, she was unhappy among these people and longed to be back among her own Huron kinsmen and the Ursuline Mothers. She remembered her prayers and said her rosary in the way her Mothers had taught her; since she did not have beads strung together, she used little pebbles placed upon the ground. She tried to be careful in avoiding all the sins that she knew were offensive to God.

Father Jogues spent as much time as he could with her, instructing and "refreshing her memory concerning her duty, and then he heard her confession to the great satisfaction of her soul." He told her that her Ursuline Mothers loved her very much and wanted her to come back to them, that the great Onontio had offered presents for her release at the council, that he himself was carrying gifts that would plead with the Mohawks, and that she, too, must pray that God would allow her soon to return to her people. Theresa most ardently desired and prayed that this could be done.

Father Jogues and his company left the fishing-grounds the next morning, June 2, in canoes which they had borrowed at Lake Ossaragué. They paddled down the stream which flowed into the

Oiogué, and then traveled in a leisurely way with the current of the river. Now that they were in the canoes again, in sheltered rivers, their progress was easy. After covering some fifty miles along the waterway, they landed at the Dutch settlement of Rensselaerswyck on June 4.

Memories flooded in once more upon Father Jogues. The Dutch had been so kindly and sympathetic that he was assured of a hearty welcome. God it was, truly, who inspired them and him to make his flight rather than to go back to certain death at Ossernenon four years before. But he was disappointed on landing. Arendt Van Corlaer, Dominie Megapolensis and others of the principal burghers had gone down the river to New Amsterdam. Isaac had wanted to see them so much. He carried a letter of courtesy from Governor Montmagny to Director-General Kieft, dated May 15. This he left at Rensselaerswyck for transmission to the lower settlement, and promised that he would return for another visit after the council in the Mohawk villages.

Jogues and Bourdon eyed Rensselaerswyck shrewdly and scientifically. Jogues had previously promised that he would write a complete account of the Dutch colony of New Netherlands; he now checked up on what he remembered from his visit of 1642 and gathered new impressions. Bourdon, with the curiosity of a surveyor, engineer and geographer, noted those details which would be informative for Governor Montmagny and the home government of France. After remaining two days among the Dutch, they paddled up the river to the waterfalls, climbed the rocks leading to the portage of the river of the Mohawks, and pulled their canoes against the stream till, on the evening of the second day, they beached their boats on the flats below Ossernenon.

Different now was Jogues' welcome as an ambassador from that as a prisoner. Quickly the news spread through all the nation that Ondessonk had come, together with another great French chief. According to Lalemant: "They were gazed at and welcomed by these people who came from all distances to see them. Those who had formerly ill-used Father Jogues no longer showed any inclination to do so. And those whom natural compassion had touched at the sight of his sufferings, felt a great joy in seeing him in happier circumstances and employed in an important office." Most of all, his dear old "aunt" was glad to receive him, for the matriarch had been as kind as a savage nature could. She now had an added reason. Her grandson, Honatteniate, had been restored to his people by the French, and he had told her of the excessive kindness shown him by Ondessonk at Three Rivers.

As soon as Jogues and Bourdon reached Ossernenon, fleet runners were dispatched to announce that a grand council of chiefs and sachems was to assemble at Tionontoguen on June 10. Two days, thus, were left to Jogues in this village. Among his first acts was that of making a pilgrimage down the steep ravine to the foot of the tree where he had buried the sacred bones of René Goupil. The cross upon the tree was seared into the trunk. He prayed there, now in a rapturous thanksgiving. René was a martyr; the blood of René was the seed from which the Iroquois Church would rise.

A strange story he heard. The two young braves who had murdered René in cold blood had both died, a year or two back, of some mysterious malady. One of them, he recalled, was the tallest and strongest of the Mohawks. Curiously, the Algonquin woman who had sawed off his own thumb, she, too, was dead. Besides, several of the warriors who had captured him and who had most cruelly tortured him, they were the ones killed by the Algonquins in the last combat before the truce was made. The same fate which overtook those who maltreated him, also happened to those who were most savage to Father Bressani.

On Sunday, June 10, Jogues and Bourdon were leaving Ossernenon. Thus it had been called in his former stay, but now he heard it referred to as Oneougiouré. He blessed this village of his captivity anew and dedicated it under the Christian title of the Village of the Holy Trinity. They took the river trail, along which he had padded so frequently, to the capital village of Tionontoguen. There they were formally met and officially received by the chiefs and elders of all the Mohawk families, and surrounded by the fierce-looking warriors, by the squat, broad-faced squaws, by the naked, intrusive children of all ages. Gone was the diabolic fury and turmoil; in its place was courtesy and profound ceremonial and a gentle etiquette.

When night had covered the earth, after they had all filled themselves with sagamité and fish and had puffed on their calumets, the council was convened in the largest cabin of the village. Ondessonk, Bourdon and the two Algonquins sat on the mat stretched on one side of the council fire. Opposite them haunched Kiotseaeton and the Mohawk leaders, sharp featured and barbaric in their head-dress of brilliant plumage. In the dim background that encircled them were crowded the warriors and squaws. The din of voices billowed through the cabin till a stentorian cry roared out: "Close your mouths. Open your ears." All hushed into solemn silence.

Ondessonk rose from his mat and strode to the open space before the council fire. He spoke in the language of the Mohawks, with an intermixture of Huron which they could understand. With gestures learned from them, and pantomime, and in their symbolism, he exhibited in succession the gifts of precious wampum he had brought from Onontio. He narrated how Kiotseaeton and his comrades had come to Montreal, after the French had looked in vain across the St. Lawrence and had nearly despaired; how they were welcomed as brothers at Three Rivers; how they had consulted together in peace; how they had feasted from the same dish and chanted in unison and slept without fear at the same fire. All the French and their allies rejoiced in the peace that was there pledged.

Here is a belt of wampum, rich and beautiful in design, Ondessonk orated. It says that the council fire is burning at Three Rivers, never to be extinguished. It invites the Mohawks and their allies to sit about the fire and pledge a closer friendship. Here is a necklace of five thousand beads. Through it, Onontio begs that the little Frenchman who lives in their cabins be sent back to his people. Here is another necklace that will console them for the Huron woman, Theresa, when they allow her to depart from them and to go to Three Rivers, where she may prepare their food as they like it when they visit the French. And here is another present which is the voice of gratitude on the part of Onontio because the Mohawks rejected the Montagnais heads offered to them by the treacherous Sokokis.

Ondessonk recalled that the Wolf clan was an ancient and powerful family among all the Iroquois nations. The warriors of the Wolfs were courageous in war but hospitable in peace. They were his friends when he formerly dwelt in the cabins of the Mohawks and they had always been the orators who advocated better understanding with the French. For that reason the French loved the Wolf clan with particular affection and looked upon them as their kinsmen. He displayed a belt of three thousand wampum beads. This, he declared, was for the Wolf clan so that they might build up the council fire in all the three Mohawk villages, and keep it always lighted, with much fuel stocked about it.

In conclusion, he shouted in a strong, confident tone the word of the Iroquois, *Hiro* ("I have spoken"). The chiefs and sachems rumbled out of the pits of their stomachs the answer of approval. All the assembly joined them in the applause. What he had said was pleasing to their ears. They marveled at this Ondessonk, at the boldness of his bearing, at the authority with which he addressed them, so different from the meekness and the docility he had shown when he was their slave. They rejoiced that he did not remember the tortures they had inflicted on him and that he did not demand revenge. And yet, in that council, waiting their opportunity, were many narrow-eyed braves of the Bear clan who still yearned to split his head open with the tomahawk. They plotted to break the peace and to go on the warpath against the French, the Hurons and Algonquins.

It was now the time for the Algonquins to address the council. One of them stood before the fire, and in his own tongue announced that Ondessonk would be his mouth. Jogues again faced the Mohawks. He explained that, since the Algonquins did not know the Iroquois speech, they had given him authority to bear their message. He related that the Algonquin chiefs sent twenty-four great skins of elks as presents; but since the weight of them was heavy and the journey over the trail was difficult, and since one of the Algonquin ambassadors had sprained his leg, they were forced to abandon fourteen of these beautiful robes at the place called Andiatarocté. For this, he said in apology, the Algonquins felt very much embarrassed and ashamed.

From the Algonquins he brought a message of friendship. They protested that good faith was deep in their hearts as it was upon their lips; that they had hurled the war hatchet so far away that it could not be recovered; that a fire was in the Algonquin cabins to warm the Mohawks, and food there to refresh them; that the forests in their land were alive with deer and elks and beavers, and that the Mohawks might hunt the animals without fear of attack or ambush.

As he was concluding, Jogues addressed the council in his own name and that of the French. He remarked that he noticed some chiefs from the allies of the Mohawks, the Onnontagehronnons

(Onondagas). He made them a gift of two thousand wampum beads. These were to pierce their ears so that they might understand the purpose of the French in visiting the Iroquois country. They must not be surprised if they saw the French coming also to their country, for these beads were a gift in advance to level the roads. In order to impress on them that the French were ready to conclude a separate peace with them, and were not dependent upon the Mohawks, Ondessonk reminded them that there were three routes which the French might follow: one through the country of the Mohawks; another across the great lake of Ontario and the Lake St. Louys; and a third through the land of the Hurons. He offered the beads to the braves of the Onondagas, who accepted them in token of their promise to tell the word to their chiefs. These proceedings the Mohawks watched in silence; the overtures of Ondessonk disturbed them.

It was early in the morning before the council broke up. The next night the Mohawks held private councils, and on the 12th of June they announced that they would return their answer to Ondessonk and the Algonquins. Their orators spoke with affection and enthusiasm of the peace with the French. They were unanimously in favor of forming one people with them. As for the little Frenchman, they put on his arm a string of two thousand beads, saying: "There is the bond which held him captive. Take him and his chain, and do with them according to the will of Onontio." In regard to Theresa, they explained that she was given in marriage to a Mohawk brave. She was absent at Ossaragué, but when she would return from the fishing she would be given her liberty if she desired it. In truth of their word, they offered a necklace of fifteen hundred beads.

The orator of the Wolf clan returned the answer of his family. He fondled a belt of wampum beads about ten feet long, closely woven in a beautiful design. It was a bond of closer friendship and alliance between the French and the Wolfs, over and above the peace established between the two nations. The French, always, would have a warm welcome in the Wolf cabins, and Ondessonk, in particular, would be under their special protection and their adoption.

The Mohawks replied to the Algonquins, but with more restraint and coldness. They made it clear that they concluded peace because that was the wish of Onontio and the French. However, they gave assurances that they would preserve the friendship. Furthermore, they sought also for peace with the Hurons, because the French desired it, and asked that two gifts be forwarded to them.

In reference to the last statements of Ondessonk, the Mohawks expressed some surprise. They were not pleased with the suggestion he had made to the Onondagas that he and the French had three roads to their nation. "It is necessary for the French to take the road which Onontio has opened," they affirmed, jealously guarding their prerogative as the authors of the peace. "The other two roads are too dangerous. One meets in them only people of war, men with their faces painted and streaked, who seek only to kill. The way to these other nations through our country is now excellent, it is entirely cleared of obstacles, it is safe from all attack." In a subsequent answer, Jogues held to his point that, though the French would accept the Mohawks as intermediaries with the four Upper Iroquois peoples, they would not bind themselves to abstain from any direct negotiations with them.

Though dressed in secular clothes and engaged as the ambassador of the French, Father Jogues was busy with the affairs of God. He made his rounds of the cabins, seeking out the sick and the dying. Some adults, nearing their end, he baptized after receiving from them expression of their desire to be with God, and thus, remarks Lalemant, "he sent to heaven these poor dying creatures, predestined, however, to riches." He found some babies also doomed to death, and forwarded them also to heaven. There were Huron and Algonquin Christians held prisoners, and these he instructed and strengthened and confessed.

With the council at Tionontoguen happily concluded, Father Jogues and his associates returned to Ossernenon, or Oneougiouré. There he encountered a difficulty. It was about the little black box that he had left in his "aunt's" cabin. It was strongly bound, and locked so that it could not be opened. That was suspicious, as was everything concealed and hidden. The Mohawks who were friendly confided to him that some of the people feared he had a demon inclosed in the box, for malicious demons lived in such things as boxes, and hollow trees, and caves in the earth. They had never had a strong box like this in their cabins, so tightly locked that they would need a hatchet to open it. The gossip was being spread that the black box of Ondessonk really did hold a bad spirit locked up in it, and that this bad spirit was being left among them in order to bring harm on them. They suspected that Ondessonk, despite his friendly words, really was waiting the chance to punish them for all the tortures they had inflicted on him.

Father Jogues smiled at them and opened the chest before their eyes. They were surprised that he could open it so easily with a little piece of iron. They laid that point aside in their minds. When he showed them that the box held only some ordinary articles of clothing, and some other garments such as they had captured from the French when they first took him, a metal cup, a book, pieces of beeswax, and the like, such things as they were familiar with, their fears were somewhat allayed. He emptied the little trunk so that they might handle it and convince themselves there were no hidden places in it where the demon might make his home. He locked it and opened it patiently, to disabuse any apprehensions of mystery there might be about the lock and key. It was just an ordinary strong box, he assured them, in which he wished to preserve the articles he would need if he came later on to live with them. They accepted his explanations, finally. But they were not wholly convinced. Still, they would do him the favor of keeping the box for him, though they hoped there was no evil genius concealed in it.

A fleet-footed messenger sped into the village. He came from the chiefs at Tionontoguen, bearing word that Ondessonk and his associates should hurry homewards. A war party from another Iroquois nation was bound for the Ottawa River and the Rivière des Prairies to waylay the Huron flotilla on its way to Three Rivers for the summer trading. The party planned to make its way down the St. Lawrence to Fort Richelieu and thence through the country of the Mohawks. The Mohawks feared Ondessonk might encounter this party if he delayed. "We do not believe that they will do any harm to you or the other Frenchmen if they meet you. We are uneasy only for the two Algonquins who are with you," the Mohawk chiefs informed him.

Father Jogues was indignant. How does this happen, he asked them, that they should permit their allies and other nations to make war on friendly peoples within the Mohawk boundaries? How was it that they did not forbid the other Iroquois nations to lay ambushes and attack their friends, the Algonquins, on the Mohawk trails? He warned them that they would be held accountable for all murders by Onontio and the French, and would be judged liars and traitors and treacherous men.

"We have warned the other Iroquois against such acts," the Mohawks assured him.

"Do they despise your commands and you?" asked Ondessonk. "Do you not understand that all the hostile acts that these Iroquois commit will be blamed on you?"

The Mohawk chiefs understood his contention and saw the warning beneath it. They promised that they would hold council among themselves, and would take efficient remedies to prevent any depredations by the other Iroquois which might be imputed to them by the French or Hurons or Algonquins. Nevertheless, now, they urged as a gesture of friendliness and good faith that the French and Algonquin ambassadors should hasten on their way.

On June 16, Jogues, Bourdon, the ransomed Frenchman, and the two Algonquins, now fearful and suspicious, left the village of the Holy Trinity, under a Mohawk escort. They had hoped to pay a farewell visit to the Dutch, but instead, they took the shortest route, across the valley to the undulating trail that brought them to the gully of the Sacandaga River, and along this stream winding its way between the mountains to the turbulent headwaters of the Oiogué River. Thence it was but a few hours' journey to the basin of the Lake of the Blessed Sacrament, which they reached about the third day.

They could not locate the canoes they had cached there, nor could they discover any other available canoes. It was the season when the bark was supple, however, when the tendrils with which to sew it were tough, and the gum to calk it oozed plentifully from the evergreens. They quickly fashioned new canoes, and started their water journey along the lakes. Ten days later, on June 27, safely and unmolested by hostile bands, they drew up below Fort Richelieu. The Algonquins pushed on ahead, for now they were no longer in the hazard of meeting enemy Iroquois. The Frenchmen did not delay, and arrived at Three Rivers on the 29th. On the 30th, they left for Quebec, which they reached on July 3. Boisterously the cannon of the fort proclaimed their coming, and exultantly Governor Montmagny, Father Lalemant and all the officers and personages of Quebec received them home.

CHAPTER XV

The Happy Night of the Martyrs

I

GOVERNOR MONTMAGNY and his Council, Fathers Lalemant and Vimont, assembled together in the home of the Governor on the heights of Quebec, listened in profound silence to the reports made by Father Jogues and Jean Bourdon. They questioned them on all details, closely, and examined their maps. They were satisfied that all signs presaged peace. Bourdon was commissioned by the Governor to draw up his complete narrative and his finished map for the official files of the colony, and Father Jogues was instructed by his Superiors to record his observations and deductions in another document. In his diary, Father Lalemant notes that these "will be found in the Archives, titulo yroquois."

Quebec was satisfied that peace was to reign. Lalemant exclaimed: "The devil foreseeing that the peace would trouble his kingdom, has striven to break it. But the angel of the Church of God has kept it fast locked. He has brought to a happy conclusion that which has been desired for so many years with a confident humility and a Christian patience." Again, he gives credit: "After all, the great God of hosts is the One and only Author of this peace. I entreat Him that He will be the preserver thereof. Our arguments were too small, weak, limited in so great a barbarism; fury was too much kindled to be quelled or extinguished by human effort. We candidly confess that if He Who has made the peace does not preserve it, we have not enough skill to restrain the inconstancy of these barbarians within firm bounds."

Speaking of the Mission of the Martyrs that would be established consequent on the peace, he declares: "Such is the beginning of a Mission which must furnish an opening to many other missions among well-peopled nations. If these roads are strewn with crosses, they are also filled with miracles. For there is not human skill nor power which could have changed the face of affairs so suddenly, and have drawn us out of the utmost despair to which we were reduced. There are neither gifts nor eloquence which could have, in so short a time, converted hearts enraged against each other for so many years. I cannot speculate what may not be hoped for, after these acts at the hands of the Almighty. May He be blessed beyond ages and beyond eternity."

Lalemant was high in his admiration for Father Isaac. "Sieur Bourdon has told me," he repeats, "that this good Father was indefatigable; he said that he suffered awfully on that road of iron." After several conversations, he put down in writing to France: "Father Isaac Jogues was entirely fascinated by and devoted to this Mission. After he had rendered an account of his embassy, he thought of nothing else but of undertaking a second voyage so that he might return thither, and especially before the winter. For, he could not endure the thought of being longer absent from his spouse of blood."

On July 8, Le Jeune arrived at Quebec from Montreal. On the following day he and Vimont, both of whom were former Superiors of New France, were called by Lalemant in consultation. Jogues laid before them his plea. He argued it impulsively and logically. The three older men were not wholly convinced that it was prudent for him to return immediately to the Iroquois. True, the peace was pledged with the Mohawks; still, it was a fresh peace that was untried for very long; besides, it was not yet clear in all its details; and then, it would take very little to disturb the status then existing. They voted as follows: "It was resolved that, if nothing else occurred, Father Jogues should not go to winter among the Iroquois, but should stay at Montreal or Three Rivers. But that, if some excellent opportunity occurred for going thither, this opportunity must not be rejected."

The decision was not at all what Jogues had hoped for. He consoled himself with the opening it forecast, and prayed with all his heart for this "excellent opportunity" to occur. What the nature of that might be he could not know; but he felt sure God would move things to His own ends. On July 14, together with Father Druillettes, he said adieu to the Governor and the Fathers at Quebec, and started up the river in the canoe of two Algonquin Christians. They stopped off at Three Rivers for some days, and held council with the French and savages. Having some leisure, he bethought himself to complete the writing of his narrative about the Dutch settlements in New Netherland, which he had long ago promised to Father Lalemant.

He signed a little cross at the head of the page, and in a flowing script, despite his mangled hands, without other title, began in a crisp, purposeful style: *"La Nouvelle Hollande que. . . ."* He stated the names given to this territory, and its latitude. Briefly, he described the lower settlement near to the ocean, that of Manhattan Island, its fort, called Fort Amsterdam, its houses and inhabitants, their religious affiliations, the scheme of grants made to new colonists, the pursuits of trade, agriculture, hunting, the climate, and the neighboring occupations of land made by the Swedes and the English. He then went on to speak of the second settlement, that of Rensselaerswyck, and noted the wretched condition of the fort, the number of its settlers and scattered dwellings, the fertility of the soil and its cultivation, the proximity of the Mohawks and the location of other savage nations between the two Dutch settlements. As if hurriedly, and by way of conclusion, he made rapid references to the wars between the Dutch at Fort Amsterdam and the neighboring Algonquins, as they were in 1642, and what he had heard subsequently during his visit in June. He covered seven delicately inscribed pages of paper, and dated the document: "From 3 Rivers, in New France, August 3, 1646."

With this duty done, Jogues continued up the St. Lawrence to Montreal. All along the river he was encountering parties of Hurons who were taking advantage of the truce and flocking down to the French settlements in great numbers. They were, for the most part, more suspicious of the Iroquois than were the Algonquins. They found it hard to believe that the Mohawks were not acting treacherously. During the winter just past and in that very summer, the Upper Iroquois nations, especially the Senecas and Oneidas, were sending parties to invade the Huron lands and all the trails and lakes to the south. And the Hurons, in turn, had taken the warpaths against these enemies. They were not too sure that some Mohawks were not among the attackers. Jogues tried his best to disabuse the Hurons of these notions, and told them of the presents for the Hurons which he had brought back from his embassy.

August advanced. More Hurons paddled down the St. Lawrence and mingled with the bands of Mohawks who went peacefully to and fro along the river. The Hurons laid aside some of their fears, the Algonquins basked in the quiet security, and the French were more than ever encouraged. Stability seemed to have arrived. Jogues pointed out the favorable signs in a letter from Three Rivers to Lalemant, and brought up again the question of his return that summer to the Mohawks. The Superior, after consultation with Le Jeune, Vimont and de Quen, jotted down in his notes among the matters settled on August 21: "3rd, *Item,* the wintering of father Druilletes among the Abnaquiois, and that of father Jogues among the yroquois."

An excellent opportunity, such as had been specified, was developing. For about that time in August, sixty of the most important Huron chiefs met Governor Montmagny in council at Three Rivers. He presented them with the presents brought to them by Ondessonk. The word which accompanied the gifts said that the Mohawks still feasted and danced in their villages; they thought nothing of war but only of the time when the Hurons would come to visit them and declare honestly their views on peace. Another important assurance went with the presents, namely, that if the Hurons killed the Iroquois Senecas and Oneidas who warred on them, the Mohawks would not consider such happenings to be an obstacle to peace, nor would they seek revenge.

The sixty chiefs, in their answer to Onontio, declared that they were favorable to the advances made by the Mohawks. They were particularly happy that they were given freedom to war with the other Iroquois, though they would prefer peace with these nations also. But they had information, they asserted, that some Mohawks were associating themselves with the Senecas, and presumably with the Oneidas; they asked for some assurance on this matter. They requested Onontio to appoint Ondessonk to accompany their ambassadors and help them treat of peace. In conclusion, they made it clear that they did not have supreme authority. The confirmation of their words had to be sought from the plenipotentiaries deputed by the general council of the Huron nations, who would arrive at Three Rivers in September.

Father Jogues remained at Montreal in a pother of doubt. He had been given assurance by Lalemant. He had heard of the decision of the sixty Hurons. All that was now needed was the confirmation by the Huron plenipotentiaries that the embassy to the

Mohawks would be approved. If ambassadors went, they would demand that he go with them. On the basis of this, he thought it better to finish the letters he was sending that year to France. To Father André Castillon, of the Society of Jesus, he wrote as follows:

My Reverend Father,

Pax Christi.

I have received what it has pleased your Reverence to write me. It obliges us to give you some information of our New France, and especially of what concerns me in particular.

I passed the winter at Montreal with Father Le Jeune. In the middle of May, I departed from three Rivers in company with Monsieur Bourdon, engineer of New France, to make a journey to the Iroquois, from which we returned in good health at the beginning of July. Monsieur our Governor was very glad to have him accompany me, that he might become acquainted with the country. We made a tolerably accurate map of these regions, and were well received both by the Dutch, through whose territory we passed, and by the savages. The principal Europeans were not there, having gone to the other settlement, which is toward the sea, and is the chief one for business. We did not lack exercise in this journey, either on water or on land; we made at least 100 leagues on foot, and were usually well laden. I baptized, in the village where we remained a few days, some sick children who, as I believe, are now with God. I confessed some Huron Christians who were there, to whom we made presents and received some in return. I am about to go back there to pass the winter, and not to return, *if I do not die there,* until the month of June next year. The matter is now being discussed at 3 rivers; they think that, if I am not sent there now, I shall be, God helping, in the spring. But I see considerable preparations made for an early departure, and our Reverend Father Superior is favorably inclined to it. It is only my own cowardice and bodily weakness which form powerful obstacles to the designs God has for me and for this country. Pray Him, my Reverend Father, that He will make of me what He desires, and that I may be a man after His own heart, "that the Lord may grant to me largeness of heart, great as the sand on the shore of the sea." Would that He would somewhat enlarge my poor heart, which is so narrow; and that by the experience of the past, and by the abundance of His goodness and mercy toward me, I may learn to entrust myself entirely to Him, being very sure that He will not draw back and let me fall, when I shall cast myself lovingly into the arms of His divine and paternal providence. Our Lord has made us a noble gift in giving us peace; pray His divine goodness which has given it to us, that it may continue, for it is from this goodness that we shall hope for the fulfillment of this prayer. This peace, together with the trade which the country now has, causes a notable change in its appearance, an increase in the number of inhabitants, and greater comfort in all respects. The country no longer seems as rough as before; and we know through experience that it can produce good wheat and other necessaries of life—especially this locality of Montreal, where we are, which is much milder and more temperate than Quebec; besides, it is in a middle latitude, namely, 45 degrees. More than 80 Huron canoes have just come down bearing a quantity of skins, which gives hopes of a still better year than the preceding one, which was very good. I do not know whether this will catch the eyes of the Gentlemen of the Company, who could scarcely furnish shipping when they had the trade. It is a fortunate occurrence that God has bestowed the peace with this change, which is very advantageous to the country. May God make it grow in spiritual blessings even more than in temporal, and if "he gives increase in peace, may he also increase the joy"; but principally may He bestow an abundance of His Holy Spirit upon those who labor for the spiritual interests of these countries. It is this for which I beg Your Reverence to entreat Our Lord, and especially to remember at the altar a poor priest, who is about to remain 8 or 9 months without Mass. It will be to me an increase of obligation to be, more than ever, my Reverend Father, your very humble and obedient servant in God.

Isaac Jogues

Montreal, this 12th of September, 1646.

About the same time, he wrote a more intimate and confidential letter to another one of his Jesuit friends in France:

Alas, my dearest Father, when shall I begin at length to serve Him and to love Him, whose love for us has been without any beginning? When shall I begin to give myself entirely to Him who has given Himself wholly to me and without reserve? Although I am the most miserable of creatures, and though I have made poor use of the graces which Our Lord has bestowed upon me in this country, and have responded to these so wretchedly, nevertheless, I do not despair in my soul; for I see that He takes care to offer me new opportunities through which I may die to myself and by which I may unite myself to Him inseparably. Because of these opportunities, He may make me worthier. Some Iroquois have come for the purpose of obtaining the liberty of some people of their nation, and to treat of peace in the name of the whole country. They brought gifts for the Governor, according to their custom. That peace has already been established, to the great joy of the French. It will last as long as pleases the will of God. It seemed necessary, to maintain the peace, and unobstrusively to see what might be done in the matter of instructing the Iroquois, to send some one of our Fathers there. I have reason to believe that I shall be employed there, for I have some knowledge of the language of that nation and country. You well understand what need I have of the powerful aid of your prayers as a protection for me living among those barbarians. It will be required that I shall live among them without any freedom to pray, without Mass and the Sacraments. It will happen that I shall be held responsible for all that may chance to occur between the French, the Iroquois, the Hurons and Algonquins, all of whom have subscribed to this treaty, if any difficulty arises, a thing not unlikely to happen. But what of that? My confidence is placed in God Who does not need our help for accomplishing His designs. Our single endeavor should be to give ourselves to the work and to be faithful to Him, and not to spoil His work by our shortcomings. I trust that you will beg this favor for me from God; after such great slothfulness in His service, I may at length begin to serve Him more diligently. And so, if I shall be employed in this mission, my heart tells me: "*Ibo et non redibo*—I shall go, but I shall not return." In very truth, it will be well for me, it will be a happiness for me, if God will be pleased to complete the sacrifice there where He began it, if the little blood which I shed there in that land will be accepted by Him as a pledge that I would willingly shed all the blood which I bear in all the veins of my body and of my heart. In conclusion, that Iroquois people "is the spouse of blood to me; this people have I espoused to me by my blood." Our Good Master who gained this people for Himself by His own blood, may open to it the door of the Gospel, if it pleases Him, and not only to this nation but to the four other nations allied and neighboring to them. Farewell, my dear Father, and beg God that He may join me with Himself, never to be separated from Him.

Isaac Jogues, S.J.

He waited at Montreal for the summons to the council scheduled for September 17 at Three Rivers. Eighty Huron canoes had swept down the St. Lawrence the week before, led by the plenipotentiaries who were to decide, after holding council with Onontio, on the Huron peace with the Iroquois. Montmagny and his suite, Lalemant and his consultors, came up to Three Rivers on September 11. Jogues was not required to attend the council unless the Hurons inclined to peace. If they voted peace with the Iroquois, if they named ambassadors to go to the Mohawk villages, he would accompany them. His flesh recoiled, his spirit flared triumphantly. He remembered what he had suffered; he knew the dangers to which he would be exposed, in body and soul; he would chance them all in the hope that he might announce the salvation of Christ to the Mohawks and through them to the confederated nations of the Iroquois. *Ibo et non redibo,* the phrase kept turning over in his mind. "I shall go, but I shall not return." He was content, if only he might go.

He was called to Three Rivers, and arrived there on September 19, as the council between Montmagny and the Hurons was being concluded. The Hurons accepted Onontio's wish that they pledge peace with the Mohawks and that they send an embassy to the Mohawk villages; but they were reluctant. They longed for peace; but they mistrusted the good faith of the Mohawks. They saw little advantage to themselves unless the four Upper Iroquois nations also entered into the negotiations. They formally requested that the Blackrobe, Ondessonk, should accompany Otrihouré and the two other envoys they were appointing.

Montmagny and Lalemant called Jogues before them. Directly and officially they asked if he still wished to venture once more into the Mohawk land, in company with the Hurons, and to remain among these savages for the winter. Father Jogues answered categorically, "Yes." He wished that beyond all things in life. He made clear his intention and his purpose. He would go primarily as a priest and a missioner, to bring the knowledge and the love of God to these pagans, to instruct and baptize them, to establish a Catholic church in their midst. In a secondary way, he went to assist the Hurons in their peace parleys. And then, also, he would forward in all ways possible the peace and the friendship that had already been established between the Mohawks and the French and Algonquins, and would strive to extend that treaty so that it would include the four other Iroquois nations. In this journey he would plainly signify his purpose and his aims by wearing his black robe rather than the secular clothes he had donned when he went as the representative of Governor Montmagny with Jean Bourdon.

Both the Governor and the Superior accepted this statement of purpose. Lalemant testified in an official communication to the Provincial of France, Father Estienne Charlet, that Jogues went "in order to return for the second time to his Mission of the Martyrs among the Hiroquois, purposing to maintain the peace there, and to manage there the interest and the affairs of Paradise." In his *Relation* he stated that "Father Jogues goes with the intention of spending the winter there, and, on all occasions which shall present themselves, to influence the minds and the affections of the savages, but most especially to care for the affairs of God and the riches of Paradise. He has much need of earnest prayers for the success of an enterprise so difficult." Subsequently, he declared that Father Jogues went "to the country of the Agneronon Hiroquois, to the end of maintaining the peace which they had so solemnly concluded, and in order to cultivate and augment the seed of the Gospel which he had begun to cast into that wretched and thankless land."

Among the orders he received from Montmagny was that of "doing all in his power to incline to peace all the Upper Iroquois whom he shall see in the villages of the Annierronnons (Mohawks); and, in case that they refused, he had commission strongly to urge the Annierronnons to prevent the other Iroquois from coming upon the Rivière des Prairies, where the Hurons pass, thus limiting their war sphere on the great River of Saint Lawrence very far beyond Montreal; or at least, to forbid the Upper Iroquois nations to approach the Island of Montreal or that land which lies directly north of their villages, as belonging in some sense to their district."

Prior to his journey in May, Jogues specified that "it is essential that he who accompanies me must be virtuous, docile to direction, courageous, one who would be willing to suffer anything for God." There was such a man at Three Rivers. Jean de la Lande was of the same quality as René Goupil and Guillaume Coûture. He was scarcely more than a lad, but he had already proved his worth as a practical woodsman, as an intelligent, prudent, virtuous and brave associate of the Jesuits in Quebec and Three Rivers. He had come out from Dieppe, his birthplace, with the high intention of devoting his life to the service of God in the New World. Upon his arrival in Quebec, he offered himself formally to the Superior as a *donné*, and vowed to work among the savages as lay assistant to the missioners, without any recompense except that of his perpetual support, to be obedient to the missioners and the Jesuit Superiors, and to live a life of celibacy.

Father Jogues, fully cognizant of what a winter among the Iroquois would mean and of the imminent dangers of the coming winter in particular, spoke to Jean de la Lande at length and in detail of what might occur. He told him of the hardships and fatigues of the journey. He explained to him the privations and sufferings he must endure, living in close contact with the savages, living exactly as the savages in all material things. He spoke plainly of the spiritual dangers, the temptations to impurity, the discouragement and despair that might overwhelm him. He pointed out to young de la Lande the necessity for patience, for charity, for the practice of all the virtues.

Warning de la Lande of the possibility of their being murdered, for the Iroquois were treacherous and the country was filled with madmen, fanatics and ruthless enemies of the French, he showed his mutilated hands and described the tortures to which he had been subjected, and those which de la Lande himself might have to endure. Worse than death was the slavery which they might be forced to suffer. All of it, without any concealment, Father Isaac related to Jean and urged the young man to stay at home along the St. Lawrence, or to go up among the Hurons, if he had the slightest tremor of fear. And he told of his own presentiment, as clear to his mind as a revelation: *Ibo et non redibo.*

Jean de la Lande listened, nor did he quail. Simply, generously, he said that he wished to go to live among the Mohawks with Father Isaac. "That good youth," declares Lalemant, "recognizing the dangers in which he was involving himself in so perilous a journey, protested at his departure that the desire of serving God was leading him into a country where he surely expected to meet death."

All was now settled. Jogues was triumphant. He added a postscript to the letter which he had written at Montreal on September 12th, to Father Castillon:

I am leaving in 2 or 3 days for the journey to the Iroquois. Again, for life complete in Our Lord.

21 Sept. at 3 Rivers.

He scribbled a short note to his confessor and friend, Father Buteux, who was absent on a mission to the Algonquins, saying: "I would like to spend another winter with you in order to train myself more thoroughly than I have done in virtue. But I would like still better to return for the third time to the country of the Iroquois."

II

A cold dawn spread over Three Rivers on Monday, September 24. It was a blue lingering of the night rather than a flushed break of the day. Father Jogues gave communion to young Jean de la Lande and finished his Mass in the Chapel de la Conception. They gulped down their breakfast hurriedly, and, accompanied by one or two of the Fathers who then happened to be at the residence, walked briskly down the road along the hillside to the strand of the river. Scarcely any of the French were about. Governor Montmagny, Father Lalemant, and all the important personages had departed a few days previously for Quebec. Sieur de la Poterie, the Commandant, had not yet emerged from his residence. Most of the people still slept, or were occupied in beginning the week's work. A knot of Hurons stood and haunched about the canoes.

All was hushed and silent, save the lapping of the waters and the muted voices which sounded hollow in the mist. The Hurons were ready to start. Jogues bundled his black cassock up about his waist, cleaned the sand and mire from his feet, and climbed into the canoe. Jean de la Lande raised himself carefully over the rim and took his place. Otrihouré and another Huron jumped in skillfully, and the Hurons in the other canoe settled themselves and held the paddles poised for the stroke. A third canoe was filled with Mohawks who were returning home for the winter. The Hurons standing about the shore uttered their guttural farewells. The Fathers raised their arms in benediction. The canoes glided into the fog.

On the second evening, Father Jogues' band turned the lip of land that banked the Richelieu River. They ascended the hill and encamped near the ruins of Fort Richelieu. The garrison had been withdrawn that summer, both because in wartime the fort had been ineffective as a barrier to the Iroquois and because peace with the Iroquois was now a certainty. The fort always had been regarded with especial hate by the Mohawks, and on its abandonment they had reduced it to a charred mound.

That night, among the ruins of the old fort, Jogues and the Hurons talked tensely. He realized fully how precarious was the situation. On the one side, the peace seemed to be firmly pledged. The Mohawk nation professed to be dealing honestly; it had faithfully fulfilled all the requirements of the code of statecraft sacred among the natives. As far as he could see, there was no ground for suspicion, no cause for alarm. And yet, there was some subtle, some intangible something that was disturbing and unsettling. As for himself and de la Lande, they were resolved to go forward and to dare what might be.

Not so with the Huron ambassadors. Neither they nor their chiefs had put such implicit trust in the Mohawk promises and fair words. They wanted peace, and they were willing to work for the peace under the moral suasion of the French; but their instincts told them to beware. Now, in the camp at Richelieu, when they were about to paddle down to and be swallowed up in the Mohawk territory, the Huron envoys were seized with dread. Their observations which could not be expressed in words, their intuitions, warned them against continuing the journey. They were convinced that somehow, somewhere, was a trap which would close in and destroy them.

Ondessonk argued with them and tried to quiet their trepidation. Otrihouré also strove to hearten them. But their courage was gone. The Huron ambassadors decided they would postpone their journey to the Mohawk villages. Pointing their canoe across the St. Lawrence, they wildly scurried back to their own people. Otrihouré, who had a special, personal claim of protection from the Mohawks, was alone resolute enough to continue with Jogues and de la Lande. About this time, there was an added cause for suspicion. The Mohawks deserted and drove their canoe off on a scouting expedition.

The three voyageurs struck out the next morning against the rippling flow of the Richelieu River. They were in the vast wilderness of the narrow river which cut its way between the close banks of the forests. They paddled for hours in the utter stillness, clambered over the rocks along the rapids and trudged along the portages. Their progress was slow, their labors were exhausting. After several days of struggle they reached the Lake of Champlain. They had expected, before this, to be meeting with stray bands of Mohawks. But not a living soul was passing up or down along the route, not a sound of anything human was anywhere heard. The quiet was strange and foreboding.

September had now turned into October. Autumn cooled the summer heats and sapped the green from the leaves and the grass. The hillsides along Lake Champlain were faded into brown and russet, and many of the trees showed their naked branches. The far elevations of the mountains were dull and depressing. All the land seemed to be desolated and so rugged as to be menacing. An ominous quiet seemed to be brooding over all the earth and the waters. Ceaselessly they pulled the canoes through the heavy calm, past the slow succession of banks until, about the middle of the second week of October, they twisted up the little stream to the rapids that poured the Lake of the Blessed Sacrament into Lake Champlain.

They climbed the trail through the woods, with the canoe over their heads, and debouched on the smaller lake. Even yet they encountered no Mohawks. They found no signs of parties who had recently passed along the way. There was nothing but the impenetrable mystery of the forests and lakes. A few days of paddling through the stupendous heights that hemmed in the Lake of the Blessed Sacrament brought them to the circular inclosure of Andiatarocté. It was about the twentieth day since they left Three Rivers. They had journeyed safely along the water route; there remained but three or four days along the trail through the mountains. Then they would be arriving at Ossernenon.

The three of them were worn out by now, and their store of food was sparse. Young Jean de la Lande had proved himself to be a lad of worth and mettle. He was more agile than René, more experienced in the ways of the wilderness, and far more venturesome. He had, too, the dogged fidelity of René Goupil and much of his simple faith. He had not been molded in the savage life, as had Guillaume Coûture, but he had the sharpness and intelligence of Guillaume.

All through the laborious days he had borne up strongly under the physical and mental strain, and his courage still flamed. He had listened eagerly to Father Isaac's instructions as to how he must comport himself among the Mohawks. He was prepared for any emergency. He prayed in unison with Father Isaac, and often expressed his spiritual joy that he should have been chosen for this service of God in the Mission of the Martyrs. His young eyes glowed and his heart expanded under the inspired words that *mon père* spoke to him. Again and again, he protested that he was ready for life or death, through love of God.

It was October 14 when they defiled along the leaf-strewn trail that led to Ossernenon. They were burdened down, all three of them, with the baggage of clothes and blankets and presents. They grew more apprehensive than ever when they were shrouded by the tree trunks and the overhanging branches. They mounted the rise of the path over the ridge of hills and dug their heels into it as they descended to the depression caused by the juncture of the Oiogué and Sacandaga rapids. A few days more and they would have the first welcome, friendly or hostile, at Ossernenon. It might be only a few hours, for most certainly there would be Mohawks along these well-traveled trails.

Father Jogues was exalted in spirit, now that he was coming back to the village he had dedicated to the Holy Trinity. He was at the ending of the journey that he had prayed for so terribly insistently, that he had longed for amid such desolation. He was back with the beloved Mohawks, he would sit at their fires in their cabins and talk to them of God and the mysteries of the Faith. He would try to convert his "aunt" and Honatteniate and other friendly ones; he would make these the corner stones for the Church, as he had helped for six years despite all the assaults of the devil to build the Church among the Hurons. He hurried his steps along the trail, so that de la Lande and Otrihouré could scarcely keep pace with him. He was never so happy, never so expectant in all his life. He had the thought that he was coming to his own home. When he had traveled this trail before, in the first journey, his steps lagged and he had begged Goupil and Coûture to escape, to die of starvation in the woods rather than face the tortures. Now he was encouraging young Jean to hurry along faster with him, and Jean, panting breathlessly, beamed with the ardor of an apostle.

A file of savages came toward them along the trail. Jogues halted, and called out a greeting. The savages melted away out of sight. He sharpened his eyes and peered anxiously through the trees. Again he shouted his welcome and announced that he was Ondessonk. The Mohawks emerged from the trees on all sides and closed in on him with blood-curdling warwhoops. Jogues stood fastened to the earth, shocked and amazed; Jean de la Lande froze beside him; Otrihouré was terrified. The Mohawks were streaked with crimson war paint. They swung their muskets before them, and held gleaming knives in their right hands. They howled and shrieked wildly, danced about him menacingly, as if they were about to fall on him and tear him to pieces.

He could not comprehend. He thought perhaps this was play-acting. He spoke to them in a friendly way and smiled but they drowned out his words with their screeches and glared at him fiercely. All of an instant the warriors leaped on him and de la Lande, bore them to the ground, pounded and rolled them around, and with violent rage tore off the black robe and underclothes of Father Jogues, and stripped him naked. They ripped off the garments of de la Lande, meanwhile beating him furiously.

Appalled, Jogues understood. This was a war party. The Mohawks repudiated the peace. These warriors were taking the trail to the St. Lawrence, to surprise the Algonquins and Hurons, to take the French unawares. His soul sickened at the terror of the thought. All was ended. There was war again. He began to understand the howls of the savages. They hated the French. They were going to massacre all the French. They hated him. He was an evil sorcerer. He plotted their ruin and death. They intended to cut him to pieces, to burn him at the stake, to split open his head, to eat his flesh.

Meanwhile, they were dragging him and de la Lande and Otrihouré along the path with them, triumphantly, to their village. They held their arch enemy, Ondessonk. They would revenge themselves on him. This time he would not escape them. Runners sped along the path as fast as their legs could carry them to announce that Ondessonk was captured and was being led into the village.

Father Jogues groaned in the abyss of his soul. He had dared death and he did not fear it. He was heartbroken for young Jean whom he had led with him; he would secure the release of the lad if he possibly could. He feared the havoc that would be wrought along the St. Lawrence; hundreds of Algonquins would be caught during the autumn and winter hunts; miserably the Hurons would perish. He was in terror when he thought of possible sudden, ruthless onslaughts on Montreal, even on Three Rivers. There would be no warning given. There was no help, now, save in the good God.

Driven madly along, he was prodded up the series of hills till he reached the ridge above the valley and river of the Mohawks. He padded down the incline with his persecutors to the flats by the bank of the river and the ford where he had first been caressed by the villagers. They mobbed about the place in a terrifying turmoil. They were struggling with one another, Jogues could see, arguing among themselves, threatening and imprecating. He and de la Lande were hurled into the midst of the throng. Some threatened him and lifted their arms as if to strike him. Others warded off the blows and pressed in to guard him. It was an angry, aroused crowd that rioted about him and split his ears with their cries. He and Jean, finally, were extricated, were hurried up the roadway to the summit of the hill, dragged through the gate of the stockade, and pushed violently into a cabin.

For the time being they were safe. They had been rescued by the Wolf and Turtle clans from the old enemies, the Bears. They were in the Wolfs' lodge, and no one of the Mohawks, however lawless, would dare to invade this sanctuary. Father Jogues "aunt," her grandson Honatteniate and some few friendly persons sat them on the mat and put food in their hands. They explained what had happened to change the minds of the people since his last visit. Part of the story was well known to him. Kiotseaeton, supported by the Wolf and Turtle and some less powerful clans, had advocated the peace with the French and their allies in good faith and with all sincerity. They had overcome the resistence of the strong union of the Bear families who raged violently, in and out of the national councils, against carrying on any peace negotiations. The Bears had aroused their kinsmen among the Upper Iroquois, the Oneidas, the Onondagas, the Senecas, the Cayugas, to support them, while the Mohawk Wolfs could not persuade their clansmen among these nations to follow their leadership. And so, after their temporary victory in pledging the Mohawks to the peace, the Wolfs were being worsted. That was the state of affairs since June when Ondessonk had visited them as ambassador.

Not many weeks after he had left them, the friendly Wolfs related, a few of the people fell sick. They were not disturbed much. But then others contracted the disease. It spread from cabin to cabin. It appeared in Andagaron, then in Tionontoguen. They invoked the sorcerers, they watched their dreams, they fulfilled the commands of their okis, they offered sacrifices to the demons, and made feasts; they danced and chanted and played games; they held sweats; but to no avail. The sickness became more prevalent during August. Many of the warriors and squaws and children died. By the beginning of September, the people were frantic. It looked as though they were being ruined by another epidemic.

There were some adopted Hurons who offered an explanation. They remembered how six or seven years before, their peoples were similarly afflicted; they blamed the disease on Ondessonk and the Blackrobes, and were on the point of murdering them time and time again. These Blackrobes were evil sorcerers, and Ondessonk was the worst of them. He and Echon and the other Blackrobes wrought frightful witchery. They wished to destroy all the native peoples so that they would have the land to themselves. They brought disease and pestilence and destruction wherever they went. They and the French were not truly seeking for peace; they were trying to annihilate the Iroquois. The sickness was brought on by Ondessonk, they asserted. Many of the Mohawks accepted their words.

In September, the corn in the fields down by the river began to wither, just when it should be fattening for the harvest. The stalks were shriveling, and the ears of corn were being destroyed by worms. There would be no corn for the winter, and without corn there would be starvation. Under this new affliction, the Mohawks grew more frenzied. Some demon was persecuting them. Again they consulted their sorcerers and wizards. Pitifully they employed their superstitions. But again to no avail. The crop was ruined.

Then they remembered the chest which Ondessonk had left in the cabin of his "aunt." The sorcerers pronounced their infallible judgment. Ondessonk had left an evil spirit locked up in this black box. They had accused him of this before he left, but he had denied it. True, he had opened the box in their presence and had shown them the articles inclosed in it. But he had fastened it in such a manner that no one of them could open it without smashing it. Why had he done this if he did not wish to conceal something from them? Ondessonk was a wicked magician, he was in league with the devil. He had left his demon, over which he had control, in this firmly fastened box. It was this demon of Ondessonk which was killing the people and destroying the corn.

The suspicion did not take long to become a firm conviction in the minds of many of the Mohawks. Ondessonk preached a strange doctrine when he was among them. He told them of a Deity who would punish them for their wrongdoings, of a place where they would burn forever after they died; he reprimanded them for certain of their actions and habits; he always sought out those who were sick and dying, and made queer motions over them, pouring water on their heads and saying some words of a charm; he made the sign which the Dutch told them was an abomination and for which they had killed the other Frenchman who came with Ondessonk. As an ambassador of the French, he did not wear his black robe, nor did he speak openly to them of his beliefs, as he did on his first visit. It was clear that he meant to deceive them and take them off their guard. He did not wish peace with them. He planned only to exterminate them. For that reason he locked up the evil demon in the chest.

They must destroy that chest left by Ondessonk. They came to the cabin where it was stored and demanded it. They would not listen to any assurances that the chest contained no evil spirit. They asserted they had proved conclusively that there was a demon in the box. They dared not smash it open, nor pry the bands apart. For then the demon would escape and would find some other place where it could lurk and continue to do them harm. Some of the more courageous among the sorcerers, those with powerful demons of their own who would protect them, took up the box left by Ondessonk and fearfully carried it out of the village and down the trail to the river. Some distance below, where the water was deep, they lifted it carefully out of their canoe and let it sink down into the water. The demon was now trapped and could not escape, but would perish. However, Ondessonk still lived. He had plotted to kill and ruin them. They had destroyed his demon. They had only to capture and murder him. Then they would be free of their curse.

At the time when the chest of Father Jogues was being destroyed, about the middle of September, the Mohawks held a council for the reopening of the discussions about peace. The Bear clan was stronger now, with the suspicion against Ondessonk and the French so clearly confirmed. Their orators pleaded with the assembly to remain loyal to the traditions of their nation and the doctrine of their ancestors. They pointed out the danger of the Mohawks alienating themselves from the alliances which their forefathers had established with the other Iroquois nations, and of their breaking all the bonds of blood and marriage with these nations which were their brothers and their children. With vivid recitals they recalled the murder of the Mohawks perpetrated by their ancient enemies, the Algonquin nations and by the Huron nation which they had sworn to subjugate.

The Bear chiefs swayed the minds of the people, now already unbalanced by the spread of the epidemic and the plague on the corn, and now quite firmly convinced that the French were contriving evil through witchcraft and the power of the evil spirit. Kiotseaeton and the peace advocates were repudiated. The council resolved to send presents and envoys to the Oneidas, the Onondagas, the Cayugas and the Senecas in order to reaffirm and consolidate the alliance and kinship of the Mohawks with them, and in order to indicate their willingness to join with them in their war expeditions against the French, the Hurons, and the Algonquins.

Father Jogues listened and understood. This was the end of all the peace efforts. The Mohawks had raised the bloody hatchet. They raised it treacherously and were giving no warnings that they were once more taking up the warpath. As for his own fate and that of de la Lande, he knew nothing. His friends told him that messengers had been sent through all the cabins and villages, announcing that a great council would be held the next night in Tionontoguen. The chiefs and the elders would then decide upon their fate.

III

It was on Wednesday evening, October 17, 1646, that Father Isaac Jogues and Jean de la Lande were brought captive into the village of Oneougiouré, formerly called Ossernenon. All that night their ears rang with threats and maledictions. "You will die tomorrow. Do not be surprised," one of the braves shrieked into Ondessonk's ear. Another, gloating, told him: "We will not torture you or burn you. Keep up your courage. We will strike you over the head with a hatchet. We will set your head on the points of the stockade, so that when we bring some of your brothers here as captives, they may still see you." Still another made as if to slash him with a knife, saying: "Let us see if this white flesh is the flesh of a manitou or demon." Jogues answered calmly: "No, I am nothing more than a man like you. And understand, I have no fear either of your torments or of death. I do not know why you threaten to kill me. I have come into your country to help you to preserve the peace, and to level the earth, and to show you the road to heaven. And you treat me like a dog. God governs the French and the Iroquois; He knows well how to punish you."

All through that night Oneougiouré was noisy with disputes. The clans of the Wolf and the Bear were in violent altercations, the one demanding safety for Ondessonk and the Frenchman, the other swearing they would kill the two of them. The chiefs were powerless to quell the rioting. They feared that the young braves, lusting for revenge and notoriety, under the impulse of dreams or their demons, would commit a deed that would be regretted. Both factions ranged through the cabin where Ondessonk lodged, and beset the doorways, some to tomahawk him if he emerged, others to obey their chiefs and guard him faithfully.

October 18th dawned. Emotions had quieted with the morning. Ondessonk and Jean were now accepted as public hostages. They were not to be troubled until the council was held and the elders had pronounced sentence. Jogues was warned by his friends that he must be most cautious, for there were many ready, on the slightest provocation, to strike him down. He was forbidden absolutely to venture out of the gates or to go beyond the stockade, unless with a strong guard about him. He was given back some of his clothes, so that he could appear in public without shame. He felt quite secure. The storm had played itself out, as usual, in the first violent gusts. Now the Mohawks would consider his presence more calmly, and with some logic reason out what had best be done. The moment of greatest peril was safely passed.

During the morning he made opportunity to talk to the chiefs, not as the docile, silent slave of four years ago, but with the air and the dignity of the ambassador he had been in June, though he did not pretend to hold that same office now. He professed boldly that he had come to them this third time as a Blackrobe, to teach them the trail to heaven, to instruct them in true thoughts, to reveal to them the knowledge of God. Facing them defiantly, he accused them of the basest treachery in violating the peace without warning, and he threatened them with the terrible wrath of Onontio and the French.

In regard to the little black box which he had left with them, he recalled how he opened it in their presence, how he showed them all the contents, how he had tried to make them see that no demon was shut up in it. He ridiculed their superstitions, and swore to them that he had had absolutely nothing to do with bringing the sickness and the blight on the corn. While he professed his sorrow for these afflictions, he begged them to rid themselves of their fancies and absurdities, to listen to the things he would tell them, to believe as he believed in the great God who ruled all men. They listened. Some approved while others flared out at him anew for being a sorcerer and a dealer in death.

That afternoon, the chiefs of all degrees, the elders of the families, all the responsible people of Ossernenon trailed out of the village and along the river path to Tionontoguen. They knew the arguments that would be presented on both sides. Kiotseaeton and the Wolfs would harangue for peace with the French and their allies. They would, failing in this, scarify those who were bringing dishonor on the nation by breaking out into war without signifying that resolution to Onontio. If they decided for war, let them release Ondessonk and his comrade, and send them back to their people to announce that the Mohawks had changed their mind and no longer were in favor of peace. Let them not commit an act of treachery that would disgrace them among all the nations, so that no one ever after would put faith in the word of a Mohawk.

The Bear orators would brush aside the thoughts of peace. They would appeal to the bonds of blood and alliances with the other Iroquois nations. They would point out that there was no need to truckle to the French for their trade, since they had the Dutch near by who would continue to supply them with guns and powder. They would instance the immemorial enmity with the Algonquins and cry for their extermination. They would demand that the Huron nations should be subdued and thus forced to form one people with them, as had been in the days of their fathers. The Mohawks had no need to placate Onontio, nor to give him warning of their change of policy, save by a sudden attack.

As for Ondessonk, he must be killed. He had wandered among them of his own free will, not as an envoy whose person must be protected. He was a Blackrobe in the employ of evil demons. Already he had committed hideous wrong by hiding his demon in his black box, by sending the disease, by destroying the corn. He would always practise his prayers and incantations and gestures. Arrogantly, he preached to them about his God; he was an offense to the gods and demons of the Mohawks. He must be sacrificed in order to placate Areskoui and their other friendly spirits.

Thus the orators would debate. Neither they nor any of the people could estimate the effect that their words would have. The nation was divided in opinion, as it had been for years. It had veered from war to peace, from peace to war. The people would listen to the speeches of the chiefs. In family groups they would weigh the arguments. In clans they would compare their findings. In the general council they would declare their decisions. Then only would the will of the nation be made manifest.

Oneougiouré was deserted and strangely quiet that Thursday afternoon. Jogues and de la Lande were in no way molested. Father Isaac spent these hours of peace in prayer with Jean, in raising the thoughts of the lad to God, in exhorting him to courage and confidence in the Providence of God. He explained the situation fully. It was possible that the council would condemn them to death, that they would both be murdered. It might be that he alone would be struck down, but that Jean would be held as a prisoner. Or else, both of them might be allowed to live but be forced to return to Three Rivers. This last, Jogues said, would probably happen. However, he instructed Jean what he should do in all emergencies.

About sundown, when the shadows were lengthening over the village, there came a young brave to the cabin. He sought out Ondessonk and invited him to visit another lodge where there were people who wished to eat and talk with him. Jogues recognized the man as belonging to the Bear clan, a man who had been somewhat hostile. To refuse this brave would be interpreted as an act of great discourtesy and would betray a suspicion that might breed greater ill-feeling. Spurning an invitation to eat in a cabin was an insult not easily forgiven. Besides, Jogues thought, to show fear of this brave would be cowardly.

He consulted with his "aunt" and the friends of his family. They were of two minds, as to whether it would be safe for him to venture out into the village or whether it would be more prudent to offer the proper excuses. Jogues was eager to make friends with the young brave and the Bears who had invited him. His "aunt" feared treachery. Nevertheless, she agreed that he should go. She sent Honatteniate, her grandson and the sworn brother of Ondessonk, to guard him. Jean was left in the lodge.

The smoky half-light of the October evening lingered over the cabins and the tang of autumn was cool in the air as Jogues emerged into the open. He and Honatteniate followed their guide silently through the subdued paths of the village till they arrived before the long house where their guide turned to pause. Jogues could discern in the dimness the rough carvings of the Bear signs on the doorpost. He looked quizzically at his guide, but the young brave gave back a stolid and expressionless stare. Jogues did not hesitate for long. Suspicion or fear, either one would give the Mohawk an advantage over him. Casually, then, he placed his hand against the stiff skin which hung down from the lintel and pushed it inward so that he might enter. Honatteniate followed closely after him. A blast of warm, smelly air assailed him. Through the heavy gloom and smoke he glimpsed the fires gleaming down the center of the long, narrow room, and saw the people dimly shadowed about them. He shoved with his shoulder against the shaggy skin and bent his head under the low doorway. He saw and knew no more.

Behind the doorpost a warrior stood, with a tomahawk poised ready to strike. The bowed head of Ondessonk came forward around the edge of the skin curtain. Honatteniate leaped into the entry, thrusting out his arm to ward off the blow he saw crashing down. The tomahawk slashed his forearm and thudded upon the head of Ondessonk. The guide sent Honatteniate reeling into a corner and with another blow the murderer smashed the skull of Ondessonk. Father Jogues lay as he fell, crumpled at the doorway of the lodge. The moment was still. No one spoke. The braves leaned over the bleeding head and the prostrate form. They whispered in awed tones that Ondessonk was dead.

Honattentiate roared curses on the murderers and rushed out of the cabin, shouting wildly. Aroused, the village came flocking to the cabin. The murderers and their friends dragged the body of Ondessonk out into the street. They set up a frenzied dance and chant of triumph. They had saved the nation. They had destroyed the great sorcerer, the Blackrobe Ondessonk. They had revenged themselves for all the evil he had brought on them. They had drowned his demon. They had split his head. They were free from his spells and charms. Into the mob, Ondessonk's "aunt" fought her way. She confronted the murderers. She raged against them: "You kill me!" she screamed shrilly in the darkness. "It is I myself whom you kill! He was my kinsman! He belonged to my family! You must pay the penalty! What will the other two villages say? You have not consulted them! You have not waited for the decision of the council! What will the others say about this murder, so unexpectedly, so rashly perpetrated?"

The people of the Bear pushed her aside. The braves bent over Ondessonk, scalped him, and with their long knives cut the head from the neck. They held it up, streaming with blood, and started down in procession through the dark lanes between the cabins, toward the corner of the stockade that faced to the north and the east. While some held flaring torches, others clambered up on the latticed scaffolding along the inner side of the palisades. They lifted up the head of Ondessonk. One of them jammed it down on the sharpened point of a pole at the angle of the walls. The face of Father Jogues looked across the valley of the Mohawks, over toward the trail which descended from the hills beyond, northward toward the St. Lawrence. With boasts and imprecations the Mohawks shrieked their defiance against the French and warned that all French palefaces would be slaughtered. Look at Ondessonk!

Another Frenchman still lived. He was concealed in the village. He must be found and killed. The mob spread out from the corner of the stockade and streamed through the lanes. Everywhere they searched for the young paleface named Jean. He was in the cabin of the Wolfs. He was under their protection. The leaders of the crowd would not dare to invade that cabin, for it would be a grievous offense to the families who lodged there and to all their kinsmen throughout the five Iroquois nations. They must force the Wolf family to surrender the Frenchman to them, or they must trick the Frenchman out into the open night.

Braves stood about the cabin, and in the darkness bellowed their threats and curses. They had killed Ondessonk. They would kill his brother. This other Frenchman was also a sorcerer. He talked to himself, when no one was listening; he lifted his head and eyes to the sky; he bent his knees on the earth and held himself upright; he made the hateful sign on his forehead and shoulders and breast; he had little beads tied together and flat pieces of iron with marks on them; he wove incantations with Ondessonk and invited deadly demons to descend on the Mohawks and destroy them off the face of the earth. He was an evil witch. He must be destroyed out of their midst, that very night, before he could do any more harm. If he were allowed to live, he would wreak a terrible revenge and call on his gods to punish them for murdering Ondessonk.

Young Jean de la Lande remained quietly sitting by the fire of Father Isaac's "aunt." The old squaw, after she had raged against the killers of her "nephew," hurried back to protect the other Frenchman from his assailants. She related to Jean what had happened, and warned him to beware. He must not move one step from the circle of the fire, she told him. She and Honatteniate, whose arm was deeply gashed by the blow of the tomahawk, and others of her young men haunched about Jean, guarding him closely. Beyond the doors and the bark walls, the village was in tumult. The raucous cries and excited voices sounded menacingly.

Jean waited. Father Isaac was dead. His body was cast somewhere on the streets, his head was pinned on the palisades. Jean prayed. He was doomed to death. Nothing could save him. He felt the tremor pass through him. He was feverish. He looked into the burning embers of the fire and watched the weird shadows that flickered through the cabin and across the posts and walls. Father Isaac was dead. He alone remained, the only white man in all the Mohawk villages. He prayed to God for courage. He examined his conscience. That day he had confessed his sins and Father Isaac had spoken the words of absolution. He was ready to die, for he knew he was in the state of grace, that he should not dread meeting God. He had pledged himself to follow Father Isaac, in life and death, for God's greater glory and service. He had known from the beginning that he might be murdered. Father Jogues had told him often that he must be prepared.

While Jean prayed and waited in meditation, the turmoil of the village softened into silence. The crowds were no longer shouting about the cabin and pressing against the walls. The savages were evidently gone off to their huts to sleep. Those of the cabin felt reassured. Nothing more would happen that night, so they wrapped themselves in their blankets and skins and laid themselves on their beds of twigs about the warmth of the fires. The silence of night brooded over Ossernenon. The fires crackled, the soft winds ruffled the bark walls, the people breathed heavily and snored. Jean stretched himself on the earth, in the darkness. Father Isaac was beyond this silence, beyond this world. He was with God, a martyr of Christ. He had hoped for so much. He was so certain that God would soften the hearts of the Iroquois. He was so brave. He knew he might die, and yet he was not afraid. He was not afraid of anything. He was a saint.

Jean remembered the story Father Isaac had told him about René Goupil; of how they had murdered René and thrown his body in the ravine; of how he had sought for the body, everywhere, since René was a martyr and his bones were sacred. Father Isaac had escaped then. He was not killed. He was kept a slave and then he managed to free himself. Guillaume Coûture had lived four years among the Mohawks. He was adopted by them, and became well liked and respected. Father Isaac's "aunt" was friendly and her family was powerful. They would probably protect him against the Bear clan. As he thought, he inclined to believe that he would not be put to death. At least, now that the village was quiet as the grave, he had nothing much to fear for the rest of that night. In the morning, the Mohawks of Ossernenon would be calmer and the chiefs holding council at Tionontoguen would make known their decision. The fires burned low. All were soundly asleep.

He grieved for his dear Father. Into his mind came the instructions Father Isaac had given him in case he survived. He must be faithful, he must have courage. The body of Father Isaac was outside, he believed, abandoned on the path not far from the cabin. Jean longed to see his Father. He wanted to recover some articles which Father Isaac carried with him. If he waited till the morning, he would not be allowed to venture out. Besides, the savages would have carried the body off and thrown it over the side of the ravine, as they did to the corpse of René. Now was the chance. It was dark, past midnight, and all the cabin and all the village was asleep. This was the time. He had a duty. He must slip out before the dawn and find Father Isaac. He would save the relics and bring them back to Three Rivers, if he were released or if he escaped. He listened intently. There was no sound.

Stealthily, Jean lifted himself to his feet and stepped slowly and carefully toward the door. It was so dark that he could scarcely see. He strained his eyes to discover the posts and the cracks of the door. He crept forward on his toes and safely reached the doorway. Cautiously, lest the skin barring the outer door creak, he pushed it aside, and felt the tingle of the night air on his face and neck. The night was clear and fresh. He could see more clearly now. The yellow paths were light, the dark cabins were heavy against the deep-blue sky. The winds sighed faintly as they rustled the dried leaves of the trees and there sounded the whir of the night creatures. No dark figures or shadows moved. He thought he knew where the body of Father Isaac lay. He would steal from the dark shelter of cabin to cabin.

More noiseless than Jean, blacker than the shadows of the trees and cabins, were the savages who lay motionless by the wall of his cabin. They were on guard through the stillness of the night. They rose like specters out of the earth, and before he could utter a cry crashed down the tomahawk upon his head. The blow felled him. Another blow, and another cracked his skull. They had the Frenchman, the brother of Ondessonk, the other sorcerer. He and Ondessonk had come together, they had prayed together, they had only one mind, to ask their God to bring ruin on the Mohawk nation. The braves did not rouse the village, but they laughed and rejoiced quietly among themselves. Expertly, they cut off his scalplock, and with the strong strokes of their knives they severed the head from the trunk. They left the body where it was, in the roadway. The head they carried over to the angle of the palisades, and there they placed it on the point of a pole, next to the head of Ondessonk.

The night passed quietly in Oneougiouré. The villagers stirred. The old squaw and Honatteniate and their families looked about for their Frenchman. They found his dead body a few steps from their door. The cabins were awake, the buzz of voices rose to a roar. In the first gleams of the morning sun the people rushed to see with their own eyes the heads of the two Frenchmen perched on the poles of the palisades. All of the Bear clan exulted and chanted and danced in triumph. Those of the Wolf and Turtle families burst with anger and threats and curses. They demanded revenge. Almost they were tempted to strike down the jeering Bears. They knew that all was over now. They were powerless.

Scarcely had the sun risen over the hills above the valley when messengers raced up the trail from the river flats and burst through the west gate of the stockade. They came from Tionontoguen, bearing the decisions of the council that had been debating through the night. They spoke to no one, nor listened to anyone, as was their custom, until they had reached the cabin where the Frenchmen lodged and had eaten of the food placed before them. Then they announced their message. The great chiefs and the ancients of the Mohawks had ordained: Ondessonk and his French brother were free; no harm must be done to them; they were ordered out of the Mohawk village and were to be escorted back to Three Rivers.

At first in silence, and then in an uproar, the villagers heard the judgment of the chiefs. It happened as the Bear clan had feared. Slyly they rejoiced in that they had circumvented the Wolf, who had sought the release of the French. They had clamored for the death of Ondessonk four years ago, but the Wolf and Turtle always obstructed them. They had tried to prove from the beginning that he was an evil genius, a malicious sorcerer, a Blackrobe who preached an unheard-of doctrine, who prayed and made signs hateful in their eyes, who was in league with the enemy demons. They feared him always, even when he pretended to be a harmless slave. He had escaped from them through the treachery of the Dutch, just when they were surely going to murder him. He had deceived the people when he came dressed like other Frenchmen, calling himself an ambassador. But then he came back dressed in his black robe, after he had begun their ruin through the demon locked up in his black box. When they killed his demon by drowning it in the river, he was in their power. He was no longer protected. Still, as they had feared, the council even then sought to let him live, foolishly, since he was an enemy who would keep on striving to destroy them. Now they had destroyed him outright, and they had destroyed his brother. There was nothing more for the council to debate.

The messengers who had come to Oneougiouré ordering the release of Ondessonk, immediately turned back along the trail to announce his murder. The chiefs and sachems, still assembled at

Tionontoguen, heard of the murders with amazement and consternation. Hurriedly they assembled in a new council. In a public session they all agreed in condemnation of the act. Even the chiefs of the Bear clan expressed regret and blamed the deed on the senseless, rash, unscrupulous young men of their tribe. The Wolf and the Turtle orators vehemently denounced the murderers and their accomplices. They cried woe on this treachery that would forever shame and humiliate the Mohawks before all nations.

Above all others, the lordly Kiotseaeton bewailed the death of his brother, Ondessonk. Untold evils would descend upon the Mohawks, he prophesied, because of this mutinous, rebellious deed carried out by the young men of the Bears. Now there was no alternative but war. This war, he foretold as one seeing a vision, was to bring ruin upon his people. The more that the hatchets and the arms of the Iroquois were raised for war, so much the worse it would be for the nation, so much the greater would be the calamities that would befall his people.

No punishment could legally be inflicted upon the murderers of Ondessonk and the young French paleface. Nevertheless, Kiotseaeton and his colleagues still hoped to preserve good relations with Onontio and the French. They were jealous of the honor and faith of their nation, as they were sincerely outraged by the perfidy of their own warriors. They therefore commissioned the Huron, Otrihouré, who had been the comrade of Ondessonk, to assure Onontio that the Mohawks had no intention of breaking the peace and waging war against the French, that they were hostile only to the Algonquins. Furthermore, Otrihouré was instructed to announce to Onontio that the Mohawks would refrain from warlike acts until they had clearly announced their intention to repudiate the peace with the Algonquins. Finally, they commissioned the Huron to carry back presents which would speak to Onontio, saying that the Mohawks apologized for the killing of Ondessonk and his white brother, that Kiotseaeton and the chiefs were so indignant that they had difficulty in restraining their arms against the murderers, that they would like to kill and exterminate all the proud, uncontrollable madman in their midst. But Otrihouré was also killed before ever he reached Three Rivers.

So grieved and humiliated were the chiefs that they counseled all the people to keep secret the vile deeds. Nevertheless, the news leaked from the mouths of some of them down at the Dutch village of Rensselaerswyck. Arendt Van Corlaer, Dominie Megapolensis, Jean Labatie and the other burghers were horrified. They were fond of Isaac, priest and Jesuit though he was. They made diligent inquiries as to the cause and the details of his death. They could learn but little, since the Mohawks were secretive. No one would admit that he witnessed the affair. Each one solemnly swore that he was not in Oneougiouré that night. All that they would admit they knew was that Ondessonk was struck down by young braves belonging to the Bear clan, and that their act was in disobedience to the desires of their elders.

Jan Labatie, the interpreter of the Dutch, collected the scant bits of information he could pry out of the savages and forwarded an account to New Amsterdam, to his friend, Johannes La Montagne, a French Huguenot. In due time, Father Jogues "aunt" came down to Rensselaerswyck and gave to Dominie Megapolensis all the goods of Ondessonk that she had been able to save from the rapacious hands of the Iroquois. His possessions were few, a pair of pantaloons, a small missal, a breviary, a ritual and a few trinkets.

Long since, his body and that of John de la Lande had been dragged down the hill under the stockade and across the flats to the Mohawk River, where they were carried off by the current. Through October, through November, through the bleak winter, on the point of the palisades overlooking the valley, remained impaled the withered heads of John de la Lande and Isaac Jogues.

EPILOGUE

How the Trails Converged

DURING the month of October, 1646, Father Jérôme Lalemant was busily engaged in his room at Notre Dame de Recouvrance, on the heights of Quebec, writing *The Relation of What Occurred Most Noteworthy in the Missions of the Fathers of the Society of Jesus in New France in the Years 1645 and 1646.* In the chapter which he devoted to a record of the peace negotiations with the Iroquois, he began: "When I speak of a Mission among the Iroquois, it seems to me that I speak of a dream, and yet it is a truth. It is with good right that it is made to bear the name of the Martyrs; for besides the cruelties which those barbarians have already inflicted upon some persons impassioned for the salvation of souls; besides the pains and fatigues which those who are destined to this Mission are bound to incur—we may say with truth that it has already been crimsoned with the blood of one Martyr; for the Frenchman who was slain at the feet of Father Isaac Jogues, lost his life for having expressed the sign of our creed on some little Iroquois children, which so greatly offended their parents that they, imagining that there might be some spell in this action, made of it at once a crime and a martyrdom."

He continued: "Add to this, that—if it be permitted to conjecture, in things which indicate great probabilities—it is credible (if this enterprise succeed) that the designs which we have against the empire of Satan for the salvation of these peoples, will not yield their fruits before they be sprinkled with the blood of some other Martyrs."

Lalemant completed the *Relation* and dated the covering letter as of October 28, 1646. He did not know that his conjectures were not only probable, that they were not only credible, but that they had become facts. He did not know, he would not know for many months, that Father Isaac Jogues and Jean de la Lande, ten days before, on October 18, had sprinkled the Mohawk land with their blood and were become martyrs of Christ.

In early November, the first snows fell along the St. Lawrence and the French at Quebec, at Three Rivers, at Ville Marie made snug their homes for the winter. They were free from the menace of the Iroquois. But strangely, unlike the early winter of last year, no Iroquois visited the settlements and none were seen in the forests hunting the moose. On November 17, some Hurons following the chase near Montreal were captured by some enemies. Two weeks later, two Frenchmen who were canoeing up the St. Lawrence beyond Montreal mysteriously disappeared. Father Le Jeune, again stationed that winter at Montreal, grew apprehensive. To his inquiries, the Hurons and Algonquins would offer no explanation. They had heard nothing from the Mohawk land. Le Jeune was troubled about Father Isaac. He stored away carefully the few scraps of paper he had found after Isaac left for the Mohawks, a Litany which the Father had devised for his own devotion, the notation of words in the Iroquois language which he had been memorizing.

December came and went, then January of 1647, and February and March. It was a mild winter, scarcely a winter at all. One would think, reflected Father Buteux at Three Rivers, that the Iroquois would be flocking up to the north, now that peace was established. But no Mohawks were seen anywhere, and no news came passing out of the forests. It seemed ominous, and Jacques Buteux increased his prayers before the Blessed Sacrament for the safe keeping of Isaac and Jean. On Ash Wednesday, while all the people were at Mass, two houses at Three Rivers were ransacked. The evidence pointed to the fact that the marauders were Iroquois. A week later, a band of Algonquins raced in with the news that they had been pursued by a large party of Iroquois. Then in quick succession came further reports of attacks, of captures, of massacres.

By April, the Algonquins were convinced that the Mohawks were on the warpath. In a council held with Governor Montmagny on April 6 at Three Rivers, they proved to his satisfaction that the Mohawks had dug up the war hatchet, and were violating the peace without having given any warning. The Algonquins resolved to start on the warpath and Montmagny finally gave his assent and added French soldiers to their band. It was war, once more a bloody war with the Iroquois.

What would be the fate of Father Jogues? He had left in September; it was now April, and nothing had been heard of him. Was he dead? Had he ever reached the Mohawk land? Was he alive? Was he held as a hostage or as a slave in the Mohawk villages? Would he escape, would he ever return? No one knew. Still, they hoped. On April 8, 1647, Lalemant and his consultors discussed the matter of sending Father Adrien Daran to the Hurons; in his diary he recorded: "Father Daran's departure was agreed upon, in case there should be found a good and prudent boatman; otherwise, he must wait for the return of Father Jogues." All through April they waited, and through May when the rivers were open and they daily expected to learn what had happened during the winter among the Mohawks.

Up at Three Rivers, on the night of June 4, Father Buteux was aroused by a pounding on the door. Ignatius Otouolti, the good Huron friend of the Blackrobes, stood on the threshold with his son. He explained that his son had been captured and adopted by the Mohawks, but had just escaped from the Iroquois party he was accompanying. He brought sad news: Ondessonk had been killed. Buteux questioned the son, but could extract little information. The fact was true. Buteux had known it in his deepest soul all winter. He knew Father Isaac was dead. Just that morning, Lalemant had sailed from Three Rivers for Quebec in the ship with Governor Montmagny. He must be informed immediately. Buteux sat down at his table and in the light of his candle wrote to Lalemant:

Dear Reverend Father: Pax Christi.

This night there arrived a young man in a wretched little Iroquois canoe: he is the son of the good Ignace, your host. This Huron was with the Iroquois that we had intended to attack. This band left the Iroquois country in the autumn, before Father Jogues arrived among the Iroquois. Here is what this young man reports, not of himself, but of others, of what he has learned regarding Father Jogues. He says, then, that some Iroquois, having resolved to take up the war again, a good part of the nation did not wish to consent. But that, at the end, the majority concluded in favor of war; that diverse bands went out into divers places, to Montreal among others, where they took two Frenchmen, of which this one knew nothing. Another band met Father Jogues at two days journey from the country; this band stripped him and his companion, de la Lande, naked. He passed beyond to the village, where they slew at once de la Lande, and a Huron who was of their canoe. They put off for a day and a night the death of Father Jogues, who was finally murdered. I have not been able to gather any other circumstance of this glorious martyrdom. Your Reverence knows well that to press a savage who does not talk, except to say yes, is to result in making him lie and be a deceiver. Following this death, the Iroquois Agneronnons (Mohawks) and others resolved to come to war in the winter to the number of 700. They set out in effect for this purpose. But the rigor of the weather made 500 return, so that there were not more than 200 who came to these parts and separated into four bands. It is a consolation for those at Montreal to have been with him during a period of two years, and it is for me a confusion on one side not to have profited by his example, and a consolation on the other side, to have been the companion of a martyr.

Your humble servant in Christ,

Jacques Buteux.

In his diary, Father Lalemant recorded the receipt of Father Buteux' letter: "On the 4th of June we set out to return from 3 Rivers; on the 5th, we arrived at Quebek. The same day, about 11 o'clock, a Shallop arrived from 3 rivers, which informed us that the son of Ignace outouolti had returned from the yroquois to 3 rivers—who announced among other matters the death, or rather the murder of Father Jogues and his companion Lalande, for whom the next day we said a high mass for the dead."

At Montreal, on June 8, a canoe floated down the St. Lawrence. A squaw, all alone, paddled it. She was a Christian Algonquin, Marie Kamakatewingwetch. They brought her to Ville Marie and nursed her, for she was in a state of collapse. She related that she had been captured and tortured in their village by the Oneida Iroquois in April. A few weeks later, while the snow was still covering the earth, she escaped. She started to journey to the St. Lawrence, without food, without weapons. All through the weeks of May she kept on with incredible fortitude and strength making her way through the interminable forests. Half-dead, she reached the St. Lawrence and chanced upon an Iroquois war party from whom she stole the canoe she paddled.

Marie had news of Ondessonk. In April, when she was captured, on the journey she asked her guard if there was not a Blackrobe in the Iroquois village. "No," he answered abruptly. "The French were killed before we came on the warpath." She did not believe the Iroquois, then. She and the other Algonquin Christians hoped to see Ondessonk and confess their sins. They reached the Oneida village, where they were exposed naked, the men on one platform, the women on the other. Marie recounted: "As soon as they were on these stages, they all requested, both men and women, to speak to Father Isaac Jogues, that he might baptize the catechumens and hear the Christians in confession. Some Algonquin woman, who had long been captive in that country, quietly approached them and told them that the Father had been wretchedly murdered."

Still other confirmations of Ondessonk's death were offered by more escaped Hurons and Algonquins. The fact was certain, but none of the details could be discovered. Le Jeune at Montreal, Buteux at Three Rivers, Lalemant at Quebec, sought everywhere for news. All was blanketed in mystery.

In late June, 1647, the ships from France began arriving in the lower St. Lawrence. One of them, which had called en route at the settlement at Acadia, carried a packet addressed to Governor Montmagny. In great haste he communicated its contents to Father Lalemant. It contained two letters from the Dutch colonies:

Monsieur:

I have already written a reply to that which it pleased you to honor me with by Father Jogues, dated the fifteenth of May. I sent my reply to Fort Orange so that it might be delivered to the said Father Jogues. But he did not return, as was expected, and so it was not sent immediately. This letter, then, will be to thank your Excellency for the remembrance which you have had of me, a favor which I shall endeavor to reciprocate, if it will please God to give me an opportunity.

I send this through the northern region, by means of the English or of Monsieur d'Aunay, in order to inform you of the murder which the barbarous and inhuman Maquois or Iroquois have committed upon Father Isaac de Jogues and his companion. Also, I would inform you of the designs they have to surprise you under the pretext of a visit, as you will see by the letter inclosed, which, although it is poorly written and spelled, will acquaint you, to our great regret, with the particulars of it all. I am grieved in that the subject of this letter is not more agreeable. But the importance of the matter has not permitted me to be silent about it. Our Minister up in the other settlement has carefully inquired of the chiefs of this village concerning the reason for this wretched deed, but he could get no other response from them except that the said Father had left the devil among some clothes which he had stored in their custody, who had caused their Indian corn, or maize, to be devoured by worms.

This is all that I am able to write to your Excellency for the present. Praying God that He may guard you and yours from this treacherous nation, and assuring you that I am your very humble and obedient servant,

Willem Kieft.

From Fort Amsterdam, in New Netherland, 14th November, 1646.

The enclosure sent by Director General Kieft was the communication forwarded by Jan Labatie, the interpreter at Rensselaerswyck, to Johannes La Montagne at New Amsterdam:

Praise be to God, at Fort Orange.
Monsieur La Montagne.
Monsieur:

My dear Monsieur, I did not wish to lose this occasion of letting you know about my welfare. I am in good health, thank God, and pray God that it may be so with you and your children. For the rest, I have not much to tell you, except how the French arrived the seventeenth of the present month at the fort of the Maquois. This is to inform you how those ungrateful barbarians did not wait until after they had actually arrived in their cabins, where they were stripped all naked, without shirts, save that they gave them each a breech-clout to hide their wretched plight. The very day of their arrival, they began to threaten them and that immediately, with heavy blows of fists and clubs, saying: "You shall die tomorrow! Do not be astonished. But we will not burn you. Have courage. We will strike you with an axe, and place your heads on the palisades, so that when we capture your brothers, they may see you there, still." You must know that it was only the nation of the Bear that put them to death. The nations of the Wolf and the Turtle did all that they could to save their lives, and said to the nation of the Bear: "Kill us first." But alas, they are no longer in life for all that. Know that, then, on the eighteenth, in the evening, they came to call Isaac to supper. He got up and went away with that savage to the lodge of the Bear. As he was entering into the lodge, there was a traitor with his hatchet behind the door. On entering, he split open his head; then, immediately, cut off his head and set it on the palisade. The next morning, very early, he did the same with the other Frenchman, and threw their bodies into the river. Monsieur, I have not been able to know or to hear from any savage why they have killed them. For the rest, their desire and undertaking is to go with three or four hundred men, that they may try to surprise the French, so that they may do the same with them as they did with these others. But God grant that they may not accomplish their designs. It would be desirable that Monsieur (Montmagny) be warned, but there is no way that we are able to do it from here. Monsieur, I have no more to write, but that I remain,

Your very humble and affectionate servant and friend.

Jan Labatie.

Monsieur, I beg you to give my respects to the Governor.
Written at Fort Orange, October 30, 1646.

During July and August, the Iroquois everywhere besieged the St. Lawrence. They were invincible. In September, a combined force of French and Algonquins went on a scouting expedition and succeeded in overpowering a small band, killing seven and capturing one. Jean Amyot, the boy whom Father Jogues carried up to the Hurons in 1636, now grown to a man, discovered a savage concealed in a tree trunk. The Algonquins claimed this sole prisoner and brought him in triumph to Three Rivers and thence to Quebec, where they intended to torture and kill him.

Governor Montmagny questioned the Mohawk Iroquois very closely, asserts Lalemant in the *Relation* of that year, "on various points; to which questions, his answers were as follows: Father Jogues, he said, was not killed by the general consent of the three Iroquois villages; he was not beaten or stripped, but simply struck down. (I will say in passing, with reference to this matter, that we attach more credence to the letters sent by the Dutch than to the words of this prisoner—because we have strong suspicions that it was he himself who killed the Father; for a Huron who had escaped from that country of the Iroquois, when he saw this Iroquois in the hands of the French, said to him: 'Comrade, what can you expect from those who have captured you, since you were unlucky enough to have slain a person whom they loved.' Furthermore, when the interpreter asked him what was the name of the man who murdered the Father's companion, he named him without delay; but when the man was asked the name of him who had taken the Father's life, he hung his head without saying aught. He was urged during two days, but would not open his lips. Finally, he spoke the name of an Iroquois.)"

The Iroquois never actually confessed to the murder of Father Jogues. But he listened to the Blackrobes at Quebec. They related: "It must be confessed that the spirit of Jesus Christ breathes where it pleases. This poor man astonished us all. He gave marked evidence of his belief, and asked pardon of God for his transgressions. 'Yes, I believe,' he said. 'I wish to go to heaven. But I am grieved to have offended Him Who has made all. Jesus, pardon me! Jesus, pardon me!' he said in his own language. 'Do not doubt,' he added, 'that I believe with all my heart what you teach me. And since we must all appear before God, according to your saying, at that time reproach me with treachery if my heart has not now the belief which my mouth declares to you.' These excellent inclinations softened all who were near. He was baptized, and was made to bear the name of Father Isaac Jogues—whom he himself had killed, as some said."

On September 16, 1647, the Iroquois was baptized Isaac Jogues by Father Druilletes. He was handed over to the Algonquins, but with an order from Governor Montmagny that they were merely "to exact justice from him," and that they must not "torture him as long as is their custom, or reduce him to a filthy nakedness, or make quarry of him like dogs."

In October, just one year after he had slain Father Jogues, he was burned to death and his charred remains were cast into the St. Lawrence.

The winter of 1647 passed, but no further revelations about the death of Father Jogues and Jean de la Lande were gathered. On May 30, 1648, while some Frenchmen were working on their nets opposite Three Rivers, a native ran out of the woods and swam toward their boat. He climbed into their canoe and explained he was an Iroquois, but friendly. Immediately, another savage appeared; he clambered into the boat, and said he was an Huron adopted by the Iroquois. Both were peaceful in their manner; they were willing to go over to Three Rivers. The French clamped them in chains, for they knew the Iroquois, who "act every sort of personage in order to deceive all classes of persons; their might is their right; their interest is their fidelity; their treachery, their politeness."

Under the questioning of Monsieur de la Poterie, the Commandant at Three Rivers, the Iroquois claimed that he was Honatteniate, the grandson of Father Jogues' "aunt." He was recognized as one of the Iroquois captured in May, 1645, and released later through the intervention of Governor Montmagny. Ever since that time, the Iroquois protested, he had been a brother to the French and carried in his body a French heart. He assured de la Poterie that he had pleaded with the Mohawks for the preservation of the peace, but that his nation rejected the arguments of the peace party.

When Commandant de la Poterie asked him about Father Jogues, he exclaimed: "I have always intended to give you information of the treason and treachery of my fellow-countrymen, but I have been unable to do so until now, when I have thrown myself into your hands." The Iroquois testified, "that he had opposed himself to those who killed Father Isaac Jogues; and that he had received on his own arm the first blow that was dealt at the good Father, of which he showed the scar." In addition, he declared "that, after the death of the Father, he had become the protector of the Frenchman who accompanied him; that he had forbidden him to go far from him, because he saw that his life was not safe; but that the young man had gone to get something, I know not what, that he had brought with him, and was killed with a hatchet by those who watched him."

The French were suspicious of this savage who identified himself as Honatteniate. At first his self-vindication was not credited and his feet were kept shackled. He was suspected of some deep treachery. Gradually, his protestations that he wished to be a Frenchman were somewhat believed. He was given the name of Le Berger and released from Three Rivers. He went off to the forests but always returned without fear. Sometimes he brought with him some of his countrymen. The French were unable to decide what should best be done with the man. Some demanded that he be killed as a spy and traitor. Others held that he was innocent and that he truly wanted to be adopted by the French. It was decided that, lest he should prove treacherous, he should be transported to France.

Le Berger never manifested any wish to return to the Mohawk village. Nevertheless, the French, when they were bringing him down to Quebec, bound him securely with cords and irons each night. Always, he was found free of his shackles. The French were amazed. His only explanation was that his bonds fell off when he prayed to the great God of the French: "Thou who hast made all things, Thou knowest well that it is wrong for the French to treat me so roughly, taking me for a traitor. Thou knowest well that I am not a traitor. Have pity on me." He begged for baptism, but the French still suspected him of diabolical intentions. On October 31, 1649, he was shipped to France, arriving at Havre de Grace on December 7. He was in poor health on board the vessel, and, in addition, suffered an injury to his leg so that he was put in the hospital at Dieppe. He edified all who saw him, and continually asked to be baptized since he knew what the Blackrobes taught and could say all his prayers.

On January 22, he was brought to Paris and four days later was found to be mortally sick with a high fever. He was loved by everyone, but even yet, despite his pleadings, he was refused baptism. It was only half an hour before he died that they poured the saving water on his head. Such was the felicity, asserts the chronicler, "of an Iroquois who had, perhaps, eaten his share of more than fifty men." Father Lalemant wrote, in reference to Le Berger's claim about attempting to save Father Jogues: "That stroke upon his arm, received through charity, was perhaps the stroke of his predestination, for it may certainly be believed that this good Father obtained from Our Lord in Heaven the salvation of this man's soul in reward for his attempt to save the Father while in the body."

Thus was completed through God's providence the drama enacted at the entrance of the Bear's cabin in Ossernenon on the evening of October 18, 1646. Father Jogues was struck down, and his soul was released for heaven. The murderer was burned to death by the Algonquins just one year later, but not before he was prepared for happiness by baptism. The loyal guard who had attempted to save Father Jogues was most certainly welcomed into eternity four years later. The prophecy of Kiotseaeton spoken as the Mohawk obituary of Ondessonk came true in the years that followed. The more that the hatchets and the arms of the Iroquois were raised in war against the French, so much the worse it would be for the nation, so much the greater would be the calamities that would befall his people, said Kiotseaeton.

And so it happened. For a few years the Iroquois ravaged and massacred the Hurons and the Algonquins and the French. But then, the penalty of temporal punishment fell upon the five Iroquois nations and they, too, were crushed and dispersed. They had shed the blood of martyrs, however, and that blood was the seed of salvation for them. René Goupil, Jean de la Lande, and Isaac Jogues interceded with God for their persecutors. In 1649, the fresh marytrs struck down by the arms of the Iroquois, Jean de Brébeuf, Antoine Daniel, Charles Garnier, Noël Chabanel and Gabriel Lalemant, added their prayers for the conversion of the Iroquois peoples. The while these eight martyrs offered their pleas before the Great Throne, their brother Blackrobes were down among the Iroquois, instructing them, baptizing them, and gathering them into the fold of Christ. From their stock, within a generation, emerged that saintliest of souls, Kateri Tekakwitha, the virgin of the Mohawks.

The centuries are lengthened out. In 1647, Father Jérôme Lalemant officially recorded in the *Relation* for that year: "We have honored this death as the death of a Martyr; and, although we were in various places, several of our Fathers—without knowing aught from one another because of the distances between these places—although they could not resolve to celebrate for him the Mass of the Dead, have indeed offered this adorable Sacrifice by way of thanksgiving for the blessings that God had extended to him. The laymen who knew him intimately, and the Religious Houses, have honored this death, feeling inclined to invoke the Father rather than to pray for his soul.

"It is the thought of several learned men, and this idea is more than reasonable, that he is truly a martyr before God, who renders witness to heaven and earth that he values the Faith and the propagation of the Gospel more highly than his own life—losing it in the dangers into which, with full consciousness, he casts himself for Jesus Christ, and protesting before His face that he wishes to die in order to make Him known. This death is the death of a Martyr before the Angels. It was with this in view that the Father yielded up his soul to Jesus Christ and for Jesus Christ. I say much more than this: not only did he embrace the means for publishing the Gospel which have caused his death, but more, one may affirm that he was killed through hatred for the doctrine of Jesus Christ, as here follows."

Father Lalemant proved to the satisfaction of himself and of those who knew Father Jogues and of the Catholics of France and of New France, whether copper-skinned or paleface, that: "Just as of old, in the primitive Church, the reproach was cast against the children of Jesus Christ, that they caused misfortunes everywhere, and as some of them were slain on that account, likewise are we persecuted because by our doctrine, which is no other than that of Jesus Christ, we depopulate, as they say, their countries. And it is for this doctrine that they have killed the Father: and consequently, we may regard him as a martyr before God."

What Father Lalemant and his contemporaries contended before 1650 has been confirmed infallibly nearly three hundred years later. Father Isaac Jogues, René Goupil and Jean de la Lande were never regarded otherwise than as martyrs and saints. The time came in 1925 when, after careful examination of their lives, after an investigation into the manners of their deaths and the motives of their assailants, Pope Pius XI decreed that it was permitted to venerate them in public prayer and to apply to them the title of Blessed. The same Sovereign Pontiff, on June 29, 1930, pronounced the final and irrevocable and unerring verdict whereby the heroic missioner and his two humble companions were raised to the altars of the universal Church as Saint René, Saint Jean, and Saint Isaac.

Imprimi Potest:
Edward C. Phillips, S.J.
Provincial, Maryland-New York

Nihil Obstat:
Arthur J. Scanlan, S.T.D.
Censor Librorum

Imprimatur:
✠Patrick Cardinal Hayes
Archbishop of New York

Bibliography

I. The primary material has been gathered from the writings of the contemporaries of Isaac Jogues. Of this, the principal sources are:

The Jesuit Relations and Allied Documents, edited by Reuben Gold Thwaites. 73 volumes. Cleveland: The Burrows Brothers Company, 1896-1901.

Rapport de l'Archiviste de la Province de Québec pour 1924-1925, edited by Pierre-Georges Roy. Quebec, 1925.

Documents in the Archives of Collège Sainte-Marie, Montréal.

Lettres de la Marie de l'Incarnation. 3 vols. Tournai, 1876. *Écrits Spirituels et Historiques: Marie de l'Incarnation,* edited by Dom Albert Jamet. Paris, Quebec. A L'Action Sociale, Lim., 1929.

Documentary History of the State of New York, Vol. IV, edited by E. B. O'Callaghan. Albany, 1851.

Documents Relative to the Colonial History of New York, Vol. I, edited by J. R. Brodhead. Albany, 1856.

Documents Relating to the Towns Along the Hudson and Mohawk Rivers, edited by B. Fernow. Albany, 1881.

Ecclesiastical Records: State of New York, edited by Hugh Hastings. Albany, 1901.

II. Supplementary material has been collected from writers of the seventeenth and eighteenth centuries who had access to documents now lost, and who preserved the traditions of the sixteenth century. Worthy of mention among these are:

Alegambe, S.J., Philippe. *Mortes Illustres,* etc. Brussels, 1655. Rome, 1657.

Tanner, S.J., Mathia. *Vita et Mors eorum,* etc. Prague, 1675.

Forest, S.J., René Guillaume. *La Vie du P. Isaac.* (Manuscript.) Orléans, 1747.

Forest, S.J., Abbé Jean-Baptiste Pierre. *Vie du R. P. Isaac Jogues.* (Manuscript.) Orléans, 1792.

Du Creux, S.J., François. *Historiae Canadensis Libri Decem.* Paris, 1664.

Charlevoix, S.J., F. X. de. *Histoire de la Nouvelle-France.* 3 vols.

Paris, 1744. *History of New France.* Translated and edited by John Gilmary Shea. 6 vols. New York, 1866.

Le Clercq, Récollet, Christian. *Premier Etablissement de la Foy dans la Nouvelle-France.* Paris, 1691. *First Establishment of the Faith in New France.* Translated with notes by John Gilmary Shea. New York, 1881.

Sagard, Récollet, Gabriel Theodat. *Histoire du Canada.* Paris, 1636. New edition, 4 vols. Paris, 1866. *Le grand voyage du pays des Hurons.* Paris, 1632. New edition, Paris, 1865.

Beauvais de Préau, Nicholas. *Essais Historiques sur Orléans.* Orléans, 1778.

Rigault, Georges. Orléans et le val de Loire. Paris. Edition, 1914.

Monumenta Germaniae Pedagogica. Vol. V. *Ratio Studiorum of 1599.* Edition, 1887.

III. Additional material that is well authenticated, confirmation of sources, deductions and observations derived from original research, and the like, have been incorporated in the narrative. These works have been published during the nineteenth and twentieth centuries. From the very great number of books consulted, the following were regarded as most important:

Martin, S.J., Felix. *Le P. Isaac Jogues.* Paris and Quebec, 1874. *The Life of Father Isaac Jogues.* Translated by John Gilmary Shea. New York, Benziger, 1885.

Campbell, S.J., Thomas. *Pioneer Priests of North America.* 2 vols. New York, The America Press, 1910, 1913.

Wynne, S.J., John J. *The Jesuit Martyrs of North America.* New York, Universal Knowledge Foundation, 1925.

Fouqueray, S.J., Henri, and Becdelièvre, S.J., Alain de. *Martyrs du Canada.* Paris, Tequi, 1930.

Becdelièvre, S.J., Alain de. *Annales Religieuses du Diocèse d'Orléans.* May 29, June 5, 1926. June 21, July 5, July 19, 1930.

Melançon, S.J., Arthur. *Liste des Missionaires-Jésuites, 1611-1800.* Montréal, Collège Sainte-Marie, 1929.

Jones, S.J., Arthur Edward. *Old Huronia.* Fifth Report of the Bureau of Archives for the Province of Ontario. Toronto, 1909.

Rochemonteix, S.J., Camille de. *Les Jésuites de la Nouvelle-France.* 2 vols. Paris, Letouzey, 1895.

Fouqueray, S.J., Henri. *Histoire de la Compagnie de Jésus en France.* 3 vols. published. Paris, Picard, 1910, 1913. Bureaux des Etudes, 1922.

Faillon, Abbé. *Histoire de la Colonie Française en Canada.* 3 vols. Montreal, 1865.

Ferland, Abbé J. B. *Cours d'Histoire du Canada.* 2 vols. Quebec, 1861.

Sulte, Benjamin. *Histoire des Canadiens-français.* 8 vols. Montreal, 1882.

Parkman, Francis. *Pioneers of France in the New World.* 2 vols. Boston, 1878. ——*The Jesuits in North America.* Boston, 1868.

Bancroft, George. *History of the United States.* Boston, 1850.

Gosselin, Abbé A. *La Mission du Canada avant Mgr. de Laval: Récollets et Jésuites.* Evreux, 1909.

Finley, John. *The French in the Heart of America.* New York, Scribners, 1915.

Wrong, George M. *The Rise and Fall of New France.* New York, Macmillan, 1928.

Bracq, J. C. *The Evolution of French Canada.* New York, Macmillan, 1926.

O'Callaghan, Edmund Bailey. *History of New Netherlands.* 2 vols. New York, 1846.

Valentine, David. *History of the City of New York.* New York, 1853.

Innes, J. H. *New Amsterdam and Its People.* New York, Scribners, 1902.

Bennett, W. H. *Catholic Footsteps in Old New York.* New York, Schwartz, Kirwin and Fauss, 1909.

Talbot, S.J., Francis X. *The Torture Trail of Saint Isaac Jogues. Historical Records and Studies,* Vol. XXIII. United States Catholic Historical Society, 1933.

Reynolds, Cuyler. *Albany Chronicles.* Albany, 1906.

Weise, A. J. *History of the City of Albany.* Albany, 1884.

Morgan, Lewis H. *League of the Iroquois.* 2 vols. New York, Dodd, Mead, 1904.

Hodge, F. W. Editor. *Handbook of American Indians North of Mexico.* Bulletin 30, Bureau of American Ethnology. 2 vols. Washington, D. C., 1907.

Ruttenber, E. M. *Indian Geographical Names in New York.* New York State Historical Association, 1906.

Beauchamp, William M. *Aboriginal Occupation of New York.* Bulletin 32, New York State Museum. Albany, 1900. ——*Aboriginal Place Names of New York.* Bulletin 108, New York State Museum. Albany, 1907.

Catlin, George. *North American Indians.* 2 vols. London, 1841.

Writings of Isaac Jogues

I. Autograph.

1. Notice sur René Goupil. Undated. (May, 1646.) Collège Sainte-Marie, Montréal.
2. Novum Belgium. August 3, 1646. Collège Sainte-Marie, Montréal.
3. Lettre au R. P. Andre Castillon. September 12, 1646. Rue St. Hilaire, 10. Lyon.
4. Letter to Mother. April 6, 1636. Orléans.

II. Apograph.

5. Letter to Provincial. August 5, 1643. Collège Sainte-Marie, Montréal.
6. Letter to Jérôme Lalemant. May 2, 1646. Collège Sainte-Marie, Montréal.
7. Illustrationes Excerptae. Undated. Collège Sainte-Marie, Montréal.
8. Recital of Vision. 1637. Collège Sainte-Marie, Montréal.
9. Letter to Governor Montmagny. June 30, 1643. Gesu, Rome.

III. Preserved by J. B. Forest in Manuscript Life.

10. Letter to Mother, October 10, 1632.
11. " " " April 25, 1635.
12. " " " February 1, 1636.
13. " " " August 20, 1636.
14. " " " June 5, 1637.
15. " " " May 7, 1638.
16. Letter to brother Samuel, May 13, 1639.

IV. Reprinted in the Jesuit *Relations*.

17. Letter to Charles Lalemant, August 30, 1643.
18. Letter to Provincial, January 5, 1644.
19. Letter to Charles Lalemant, January 6, 1644.
20. Letter to Jesuit, September, 1646.
21. Recital of Captivity. (More complete version in Alegambe.)

V. Felix Martin, S.J., in his life of Bressani, p. 244, n. 3, states:

"The account of Jogues' second voyage, written by himself, was preserved in the archives of the College of Quebec until 1800, about the time at which the last Jesuit died. Unfortunately, this, with other rare documents, has disappeared, since those archives were deposited in the Provincial record-office" (Thwaites, Vol. 39, p. 267, n. 19). Jérôme Lalemant states in his diary, under date of June 30, 1646, in reference to this document: "All that concerns his journey will be found in the Archives, *titulo* yroquois." (*Jes. Rel.* 28-213.)

Three previous letters written by him were referred to in Father Jogues' letter to Governor Montmagny, June 30, 1643. Barthelemy Vimont, in his *Relation of 1642-43* states: "It is a great pity (un grand dommage) that three others, which he wrote to us previously, have been lost" (24-295).

In his preface to his Manuscript Life (1792), J. B. Forest indicates that he consulted some other letters which Father Jogues wrote to several of his religious brothers. These have remained unrecovered. Forest also states that the Latin poem on St. Nicephorus, written at Rouen, was in existence: "At the opening of classes he recited a Latin poem in that fashion still followed among us. It is written in his own hand, and we shall give some portions at the end of this work." No extracts of this poem have been discovered in any of the copies of Forest that are extant.

Notes and References

Abbreviations Used

4-259. Jesuit Relations. Quotations from and references to the Burrows Edition are indicated by numbers separated by hyphens. Thus the first reference, occurring on page 27, indicates Volume 4, page 259.

Al. Alegambe. Mortes Illustres.

Bec. Becdelièvre. Annales Religieuses.

Beau. Beauvais. Essais Historiques.

For. Forest, Jean-Baptiste. Vie du P. Isaac.

Fouq. Fouqueray. Histoire de la Compagnie de Jésus.

Fouq. Mart. Fouqueray. Martyrs du Canada.

Mon. Ped. Monumenta Pedagogica.

Q. A. Rapport de l'Archiviste de Québec.

Roch. Rochemonteix. Les Jésuites de la Nouvelle-France.

Notes and References

Chapter I

P. 6. The Jogues family developed two branches through Philippe and Pierre II in the sixteenth century. The branch of Philippe, in the seventeenth century, came to be known as that of the Jogues de Saint-Mesmin, and was perpetuated through Philippe, the brother of Isaac. The branch of Pierre II divided into several families, the Jogues de Guèdreville, de Bouland, de Neuville, etc. Both branches extended their commerce beyond Orléans, and both were classed among the nobility in the eighteenth century. Many members of the family still reside at Orléans and in various parts of France.

P. 8. The name of Isaac was apparently a favorite one in his family, Father Wynne notes. Holweck lists forty-eight saints of that name. The baptismal register which contains the record from 1602 to 1629 "is not in a good state," writes Father Becdelièvre. "Many pages are wanting, and among these that on which were written the baptisms administered between October 16, 1606, and February 8, 1607, has evidently been torn out. Through a devotion badly conceived, a researcher not of delicate conscience has probably appropriated this relic of the illustrious martyr."

Page

5. Bec. July 5, 1930. May 29, 1926. For. 5, 75. Arch. Orl.
6. Bec. May 29, 1926. For. 75. Beau. 179, 182.
7. Bec. May 29, 1926.
   Jog. Let. from Diepp. Beauv. 69. Bouvier Plans.
   Bec. May 29, 1926. For. 76.
8. Bec. May 29, 1926. For. 5, 75. Beauv. 95.
9. Bec. May 29, 1926. Fouq. Mart. 38.
10. Fouq. III. 489.
11. Mon. Ped. V. 5, 9, 458.
12. Fouq. III. 490. Beauv. 66. Rig. 93.
    Mon. Ped. V. 9, 398, 442.

Page

13. For. 6, 7, 9. Q.A. 27.
14. For. 6, 9.
15. Q.A. 26.
16. Fouq. II. 2, etc.
    Fouq. II. 598, 664.
17. Fouq. III. v, 151.
18. Fouq. III. 209, 606, etc.
    For. 14.
19. Fouq. III. 13, 230. For. 10.
20. For. 9. Q.A. 27.
21. For. 13.
22. For. 10, 14.
23. Fouq. III. 166, 268.
    Q.A. 27.
24. For. 15.

Chapter II

P. 37. April 6, 1636, fell on Sunday. The letter was probably written on Saturday, April 5, for the postscript speaks of "tomorrow . . . the 2nd Sunday after Easter." Forest and Martin, followed by Shea, date his arrival in Dieppe as the 1st of April. Fouqueray places it in the middle of March.

P. 42. Le Clercq's description and location of the Jesuit residence of Notre Dame des Anges, and its first establishment, does not tally with that of the Jesuit writers. He states truly, however, that it was 40 by 28 feet, and was about 800 paces from the Récollet establishment.

P. 42. In terms of today, the Fort of Three Rivers occupied the square where now stands the Post Office. At the intersection of rue du Château and Notre Dame, where is erected a statue of the Sacred Heart, is the site of the first Jesuit residence and chapel. Confer, *Historical Records and Studies,* Vol. XXIII, p. 29.

Page

26. Roch. I. 70, etc.
27. 4-259. Roch. I. 124, etc.
28. Roch. I. 167, 181, etc.
29. Roch. I. 416. Jes. Rel., passim.
30. For. 15, 16, Fouq. Mart. 43.
31. For. 15. Let. from Dieppe and Three Rivers. Fouq. Mart. 43.
34. Al. 618.
35. 27-311. 8-221, 309. 9-185. Sult. II. 60.
8-306. 9-207. 11-47. Roch. I. 227, 307.
5-13. 9-312. 28-83. 30-149. 32-63, 145. 2-209. 71-122.
36. 13-19. For. 20, 21.
37. Arch. St. Mary's College, Montreal.
Q.A. 27.
38. 5-43. For. 20.

Page

39. 13-89. For. 20. Roch. I. 196, etc. Jes. Rel., passim.
40. 7-263. 8-293. 9-135, 301. 12-263, 312.
13-89. 9-227. 8-292. 12-263.
41. 5-15. Roch. I. 253. Jes. Rel., passim.
For. 20.
42. 9-301. 8-221. 9-227.
6-69, 326. 9-107. 73-107. Jes. Rel., passim. Roch. I. 155.
43. 4-256. 6-103, 326, 81. 7-293, 309. 8-217, 221. 9-145. 42-269, etc. Roch. I. 200.
44. 9-229.
8-19. 6-43. Roch. I. 202, etc.
45. 9-137, 235.
46. 9-247, 251, 257.
47. 9-261.
49. For. 20.
50. 9-271, 279. 13-7.

Chapter III

P. 52. Thwaites, in his Index to the *Jesuit Relations*, supplies one with all possible data in regard to the Hurons, their country, language, tribal characteristics, social life and customs, events in their history, relations with other tribes and with French, etc. Father Jones, in *Old Huronia*, devotes an interesting appendix to a summary of the subject.

Page

52. 1-279. 5-23. 15-155. 16-229. 27-299. 38-249, etc.

53. 9-281, 291.

54. 9-293. For. 20.

55. 30-304. Jones. 301, 310. 6-67. 8-179.

56. 12-117 to 123. 26-316. 50-171.

57. 3-83. Jes. Rel., passim. For. 24.

58. 22-205. 9-237, 241, 314. 12-133, 272. 8-294, etc.

59. 8-294. 12-133. 10-89. 15-151. 13-87, etc.

60. 13-87. For. 24.

62. 13-21, 89. 8-105, 109. 10-91, 247. Roch. I. 339. Jones. 299.

Page

64. For. 24. 9-299. 16-239. Jones. 301.

65. 10-237. 3-73. 1-281. 3-75, 101. 7-11. 38-245. 15-75. 18-211. 26-123, 213, 315, etc.

66. 10-211, 241, etc. Roch. I. 323. 8-105. 10-91. 15-153, 246. 38-247. 39-107. Jones. 30, 185.

67. 16-225. 8-115. 5-278, etc. 8-294. 10-235, etc. 11-17, 225. 13-125, 270. 15-39, 153. 16-225. 17-87, 195. 19-269. 20-19, etc. Jones. 419. Roch. I. 322.

68 to 72. 10-91 to 115.

73 to 76. 13-89 to 113.

Chapter IV

P. 79. Through very careful calculations, Jones and Martin have determined the locations of the principal Huron villages. They are in the townships of Tiny, Tay, Flos, Medonte, Oro, and Orillia in Simcoe County, Ontario. In his tabulated list in *Old Huronia*, page 262, he places Ihonatiria in Tiny, near lot 6, concession xx, xxxi. Ossossané he locates on two sites, Tiny, lot 18, concession viii, and lot 16, concession vii. The smaller villages he determines as follows: Wenrio, near Tiny, 5, xvii; Anonatea, near Tiny, 10, xvii; Onnentisati, on Tiny, 10, xiii; Angwiens (Angoutenc), on Tiny, 10, x; Arontaen, on Tiny, 20, xvii.

Page		*Page*	
79.	13-115, 103. 22-293. 12-25.	90.	10-117, 123. 15-155. 2-11. 39-121.
80.	13-131, 213.		14-11.
	10-185. 12-25. 13-33, 175, 189, 195, 203, 229, 263.	91.	14-39, 47.
81.	13-115, 127, 175, 189, 203, 229, 263. 12-113, 141.		14-15, 35, 43, 51.
82.	13-117, 127, 179, 143, 125.	92.	10-235, 294. 13-185. 17-179. 14-59, 75.
	13-137, 145, 149, 249.	93.	14-77, 97. 15-131.
	11-17, Jones. 25, 184.	94.	14-103. 15-17.
83.	13-147, 149, 159, 209, 213.		11-19. 12-127, 235. 13-17.
	13-151, 159, 163.	96.	For. 23.
84.	13-171, 175, 187.	97.	14-11, 51. 15-13, 31, 53. 12-237.
85.	13-191, 211, 181.		
86.	13-217. 233.	98.	15-29, 35, 49.
87.	13-235, 241.	99.	12-161, 195, 235, 255. 15-55.
88.	13-247.	100.	15-13, 59, 19.
89.	14-109.	101.	15-63.
	14-9, 11.	103.	15-67.

Chapter V

P. 108. The manuscript of Jogues was found after his death. Its authenticity was attested by Joseph Poncet and by Paul Ragueneau, dated August 25, 1652. Ragueneau states that the experience occurred in 1637, but Ascension in that year was May 21. Since Ascension in 1638 fell on May 13, the vision happened in that year, since Jogues states: "On the eleventh of May, which fell on Tuesday, the day before the vigil of the Ascension. . . ."

P. 109. Forest, Martin, and Shea combine these excerpts and others that follow, and date them in 1639. The portions here given, from internal evidence, are evidently of 1638; the remainder are of 1639.

P. 111. According to Jones, the village of Teanaustayaé occupied the site that is now in the township of Medonte, west half of lot 7, concession iv. Scanonaeenrat is identified as Medonte, west half of 17, iii.

P. 121. Sainte Marie is definitely located, in modern terms, in Tay, 16, iii. It is on the east bank of the little Wye River which flows from Mud Lake to Midland, or Gloucester, Bay, one of the inlets of Matchedash Bay. Parts of the walls of the fort which was begun under the direction of Jogues are still standing. On the hill overlooking the site has been erected the Shrine of the American Martyrs. It is near Midland, Ontario, about ninety miles above Toronto.

Page		Page	
105.	15-157. 28-63. 26-125, etc.	117.	17-113, 117, 125, 31, 81, 85.
106.	15-113, 121, 155. 12-61. 10-67, 227. 38-269. Roch. I. 116.	118.	17-33. 15-139, 175. For. 32.
107.	13-270. 9-112, 207. 12-7. 22-317. 10-169, 193, 201. 15-139. 17-119.	119.	17-39. 16-277. 17-89, 93. Jones. 25, 178, 422.
108.	15-77, 101, 123.	120.	19-125. 18-11. 17-25, 37, 45, 61, 97. 15-189. Roch. I. 384.
109.	Q.A. 69, 26.	121.	19-133, 269. Jones. 8, 308, etc.
110.	For. 26, 30, 31. 17-11, 61. 15-141.	122.	19-137.
111.	17-59. Jones. 15, 250.	123.	19-77, 89.
112.	17-11, 61.	124.	19-93, 111.
113.	17-67 to 77. 17-25.	125.	19-93, 115, 227.
		126.	18-25. 19-117.
114.	14-273. 15-153. Roch. I. 381. 16-249.	127.	19-125, 167, 175, 183, 207, 232, 265. 20-21. Jones. 315. 20-43. Jones. 214, 226, etc.
115.	16-241. 15-167.		
116.	17-115.	128.	20-45.

Chapter VI

P. 129. "After the year 1639, the bulk of the Petun nation was concentrated in that portion of their territory known today as the Blue Hills" (Jones. p. 220). Their land included the western part of Nottawasaga township in Simcoe County, and practically all of Grey and Bruce counties, Ontario. The village of Ehwae is tentatively located by Jones as "corresponding to a point in Arran township a little to the northeast of Mount Hope."

P. 144. The villages of the Ataronchronons are located as follows by Jones: Ste. Anne, Tay, east half of 9, iii; St. Denis, Tay, west half of 3, v; St. Louis, Tay, west half of 11, vi; St. Jean, Tay, west half of 6, x.

Page		Page	
129 to 138.	20-45 to 65. Roch. I. 414.		21-293, 305. Roch. I. 388. Jones. 321.
139.	20-43.	144.	19-135. Jones. 312, 321.
140.	2-75. 19-177.	145.	21-131, 145. 20-93, 97. Roch. I. 399. Jones. 321.
141.	19-177, 79, 199. 20-69. 17-229.	146.	21-129, 149. 20-99. Jones. 97, etc. 18-19.
142.	19-137, 151. 20-47, 77, 83, 97. 21-147.	147.	23-35. Jes. Rel., passim. Jones. 10, 313, 333, etc.
143.	21-141.		

Page		Page	
148.	23-223. Roch. I. 418.	154.	22-311, 23-23.
149.	23-225, 215.	155.	23-39, 43, 55, 75.
150.	23-217.	156.	23-83, 79, 115, 135, etc.
151.	23-225, 215.	157.	23-27.
152.	23-227, 181.	158.	23-31, 23. 22-309.
153.	23-19, 227.	159.	Q.A. 25. 31-17. Al. 618.

Chapter VII

P. 160. An immense amount has been written about the Iroquois Confederacy and the Mohawk nation. The information obtainable from the *Jesuit Relations* is dated later than the years of Jogues; it was secured by the missioners who followed him. Thwaites, in his Index, very carefully lists the abundant references. Morgan is the best among the earlier writers, but many later studies have clarified much about these amazing peoples. Jameson in his *Narratives of New Netherlands*, reprints the "Narrative of a Journey into the Mohawk and Oneida Country, 1634-35," written either by Marten Gerritsen or Van Corlaer; also, "A Short Account of the Mohawk Indians, by Reverend Johannes Megapolensis, Jr., 1644."

P. 163. Shea in his *Life of Father Jogues* (p. 66) states that twenty-five persons departed from Sainte Marie on June 2, 1642. Bressani and Alegambe give the number as twenty-three, but Jogues himself makes the total twenty-five in his letter to the Provincial. The date was definitely June 13, as recorded in 31-17; 39-177; Alegambe, 618.

P. 169. A *Journal of New Netherlands*, written from 1641 to 1646, deplores the avarice of the traders in illegally supplying the Mohawks with firearms. Confer, Brodhead, I. 182.

P. 180. The place of the Iroquois attack and the capture of Father Jogues has been calculated by the present writer to be on the north bank of the North Channel of the St. Lawrence, opposite Ile à l'Aigle, near the dividing line between Berthier and Maskinonge counties, Quebec. (*Historical Records and Studies,* Vol. XXIII, 1933). In contradiction to this, Rt. Rev. P. S. Desranleau, of Sorel, contends: "This historical spot must be looked for on the Ile Saint-Ignace, opposite Sorel, not very far from the Jesuit Fathers' summer camp, in the immediate neighborhood of the little village of Alençon."

Page		Page	
160.	23-305.	163.	26-233.
161.	Q.A. 25, 30. Al. 619. 31-19.	165.	31-19.
162.	Al. 619. Q.A. 13, 29. 31-17. 39-177. Jones. 332.	166.	31-21. Q.A. 30. 39-117.
		167.	25-33. 28-117. 24-312. 39-203.

Page		Page	
168.	25-23. 28-119. 21-303, 318. 24-312. 25-21. Jones. 321.	176.	26-183. 31-23. 28-119. 26-189. Q.A. 3, 30.
169.	21-117, 247, 259. 22-33, 127, 253. 22-251. 32-31.	177.	26-183.
170.	17-223. 20-119. 22-31. 20-19. 21-169. Roch. I. 387.	178.	31-21.
171.	22-89, 203, 247. 22-35, 43, 89, 217, 247. 21-125. Roch. I. 246.	179.	Q.A. 30, 3. 31-21. 39-179. Al. 620.
172.	19-9. 16-9. 24-157, etc. Roch. I. 295, 304. 16-9. 22-145. Roch. I. 307. Mère Marie.	180.	26-185. 31-21. Al. 620.
173.	Mère Marie. II. 430. 25-231. 23-61, 145. 22-135, 193.	182.	Q.A. 30, 31, 3, 4. 31-23. 39-179. 25-69. 24-281. 28-119. 26-189.
174.	25-29. 31-21. Al. 619.	184.	Q.A. 31, 4. Al. 620. 24-305. 31-25. 24-28.
175.	22-197.	185.	Q.A. 31, 4. 31-27. 24-281. 28-119. 22-269. Al. 621. Jones. 332.
		187.	24-305.
		188.	31-29. Q.A. 5. Al. 621. 22-283. 12-215.

Chapter VIII

P. 189. A reconstruction, in terms of today, of the torture trail of Isaac Jogues from the time he left Three Rivers till he reached the first Mohawk village of Ossernenon has been attempted by the present writer (*Historical Records and Studies,* Vol. XXIII. pp. 7 to 86). Briefly, the route, from August 2 to 5, 1642, was along the Richelieu River. On August 6, 7, 8 and 9, they paddled down Lake Champlain. On August 9, occurred the torture on the island. In my original determination I identified this island with what appears to be an island, the western tip of Crown Point, opposite Port Henry, Lake Champlain. Fathers Wynne and Campbell, with much greater probability, specify that the island is that known now as Jogues Island (sometimes called Albany or Cole Island) in a little bay about three miles south of Westport, New York. In my narrative, also, I stated that Jogues followed the trail through Lake George (Lake of the Blessed Sacrament). Further consideration leads me to believe that he was taken to the lower end of Lake Champlain. In the land journey, from that point, on August 11, 12, 13 and 14, 1642, he followed the trail to the junction of the Sacandaga and Hudson rivers, below the town of Luzerne, and thence along the course of the Sacandaga River near the towns of Conklingville, Broadalbin, Vail Mills toward West Perth, New York. The Sacandaga Reservoir now floods this valley.

P. 203. The time of Jogues' arrival at the first Mohawk village was stated by him to be, "On the vigil of the Assumption, about the third hour." Shea translates this, "On the eve of the Assumption, then, about three o'clock." The present writer, from consideration of other elements, takes it to mean the third hour of the march, that is, about seven o'clock in the morning. Bressani states the time of the arrival to be "about the twentieth hour" (39-189).

P. 203. The three Mohawk villages have been definitely located by John S. Clarke, Fathers Campbell and Wynne, on the south bank of the Mohawk River. Beyond any doubt, Ossernenon was on the elevation now occupied by the Shrine of the North American Martyrs, near Auriesville, in the town of Glen, Montgomery County, New York. Tionontoguen was located on a magnificent height near what is now designated Sprakers.

Page
189 to 198. 31-29 to 37. 28-21, 123. 26-187, 189. 39-185, 187. Al. 621, 624, 626. Q.A. 5, 6, 32.
198 to 207. 31-37 to 43. 28-123, 125. Q.A. 6, 7, 8, 33. Al. 622, 623. 24-299, 301. 26-193. 25-69. 39-189 to 193.
208 to 217. 31-47 to 51. 28-125. Q.A. 9, 10. Al. 623, 624. 39-195, 199. 25-71. 22-273. 26-187, 195.

Chapter IX

P. 226. Contrary to all the other available facts, and contrary to the very nature of Father Jogues, is the statement made by Arendt Van Corlaer in his letter of June 16, 1643, to the Patroon in Holland. After stating that he visited the Maquas country, for the purpose of releasing the three Frenchmen, "among them a Jesuit, a very learned man," he asserts: "The Frenchmen ran screaming after us and besought us to do all in our power for their delivery from the barbarians." And again he says: "Two of these Frenchmen, of whom the Jesuit was one, were at my house last May. They expressed their hope that means could be found to procure their release" (Fernow, XIII. 15).

Page
219. 22-283.
220. 22-265, 271, 283, 22-35.
222. 22-247, 279. 25-71.
224. Al. 625.
225. Al. 625. 39-201, 266. 24-283. 25-287. Fern. XIII, 15.
226. 24-283. 31-53. Morgan. 333.
227. Morgan. I. 75, etc. II. 225, etc.
228. Morgan. I. 104, 231. II. 6, etc. 31-53. 39-201. 28-127. Al. 625.
229. Morgan. I. 308, 305. II. 298. Jameson. 141. Q.A. 11.

Page
231. 28-127, 133. 24-281, 127. 31-55. Al. 626.
232. 31-55. 28-133. Al. 626. Q.A. 11.
233. 28-127. 29-227. 31-57. 24-281. 39-201. Al. 626.
234. 31-59. Q.A. 12. 28-129. Al. 626.
235. 31-59. 39-203. Al. 626.

Page
236. 28-129. 31-57. 39-203. Al. 626.
237. 28-131. 31-59. 39-205. Q.A. 12. Al. 627.
239. 28-131. 31-63. 38-129. 39-207. Al. 627. Q.A. 34, 36.
241. 28-129. 31-61. 39-207. Al. 627.
244 to 247. 31-63. Q.A. 34 to 36.

CHAPTER X

P. 250. It is quite probable that Jogues was taken for the winter hunt to the vicinity of Lake Saranac. On this basis, he could be said to be the first white man who ever penetrated among the Adirondacks.

P. 269. An attempt has been made to harmonize the details offered as to what Jogues did with Goupil's bones: "I committed them to the earth" (letter to Provincial); "I buried them" (Goupil narrative); "I finally buried them" (Bressani adaptation); "Hides them in the hollow of a tree" (Lalemant, 31-57); "les caches dans trois ou quatre creux d'arbres" (Buteux, Q.A., 12). The place where they were deposited is probably along a line about twenty paces above Auriesville creek, most certainly somewhere in the ravine that cuts the western edge of the plateau on which the Shrine of the North American Martyrs is built.

Page
249. Morgan. I. 337, etc. Q.A. 13.
250 to 260. 31-71 to 81, 131. 39-207 to 211. Q.A. 13, 14, 15, 36. Al. 628, 629, 634. 28-133.
261. Q.A. 15. 31-81.
262. Al. 629, 635. Q.A. 15, 16, 31-83. 39-213.
263. Q.A. 16. Al. 630, 635. 31-129, 83.
264. Al. 630. 39-213.
265. Al. 630. 31-133.
266. Al. 630. 31-83, 137. 39-215. 24-285. 37-175. 26-195.
267. 23-297. 24-281, 283. 26-197.
268. 31-57. 28-135. Q.A. 12.

Page
269. Al. 627. 28-133. 39-205. 31-57. Q.A. 12.
270. Al. 630. 31-83. 39-215.
271. Al. 630. Q.A. 16. 31-85. 39-217.
273. Al. 631. Q.A. 16. 31-83. 39-215.
274. 36-105. 25-53. 31-87. Q.A. 17.
275. 25-53. 31-87.
276. Al. 631. Q.A. 20. Fern. XIII. 15.
277. 39-223. 25-71. 24-297. 31-89.
278. 24-275. 39-219. Al. 631.
279. Al. 631. 23-249, 267, 327. 24-297, 312. 25-67.

Chapter XI

P. 285. The embassy of the Mohawks was toward the south, to the tribes of the Huron-Iroquois stock who had much earlier spread through that region which is now identified as the lower portions of New York State and northern Pennsylvania. It is quite possible, judging by the time element, that Father Jogues followed the Susquehanna River as far as Harrisburg.

P. 288. In 1630, Kiliaen Van Rensselaer acquired land extending from Fort Orange northward, on both sides of the Hudson river. In 1631 he secured from the natives a tract on the west side of the Hudson from Beeren (Bears) Island northward to Smacks Island, and in breadth, "two days' journey inland" (Reynolds, p. 24, and Documents, Colonial History, New York, Vol. II). The determinations made by Reynolds, according to a map of Albany, by John Miller, British chaplain, in 1695, enclose Rensselaerswyck within the boundaries of Hudson River on the east, Lodge Street on the west, Steuben Street on the north, and Hudson Avenue on the south. The fort was along the southern stockade. The Dutch church and the dwellings of the village were along Broadway (Handlaars Street), James Street (Middle Lane), Court Street, States Street (Yonkers Street), Pearl Street, etc.

P. 293. The fishing-place here mentioned was along the Hudson between Coxsackie and Hudson.

Page
280. 24-273. 26-175.
281. 24-273, 279, 289.
282. 24-283. 26-21, 183, 219. 23-297.
283. 25-45. 24-305.
284. 24-295. 31-135.
285. 31-89, 91. 39-229. 25-71. Q.A. 17.
287. Al. 632. 24-297. 39-223. 25-71. 31-135.
288. 25-43, 57. 31-93.

Page
289. 28-111, 113. 31-131.
290. 25-49, 71.
291. Al. 619, 39-175.
292. Al. 632. 39-223, 266.
293. 25-45, 49.
294. 25-47. 24-293, 305.
295. 25-49.
297. 25-55. Q.A. 18.
298 to 307. 25-55 to 61. Q.A. 19, 20. 31-95, 97. 25-61.

Chapter XII

P. 311. Fort Amsterdam occupied the site now covered by the Custom House, Bowling Green, New York City. The Marckveldt is identified as Whitehall Street, the extension of Broadway. Parel and Brugh and Hoogh have become Pearl, Bridge, and High streets, while the promenade along the "Ditch" is now known as Broad Street. The Stadts Herbergh was built on ground that lays, now, just west of Coenties Alley, "a curious little dark street between high and almost blank walls; it is overhung by rusty fire-escapes, and furnished with miniature sidewalks, of about two feet wide" (Innes).

P. 324. "Creuxius gives some details as to his landing in France which are not in the *Relations: Historia Canadensis*, p. 391." (Shea's Charlevoix, II. 160). In his *Life of Father Jogues* he states: "The account in Creuxius, which has not been followed by Charlevoix, is very confused as to what happened in England and on the Breton coast" (p. 160). Since there was not proper documentary authority, the present writer has not followed Martin in asserting that "the Dutch captain was loth to let his passenger go unless he paid his fair"; that "Berson came on board (the collier) to arrange some affairs with the captain. . . . Seizing a favorable moment, he (Jogues) approached Berson, and touching him gently asked him to take pity on him," etc.

P. 332. Forest, in order to draw a spiritual lesson of renunciation, declares that Jogues, after the example of Saint Francis Xavier's reputed refusal to visit his mother, did not go to Orléans. As stated in the text, he could scarcely have avoided passing through the city.

Page
308. Q.A. 21. 31-97. 25-63.
310. 31-97. Q.A. 21.
311. Innes, passim. Valentine, passim, etc.
312. 31-97. 25-63. Q.A. 21.
313. 28-106, 115.
314. 28-107.
315. 31-99. Q.A. 21.
316. 28-109. Q.A. 21.
317. 31-99. 25-65. Q.A. 22.
318. Brod. I. 139. Q.A. 22
319. Hastings. I. 168.

Page
320. Q.A. 22. 31-99. 25-65.
321. Q.A. 22. 31-101. 25-73.
323. Q.A. 25, 22, 23.
324. 25-65. 31-101, 103. For. 70.
326. 23-237, 249. 26-197.
328. 39-175. 31-105. 25-403, 65. Al. 619. For. 70, 71. 31-103.
331. 25-65. For. 72.
332. 25-73. 31-105. For. 73.
333. 24-301. 26-197. 23-249, 237. 25-43.
334. For. 72. 31-105, 125.

Chapter XIII

P. 345. The fort at Ville Marie stood near the river. In the terminology of today it was on Commissioners Street, behind the old Customs House.

Page
336. For. 72. Hastings. 437.
337. Charlevoix. II. 167.
338. Q.A. 27.
341. Q.A. 27. 26-29, 35. 39-54. 25-193.
342. 25-107. 27-63.
343. 22-203, 207. 12-273. Roch. I. 309.
344. Roch. I. 314. 22-203, 213. 31-107.

Page
345. 22-205. 24-22.
346. 26-49, 59, 65, 69. 27-253, 297.
347. 27-221.
348. 27-77. 26-115. Q.A. 27.
349. Q.A. 25, 26.
350. 24-223. 27-221, 231, 241, 267.
350 to 356. 27-249 to 265.
357. 27-269. 28-151, 245.
359. 27-279. 28-39.
361. 27-297, 79, 303.

Chapter XIV

P. 382. In his embassy, Jogues followed the route through Lake George, thus walking, during the portage, through what is now Ticonderoga. The details in modern terminology will be found in *Historical Records and Studies*, Vol. XXIII, p. 71, ff. Historical appreciation would require that Lake George, a name which has no significance of value, should be given its first name, Lake of the Blessed Sacrament, or should be called Lake Jogues after its first namer.

Page
363. 27-77, 93. 28-137. 31-125, 127.
364. 27-77, 137. 29-171, 145, 155, 181, 149.
365. 29-153. 27-79, 93, 101. 28-77.
366. 29-147. 28-147.
367. 28-149, 155. 29-181.
368. 29-17. 28-163, 281, 291.
369. 29-49, 285. 28-283, 287, 171, 291.
371. 28-183.
374. Q.A. 38. 31-107. 28-119.
375. 28-117 to 135.
376. 28-293, 283, 287.

Page
377. 28-301. 29-47.
378. 28-303. 29-47.
379. 29-49. 31-115. 27-87, 203. 29-55.
380. 11-277. 28-137. 31-290. 29-47.
29-45, 294. 28-137, 189.
382. 29-49. 51-181.
383. 29-51, 293.
384. 29-51. 28-297.
385. 29-51. 28-137. 31-290. Q.A. 40.
386. 29-53, 227.
387. 29-53, 294. 31-290.

Page
388. 29-55.
390. 29-59. 28-137.

Page
391. 29-59. 28-213, 137. 29-61. 31-109.

CHAPTER XV

P. 403. Martin, followed by Shea, sets the date of Jogues' departure from Three Rivers as that of September 27. Lalemant in the *Relations* (pp. 29-61 and 31-111), distinctly mentions the day as that of September 24, and Alegambe (p. 639) also specifies the same. In his diary (pp. 28-231) written during the week after September 12, Lalemant says that "Jogues was to start on the 29th."

Page
393. 28-213, 287, 137, 279. 39-267.
394. 29-61. 31-109. 28-217, 105.
395. 28-105 to 115. 29-249.
396. 28-227. 29-233.
398. 28-137 to 141.
399. 31-111. Al. Shea. 60.
400. 28-141, 229, 29-233. 31-113, 127. 39-237.
401. 30-221, 227. 29-63, 183.
402. 31-111, 123. 30-229.
403. 28-141. 31-127. 31-111. 29-61, 261. Al. 639, 28-231.
404. 29-61.
407. 31-117. Q.A. 28. 30-219.
408. 30-219, 227. 31-117. Q.A. 27.

Page
409. 30-227. 28-289. Q.A. 28.
410. Q.A. 29. 30-227.
411. 31-117. Q.A. 40.
413. 32-235. 31-115. Q.A. 27.
414. 31-117. Q.A. 27. Al. 639.
415. 32-25, 15. 30-221, 229. 36-23. 31-117. 39-235. Q.A. 29, 40.
416. 32-27. Q.A. 40.
417. 32-151.
419. 31-117. 32-151, 25.
420. Q.A. 27.
421. Q.A. 28.
422. 32-145. 31-115. Q.A. 39. Corwin. I. 437, 214. O'Call. II. 299.

EPILOGUE

P. 428. Lalemant, in the *Relation* of 1647 (pp. 31-117) states: "The inclosure, mentioned in the preceding, written by a Dutchman to Sieur Bourdon. . . ." The text of the letter preserved at Collège Sainte-Marie, Montréal, published in the Quebec Archives, 1924-1925, p. 39, shows that it was addressed to Monsieur La Montaigne, and the contents indicate that Labatie had no way of communicating with Bourdon, whom he had met on the latter's visit to Rensselaerswyck in June. Neither was the letter addressed to Governor Montmagny. Johannes de la Montagne was a French Huguenot who became a Councilor at New Amsterdam. Complaints about him and Megapolensis, as being creatures of Kieft, were sent to Amsterdam in 1652 (Brodhead. I. 496).

Page		Page	
423.	29-45, 63, 235.	429.	Q.A. 39. 31-117, 290.
424.	28-243, 251. 30-229, 231, 161, 171. 31-77.	430.	32-23. 30-193.
425.	29-167.	431.	32-153. 36-21, 27. 32-149, 151.
426.	Q.A. 28.	432.	36-31, 23, 45.
427.	30-175, 237, 243, 273, 257, 269. 31-119.	433.	31-119, 129, 30-229. Mère Marie. I. 334, 378.
428.	Q.A. 40. 31-115.		

Index

To SAULT STE. MARIE
LAKE NIPISSING
French R.
Island Algonquins
Georgian Bay
Lake Huron
IHONATIRIA
SAINTE MARIE
OSSOSSANE
Hurons
PETUNS
Ottawas
Lake Ontario
NEUTRALS
IROQUO
LAKE St. Clair
Lake Erie
Senecas
Cayugas
A MAP showing the TERRITORIES through which ISAAC JOGUES traveled 1636 ~ 1646
GEORGE ANNAND 1935